THE BRONX/BROOKLYN,
73-1978

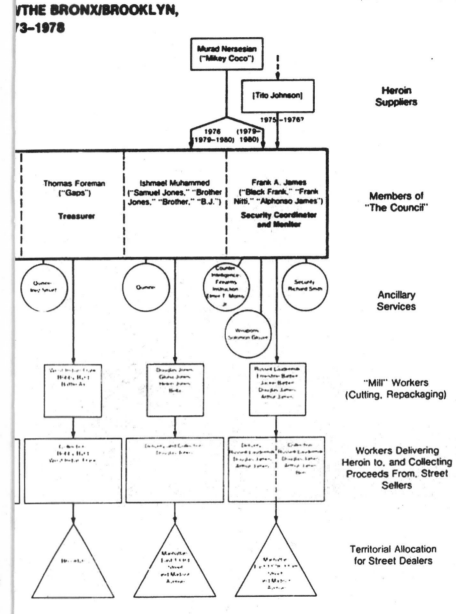

Murad Nersesian
("Mikey Coco")

[Tito Johnson]

1975–1976?

| Heroin Suppliers

1976
(1979–1980)

(1979–1980)

Thomas Foreman
("Gaps")

Treasurer

Ishmael Muhammed
("Samuel Jones," "Brother Jones," "Brother," "B.J.")

Frank A. James
("Black Frank," "Frank Nitti," "Alphonso James")

Security Coordinator
and Monitor

Members of
"The Council"

Ancillary
Services

"Mill" Workers
(Cutting, Repackaging)

Workers Delivering
Heroin to, and Collecting
Proceeds From, Street
Sellers

Territorial Allocation
for Street Dealers

...ing network co-founded and directed by Leroy "Nicky"

MR. UNTOUC

by Leroy "Nicky" E

and Tom Folsom

RUGGED LAND | 401 WEST STREET · SECOND FLOOR · NEW YORK CITY · NY 10014 · USA

RuggedLand

Published by Rugged Land, LLC

401 WEST STREET • SECOND FLOOR • NEW YORK CITY • NY 10014 • USA

RUGGED LAND and colophon are trademarks of Rugged Land, LLC.

Library of Congress Cataloging-in-Publication Data

Barnes, Leroy, 1933-
Mr. Untouchable / by Leroy "Nicky" Barnes and Tom Folsom.
-- 1st ed.   p. cm.
ISBN-13: 978-1-59071-041-8
ISBN-10: 1-59071-041-X
1. Criminals--New York (State)--New York. 2. Organized crime--New York (State)--New York.
3. Barnes, Leroy, 1933- I. Folsom, Tom, 1974- II. Title.
HV6795.N5B37 2007
364.1092--dc22
[B]
2006036665

Book Design by
HSU+ASSOCIATES

RUGGED LAND WEBSITE ADDRESS:WWW.RUGGEDLAND.COM

MARCH 2007

1   3   5   7   9   10   8   6   4   2

First Edition

For Prisoner #05404-054,

Allenwood Federal Penitentiary

Everything you had came from me. I turned you on to making money, and then I showed you how to spend it. You drove a Benz because you rode in mine. You lived in a penthouse because you'd been to mine. You didn't even have jewelry till you saw mine! And what did you do in return?

You disrespected me. You betrayed me.

See where that got you?

I want you to read every word of my story. And when you finish the last page, I want you to look up, see where I put you and ask yourself, was it worth it? Ask yourself that every day until you die.

Keep this in your cell as a reminder. I dedicate it to you.

AUTHOR'S NOTE

You have to understand there's no statute of limitations on murder. So anything involving murder will have to be in the documents already, will have to be solved already. If it's an unsolved murder, I'm not going to solve it! That ain't happening, man.

And I have omitted a few details to prevent anyone else from getting killed.

ACT ONE

THE COUNCIL

1973-1977

The Package

IN A SUITE AT THE CARLYLE HOTEL, Matty Madonna dropped three coffee beans into our long-stemmed glasses of Sambuca: one for health, one for wealth, one for happiness.

If it all worked out, at least we'd get the wealth.

Madonna was a big name on Pleasant Avenue in East Harlem. That was Italian turf. Uptown's Little Italy. There, inside the tenements lining the stretch between 114th and 120th, the Mafia stockpiled pure dope like gold in Fort Knox. But to move that powder west, to get it in the veins of the city's biggest concentration of junkies, the Italians had to go through men who could work the streets.

They had to go through us, the black dealers of Harlem.

"Look, Matty, I got a group of dealers with me now. As much powder as you can give us, we'll turn."

"Shipment of 200 kilos is comin' in. That's a lotta powder."

"We'll take care of it, man. *All* of it."

He didn't doubt my word. I had this overpowering reputation with the Italians. All the suppliers on the Avenue knew if you can get Nicky Barnes's business, you've got it *made*—Nick's going to take care of your package. He's going to take care of your money. I could've picked any one of those guys to be in on this, but I only wanted Matty. We had history. We trusted each other implicitly.

He struck a match and held it over the tops of the Baccarat glasses until the alcohol caught flame. My next request struck him silent.

"Matty, all seven of us need to have access to you."

It was an unusual request, 'cause in the dope game, dealers don't share suppliers. Take these two friends of mine—Mac and Vince Hunter. Neither was doing really well, but Mac got some powder on consignment and took it to the streets with Vince. But when they finished sellin' their powder, put all their money in a pile to give to the supplier?

Vinny pulled out his shit, shot Mac and watched the bullet come out the front of his head. Sparked his own partner, just so he could have that supplier all to himself. See, a dealer can't just go stroll down Pleasant Avenue to find a supplier. You don't find them. They find *you*. And if a supplier chooses you to be the man for his goods, you're at the top of the heap. His powder's flowin' through you, and that means the *power's* flowin' through you, too.

But for my thing, temptation had to be eliminated from the start. We were seven equals hooked up for the long haul. And like I told the brothers, "If we're all going to treat each other as equals, we *all* should have access to the source." All of us had to push the powder hard. All of us had to feel stake in what was going on. It was just too dangerous for power plays.

The heat of the fire forced the oil from the beans and a thin brown trickle floated to the surface of each glass. When the oil dropped to the bottom, Matty snuffed the flames with a folded-over, $100 bill and gave his answer. "I don't wanna meet with all these different guys. I only wanna meet with you."

I gave him that concession. The Madonna connect meant a consistent flow of top-shelf powder, whenever I wanted it. I couldn't jeopardize that windfall over an ideal.

We lifted our glasses to toast the shipment. A month later, it arrived. Probably from Marseilles, maybe Amsterdam. As for how it got here, I had no idea. A car over the Canadian border, a container off-loaded in Jersey, as cargo at JFK, where guys are paid not to look...

I didn't know and I didn't care. I didn't ask a lotta questions, 'cause I let the Italians handle that end. They'd been smuggling drugs into Pleasant Avenue for at least fifty years, so they had it down to a science. Let *them* bring it in. Let me pay for it when it got here. Long as I was hittin' the streets hard, that was good enough for me. 'Cause that was my science, and nobody had it down better than me.

My next meet with Matty was on the night of January 27, 1973, at the Colossus, a lonely diner in Astoria, Queens. The old Greek owner brought the menus and pushed the spinach pie.

"My mother's recipe," he said, beaming.

"Just coffee," we said.

For a restaurateur like Matty and a gourmand like myself, the food in this joint wasn't worth eating. Nobody'd ever expect us in a place like this, which made it perfect for our meet. True, underlings could've filled in for us, but Matty insisted on a face-to-face—"You come, I'll come. You won't let anyone trail you to get to me, I won't let anyone trail me to get to you."

That was important. It was our bond of trust.

The Greek filled our cups as we watched Willis Reed tip off on the black-and-white TV behind the counter. The Knicks had an early lead when I brought up Matty's imports—a stable of blonde Vegas showgirls he'd flown in for our after-party at the Carlyle.

"I don't understand, man. You got three million women in Manhattan to pick from. Why you flyin' in pussy?"

Matty lit his Cuban cigar. "'Cause my wife's in Brooklyn. My girls need to be as far away as possible." That was typical of Madonna, trapped in that Italian family man bullshit. We drank our cups and caught up on our gang from Green Haven, Marty Yamin and Sammy Katz and Joey Gallo, shot to death at Umberto's Clam House a few months ago.

"Too bad," said Matty, "but he had it comin'. Got cocky, like he couldn't be touched, you know? Can't act like that in this business."

"Unless you the strongest out there," I said.

And that's how it went. We enjoyed each other's company, talking about everything but the business at hand. The Celtics were up by six at the end of the quarter when Matty slid a velvet jewelry box across the table. I hesitated to take it. This wasn't the plan.

"Go ahead, open it. I designed it myself."

Inside was a solid gold Madonna on a link chain, a token of friendship to hang on my neck. The Greek was in the kitchen and the diner empty, so when I stepped up to leave, nobody saw Matty reach into his pocket, shake my hand and palm me the real gift.

"Blue Ford Granada, 120 Overlook."

I walked out to my white 1972 Benz and opened my fist. There it was, the key to my kingdom. I slid it onto the key ring, warmed up my ride and eased off to get the goods. But don't get me wrong. There is no such thing as me sitting in a car with a trunk full of drugs. I'm just not going to do anything like that. Sure, I had some sniff coke in my pocket—but I could swallow that, and if I ended up taking a misdemeanor pinch, so be it.

Getting caught with thirty kilos of heroin is a whole other story. That will put you down for a long time, and me and Matty had spent too much time in the joint to go back again. So we arranged a system to leave us as far away from the drugs as possible.

An hour before our meet, Matty's lieutenant put my package in a two-year-old blue Ford Granada. Like all our delivery vehicles, the motherfucker was a vault on wheels. Steel plates reinforced the trunk, so you'd need a tow truck and a chop shop to break into the thing.

The car itself was ideal for the job, well-kept but nondescript. You could leave it in front of the Plaza Hotel or on the streets of Bed-Stuy without suspicion. Any safe place would do, long as it wasn't by a hydrant or in front of a precinct, and tonight, Matty's lieutenant parked it in Hackensack, the city we'd agreed on, then gave the key to Madonna to give to me.

That way, I was bulletproof. Even if the cops pulled me over and asked for that key, what could they do? I had five on my ring, to a Benz, a Citroën, a Jensen Healey, a Chevelle and now, a Granada. If the NYPD picked the right key, they'd have to go around trying every Ford in the five boroughs. And the dope car was parked in Jersey!

A flawless system, with one vulnerable point.

I parked on a quiet street in LeFrak City, Queens, a nice block so the Benz wasn't out of place. My senses sharpened as I walked street after street to the seedier side of town, past the abandoned storefronts and the low rooftops, all perfect spots for a narco stakeout. And if the cops were really on game, catching this handoff meant a conspiracy charge.

My top lieutenant, Curt Molette, emerged like a ghost from the darkened alley. I let my instincts take over. *Nobody is watching.* I slipped him the key and the coordinates, "Blue Granada. 120 Overlook," and he took off into the night. I knew it'd be taken care of. Dude came out of two tours in Nam without a scratch and picked up countless packages for me without a hitch, a lucky motherfucker in the combat zone.

I drove back to the garage below my Washington Heights penthouse, and the elevator door opened to the shit-eating grin of the attendant, dressed in a blue bellhop cap and uniform.

"Nice trip, Mr. Darling?"

The fuck do you care?

I was not happy with the nosy new help. Like that doorman. When I told him the guys were coming over tonight, what did he say? "Absolutely, Mr. Darling. Just give me the names and I'll let them right in." Have to train these two how to handle me.

The fewer questions, the better we'd get along.

I stepped into my pad and there they were, bunched around the state-of-the-art, big-screen projection TV. The Celtics were up by one with a minute left on the clock, but with a little shakin' and bakin', Walt Frazier took the jumper and clinched the lead!

Frank, Ishmael and Wally leaped off my white leather sofa and passed high fives. Gaps showed a little fire with a pump of the arm, all you were gonna get out of that laid-back a dude. As for Jazz? He did the reverse, dancin' around the room like the sixth man of the Jackson Five. Guy got up from my Eames lounge chair and offered me the throne.

These were my warriors, these were my brothers.

I couldn't pull off something this big with just anybody. It took a lot of coordination by guys truly committed to making the dollar. I needed dealers who could turn the powder, were tough enough to protect the package and weren't going to present problems to where I'd have to take them out. 'Cause court wasn't gonna do me a bit of good if they fucked me over!

But after a lotta searching, I found the right men. They were street guys who had street smarts just like I had and, in my mind's eye, were gonna be excellent allies. And that's what I wanted.

There was Frank James. The legend himself. Behind his smooth baby face lay one of the most feared dudes on the East Side. A thick guy who looked like a slimmed version of Idi Amin, Frank carried a fierce rep on his shoulders. If somebody had to be taken out, physically interrogated or shown the brutal side of what we do, Frank was the man.

Ishmael Mohammed. "Brother." A lean soldier trained by the Fruit of Islam, a deeply spiritual dude who came up with our oath after an all-nighter of cocaine and the Koran. We all turned to Islam in the joint, so Ishmael would keep that bond strong. Might murder on Thursday, but come Friday morning, we'd be at the mosque.

Wally Rice. A prime mover in numbers till the Cubans inched him out, but once he turned to dealing, money just rolled in. With all that profit, Wally established himself as a real estate man. I wanted to be down with his business expertise, 'cause I had big plans for turning our organization legit.

Thomas Foreman. "Gaps." A real underground dude from Bed-Stuy, Gaps was an easygoing guy with a kind of sinister aura about him. You could just tell. This muthafucka was dangerous. You knew that. Even though he'd give you a smile, flash that gap in his bottom front teeth. He'd store our money out there in Brooklyn and be our treasurer.

Jazz. Got him right outta state prison. A good hustler with a lotta energy, lotta heart. Who knew what role he'd play, but for now, I charged him with getting our quinine and cut.

Guy Fisher. "Sugar Pie Guy." Even though he was a smooth kid—six feet tall, slim and good looking—with a real air of confidence, we were all seasoned veterans pushin' or past forty. Guy was just twenty-five and didn't have our experience. But I gave him a chance, figuring young blood might do the old guard good.

The thing I treasured most about these guys was loyalty. Didn't give a fuck if A turned more powder than B; if B was trustworthy, that was it. Long as they looked out for me, watched my back and provided for me, I'd look out for them. It's how it had to be.

For now, there was nothing any of us could do but wait, so we just poured all our energy on the game. With seconds on the clock, the Celtics tossed the inbounds pass, but Frazier stole it from Don Chaney and sunk it for two! Game over! We were shoutin' so loud, I barely heard the phone ring once, stop, then ring three more times. That was the signal from Curt, so I went back to the garage and drove the three blocks from my penthouse to the pay phone. A wiretap sent me to the joint once before. No way I'd let it happen again.

I dropped in a quarter, then dialed the number to another pay phone on the West Side. Curt picked up on the first ring. "Yo, boss. That car was parked right under a bright billboard. Lit up in plain sight! My instincts weren't going the right way, so I just walked on by."

Matty's lieutenant fucked up.

That's the thing with an operation as big as Matty's or mine. It can't be a one-man show. You have too many critical decisions to make all day, all the time. Ultimately, you gotta rely on other people, and occasionally other people do stupid shit, like parking a car under a billboard during the day, not thinking the goddamn thing is gonna light up at night.

"It's fine," I told Curt. "Go back there and pick it up."

All of a sudden, the hairs on the back of my neck shot straight up. True, it was cold as a motherfucker outside, but that wasn't the reason. I can't describe the sensation exactly, but it's like this old joke we used to tell in the joint:

This woman's coming through the park late one evening, and when she sees this shady dude walkin' toward her, she kind of holds on to her purse. "Excuse me, ma'am," he tells her, "I am so hungry, and I don't even have a dime in my pocket. The only thing I got in there is this nine-millimeter pistol. I sure wish you'd give me a few dollars."

We thought that was a riot, but the point is, right when that woman saw him, she knew something was wrong. And if there's any hard and fast rule I followed in the dope game, it's trust your instincts. That's big, man. Like if I came out of the after-hours joint and two guys were by my Benz? Instincts told me to put my hand on my shit. That way, if these guys didn't give me some goddamn space, I was ready to spark first. It's just self-preservation.

And right now, my instincts were on full alert that someone was watching me talk on the pay phone. I couldn't see him, but I'd been under enough surveillance in my life to know a presence was there. Didn't give a fuck about him listening to me—he wasn't gonna catch me sayin' anything that could harm me—but if the cops were spying on me, maybe they were onto Curt, too.

You just never know. If he led them to that Granada, we'd *both* go down on conspiracy, and even the remote possibility wasn't worth the risk. I'd seen too many guys go down by not being extra careful.

I caught Curt right before he hung up.

"Hang on, dude. Just wait till you hear back."

"Quick trip, Mr. Darling?"

The attendant kept watching me from the corner of his eye. I looked into the lens of the newly installed security camera and it all made sense. The dude was a narco! I had no idea what was known or unknown, but one thing was clear.

This shit went deep.

I dialed up the volume on the postgame show till Frazier's trash—"I knew I was fast, but didn't know I was that *quick!*"—filled the room. The Council picked up the cue. We stood on the white shag, crossed arms and linked hands in a tight circle. Each man spoke one word of the oath.

"Treat my brother as I treat myself."

The vow complete, I laid down the situation to the brotherhood.

"I'll pick up the car," said Guy. "I'd walk into fuckin' DEA headquarters for thirty kilos."

The kid was eager to step to the plate, to get our thing rolling, but I didn't want any of the brothers taking unnecessary risks. That's why we each had crews in the first place, to do our dirty work on the streets.

"Slow down. You all got your lieutenants on deck, right?"

"I dunno," said Jazz, "if I send my dude and he gets pinched, he might flip, you know, figurin' I sent him into an unsafe situation."

But as far as I was concerned, even with all this surveillance, the situation *was* safe—for anybody but Curt.

"Is it really safe?"

All eyes turned to my woman Thelma, or as we called her, Tee, who'd been keeping an ear on the situation. She blushed at the attention, but spoke with confidence.

"I mean, if you think it's safe, *I'll* go and get it."

Now there are a lot of good reasons why you want a woman hooked up with your thing. A man looks less suspicious when he's with a woman, and if a cop pulls you over, he'll think you're a couple going out. Two guys and two gals are fine too. That's a double date. But four guys in a car? That's either a drug deal, a conspiracy or a hit team.

At the same time, no woman gets in your thing because she looks good. To be considered for a relationship, she's got to pass tests to prove she's 100 percent in your corner. No way around it. If she don't stand and hold, she don't get the trips to Bergdorf's and Bloomie's. If she don't strut, she don't get her wheels. As for a penthouse? A whole other deal. Only your wives get a penthouse.

Now, when Tee told me she was pregnant after our first fuck date, my first reaction was shock, 'cause I'd been strict about takin' care of business—held till she was ready to skeet, put the condom on and finished the job. But lookin' at her long, lean legs, dancer's body and big, pretty nipples? Shit. I just had to go right back in there, and that was my mistake, bein' unprotected for that initial penetration on round two. Extra liquid must've still been in me.

Once she broke the news, I said, "Fuck it." Bought her a leather coat from Spain, a two-seater ragtop Mercedes with a separate metal top she could snap on in winter and this beautiful Washington Heights penthouse. I showered her with more luxuries than she'd ever seen in her life, but that didn't mean she was my woman. She was just a girl I knocked up on our first fuck date, whose needs I provided for as a gentleman.

Tee decided on her *own* to position herself as my woman. She took it on herself to become a stand-up ho.

Now, how does a woman do that? Is the barrel in her pussy? Are the muscles holding it up? I don't know. That's something we didn't teach our women. That was their thing, their code, their way of showing "Yes, I have absorbed the Council value system as a part of me."

Tee didn't have problems standing and holding but was frustrated by the strut, so Ishmael's wife Helen had her and Renee, Guy's girl, over for pinochle and practice sessions.

"Know why Helen's so good?" Tee told me. "Notice how her ass rolls while she walks? How her cheeks move independently? Her thighs rub together and she can hold it in tight, but I got bow thighs. I got too much space under my pussy, and that's why I'm havin' a hard time."

I wasn't interested in updates. All I wanted to know is when a cop pulled me over, Tee was gonna grab my rod, shove that motherfucker between her legs, step out the car, strut a few paces, then take a frisk without dropping.

But I had to give it to her. Tonight, when she asked to pick up that car, she didn't see it as a chance to step in and save the day. It was an act of submission, a plea for acceptance. Her eyes begged me to let her do it, and whether she could strut or not, I knew she'd truly absorbed the values of a stand-up ho.

"Go and get ready, baby."

Tee emerged from the bedroom in her sable coat, dressed as a Fifth Avenue princess out for a big night on the town, honored to be part of the inner mechanics of the Council. With a rush of adrenaline, she strutted past the men in her boots, customized by Capezio with skins boosted from Louis Vuitton, walked out the door and into the fire. That really tightened her up to the brothers.

"She's a brave woman for pickin' up that powder," said Guy.

"She'll be fine," said Frank. "She's so young, she could do that five or six years on possession easy, even if somethin' did go wrong."

But that wasn't the case when a half hour later, the phone rang the signal. I headed to the pay phone and dialed the spot.

"Hey, baby," answered Thelma. "It's all taken care of."

"You did good."

"Well, I'm gonna go over to Helen's if that's okay. Renee bought a nice bottle of Marsala wine, and I'm gonna get the ingredients to that spaghetti allo…"

"*Alla Bolognese.*"

It was a special recipe from Nicola Petrizzio, Matty's chef at Tre Amici Ristorante.

"Yeah, that. Helen's gonna cook it while we help out Renee with her strut. She still can't get it down like I can."

Once Tee passed Curt the key, my operation launched forward like the four-cylinder Maserati engine under the hood of my Citroën. A well-oiled, finely tuned machine.

Curt drove the Granada inside a Hackensack auto garage. The owner got $500 to split for the night, so the place was secure when Curt reached under the dash and pushed two buttons to pop the trunk. That's how easy it was to get to the goods in a delivery car, but you had to know the trick: keeping the ignition on when you hit those buttons.

He divided the thirty plastic kilo bags into seven grocery sacks, one for each member of the Council. Guy had his lieutenant Whop there—called him that 'cause for a little guy, his head was big like the Burger King Whopper—so Whop split with six of the sacks and distributed them to the other lieutenants, from Ishmael's man Dougie to Jazz's man Scrap.

Since I had the biggest operation in the Council, my sack was heavier than the others combined. Curt was responsible for my share, so he drove it to a middle-class apartment in Fort Lee where a young couple, forty-hour weekers who didn't attract suspicion, lived in rent-free luxury in exchange for one night of work a month.

"Put an eight on it," he told them.

That's how you make real money in the heroin business—turning one kilo into nine by diluting it with cut. I could've gotten away with a nine or even a ten cut, but I wanted to make sure my goods were the strongest on the streets, so I didn't get too greedy with it.

As for the cut itself, it was top-quality mannite, a lightweight laxative that gave my heroin that nice, fluffy texture. Plus I spiced it up with a little quinine. Q gives a hot flash to accompany the injection of the drug, and I knew from back in the day that if I didn't feel the flash, even if it was great shit, I wouldn't think the package was any good. So I had to have that Q in the bag.

The couple opened a kilo of pure, put a few ounces on a cutting board, added the cut, then shuffled it all up with two playing cards. When the powder looked uniform, they put each kilo in a plastic bag, closed it up with a sealing iron and earned their rent within an hour.

Curt's next stop was a tenement apartment on 155th and Bradhurst in Upper Harlem. Strapped with a sawed-off, Thelma's brother Duke checked the peephole and let him in as ten women—all under thirty, all related to Thelma—undressed and got ready for work. Keeping the mill in the family is important. Pulls everyone together and prevents informing.

Having all girls isn't some sexual thing, either. If men work the mill, they'll drink, smoke weed and turn on the TV. Takes twice as long to do the work, giving cops twice the time to bust your operation. But women? They just wanna be done and get away. Besides, you need your men making drops, dealing powder and takin' out muthafuckas who need killing. Puttin' shit in bags seems like something a woman should be doin' anyhow.

Curt watched like a doctor as the girls on the assembly line, completely naked except for surgical masks, went to work on the first of his kilo bags. It was a real blue-collar assembly line, with each girl mirroring her opposite across the huge sheet of plate glass, propped up by two couches.

The baggers grabbed a bundle of little glassine envelopes from the box on the center of the table, then squeezed it so the top bag flipped out—one to the left, one to the right. The spooners pinched open these bags, scooped 'em down on the mound of powder and lifted up with a quarter spoon worth of heroin.

The tapers did the packaging: sealed up the bag and folded it over—this way, the bag looked bigger than it really was—added a piece of black tape to close the fold, then put it in a brown grocery sack. Once that sack was full, an empty one replaced it.

It had been a straight day of tedious work by the time the girls bagged the 140 kilos of heroin and rubber-banded them into "New York Loads," bundles of ten quarters, my patented manner of distribution.

On Curt's orders, the girls put 200 loads in a brown sack marked Flower, 200 loads in a sack marked Sugar and so on, until all the loads were accounted for.

Now came the wipe-down. A morning fog of powder filled the room—clogged the air-conditioning, covered the rugs and turned the women white with heroin dust. But any trace of heroin could be the building block of a conspiracy, so the girls vacuumed the rugs and couches, changed the AC filters and scrubbed the floors. Like bagging, it was woman's work, so Duke just watched over it all with his shotgun. Once it was clean, Curt changed his clothes and wiped the soles of his shoes—otherwise, he'd leave powder tracks in the building.

Tossing the ten sacks into the trunk of the Cutlass, Curt drove to a secluded Bronx parking lot and passed the key to Flower, one of my ten middleman street dealers. Flower drove it to Morningside Park, pushed the buttons under the dash and a took a sack. He walked three blocks and, without a word, passed the key to Sugar.

And on it went—get in the car and go, park it and take the goods, pass the key and split. In an hour and a half, the Cutlass came back to Curt completely clean, so he drove it to his wife's, had a freak and a hot bath, then slept for a day straight.

By the time he woke up, New York City was flooded with powder.

I made it clear when I started our thing that I wanted the street *saturated*. "Every time a buyer wants a fix, our product has gotta be out there."

Well, we did just that, in tens of thousands of tiny quarter packages across the top markets of the city. Guy took the South Bronx and Gaps took Brooklyn. Ishmael, Frank and Wally took the East Side—Ishmael on Madison and 132nd, Frank on Madison between 117th and 120th, Wally on the corner of Fifth and 117th. Me and Jazz covered the West

Side, but only I got the Marketplace on Eighth and 116th, power alley of the Harlem dope scene.

It was just spectacular.

After years of plotting and waiting, I pulled off the boldest score in the underworld—seizing the distribution of heroin on the streets of New York City.

"Nice work," said Matty the next week in a Mount Vernon diner, passing the key to a Plymouth with another installment in the trunk. I passed the key to a Skylark in return, parked by Curt with $750G in the trunk.

Week after week it was the same routine, and by the time I passed the last key, the Council had turned the entire shipment of 200 kilos, paid for it in full—$5 million—and between street and weight sales, made over $20 million. And that was in *1973* dollars!

But it didn't end there, 'cause en route from Marseilles, or maybe it was Amsterdam, another shipment was comin' our way. And they say crime doesn't pay. The only question was—what were we gonna do with all that money?

The American Dream

THE CITY WAS MINE, all spread before me. Pushers in the streets, raking in the cash. Junkies in the dens, getting the high of their lives. I took in the view from my private yacht, cruising up the Hudson as the sun set on Manhattan. Tee held the arm of my blue blazer. Her Hermès original, a red, white and blue head scarf, flapped around like a flag. Who knew? Booze worked for the Kennedys, maybe junk will for the Barneses!

The brothers sang along as the jazz quartet kicked off our favorite song—"God Bless America." Goddamn right. Our powder was so good, dealers were coming into New York from Baltimore, Philly, Washington DC, even as far as Oakland to buy it. I'm not even talkin' about weight, this is *street* stuff! They'd spend fifteen to twenty thousand dollars, take home the merchandise and kick ass with it! That was just a real good feeling, knowin' America was hooked on our shit this happy Fourth.

"Capt'n Barnes!"

Frank James in an ascot. Never thought I'd see that.

"What's happenin', Frank? You got the works ready?"

He handed me a bottle rocket and looked to the NYPD chopper looming over our party. "Wanna take a shot?"

I lifted an ice-cold martini instead. It's the only way to live in the face of round-the-clock surveillance—*extremely* well.

I almost felt sorry for the cops, so used to trailing Superflys in customized Cadillacs, chinchilla coats and purple fedoras. They could laugh at that shit, but my tastes cut to the bone. I mean, wouldn't *you* love a Corniche, a gold Piaget and custom-tailored, designer threads? Or an evening cruise with exotic beauties, French wines, Beluga caviar, Colombian coke and M&Ms? (That's Château Mouton and motah, a breed of Jamaican weed mixed with dust. Excellent combination.)

But after all my years on the wrong end of trumped-up charges, illegal wiretaps and planted evidence, I *deserved* to dish out the best revenge—livin' the dream with a big belly, Van Cleef bracelet and a huge goddamn Tiffany diamond on my platinum ring.

Of course, not all cops got shut out from the good life. I'd see detectives from the Special Investigations Unit, the elite force of the NYPD Narcotics Division, cruisin' the city in sharp Italian suits and gold Rolexes. Think they got all that from a government salary? Only difference between them and me was they got caught, busted the Christmas before when Commissioner Murphy revealed that all the heroin seized in the "French Connection" case was missing from the police vault.

Millions of angry voters wanted to know why. Was the clerk behind the desk gettin' high as a motherfucker? Or was it true that the city's top detectives were the city's biggest pushers? All the dealers knew these guys offered product as good as any Italian on Pleasant Avenue, but Governor Rockefeller dodged the issue altogether by pushing the toughest anti-drug law in America: Get caught selling dope? Go to jail for life without parole.

No plea bargains. No exceptions.

Mayor Lindsay called the governor's law vindictive. Harlem called it a plot to lock up the little man, the nickel-and-dime pusher who had a habit. But the Special Narcotics Prosecutor? He called it opportunity. If he busted a high-profile dealer as the very first arrest under the Rockefeller Law, he'd prove the law worked against the big men, and wouldn't that make the governor *real* happy come budget time.

Now it just so happened on January 8, 1973, days after the governor announced his law, *New York* magazine profiled "The Untouchables," eleven top names in the city dope trade. And while people in this town pay good money to have their picture plastered in the papers, for a drug dealer, publicity is a real bitch. The fact that they called us "difficult to catch and even harder to get into court" was like a big dare to the prosecutor, making us prime candidates to be the poster boys for the Rockefeller Law.

So why did he pick me? Could've been the buzz on the wire: *Nicky Barnes got a Black Mafia, an uptown Cosa Nostra.* Maybe it was just my pretty face. Jose Rosa might've been the biggest dealer in Spanish Harlem, but who'd want his ugly mug on a poster? Whatever the reason, the prosecutor launched a coordinated investigation by the finest of New York's Finest, three teams that would shit, eat and breathe Nicky Barnes over eight months of 24-7 surveillance.

"Operation Slick" hit the back alleys of Harlem, where informants revealed I was Muslim, *right*, in the Black Liberation Army, *wrong*, didn't drink or use drugs, *everything but heroin*, a protégé of Joey Gallo, *not exactly*, and an organizational genius—*absolutely*. The cops filed all this bullshit as "evidence," leaving me with the biggest file in the records cabinet of NYPD Intelligence. With the price of real estate in Manhattan, it was a criminal waste of space.

"Operation Charlie" of the Manhattan DA's Special Narcotics Unit was headquartered in the basement of the building across from my Haven

Avenue penthouse. They listened to bugs on my phones and in my living room and snapped photos of me coming to and from the garage.

"Operation Get Our Shit Together" of the Special Investigations Unit, still reeling from the worst scandal in NYPD history, went one step further. A fresh batch of young Serpicos trailed me 24-7 in a no-holds-barred last shot at redemption.

As I saw it, there was only one reason why everybody wanted to take me down so bad. See, the city was just filled with junkies, more users than at any time before or since, and nobody could do anything about it, from the cops to the prosecutor to the governor. But if they got Nicky Barnes when the Rockefeller Law kicked in on September 1, 1973?

At least they'd have a reason to keep their machine running.

Well, I hated to disappoint everybody, but no way were they gonna catch me near anything that could hurt me. That ain't happenin'.

"Yo, Nick! You gonna beat Rock?"

My fans surrounded me on 125th Street, calling out support, counting on me to shove Rock's evil law up his ass. They were sick of being fucked over by dirty cops, tired of being stepped on by the government. They couldn't wait to see me stick it to the man, but for now were happy enough watching the sparks rain down in the biggest fireworks display ever to hit Harlem.

Gotta give it to the Council; we knew how to put on a show. But the best was yet to come...

See, we *always* had somethin' goin' on at the Hubba Hubba. Like all our after-hours joints, the Hubba had glitz and glamour, and every night big Continentals and double-parked Cadillacs lined the street. With strippers, deejays and spots to freak off, the Hubba had a little for everybody, but of course, not everybody could get in.

We had double steel doors at the entrance with a peephole we could slide open, like in a speakeasy. If security saw you were a friend of the Council's, they searched you with a pat-down and an Amboy metal detector. You'd have to pay a $100 bill for cover, too, but nobody minded that 'cause in return you got an eight ball of coke worth more than the cost of entry. Plus, the drinks were free, everything but the champagne and international wines.

Above the bar was a wooden sign—"The Pedigree of the Honey Does Not Concern the Bee." In other words, no woman's comin' through the door unless she's honey, so go on and get your stinger ready. Or try your luck with the go-go dancer, shakin' her thing on an elevated table. Depending on the tip you gave, she might even take her clothes off!

On weekends we cleared room for a small stage. It was *the* show to see on Friday or Saturday night, and if you picked the short straw from the hat, you had to be a judge. No experience necessary, but on a night like Piece of the Rock, where lesbian couples competed for a baseball-sized chunk of cocaine, you'd have to weigh several factors into who was the winner.

Oral sex was a must—the girls might get booed off the stage otherwise, and while sixty-nine was a crowd favorite, it all came down to the gratification level each woman experienced. If she faked it, she'd have to convince you she hadn't. Same deal for our signature contest, the legendary Freak of the Week.

"Ladies and gentlemen," said Jazz on the mike, soakin' up the limelight. "I'd like to welcome y'all to tonight's star-spangled event!" The diamond JAZZ glittered off his gold medallion, but he didn't need introduction. Nobody looked like this dude. He was a short guy with real angular features who could've been the child of Sammy Davis Jr. and the Bride of Frankenstein. It seemed all the energy in his body rose up to that shock of hair on the peak of his Afro, worn high to give him a few extra inches.

"So without further a-*doo*…it is my distinct pleasure to introduce the first contender for this week's Freak. Red Ronnie from 135th Street!"

A sweet sweetback in a close-cropped Afro took the stage as Isaac

Hayes crooned "Your Love Is So Doggone Good" on the speakers. A comfortable couple made for a better show, so we always played their favorite music in the background.

"Red Ronnie, meet Pumpkin, a nice girl from the South Bronx!"

Pumpkin strutted onstage, kinda wild like a street cat. It was all part of the act, pretending they just met each other. But while the initial meeting was simulated, the fuckin' got real and raw.

The audience chilled at the bar as Pumpkin took off Red Ronnie's suede jacket. A good crowd tonight, from the powder people to the hustlin' crew. It's why we charged the high cover, to keep certain types out. Freak of the Week was a ceremonial event. No peep-show weirdos were gonna jack off on my stage.

I watched from the maximum privacy of my velvet-lined banquette, my throne to watch over court. Everybody knew the rules on dealing with me. Same deal with the go-go dancer. Look all you want, but don't touch. Course I let our new waitress slip me a tongue to go with my big shot glass of Remy and water. Both slid down smooth and easy.

Ishmael took a hit and checked her out, tense. "You sure she's cool?" he whispered. I loved Ishmael. His mission in life was to watch my back. But all the same...

"The fuck are you worried about the waitress for, Ishmael? The fuck she gonna do to me?"

Ishmael had a habit of getting paranoid, especially on the last leg of his ritual—smoke Buddha, drink Remy and water for a few hours, then start sniffin'. Each stage was separate. Wouldn't mix one with the other, 'cause for him coke just tasted too good. That's what happens with topshelf blow. It gives your taste buds an ongoing sensation of ecstatic feeling that rises through your nostrils to your brain into the center of your whole being. Not quite like an orgasm, but covers your body in almost the same way.

I was mellow when I sniffed, 'cause like tonight, I drank and smoked weed at the same time. That balanced everything out. But Ishmael didn't want to spoil that good coke flavor, so the paranoia caught up to him. It got in his eyes and kind of took over, made him think everybody was a potential threat who had to be killed.

"Great shit," said Frank, sniffing the tiny gold spoon and scooping a hit for Guy. "Time to get hair on your chest, Wonder Boy. Get some ping in your thing!"

Fuckin' Frank. Always undermining the brothers, from insidious little nicknames to strong-arming. True, he was my first choice to be in the Council, but that didn't make him first among equals! Frank didn't see it that way. He thought he had the right to treat everyone like a subordinate, especially Guy.

"Naw, man. I gotta split," said Guy. And he did.

"Frank! Why you gotta mess with Guy like that?"

Guy didn't touch coke, weed, alcohol, nothin', but Frank interpreted that as some kind of weakness. I valued Guy's decision as a real smart choice for a young hustler. The fast life could overwhelm a kid. Keeping clean gave him some distance, kept him focused on building his street biz.

"I'm telling you, Nick, that boy needs to get fucked up! How he gettin' his high otherwise?"

"Uh, I'll take that hit for him," Ishmael said.

Red Ronnie was really diggin' into Pumpkin's pussy. He rode her like a beast as her heels arched to the ceiling in a real show-stopper.

Big Smitty pushed through the cheering crowd. Comin' in at 6'4" and 300 pounds, a convicted felon who machine-gunned a man to death, he was a natural choice on security. Nobody fucked with Big Smitty.

"Yo, Nick, these Italians want in. Paulie and your pal Sally. Sally says he don't have enough to pay the cover."

"It's cool. Send 'em to the office."

"I'd hate to be on his end of that sit-down," said Wally.

"Well you be on my end. All you."

"Yeah," said Ishmael, "we'll put the fear of Allah in that muthafucka!"

When Paulie came into my wood-paneled, soundproof office, I could tell he was taken aback by the show of force—me sitting at my desk, the brothers standing behind, rock faced like terra-cotta warriors. He tried to brush off the show of force, but his hands shook as he lit his Camel.

"Nice to see you again, Paulie."

Joey Gallo had hooked me up with him a while back, although it didn't work out too well. Just like an Italian, Paulie charged a price for a "white kilo," then jacked up his rate for a "black kilo." The major difference was the color of the buyer, although his black kilo had so much cut on it, it was too fucked to sell on the street! Too bad for Paulie. Could've made him a lotta money if he'd only played fair.

"I gotta virgin fuckin' package," slurred Sally Moon. "Nobody put *nothin'* in it! Ain't whacked up a bit!"

You always knew what you were getting with Moon. Had a rep for being flaky on his packages—always top quality, never on time—but damn, he was a great guy. A fabulous lifestyle, a pricey duplex near Lincoln Center, the latest Cadillacs and the finest women…

No wonder he was always broke and desperate for a deal.

"We'll talk later, Moon."

Even if he did have a package, he was drunk and full of cocaine and in no shape to do business. Paulie only brought him for protection, knowin' the two of us were cool. Hopefully he was more sober, 'cause he needed to listen to my words very carefully. I'd been waiting to say them for some time.

All my life, to be exact.

When I was a kid we had to respect turf. If my gang went to Pleasant Avenue to play basketball at Benjamin Franklin, we had to give propers to the Italians. That was cool with us, 'cause we were playin' ball on their court. And if the Italians came to the West Side, to play us in stickball at St. Nicholas Triangle, they knew to give *us* respect.

Recognizing territory kept our games friendly, but once the Italians took over illegal money in Harlem, they dropped that territorial respect.

They inched us out of numbers and brought in heroin. They bought mom-and-pop stores on the West Side and built pizza parlors. If we needed cash, we'd have to go to the Italians. If we needed jobs, we'd be put to work as numbers runners or dope pushers in the Italian machine.

No way around it. The Italians had the upper hand.

To protect their financial interests, whether it be policy, weed or hard drugs, the Italians were known to use enforcers. You'd see their goons coming into the spots, and the blacks practically turned white. "The motherfuckin' guineas are here! You'd better pay them their money."

Of course, I assumed we'd all moved beyond that. This was 1973, a new era of Black Power and pride. So imagine my surprise when I'm enjoying my drink at the Purple Manor, and two goombahs approach this friend of Wally's.

"You know," they told him as they cracked their knuckles, "Paulie ain't too happy about your debt."

There's something you've got to remember about the Manor. This bar and grill is right on 125th Street between Madison and Park. Two blocks down is Sam Windham's Church of God in Christ, a cornerstone of the Harlem church scene. Two doors down is the Sandwich Oasis, owned by Frank James. It's clear that this block is our turf. No pizza parlors. No cannoli shops.

What got me was *everybody* knew the Manor as a Council hangout. And for an Italian to muscle in on a debt was not just an act of disrespect to Harlem, it was a dis to the Council. I couldn't allow that.

"So why don't you two step back cross town," I told these goons, "and tell Paulie to come see me at the Hubba…"

Never one for Cuban cigars, I lit up a straw-sized dust joint and put on my game face.

"I appreciate you coming on such short notice, Paulie, but I couldn't help notice your guys at the Manor—"

"I didn't mean no disrespect," he said, putting up his hand. "If I'd known you were hooked up with that guy, I never woulda sent—"

"Stay cool, Paulie. I just saw your guys talkin' to him. I wasn't hooked up with him at all."

"Good. 'Cause that motherfucker's a *deadbeat*. Owes me fifteen Gs. Hate getting it the hard way, but that's how it's gotta go sometimes."

"I understand. And I know the higher-ups are breathin' down *your* neck, 'cause you gotta get them *their* money."

"Crazy business we're in, ain't it?"

"So I want to make it easy for everybody. In the future, if a problem like this happens again, don't send anybody into Harlem. Just come straight to me and I'll see what I can do."

"Really, Nick. We wouldn't wanna trouble you with that."

Fuckin' Paulie. Nobody ever talked like this to him before, so my message didn't even register in his brain.

"Paulie, the Italians can't have physical presence in Harlem no more. You need to collect money, you got to see *me*. No more threats, no more pushin' that strong arm. You send the word to the top. That shit is *out*. If it happens again, somebody gonna end up gettin' hurt."

Paulie was speechless. Poor Sally was passed out in the chair, sleeping through a real milestone in history—the first black man *ever* to tell the white boys, "Look, you muthafuckas can't come over here, fucking around in Harlem!"

A perfect cap to a fine day for independence.

The Freak of the Week ruffled through her prize money, ridin' shotgun in my tan Citroën.

"Fourteen hundred! Fifteen hundred dollars!!!"

Damn, girl, get over it. Got to chill this bitch out.

"Here, baby, smoke this."

Pumpkin sucked a drag of the zing. I did the same. I loved dust. Only thing that wiped me out since I gave up junk. I eased lower and watched the white lines of the Major Deegan float to the stars. This was a problem. Dust made me hallucinate.

Please, car, just get me home tonight.

The high beams hit from behind. Another tail. But after seven months of this shit, I had my moves down pat.

On sunny days, I'd treat 'em to long, leisurely drives in Brooklyn. I might step out of my car, walk around a random building to keep it interesting, do a few U-turns comin' home. Then there was my driving tour of Harlem, stopping at all my favorite spots, all hundred of them. A master of the goose chase!

This time I'd pull an old-fashioned cat and mouse. I'd take that exit up at the little hill in the 140s, right near the exit. Make that right like I'm getting off, but peel out immediately at the U-turn. The tail would fly by, 'cause he can't react that quick, then I'd just go up the one-way street, drive down to Joe-Boy's garage midway down the block, borrow one of his cars and ease on home.

But when my tail pulled beside in the left lane, I thought I was *really* banged out.

Cops don't drive yellow Cadillacs?

But Guy Fisher did. I looked at him cruisin' beside me, and he flashed a grin like he wanted a challenge...Did Guy think he could take me in that ratty Caddy?

Couldn't be happenin'. But there he was, inching forward with Renee riding shotgun. I hated to make him look bad in front of his woman, but no way was he gonna get away with this.

"You know, Pumpkin, this car got a Maserati engine."

"What's that do?"

"Makes it good for racing."

I pulled down the lever, dropped the car to a few inches off the ground, hit the accelerator and—bam! Poor Guy couldn't do a thing as I blasted off. Pumpkin squealed in delight, so wet she slid all over my tan bucket seat.

Sorry, Red Ronnie, you got nothin' on *my* foreplay.

LEROY "NICKY" BARNES

Caught Holding
The Bag

IF YOU DRIVE AROUND in a Maserati-Citroën, own a couple penthouses and report only $30G at the end of the year, the IRS is gonna audit your ass with a lifestyle profile. My luxurious life already landed me one, and if I got busted again, I'd go down like Capone for tax evasion. But I was smarter than that guinea, so I made the system work for me.

See, the Republican administration was eager to provide tax breaks for the wealthy, so those who invested a few million in FHA housing got incredible incentives. I could pump drug money into these housing complexes and once my investment matured, end up with millions in perfectly legitimate cash. Until then, I got a two-for-one tax write-off that applied to back taxes! It was all too good to be true, and as far as I could see, there was only one problem.

"Why do I gotta give money to this white guy Goldberg for settin' up the deal?"

"Marty Goldman has the connections to the tax shelters," said Carl

Bolden, a black lawyer from Detroit.

"We don't," said Benjamin Blake, his partner.

"Well, you gain the expertise you need from him, get his connections, then step away from him.'Cause we can do this on our *own*. An all black thing."

"Absolutely," said Blake, handing me the papers. "We see a real future in a partnership with you."

"Black is beautiful," said Bolden.

Riding in first class back to LaGuardia, I eased against the leather headrest and dreamed of all I could do with millions in clean cash. Open strip malls in Harlem, move on a nationwide chain of automated car washes...the Council could turn legit in no time.

When I stepped off the plane, the terminal was completely dark from the first blackout of the summer. *Fuckin' Con Ed*. Criminal how they couldn't get their shit together. I looked for Thelma, but she was nowhere in sight. I called home to find out the situation.

"Tee? Why ain't you here?"

"I'm so sorry, baby, but we lost power and the elevator ain't workin'. I got the baby and she's cryin' from the heat and I didn't wanna walk down all those stairs holdin' her."

"Stay cool, girl. I'll take a cab and see you at home."

DON'T GET CAUGHT HOLDING
THE BAG ON SEPTEMBER 1

The bold block letters of the billboard greeted me back to Harlem, and I thanked the governor for that reminder. Glad to see my hard-earned tax dollars workin' for me. I'd gotten so used to surveillance, I almost forgot why they were doin' it! But in two days the Rockefeller Law was gonna kick in, which meant the cops were gettin' ready to pounce all over me.

Good luck, muthafuckas.

Back at Haven Avenue, a couple cars blocked up the horseshoe driveway, waiting for the elevator to kick in. I just hopped out the cab and ran up the thirteen flights, the only time I regretted penthouse living. *Goddamn!* That wore me out. I was hoping to hit the Hubba for some action, but fuck it, I drew a scented bath and freaked off with my woman.

Come morning the power was still out, so I figured I'd face the heat, ninety-five degrees and muggy as hell. I revved up my Benz and cranked the AC, but right then three black-and-whites peeled in behind me. With all those flashing blue lights, fuckin' garage looked like the Hubba discotheque.

"Stay where you are!" screamed the bullhorn. "Don't turn around! Down on the ground and spread 'em! Don't turn around!"

"Man, I ain't turning!" I went down to the ground. It was some crazy shit, man. Fifteen cops in full riot gear, all with their heads down, all ready to kill. I was certain I'd get a bullet in my black ass, but finally they let me up.

"We're disappointed in you, Barnes! Thought you were gonna shoot it out with us!"

Like I was dumb enough to shoot it out against fifteen cops!

I marched back up the steps to door 13E, handcuffed, pissed and defiant. The pigs heaved as they lifted the battering ram, but I just told 'em to use the gold key in my pocket.

"What about this silver key? Huh, scumbag? Does this go to that nice Benz you got?"

"Ask my lawyer where it goes."

Jealous motherfucker.

They barged on in, dumbstruck at the scene. I guess they expected a huge heroin mill, but instead saw Tee nursing our baby girl.

It all just blew their minds.

Unlike the typical dope dealer pad—gaudy red velvet and silk sheets—I had an immaculate white shag on a white wood floor, a $4000 white sofa, wall-to-wall mirrors and bookshelves of ancient and black history.

The cops took all the time in the world to snoop through my kingdom—walking into the closets, gaping at the sixty pairs of custom-made shoes and the twenty-seven full-length leather coats. Of course, they found the good stuff, too—$50G cash in my oak bureau drawer, a loaded sawed-off next to the king-sized bed, a .25, a .32 Smith & Wesson, a .32 Clerke and a .38 Colt. Big deal. But when a detective pulled my leather travel bag from the bedroom—"We got ya, Barnes"—I thought I was a goner.

No stranger to planted evidence, I was sure the detective stuffed a few kilos in that bag, so I'd say we were both surprised when he only pulled out clothes and tax papers.

And then came the barks from Prince and Duke, two German shepherds who were by far the smartest cops in the room.

"Look what the K-9s found!"

An officer stepped out of my chrome-fixtured bathroom with a plastic evidence bag, grinning away at his big score.

They'd been looking all over for me while I was in Detroit, figuring I split for the Caribbean to ride out the Rockefeller Law. But when Operation Charlie heard the wiretap on my phone, they thought they'd finally hit pay dirt.

To them, "Stay cool, girl. I'll take a cab and see you at home," sounded like a cryptic message. Seeing me step out of the taxi with a leather travel bag added a degree of suspicion, and when they stopped the driver and discovered I'd just come from the airport, they assumed my bag was stuffed with kilos from France, Hong Kong or somewhere else exotic. In those days, airport security wasn't too tight, so people stuffed dope into their carry-ons all the time.

What really closed the deal was the surveillance cam showing me run up thirteen flights of stairs. They thought I was trying to evade the undercover narcos at the door and elevator, forgetting the fact that the goddamn elevator wasn't workin' in the first place! Fucking keystones. So they went to the judge, secured the warrant and waited all night in the garage, thinking they were gonna catch me coming down with that travel bag.

After all, they were hoping to find *something* after an eight-month intense investigation, a big chalkboard of who's here and who's there, where I'm going and who's dropping me off. Surveillance comin' from wiretaps, choppers and cars and cameras. Detectives trailing me at all hours. Three narcos working my building in eight-hour shifts. Two people across the street working twelve-hour shifts. A whole network of street informers. Trusty Prince and Duke sniffin' my cars every night...

But with all these war rooms, all these informants, all this technological shit they had going on, what drugs did they find? A fucking joint! I'd smoked it in the tub with Tee, but the shit was so good, I forgot to flush it! That was a riot, man. My major drug violation. Possession of a reefer stub. And the Council had powder flowing in the street the whole time! The cops couldn't connect one *ounce* of that dope with me. Why?

'Cause our surveillance was better than theirs.

If an apartment on the block got busted with a search warrant, that was a tip-off the cops had a division post in the area. If we saw a Con Ed truck on our turf? Well, that had to be a surveillance truck, 'cause those motherfuckers *never* did maintenance up in Harlem.

We had lieutenants and soldiers lookin' out for us, reporting the day-by-day activities of our operations. And we discussed these reports in our Council meetings. By talkin' about things, we keep on our toes!

If a brother needed to check out a suspicious situation himself, he'd shut down his operation for the day, go to his area in a tinted van or inconspicuous car. If the heat was on, he'd take our powder off the block till it cooled. He didn't lose business, 'cause all he had to do was move the pushers a few blocks away. Customers sniffed them out well before the cops did. And by the time the cops secured new observation posts, got people to operate the cameras and monitor the electronic devices, went through all that red tape to make their move, we'd just go back to our old location!

We stayed ahead of the heat because we were careful. They couldn't catch a Council meet, 'cause we didn't keep a formal schedule they could nail us on. We moved from place to place, safe locations picked round robin by the brothers. When we came to our meetings, we entered individually or in pairs to avoid suspicion. We didn't even want security standing watch.

That was the rule. No outsiders.

Our operation was tight and we had our shit together, but I couldn't say the same for the NYPD. Somebody's ass was *grass* for wasting hundreds of thousands of dollars on my nickel-and-dime charge, and since the top brass doesn't have money to investigate a target indefinitely, their best tack was to save time, dollars and future embarrassment by just leaving me be.

New York City was now my playground.

I was home fuckin' free.

"Only the grace of the Almighty can deliver us from the *plague* in our community!" spewed Reverend Windham, all fire and brimstone on the pulpit. I scanned Samuel's Church of God in Christ for my wife.

She hadn't arrived.

Thank you, Jesus.

I was hungover as hell and ten minutes late. Last night was some victory party, my stick-it-to-the-man celebration at the Hubba. I took a seat beside a church lady in a flowery hat and she turned up her nose, her fat ass filling up half the pew.

Sista was getting chunky, too, chubbier by the day since she found Jesus. I was sick of her talking about this white man like he was her father, so I kept her under wraps, stashed up in a Mount Vernon penthouse. Still, I had to spend *some* time with my wife of seven years, and while Sunday morning was one of those times, she was nowhere in sight as the electric organ played the benediction, "I'll Fly Away."

The reverend opened his arms as soon as the church cleared.

"Deacon Barnes! We've been praying for you. I hope our contribution helped out."

To post my $15G bail, I had to funnel money through Windham. If I put up cash myself, the DA would claim it was tainted and press the judge to hold a hearing on the origin of the money. But I figured nobody would question a man as holy as Windham.

"And we all thank you for your generous donation last week."

"You got another $200G comin' this afternoon."

"Hallelujah! Even the Lord can't open the bank on Sunday, but I'll burn that money *clean* by Monday."

That was good, 'cause August had been a bad month to keep cash in our money houses, apartments we had around Harlem to store the collections of our street dealers. To keep from passing out, the guards had to turn on the AC, but then the scent of ceiling-high stacks of singles, fives, tens and twenties wafted through the whole building. Believe it. Money got a real smell, and I didn't want that odor to travel.

I needed Windham to launder it as soon as possible, and luckily, he had his operation down pat. He'd walk into the bank with sacks of small bills—"Really *moved* the flock this week"—and step out with crisp, unmarked hundreds ready for the safe-deposit box. Since he got 2 percent of everything he changed, he was well on his way to building that chapel in the Bahamas.

"And Deacon Barnes, please tell Sista that her friends in church are so sorry to hear about her troubles."

Oh Christ...

"Listen, baby, I had no idea they were gonna come here too. You know a weapons charge ain't nothin'. I can get that tossed in no time."

"I was in my *nightgown* when they busted down the door."

Sista didn't say another word on the trip from the Mount Vernon jail to our penthouse, where she started packing her clothes from Bergdorf's and Bloomie's.

"Where exactly are you leaving to anyway?"

"My sister's place on the East Side."

Bullshit. She couldn't even fit in that place.

She collected her makeup from our marble bathroom in a big charade. No way was she gonna leave. I'd put at least a million in this place and, only a month ago, bought a Persian carpet to give our bedroom a sensual, Mediterranean vibe, although her oil paintings of Jesus managed to kill it.

"God does not want me living in a home bought with your evil blood money," she said, snatching her Louis Vuitton suitcase and leaving behind her 24-karat diamond ring. This was getting out of hand. I grabbed her arm on her way out the broken-down door, and as I touched her warm cheek, a tear welled in her eye. She was still so attractive.

"Look, why don't we check in at the Four Seasons for a while? We haven't done that in ages."

"I fear for your *soul*, Nicky."

"I got soul in spades, baby."

We laughed like we did in the old days, and I knew she wouldn't leave. But she walked away from the penthouse, the Cadillacs, the jewelry, the life and me. Forever. When I checked her safe-deposit box the next day, the stacks of crisp hundreds were gone and a note remained—

I gave it to the church. A real church. Not Windham's.

Sista.

I don't know where you are now, Sista. I'm still pissed about that money, but you did the right thing by leaving. You're the only one who walked away clean.

Nicky, the Preacher & $50,000 Bail Money

"GOOD WORK, GUY."

Guy was getting a real handle on the business. At first I wasn't sure he had the years under his belt to handle the South Bronx, a huge market and a lot of responsibility, but he rose to be a sharp dealer under my watch. Did things like I did. Kept his table tight, the cut low and moved that powder smooth and quick. But Frank James, the old pro? His turnover was so slow, you'd think he was pushin' molasses.

"Well, the man said we could put a ten on it!"

"Forget about the man, Frank! There ain't no man! *We're* the man! You know what I mean?"

Frank just didn't get it. He always had problems collecting money, 'cause he always cut his dope to the bone. Put weak-ass powder on the street, wanted people to buy it and expected his dealers to turn it.

"If you put out a good package, people are going to be standing on line, begging to get your goods. You're gonna have to send out *patrols* to get your money, Frank. Can't you understand that?"

"Well, I'm making more off my package than you are off yours."

"So? By the time you turn that one package, I'll turn two!"

"Yeah, but you got twice as much work."

This was getting us nowhere.

"Listen, dude, we got another shipment comin' this week, and when you get your package, whack it like I do. Make your customers think Christmas came early. Just do that for me, please. Brother to brother."

That's how it worked in our Council meetings. Mostly we talked about goods: When's the next shipment? What's the quality of the powder?

But now and then a situation arose, like the Lucky incident.

"That broad who's fucking Curt," I asked Frank, "you know her? Nineteen. High yellow. Real beautiful?"

"Except for the black eye," said Jazz. "Curt smacked that bitc—that *woman* good at the Shalimar the other night."

I was glad Jazz corrected himself. Council rule was to address women with the same respect we gave each other. Jazz had problems with it at first, slipping out with "What's up, muthafucka?" or "What's happening, nigga?" But offensive terms were a step backwards in self-respect, and I told Jazz if he used that type of language toward another brother and didn't correct himself, we'd take him out. So Jazz cleaned the edges off.

I handed Frank the scrawled note and he read aloud. "*Curt, Fuck you and your money. Lucky and Judy.* Who Judy?" Judy was Lucky's girlfriend, although I doubted Lucky was a true lesbian. Just young, confused and extremely jealous of Curt for having a wife.

It was too bad. We all were fuckin' young, twenty-something girls at the time—they'd be waiting at Small's or the Gold Lounge, no strings attached—but in a rare case of bad luck, Curt got to banging Lucky, a possessive type. Bought her a Fleetwood and an apartment to try and cool her out, but that only made it worse for Lucky.

She hated Curt comin' over for a few hours, then goin' home to his wife, so she got herself a little freak lesbian and moved her in. Seemed an ideal situation to me, but Curt was a missionary man and wouldn't have it.

"That bitch's bras are hangin' all over the bathroom! I like my place clean."

"Ain't *your* place, Curtis! It's mine and Judy's!"

That fired up Curt real good, so he cracked her in the eye, right there in front of everybody at the Shalimar. Lucky hurried home to Judy and got dusted, but on their way out the door, stole $33G Curt had stashed in the closet, all profit going to the Council.

"You want the work done?" asked Frank, stubbing his Parliament.

"No. Do a little undercover work, find where they are so we can fix the situation. I don't want a lot of commotion, so work around the edges, you know, keep it low."

But what did Frank do? Told *everyone* he was on the hunt—and believe it, hard muthafuckas trembled when Frank James was on the hunt. Once word got to the chicks, they took the money and split town in the Fleetwood.

I was mad as a muthafucka.

"How are we gonna get our money back now, Frank? You gonna follow the tire tracks across the country?"

"Listen," said Frank, eyes gleaming, "that dyke cunt has a fag brother, Cliffy. I'll push in his door, find where his sister at. Hit the road and come back with heads."

"Ain't worth killin' over pocket change," I said.

"But if we don't knock 'em off," piped Jazz, "we'll look soft!"

Man, what is this? I could've swatted Jazz off the chair.

"What do you say, Youngblood?" asked Frank. "You wanna let anybody just run off with our money?"

Guy kept a steel eye and threw down his answer, not takin' any more of Frank's bullshit.

"Termination on the table."

"I second the motion," said Wally. He usually wasn't the prime mover on matters of muscle, mainly advised us on the quiet things. But rules were rules, and now we had to vote on the homicide.

If a brother wanted to do work on a guy, I didn't want it to be us sittin' around in a bar sayin', "I had a problem with this guy. I'm gonna go take him out." We all had hot tempers and private graveyards, but now that we were hooked up together, being fired up about killing someone wasn't reason enough. The victim might have sympathetic forces. We needed to know what we were dealing with to weigh consequences.

As the yeses piled on the girls' death sentence, it came down to me. The vote had to be unanimous, plus I had veto power over everything. I seldom used it 'cause I wanted everybody to feel they had a say, but it was time to take control.

"Homicide is a last resort, reserved for threats to our survival. We ain't gonna waste it on a barely bruised rep."

And that was that. No more words on the situation. We may have been equals, but my decisions were not subject to discussion.

I loved having money. I never saw it as the root of all evil. The dark side is *not* having money. I even loved the smell of money. I loved the feel of it. Just knowing I had safe-deposit boxes across the city, packed full of crisp $100 bills, left me with a really good feeling. Wasn't so much I loved the things money could buy. It was the money itself.

Maybe it was 'cause I used to be an addict, but I could never get enough money. And even though I had millions, it really disturbed me how Curt's no-good woman ran off with 33,000 of my precious dollars. Had no problem takin' her out either, 'cause if you're not willing to use violence in the drug game, you're not gonna survive. It's street-corner Darwinism.

But killin' all your problems don't necessarily get you the most money in the powder game. Customers don't ask, "Who the most ruthless muthafucka out there? That's who *I'm* buyin' my powder from!" They ask, "Who got the best powder?" And the reason why I had the best powder was I built the machine to move it. Took *years* to find the right people, and believe me, when you find a good worker in this business, you wanna make sure he keeps workin', keeps movin' your goods to the street.

So how do you do it? I used to read *The Prince* in the joint, and Machiavelli said if you've got a choice between your warriors loving you and fearing you, it's better to have them fear you. If he were in charge of the Lucky situation? "Hell, yeah," he'd say. "Knock that bitch off! No question!" But I chose to treat my people as family. That made 'em work hard. Made 'em feel stake in what was goin' on for the long haul. A loyal crew is just good for business, and good business got me more money!

Nobody was more loyal to me than Curt, and whatever kind of pussy his troublesome bitch had, he was all hung up in it. He'd never asked me for a thing in all our years together, but when he laid down what happened with Lucky? He *pleaded* for her life to be spared. He didn't have a heart with a dagger tattooed on his arm for nothin'. The dude bled love.

So I treated him how I'd want to be treated. I let Lucky live.

"Her brother's name is Clifford Haynes. He lives in the Bronx at 970 Simpson. That's the only lead Frank found, but you can take it from there."

"Thank you, Nick," he said, sighing relief. Curt seemed like a new man. He'd never forget my gesture of affection. "I'm gonna go to Cliff's and track your money, right away."

"Have one of your dudes back you up. Cliff has to have heard we're on to him. Might be ready to spark."

"Maybe you can back me up? I mean, he might ease his guard that way. Gotta know your rep as an honorable dude, and he'll know we ain't settin' a trap on him."

I trusted Curt's instincts in all situations, but he was either short of sleep or too emotional, 'cause he knew better than to be with me in public, let alone in a compromising situation. At the same time, there'd be better odds of things goin' smooth with me there. And I *really* wanted to get back my money.

In light of the events that morning, March 8, 1974, I'll state for the record I told him no, that Curt got Freddie—heavyset, dark complexion, moustache, wearing a black ski cap and leather jacket—to back him up.

Freddie leaned next to the peace sign spray painted on the peeling, fifth-floor wall while Curt knocked on Cliff's door.

"I ain't strapped, and I got no problem with you. Open up."

Cliff cracked the door and spoke through the taut chain.

"Well, bitch, I *am* strapped, so what you want?"

Tough talk for a junkie faggot.

"I wanna see Lucky. Where she at?"

"Fuck yo' mamma!"

The chain snapped as Curt came in the hard way, slamming Cliff beside the African mask hanging on the wall, kneeing him in the nuts. Cliff had to vomit before he could beg.

"*Pleeease!!!* I don't know nothin'. Jesus, I swear they left days ago and those dumb bitches didn't even call—"

Curt rammed the gun inside Cliff's mouth.

"What'd you call Lucky!? Say that again, cocksucker!" His eyes lit with fury and his trigger finger glistened.

"Cool out," Freddie said. It's a bad move to open fire on an upper floor. If neighbors run out to the stairwell, coming down means spilling innocent blood. He grabbed a garbage bag from the filthy kitchen, looked for an ice pick but only found a dull steak knife. "We don't wanna hurt anybody," he told Cliff, real easy. "Just tell us where the money at."

"I swear!!!" shrieked Cliff, "I dunn—"

Freddie tossed the bag over Cliff's head and pulled it tight against his face. The plastic fogged as Freddie pressed the knife to Cliff's heart and spoke right in his ear, coolly.

"Just hand me my muthafuckin' money, that's all I want."

Too bad Cliff resisted. Freddie had no choice but to stick him. At least looked like a typical junkie stabbing, a random act of violence with no motive. But sure enough, the streets got the message.

You don't fuck with the Council's money.

Bronx man Curt Molette was arrested this afternoon for the stabbing murder of Clifford Haynes. His accomplice, Leroy "Nicky" Barnes, alleged Harlem drug dealer known as Mr.——

I snapped off the radio and threw my evening plans out the window. *Man.* I was all decked out for the grand opening of Jegazzy's in my new fit from Brioni. At least I'd be the best dressed dude on the run!

I drove deep into Jersey until I found a nice hotel, checked in under my fake name—"Wally Rice," ordered room service, took a long, hot shower, put on the terrycloth robe, lay on the bed and considered my situation.

The fuck am I gonna do now?

Now that the cops linked me to Curt, it was like my right hand got cut off. I sure couldn't pass him Madonna's key anymore. It'd be much too risky. Shit! I couldn't even meet with Madonna anymore!

I was on the fuckin' lam!

But with that shipment comin' into the docks, I couldn't let Madonna's powder just sit there. Neither could he.

I figured Frank could meet him till things cooled, but Frank wouldn't meet anyone without his iron. And Matty wouldn't meet if you were strapped. Plus if Frank got the driver's seat, even for a moment, he'd have an excuse to put brothers under his thumb. I couldn't have that.

I needed someone who'd be a natural extension of me, who wouldn't dare question my authority.

Someone I could control with a tight rein…

An hour later, Guy pulled me into his Hackensack highrise, closed the blinds and turned on the blender. Good to see him careful, taking a cue from me, but I doubted he was a target. I turned it off and laid it down. "We don't have time to get down to the Council thing. I'm going to take you out tomorrow and introduce you to Matty."

Guy didn't say a word, just played it cool like it was coming all along.

I groomed him on the specifics, from getting a fake driver's license to the meet itself. "Madonna picks the places where you'll swap keys. If he ain't there, expect him the next week. Same time. Same place. If you pick up heat on the way, lose it, but if it ain't gonna work out, same deal."

Guy listened close as I talked into the night.

I grew comfortable with him leading things while I was away. It was good training. I hadn't built the Council for just my generation, and one day, when Guy was my age, I'd be sunning in the Caribbean while he ran the show. I spoke my last bit of piece shortly before dawn—"Trust your instincts"—and sank right into the white leather couch.

That's just how tired I was. Bleary eyed and bottomed out.

Guy sat straight, looked me in the eye and said the right thing. No "you won't be disappointed" or any other bullshit, but a simple show of brotherly affection—"I stayed in tonight to stay *out* of trouble. Didn't think I'd be harboring a fugitive!"

We laughed as Guy showed me the guest room.

After a few hours sleep, we headed to the courts by Washington Square for the meet. Nobody recognized me with my cap low and my sunglasses off. Besides, the main attraction was the other legend—streetball king Pee Wee Kirkland, soaring up for the alleyoop, bringin' it home for two.

"Think I got time for a quick game?"

"Just chill, Guy. Don't go drawing attention to yourself."

"Yeah. Probably make a scene showin' up the amateurs."

Madonna arrived on time in a blue tracksuit. He sat on the bench beside, keeping his eye on the game as he laid down the rules—"We meet here, only in the daytime. Dress like a ballplayer."

Guy handled it perfect, acted smooth and respectful. When it was all over, he split for the subway, just as planned.

"Kid's got some spring in his step," said Matty, getting up to leave.

"He's good, Matty. Treat him the same way you treat me."

"There's only one Nicky Barnes," smirked Matty, "and only one Matty Madonna."

You can't be on the run forever, and on May 11, 1974, the cops tracked me down at my Riverdale penthouse and booked me on murder. The judge only hit me with $100G bail, so I funneled the cash to Reverend Windham, thinking I'd hit the streets in no time. But just to be a hard-on, Bronx DA Mario Merola, a hated and feared, old school crime fighter, convinced the judge to hold a discovery hearing on the source of Windham's money.

Taking the stand at the Bronx County Courthouse in a black suit and patent leather wingtips, Windham said I was a minister of the church in good standing since 1966. "And I don't know nothing about pushing charges. I have *fought* pushers." The congregation from the Church of God in Christ gave an "Amen!" from the spectator section.

When the DA's goons asked how the church could've possibly put up $50G towards my bail—at the time of my arrest, its account only had $334.40—Windham said church trustees stored it long ago in a safe-deposit box, an "emergency fund" for helping members in legal trouble.

"Snake in the grass," shouted the prosecution.

This argument didn't quite fly with the judge, either. He rejected my bail with a smack of the gavel and sent me back to Riker's. Oh well. At least Riker's gave me a chance to catch up with guys from the neighborhood. Plus, waiting for bail ain't like waiting for the parole board. The vibe is totally different, 'cause no matter what Merola threw out at me—hearings, technicalities, roadblocks—as soon as my lawyers negotiate through all that shit, I'm comin' out!

But Merola was tenacious. He threw four of my bail attempts out of court, proving I funneled the cash each time. After about two months in the joint, I was ready to end this bullshit.

I told Tee to see my Plan B person.

"Go to Detroit and see if my man Chuck Goldfarb is back from Russia."

A few nights later, early in the a.m. on July 19, 1974, Goldfarb walked into Riker's, opened a black briefcase of $100G in tens and twenties and asked for my release. The DA's goons were there within the hour, accusing him of taking the money from me.

"No," said Goldfarb, a notorious player in the casino business, "I didn't get the money from Mr. Barnes. I got it from selling the Silver Slipper to Howard Hughes."

It was true! And he had a certificate of deposit to prove it. But now that Howard Fuckin' Hughes was involved in this thing, the press packed court the next morning, watching Merola attack Goldfarb on running an illegal bond business in New York City.

Goldfarb claimed that wasn't the case—after all, he wasn't charging me a fee. He was simply "irate" at the violation of my constitutional rights, like the time he posted $100G bail for the 1967 Mississippi Freedom Riders, free of charge. The media circus loved that. Nicky Barnes. Civil rights hero!

As for the collateral behind his bond, Goldfarb said I put up my 90 percent share in a $4.6 million, federally funded housing development called Oakwoode, an investment checked and approved by the FHA. Merola was stunned at how I wound up in a partnership with the U.S. government to launder drug money, but all Goldfarb had to say was, "I think it's a super investment."

For the press, this was all too good to be true. The *Daily News* recapped it in a three-part series—NICKY, THE PREACHER & $50,000 BAIL MONEY, and when I finally walked down the courthouse steps, the paparazzi crowded for a shot.

I wasn't gonna mug for the cameras and smile, so I just kept my head down, 'cause that's what people like to see. They don't want you smiling, like you some bad motherfucker. They want your head *down*. They want you to say, "Oh, I'm an asshole, please forgive me," and that's the role I took. But that made it worse, turning me into an *elusive* celebrity, like Greta Garbo or my man Howard Hughes.

Everybody wanted a piece of me, and it only made sense Hollywood cashed in on the action. Downtown at the Cinerama was whitey superspy James Bond, saving the world from evil black dope dealer Mr. Big. Some fantasy. At least they got it right uptown at the RKO. Fred Williamson stickin' it to the man in *Black Caesar*. Now that was a movie!

Wasn't just movies, either. Sinatra recorded a special version of "Bad, Bad Leroy Brown"—*baddest man in the whole damn town*—a tribute from one high roller to another. Got to where every time I walked in a bar, the crowd parted as that song played on the juke.

Yeah, fame had its ups and downs. Got me the front tables at the Copa, but got me the pitfalls, too. Since every tabloid reader knew my face, it was too risky to resume meets with Madonna.

So I let Guy keep doin' it. Besides, while I was locked up, he put a million in cash in my stash house, all the profit I had comin' from the streets. He'd really been on top of things in my absence.

Of course, Frank James was the only one who had objections.

"Madonna don't respect Guy, 'cause he ain't givin' up the powder he used to. We only gettin' ten packages at a clip! I dunno, man. Maybe I oughta handle the connect. Show Matty he ain't fuckin' with junior leagues."

I met with Madonna to clear up the situation.

"You want me to treat him like I did you?" asked Matty, sipping his espresso in an Italian restaurant. "Well he's gotta treat me the same way *you* did. Soon as he tightens up the paper, I'll take care of you guys better."

The next morning, I called the brotherhood to an emergency meeting at Frank's house to discuss the situation. Ishmael spoke first.

"You know how it is, they had the *eye* on me. Motherfuckers were right on my ass, all the way to my stash."

He went on to say he ran up the back stairs of his stash house and flushed a whole lotta shit down the toilet—a quarter million in dope, to be exact. Now, I was no stranger to surveillance, but I had doubts. There'd been serious discussion whether Ishmael was too zapped out on that ping.

"Ishmael, what were you doin' before the pickup?"

"Hangin' at the Shalimar, then a few hours at the Hubba."

"Well, do this. Get the rocks out yo' head! If you don't sniff, you won't see narcos in the mirror! Better yet, have your lieutenant do the pickup for you! The fuck you doin' pickin' that shit up yourself anyway?"

Ishmael promised he'd have his man Dougie pick up goods in the future. One problem down, one to go.

"What about you, Frank? How come you didn't get Guy your payment on time?"

"Muthafuckin' dope fiends flipped on two of my street people. *Po*-lice busted 'em and took all they money and dope. That's why I'm short. But it ain't gonna happen no mo'. I fixed the situation."

"How'd you do that?"

Frank stuck out his index finger and thumb. "Pop! Pop!"

"You lay 'em down?"

"Had to teach my crew a lesson. Muthafuckas gotta pay back my money. No excuse."

"Frank! The Council has rules on termination!"

"Those dealers were my underlings. I don't need permission for that."

My nostrils flared and my jawline stiffened. "Why would these customers turn your people in out of the blue? Don't make no sense! Were they dissatisfied with the goods they got? Frank? Frank, don't tell me you whacked your package too much. Please, man, anything but that."

Frank shrugged in silence.

What was his problem?! Even his workers told him, "Look, if you give us good product, give us somethin' to work with, we can get the paper no problem!" Frank didn't accept that. He wanted his money no matter what kind of package he gave.

But his dealers couldn't turn it, and now two dealers were dead. That's what happens when you put weak powder out on the street.

That's what happens when you get greedy.

Despite these problems, it didn't take long to collect the money owed to Madonna, and on the afternoon of September 30, 1974, Guy took the key to the '72 Chevy, dressed for the occasion in a tee shirt and tracksuit.

"You don't have to do this yourself, Guy."

"I wanna handle it personally. Gotta make sure everything runs smooth."

Guy split for the drop-off.

First he weaved through Houston Street traffic like Mario Andretti, but when a patrolman pulled him over for not signaling, Guy gave his phony license. Should've been fine, only his *real* license was stuck right underneath! Now they had reason to search the car, and when they saw that hundred grand cash in the trunk, Guy offered it to 'em to walk away clean.

"Just take the pie and let me go."

 Police threw the pie in his face instead, booking him on bribery and criminal impersonation, confiscating all that money meant for Madonna. Well, shit happens, man. I pulled enough from the stash to post his bail and pay Madonna, too, but as I checked that million Guy gave me on my return, I noticed he was about five grand short.

I had absolute trust in Guy, so I figured it was a mistake. I mentioned it only in passing when he came home, and he just shrugged it off like it was no big deal. Which it wasn't. Five grand was like a drop in the ocean. But if I had been Guy, I would've taken responsibility and paid the difference. He didn't. He should have.

That was a clue.

The Father Image
Or How Bobby Monroe Got His Gun

"HOW'D YOU DECIDE on this particular car, Guy?"

"You know how it is. American cars just don't have that independent suspension. Can't beat a Benz for cornering."

At least Guy chose a different color. Mine was white. His was black.

"Your damn Benz is ugly," cracked Frank James. "Don't know what you're doin' with that."

"You mean to tell me that ratty-ass Cadillac of yours is better than a Benz?" snapped Guy, throwing it back at Frank for a change.

"We gotta settle this once and for all," I said. "Frank, we gonna switch cars over the weekend. And if you don't want a Benz come Sunday, then drinks on me, all night."

"And if you don't want my Cadillac," said Frank, "then drinks on *me*."

We shook on it and swapped keys.

That night I detoured through Central Park on my way down to the Copa. Everybody cruised the park on a cool summer night, and while I didn't want to be caught dead driving this thing, a bet was a bet.

"Ride's got some rattle," I told my old lady. "Check the glove. Maybe Frank stashed some marbles in there."

Then this big, brand-new Cadillac, jacked up high, pulled right beside us at the light. "Yo! Yo, Nick!" Frank Lucas. Flashin' that dumb-ass grin in my face. He looked through his window and preened, like he'd won the game 'cause his ride was newer than mine.

"Nice Cadillac, Nick..."

I don't know what his problem was. He was a two-bit dealer obsessed with proving his superiority over me. In Frank's mind we were in competition, but he was no rival, on an entrepreneurial *or* intellectual level. He was just a bumpkin from the word go, just like the rest of his bumpkin gang. They all had some vague blood link, so you could technically call them brothers, but I called them a pack of clowns who'd throw a rock at a baby carriage for a dollar.

Everybody else called them the Country Boys. And why were they called that? 'Cause that's what they were! They acted country and dressed country. If you asked a Country Boy, "What does it mean when they say, 'Dress to your left?'" he wouldn't know what the fuck you meant. He'd go to Frank Lucas and ask, "What does that mean, Frank? Dress to your left?"

Frank wouldn't know what the fuck they were talking about, 'cause he's off the rack! He don't know when you go to a tailor, "dress to your left" means pull your dick to the left so he can make your pants!

Frank Lucas. Wasn't international in any sense of the word, but *loved* to gloat about his Vietnam connection. Even claimed he fought jungle beasts and the Vietcong to set up that pipeline. Come on, Frank! That's pure fantasy created in your country head. Your man Ike Atkinson told me the truth. He just threw that whole Nam connection into your lap, and you know it.

Here's the real story. Ike was a sergeant comin' home from the war, and went to collect from this Vietnamese dude who owed him a craps debt. The guy gave him five kilos of powder instead.

"What am I gonna do with this shit!?" asked Ike. "I want money!"

But that was all he had, so Ike took it. Ike wasn't in the powder game, although his cousin was married to Frank Lucas. Ike saw he could make some money off this clown, so he flew back to Nam, started smuggling goods in the nose cones of jets comin' home to America.

And that's how Frank Lucas got his powder. Straight up.

I'm not gonna bullshit like Frank. I would've loved an overseas supplier. That would've been perfect. But I didn't know anything about importing. I didn't wanna take that chance of exposing myself. Besides, I was doing just fine, a thousand times better than Frank Lucas could ever dream of. He only competed with me in one area—the Marketplace on 116th Street. And that didn't bother me a bit. Shit. I welcomed the Country Boys with open arms!

The more pushers on my turf, the more shade on my activity from the heat. I needed all the help I could get, 'cause when my people yelled "Black Tape," customers stood in *line* to get my thing.

So if Frank felt some petty little victory by making fun of this Cadillac, let him.

At least it wasn't mine in the first place.

By the next day I'd had enough of driving around in Frank's ratty Caddy, so on my trip upstate to Green Haven Prison, Big Smitty took me in the Lincoln. My spine chilled as I looked at those stone walls, but as Bobby Monroe shuffled out the door, my face just lit up. After twenty plus years in the joint, he was finally free. We hugged and he stepped into the car, bottoming it out with his size, bigger than even Big Smitty.

We scraped all the way home to his welcome-back freak party.

It was a real motherfucker, man. Everybody spread across this great big apartment on 110th Street, four titties, two pussies for every dick in the house. I was diggin' into the go-go dancer from the Hubba, just zinged *out*. Now, I hadn't touched heroin in years—that was a high I couldn't control, but everything else? Fair game, so I put all of it in a zing.

I'd lay a line of hash oil onto a real big cigarette paper, add black motah, put on the angel dust real thick, sprinkle on crystal coke and roll it all up. We'd smoke that shit regularly! Zings were the thing, great for laying the skins. Wouldn't give you a hard-on, but got you to an Arabian Nights floating sensation, a cosmic flow between you and your partner.

"Don't fuck me so hard!" yelled the go-go girl, but she was just playin'. She *loved* to deep fuck. I grunted louder when Guy lifted from his woman and yelled across the room.

"Keep quiet! Can't concentrate with all that noise!"

I didn't wanna disturb my groove, 'cause the way a zing works is when you come, it prolongs your orgasm and extends your ejaculation. And I was really looking forward to that.

But I had to cap Guy.

"The fuck you got to concentrate about, dude?"

Everyone busted out laughing, everyone 'cept the one with most to celebrate.

"Don't you like your new spot, Bobby?" I asked, sitting next to him on his brand-new leather sofa.

"Naw, man. It's cool. Thanks a lot."

"Well, what's the matter with you?"

Then this big freak Alice slid behind and whispered in his ear, "Maybe next time, daddy." Man, I tried not to laugh, but you gotta understand the irony of the situation. Now that Bobby was out of the joint, he couldn't even get a hard-on! He got so used to fuckin' men, he couldn't get it up with a woman!

"Nick," he finally said, lookin' right at me, "I need my own piece."

That's the one thing I didn't want him to have, so I employed a little child psychology.

"You don't have to be strapped, Bobby. See, people know you're my dude. You gonna be strapped with the Council's reputation!"

"Yeah, but I wanna be down with what you doin'."

"Naw, Bobby, you just chill. I'll get you a phony job and fake pay stubs for your parole officer. I'll even give you $1,000 a week!"

Bobby didn't brighten much at the good news.

"Tell you what I'll do, Bobby. I'll have you ride with Smitty. I want the two of you filling up that Lincoln Continental, checking out my spots, looking like tough guys. When people say somethin' to you, don't say nothing back. I don't give a fuck who it is. Just stare in his eyes and swell up. Just be big, Bobby."

Bobby seemed pleased as he scraped the last bit of coke from the marble coffee table and passed right out.

Thought I made him real happy by setting him up with a new apartment and a big income, but after a few weeks of riding around with Smitty, Bobby broke the news.

"Hey Nick, I'm kind of bored."

I kept beating the bag at Jegazzy's, a new five-story club I'd bought for Jazz on 117th and Lenox. From the bottom up was a Chinese restaurant, discotheque and velvet lounge casino. The fifth floor was off-limits to everyone but the Council. Mainly it was a meeting room, but since we all worked out in the joint, we installed a gym with free weights, plus a heavy bag and a speed bag. Though we rarely used any of it, we flattered ourselves that we did.

"Well, go and get some gloves, Bobby!"

As kids, the two of us used to train for the Golden Gloves at Fred Irving's Gym, a block down on 116th. Bobby was a good-lookin' prospect for the pros, and the heavyweight champ, Ezzard Charles, used to knock him around. But like the rest of us, Bobby was wild and used too many drugs. So his star began to fall.

"I dunno, Nick," he said, taking a weak swipe at the bag. "I just see these young kids working for you, riding around in their Mercedes... Well, sometimes? I wanna pull 'em out the seat, fuck 'em up and take their wheels!"

Poor Bobby. He'd been away from the street so long, he didn't know what the fuck was goin' on. He thought he should be getting the kind of money these kids were.

"Look, Bobby, those guys have crews and real operations going on."

"Why can't I have that, too? I want a operation! Just tryin' to help, you know, 'cause I'm getting your money and—"

"Bobby, you *are* helping out. You're doin' okay, dude! If you need more money, I can arrange that for you. But don't fuck with selling drugs. There's nothing in the business that I want you to do."

That really hurt Bobby's feelings, so I softened the blow.

"Listen, dude, you've been in the joint for almost twenty years. You don't have that same kind of feel of the street. But you'll get it back! Until then, just ride your car during the daytime, hang out with Smitty at night and have fun!"

"How 'bout gettin' me a gun, then? 'Cause these Latino muthafuckas just got outta Green Haven, and they got some beef with me, and—"

"No, Bobby. I don't want you to have a gun."

"Well, can I get a hot license?"

"Bobby! What good is a hot license gonna do you? You can't even drive!"

By now he looked like he was gonna unravel, so I said, "Fuck it, Bobby. Follow me to the Benz." And I taught him how to drive, right there on 117th. Bobby really wanted to take the Citroën instead, but was much too big to fit in that.

On the big day, Bobby took his DMV test while we watched the Jets at Jegazzy's on our new big screen. Unlike the gym, this addition to the fifth floor got a lot of use. Not all of New York was hooked up with cable at the time, so we thought that was a real treat.

Only Ishmael shook it up with a better one.

"I've got the motherfuckin' joint, man. It's crystal that gives you the *bells*."

"What!? You've got bell ringers?"

Bell ringers usually come from speedballin' high-quality shit, levitating you to this mystical state where bells go off in your head. Ting! Ting! You feel it, man, and it's *really* good. Hadn't heard the bells in a long time, so when Ishmael pulled out his bottle and poured the stuff on the aluminum foil, I *had* to try that out. Everybody but Guy did, too.

"Dang," said Gaps, hearin' the bells. "You sure this is just coke?"

"Yeah," said Ishmael. "It's just that good."

But after about twenty minutes, we all got heavy eyelids.

"Ishmael? The *fuck* did you give us, man?"

Ishmael called his source from an outside payphone, and came back with this pale look on his face.

"Yo, there's a fuck-up some kinda way. My dude, well…There's some *monster* in there."

Motherfucker. That just struck us to the bone. Dead silent.

People used to ask me—"How can you be selling all that stuff and not use it?" The answer was that I wasn't *around* it. I had underlings handle that stuff for me. All of us did, 'cause that's what you do as a sharp dealer. Bein' in the Council kept all the brothers from slippin' back to the junkie life. Worked a whole lot better than NA ever could.

Sure, we'd passed the point of temptation to fuck with heroin anymore—it wasn't even part of our lifestyle—but those needle marks in our arms were like a warning. *One more mark from goin' back in the grave, dude*. And as we're all brooding these dark thoughts, all making an effort to keep our shit together, in sulks Bobby Monroe. He's just taken his driver's test and is waiting for the results.

"Goddamn. Waiting for this license is like waiting to see the parole board."

Waiting for the parole board? Is that what he said?

Muthafuckin' tears came to my eyes! That tore us up! 'Cause we all knew that feeling, waitin' for the parole board—"Why won't you mothers just let us go!?" After the ice broke, we just laughed and talked about our days in the grave, how Frank used to rob my workers, how we'd be sick and have to stick up people…

Man, what a fucked-up scene that was.

That night we took Bobby to the Playboy Club to celebrate, but as we waited in line, Frank the underminer took a crack at Bobby's blue-grey threads.

"Damn, Bobby, why you buying that color?"

That's the color the warden wore in Green Haven. If anybody bought that certain shade, we'd ask, "You still searching for the warden to take care of your ass? The great white father?" Or as Frank said to Bobby, "You still searchin' for the father image?"

Bobby shrugged as we made our way to the door, but the motherfuckin' bouncer wouldn't let me in 'cause I had on jeans! Obviously this guy wasn't up to speed on the latest. These weren't any old pair of Levi's. These were Calvin Kleins! Designer jeans were the new thing! Smitty raised hell (he wanted designer jeans too, but Calvin didn't make 'em in his size) but got so heated, the bouncer threatened to call the police.

Course I cooled the dude out quick with a few hundreds, so he slid us right on in. What a place! That great disco music was pumping and people were jiving. We were all up on coke, smoking weed and real high as the bunnies hopped all over Bobby and Smitty.

"You know, Frank, I think those two broke that front seat of the Lincoln from bein' too big. So I'm gonna take that in, get Bobby a new Lincoln. That'd be a good present for getting that license. Then I'm gonna go out and get Smitty a new Benz."

A great look of concern crossed Frank's face.

"How are you gonna do that?"

"I'll take him to the Benz dealership, how the fuck else?"

"But if Smitty has a Benz…well, *I've* got a Benz. Can't have him in a Benz and me in a Benz."

"Fine, Frank. Fuck it. I'll just keep Bobby and Smitty in the Lincoln."
The fuck was his problem? Killed my buzz with that bad attitude.

Months later, in a small office in the back of the Mark V Lounge, Wally
raged about this motherfucker Billings who needed to die.

"I *trusted* that bitch-style muthafucka, goddammit! I *trusted* him! I
gave him that shit and he ain't payin' up. He broke in my office, took my
money. He disrespected me and, and...and he's a *snitch*! A fuckin' DEA
snitch! Gotta take him out. Tonight! Rip his eyes out through his asshole!
Cut off his head, eat out his heart, snap his..."

I siphoned the proper information through Wally's pent-up, repressed
anger. Billings supplied us with Q and was a friend of Wally's. Clearly
he dished some kinda static, and we'd have to deal accordingly. Wally
had given Billings some powder on consignment, so if Billings owed him
money? We'd send Big Smitty to rough him up. If Billings broke into
Wally's real estate office? Smitty'd have to break his knees, too. But if he
was an informant for the DEA? Yeah, muthafucka *did* need to die.

"We gonna have Guy check out his source," I told Wally, "and if it's
true about the DEA, you can contract the work."

That was the rule. Homicides were to be handled by the brother most
involved. If Billings was a snitch, Wally would have to get the money
from Gaps, hire a hit man to prevent any link back to us.

"No, I gotta take him out *myself*," said Wally, hot from fury. "I gotta
do to him what he tried to do to me."

"Wally, you're too emotional. If you wanna help, bring coordinates.
We need to know how to locate Billings so someone *else*, not you, can
take care of him. If the situation indeed warrants that. Understood?"

With the issue settled, it was time for the Council Christmas
party. Wally decked the Mark V with tinsel and put "Silent Night"
by the Temptations on the juke. I treated everyone real good over

Christmastime, so I gave each brother a ring with a precious stone—the Hasids just loved me down at the Diamond District. As for Big Smitty, he got a pair of custom-made Calvin Kleins, and I even stuck a hundred in the G-string of the go-go girl at the bar.

"Gimme a peek at that!"

She pulled it down, leaving nothing but a Santa hat. A fun girl, man. We'd always get dusted and deep fuck. I got to eyeballing her, throwing her bills till long after the Council split, then turned my attention to the velvet portrait of Wally hanging above the bar.

Man. What was up with that dude?

He'd been trying to build up his legitimate sidepieces lately, selling auto, fire and home-owner insurance. Did that shit well, too. Seemed to be moving away from the thug life, so why would he wanna fuck around with killing? Maybe he wanted to prove something, show himself capable of doin' more than the quiet things.

The telephone rang and the bartender answered—"No, Wally ain't here... Frank ain't here, either..."

"Yo! Hand me the phone."

It was Big Smitty on the line.

"What's up, Smitty? I'm gettin' ready to leave."

"Man, I got a problem. I let Bobby take the wheel of the Lincoln and he smashed it. I got the shit out the trunk, but we're stranded."

"Get in a cab and hop up to the Mark." I hung up and called Curt at the spot. He answered on the first ring.

"Yo, man. I've been waitin' over an hour for Smitty."

"We just talked. He got a problem. Come to the Mark."

"Okay, but I was hopin', uh..."

"Shoot, bro."

"Well, I got hung up waitin' for Smitty and now I'm late."

"Late? The fuck you got somethin' to be late for?"

"For my date, man!"

Curt and his multiple women problems.

But what the hell? I was feelin' the Christmas spirit.

"Don't sweat it, bro, I'll take care of it."

"Yo, man, thanks! And thanks for that emerald, too! Maybe it'll bring me luck tonight!"

By the time Smitty and Bobby showed with the bulging duffle bag, I was in a hurry to grab Tee and go to the Copa, so I figured I'd shoot over to Smitty's in the Benz and drop 'em off.

"Just toss the bag in the trunk."

"Can I drive?" asked Bobby.

"No, Bobby. You've done enough driving for one night."

Now right at this time, one in the morning on December 17, 1974, it just so happened the cops were cruising the block. And while it wasn't a big deal to see a Benz in a high-crime neighborhood by now—everybody caught onto my trend, and believe it, I was the *first* to be doin' that—the cops decided to tail us.

Whatever. I coasted at my usual pace. Tails were like nothing to me. But my man Bobby? I'll put it this way. He'd developed this incurable instinct that turned his head whenever police passed. Plenty of times I told him, "Bobby? You can't look every time you see those muthafuckas. They gonna think you nervous, that you got a gun or somethin'."

But Bobby is so gun-shy about police, so worried about twenty more years in jail, he can't help but look behind at this tail. Part of me empathizes with him, but that part isn't present tonight.

"Bobby! Stop doing that! *Turn your fucking head frontward!*"

When the sirens flash, I get this bad feeling. Just like Bobby's.

"Are you the guy who's recently been in the papers?" asks the cop.

"Yo, man, we ain't doin' anything wrong."

But we're doing *everything* wrong. Got money in the car, been drinkin', sniffin' cocaine, gettin' stupid…So the cop looks in the back window and says, "We have a robbery report about these two guys who look a lot like your pals here. Let's get out of the car, fellas."

Man, we *really* needed a stand-up ho, 'cause when the cops frisk Bobby, they pull a gun from his coat pocket.

"What do you need a thing like this for, Mr. Monroe?"

I'm asking the same question. Since Frank was all bent out of shape about putting Bobby in a new Lincoln, I felt I had to give him *something* for Christmas.

So I broke down and got him a Beretta.

Only now the cops have reason to toss the car, so they open the trunk and find the money in the duffel bag. I guess I hadn't thought about driving around with this much cash. It wasn't even payment for drugs. It was to give out for Christmas! I'd see somebody in need and say, "Yo!" And give out one to ten of those hundred dollar bill stacks.

That's what I planned to do!

"Don't worry, Nick," the officer tells me. "We know what's in the trunk. Maybe something can be worked out if you do the right thing."

So they take us to the 48th Precinct in the Bronx, dump all the cash on the table and start counting the $133G. And their pals come in and start talkin' about the Christmas gifts *they* wanna buy. A boat. A Mercedes. A diamond ring...

All the luxuries they've seen me with.

It's a feeding frenzy in the making, and before long, the cops have a heated argument on who's gonna get what share. Clearly this thing is gonna get ugly, with no resolution in sight.

"Sorry, Nick. These guys smell money. Maybe our deal ain't gonna work after all."

So what do those motherfuckers do?

"I understand," said Judge Hughes later that afternoon in Bronx Supreme Court, "this is a bribery charge concerning an offer of over $130,000 to police. I will set bail at twenty times that amount—$2.6 million."

Wearing my most humble suit, light blue denim with white stitching, I turned to the packed spectator section, raised my hand to my forehead and saluted my fans goodbye.

Off to a rubber chicken Christmas dinner, courtesy of the Bronx House of Detention!

Two weeks into the new year, 1975, Guy laid it down for me in his visit to the House of D. Turns out Wally did exactly what I told him *not* to do. He called Billings on the phone, forgave him for fucking him over, then promised to give him a package in good faith. Don't know how Billings was dumb enough to fall for it, but Wally lured him into his wife's station wagon, shot him three times in the head, yelling "You set me up!" with each bullet.

To do the work, Wally used his favorite gun, the .32 long. Wasn't so much the caliber he liked, but the fact it had a silencer. But you needed to put it in the right place to kill someone, and instead of blowing Billings's brains right out his head, Wally just blew off Billings's jaw. And despite not having that fuckin' jaw, Billings managed to make a deathbed confession.

"Wally, Nicky Barnes and them did it to me."

The cops arrested Wally for attempted murder the next week, catching him in his wagon, finding a .38 under the console, plus a .25 in the glove. Seems Wally had turned into some kinda gun nut.

"You better have an outside witness!" he screamed at the cops.

Which they did. *Billings*. Muthafucka didn't even *die*.

"Get ten grand from the treasury," I told Guy, "and stretch out to Billings in his recovery room. I don't want him sayin' a goddamn thing against me, *or* Wally."

Wally sent an emissary with some hospital blues and a brown sack of cash to Billings's recovery room, only Billings wouldn't take the money.

"Then up the offer to $20G."

But by then it was too late. Billings was gone, moved into protective custody at an undisclosed location, a material witness against me for attempted murder.

"Guy, you give Wally the message. I don't know how he's gonna find

Billings, but he either gets to him or he gets his ass out the Council."

I hated being trapped here in jail. I hated not being able to take over the situation myself.

When I finally got out on March 7, 1975, DA Merola wanted me back under, right away. With two chances to do it, Merola pushed the bribery case first, thinking he could earn me seven years easy, then nail me later for murder.

Only a week after my release on bail, Merola summoned me to our old battleground, the Bronx County Courthouse, leaving me little time to prepare a defense. At least my top lawyer, David Breitbart, was up on all the dirty tricks Merola might throw. He'd been a prosecutor for the Bronx DA's office himself, but turned to criminal law to pay the bills.

A natural-born fighter and a black belt in jujutsu, Breitbart clawed his way through jury selection. That was important, 'cause to me, voir dire is where you really win a case. What you want is as many blacks and Italians as possible on your jury. Seemed every trial I went to, Italians were on my side. But you gotta strike all conservatives, so if they attend church regularly or have relatives in law enforcement? Lose 'em.

It was getting down to the last few jurors in the pool when this white guy glared at me with anger and a guilty verdict in his eyes. The dude just didn't get it. He was an immigrant from some country ruled by a dictator, but like the judge says, here in America, the defendant is innocent till proven guilty. That's the law! You can't prejudge!

The DA sure wasn't gonna strike him—he always considered me guilty until proven innocent—but we didn't want to waste a preemptive challenge. You only get so many of those, and they get used up quick. What we needed was legal cause to prove this juror wouldn't be impartial. We needed the judge to toss him for us.

That's why Breitbart moved behind my chair and asked the juror, calmly, "Do you have something to say, sir?"

"If he is innocent," the juror screamed, "why is he here!? Why is he here!?" That guy was something, man. Obviously he was predisposed for conviction, so the judge dismissed him for cause, leaving us with a jury of five women, seven men—a good mix of blacks and Italians.

"I don't know how you got that jury," I told Breitbart, "but it's perfect."

Not to mention they were all from the Bronx, and people from the Bronx know what it's like to be fucked over by police misconduct. They respond to street-smart questions—If Bobby Monroe is the one with the gun, why didn't *Bobby* offer the bribe? What did Nicky Barnes have to gain from giving a bribe?— 'cause they're asking the same things themselves!

We hammered in plenty of doubt over the three-week trial, and when the jury retired on May 8, 1975, I felt great about my odds. I even napped on a wood bench in the courtroom, just so I'd be fresh and ready to hit the town when the foreman announced "not guilty." And he did.

"Breitbart, we got to celebrate."

We stuffed him into the Lincoln and headed to the Purple Manor. Breitbart lived on the Upper East Side, the whitest neighborhood in Manhattan, and didn't quite know what he was getting into, but Guy wanted to make him feel at home, like he was part of the group.

"If you're gonna roll with us," said Guy, "we *got* to get you a nickname." That was Guy's territory, givin' out the nicknames. He'd come up with great ones for his crew—"Farmer Brown," "Chico Bob," "Whop"—and got us calling Wally Rice "Birdcage" 'cause of his bushy fro. (Wally hated that.)

After some serious thought, Guy finally found the perfect name. "Mighty Whitey! That's it! From now on, you gonna be Mighty Whitey!" That stuck for good, 'cause as we stepped toward the Manor, this wino poked at Breitbart and said, "Gimme two dollars, whitey!"

Big Smitty didn't like that. He picked up the wino by the butt and the back of the neck, then piledrived him into the concrete.

"Are you crazy, man? That ain't whitey! That's *Mighty* Whitey! You can't bother Mighty Whitey."

Mighty Whitey had his work cut out on my next case. This time it was murder one with a deathbed confession by the victim, Clifford Haynes. The one who really *did* die.

Merola thought he had it in the bag, and wanted that glory as the one who took down Nicky Barnes for 25-to-life. But Breitbart did his homework and discovered strict legal guidelines as to what can be admitted as a "dying declaration," foremost being that the victim has to have not been *dead* when he gave it. Breitbart studied the ins and outs of heart surgery, put the doctors on the stand and proved Clifford Haynes had been dead *two hours* before he supposedly made his confession. Merola was in such a hurry to bring me down, he didn't even check that out!

Since rising from the grave didn't fly with the Bronx jury, Curt and I were promptly acquitted. Breitbart interviewed one of the jurors after the case, and the juror summed it up better than anyone—"If Nicky Barnes is supposed to be this big drug kingpin, if he's got like 300 people working under him, why would he go out of his way to walk up four flights in a Bronx shithole, then stab a gay guy with a penknife? That ain't how Nicky Barnes would do it."

Thank God for the Bronx.

Don't know how Wally pulled it off, but he found where the cops stashed Billings—in a third-floor room at the St. George Hotel on 28th Street. He'd been stuck for seven weeks, not allowed to even leave his room, with cops waiting outside his door and checking in every thirty minutes. But I must've lit a fire under Wally, 'cause he pulled off the impossible. When the cops peeked into Billings's room at 5:30 a.m. on March 20?

Billings was gone!

Motherfucker tied bedsheets down his window, shimmied down three stories, grabbed the twenty grand from Wally's emissary and ran off. The great escape! That money was more than enough for Billings to get a new jaw and keep that motherfucker shut at Wally's attempted murder trial, so he denied knowing anything about Wally, or me.

But even though I slipped by that one, just like all my other brushes with the law, I didn't walk away completely clean. I escaped prosecution, true, but I'd left a long paper trail through the Bronx, from Windham's $50G up to my $133G. If it ever came down to a conspiracy charge, all these sums could add up to proof of a larger, illegal operation.

From here on out, it was gonna be a lot harder to surface legitimate cash, too. Once Merola exposed my "partnership with the government" to launder drug money through housing projects, the FBI looked into my financial holdings and the FHA promised to be more thorough about screening applicants, aka me.

And that Billings situation *really* nagged at me. If you want to nail the guy running a criminal enterprise, you don't do it through surveillance and drug-sniffing dogs. The only way a case happens is through an informer—a genuine, inside connection to the big man.

The fact the Feds got to Billings in the first place, a guy directly connected to the Council, was serious shit. The guy was one of our sources for quinine! He could've brought us *all* down with that information!

As I looked to the future, I remembered a warning from the past, from Joey Gallo—"If we do this thing," he said, "if we rule the streets, the Feds are gonna come after us with everything they got."

Plans fell through with Joey, but now that my Council was on the federal radar, I expected real blows to come. We'd have to tighten up. No more mistakes like killing dealers, cutting dope thin, sloppy hits and driving around with money in the trunk. You can get away with that shit under the NYPD's watch.

But the Feds? They're a whole other story.

The Wise Man
and the Fools

WE WERE ALL MEMBERS of Mosque No. 7 on 116th Street, Malcolm's mosque, and on certain holidays we'd pay our respects and hear Farrakhan preach. At the same time, we didn't want law enforcement trailing us in, branding the mosque with what they couldn't catch us doing, so we usually held our own services at Ishmael's home in Jersey. His basement was well put together, and when Ishmael held Friday prayer meetings, our jumu'ah, we'd sit in a circle on cushions. He sat at the head and I sat directly across, but there was no competition between us. In that arena, Ishmael was the man. Our Imam and teacher.

I liked to hear Ishmael talk about the things Farrakhan talked about— self-improvement, the Koran, the positive things Allah says about black people. I felt animated when he held services. A certain kind of sacredness floated in the atmosphere, with no drug business going on at all.

Today, Ishmael closed his jumu'ah with a lesson from an ancient Arabic proverb:

He who knows not, and knows not that he knows not, is a fool. Shun him.
He who knows not, and knows that he knows not, is a child. Teach him.
He who knows, and knows not that he knows, is asleep. Wake him.
He who knows, and knows that he knows, is a wise man. Follow him.

But when we stepped upstairs, linked arms and spoke the oath—
"Treat my brother as I treat myself"—we came together first as brothers
in the trade, not as brothers in Islam.

Jazz brought up the first order of business.

"You're not gonna believe this. I got this Italian guy, Mikey Pugliese,
who can hook us up. He got powder that's just as good, if not better than
Madonna's!"

I didn't care about the quality of the goods. I cared about the quality of
the supplier. My freedom and safety were well protected with Madonna,
and I wasn't willing to trade that off.

Besides, Jazz had a creeping habit of tryin' to one-up everybody. We'd
talk about practical things, like gettin' a few drums of Q, but Jazz got
all insistent he could work a better deal. Then he'd come back and say,
"Well, my guy's a little overloaded to do it this time…"

I was gettin' tired of that shit. At the same time, I didn't want to be a
dictator, so when Jazz went on about Pugliese, saying we should open our
lines to another source of supply, I put it on the table.

"If the Council approves," I said, "we'll take a sample." That was our
policy. Always test the merchandise before you buy. A few days later Jazz
passed the sample, and when each brother approved the quality, I had to
say I was impressed—Jazz had hooked us up with some really strong
product.

We pooled $250G for the goods and got 'em to the streets, but only
a few days later, Frank James called an emergency Council meeting to
discuss the package—"I cut my shit *strong*, swear to God. But my guys
are sayin' it's too weak to sell!" Guy and the other brothers said it was the
same deal for them.

"Well, Jazz, seems your man Mikey Pug has sold us synthetic."

Synthetic heroin is created in a lab, and while it tests strong, the quality plummets once you cut it. By the time the customer shoots it, he barely gets his fix.

We ordered a street-wide recall and demanded a refund, but Pugliese only gave us $200G back. Jazz tried to contact him for the remaining fifty but couldn't find him; nobody could. Who knows? Maybe he got whacked, but whatever the reason, I considered that money the cost of a good lesson—if you've got a good supplier, don't fuck around with others.

It was late September 1975 when Big Smitty came up to me at the Hubba. "Yo, man, this guy Joe Beechum wants in."

"Yeah, I know Joe, let him come in."

Joe and I were friends from years back and had made a few deals together. I invited him to my booth and we caught up before he spoke his business.

"I need some powder, Nick. I'm out of action."

"Well, right now, ain't nothing happening because I don't have anything. But if you got any interest, Frank's got some garbage."

I didn't expect Joe to bite. Unless you're a low-level dealer, or unless there are no goods on the street, synthetic is not something you wanna buy. It still sells on the street, but moves really slow—perfect for Frank's pace, which was why he kept a stash of Pug's junk on reserve.

"Sounds perfect," said Joe, scratching his lapel. "When can we set this up?"

I went to the back room and told Frank I had a dude who could turn some of his thing. They sat and talked a couple of hours, and on his way out, I asked Joe how he made out.

"Everything's set. Frank's gonna give me a sample and if I'm satisfied, I'll come back tomorrow. But look here. I got a lotta static getting in here tonight, so tomorrow, I'm gonna say you said it was all right to come on in."

"Cool. Do it just like that."

Joe split as Solomon Glover came to my booth. A stocky guy who was our arms supplier—got us guns and silencers—he was just a really dangerous dude. Solly.

"Who that little fat boy talkin' to?" Solly asked, looking behind.

"Joe? He was talking with me and Frank."

"Man, that guy is *bad*."

Everybody was shocked. So I split, got in the Citroën and shot over to find Guy at his house in Hackensack.

"You got to get on this right away, Guy."

"I'll put Coco on it, immediately."

Coco Morris was Guy's half brother, a cop with the Tuckahoe police and our source on the other end of the law. His information came at $5,000 a shot, but was well worth it. Always had ways to find what we needed, like paying off a radio patrolman to see if we were under surveillance, or checking his contacts to see if a guy was an informer for the NYPD or the DEA.

Back at the Hubba, me and the brothers waited all night for Coco's report, and by daybreak, Guy came in and said it was true. Joe was a snitch for the DEA.

"We got to move on this," I said.

"I'll put him on the dummy meet tonight," said Frank. He was gonna take Joe in his Mercedes, make him think they were going to pick up the synthetic. "Solly'll ride with me and we'll do the work."

The next night, Joe came to the club, just as planned, so Frank and Solly put him in the car and drove out to Long Island. They passed the tollbooth on the LIE, then Frank pulled the car to an isolated spot on the side of the road.

"What's happening?" asked Joe, a little nervous.

"Just chill," said Frank. Then he turned around and shot Joe a couple times in the face.

Sparked him up right there in the car.

Black Crip was a tough guy despite that bum leg, and rode shotgun with Atlantic City Pete, a treacherous dude who was always strapped. Guy sold Pete some powder now and then, so we'd see him and Crip limpin' behind, hangin' around and comin' to our spots. No, I didn't think it was cool to have clients around me, but that's how I handled my thing. I didn't condemn Guy for acting different.

But then rumors reached a high level of persistence that Crip was an informant. None of us believed them at first, although Crip *had* been talkin' a lotta narcotics at the Hubba. Then Ishmael got some news from a trustworthy guy, right out of jail, that Crip was a snitch for the DEA.

"Let me touch base with Coco to find out for sure," said Guy. Hours later, he had his answer. "Crip's bad, but that ain't all. Pete's bad, too. Coco found out they were *both* workin' for the DEA."

Once we voted on elimination, the only question was how to do it.

"I'll take both those muthafuckas out," said Guy.

But I told him the best way was to have Crip and Pete come around to the Hubba on a dummy run. Ishmael and Guy would warm them up for a later meet, to a place where Solly could do the work. The plan sounded solid, so I left for Detroit knowin' it'd all be taken care of...

Having the Feds all over our ass, sending informants right and left, only bolstered my belief that the Council was in a race against time to step away from the drug biz. But if we were gonna do it, we had to do it right. We'd been used to living on a certain scale, and I didn't want our transition to the square world to compromise that.

Now that the housing complexes were out of the picture, Bolden and Blake brought a new opportunity to their leather couch, a black guy who worked in management at the Parks Food Company.

"And I have access to all their sausage recipes," this guy said. Then he offered his deal—if I wanted to start a sausage company, he was willing to hijack those recipes for me.

I didn't wanna get involved in no corporate espionage, but then he went off on another business he wanted me to start, one that really caught my eye. It was the flake-burger business—making hamburger steaks out of discarded beef accumulated in the butchering process.

This guy said he could run the flake-burger business if I wanted to start it up. Having once run a car wash with Frank James, I knew you needed to put in twelve or fourteen hours a day to get a legitimate business running. But this flake burger guy was financially secure and had solid insights on upper-level business management. I knew he could do it, but I played it cool.

"What do you want for your recipes and time?"

"I don't want money, but if you start up this business, I'd like a management position. Plus stock options."

As I flew back home, I had my mind on being the future flake-burger king. Seemed like a good idea! Had great tax incentives too! Once the Council got that rolling, we could move to bigger things, build a legitimate empire!

Frank met me at the gate with a dose of reality.

"Don't go to the Hubba, there's trouble."

I got the story on the way back to Harlem. Guy and Ishmael brought Pete and Crip to the back room office on the dummy run, but Crip kept sayin', "Speak up, man, I can't hear you."

Ishmael asked, "What's that, Crip? You talkin' like you got a fuckin' wire on you!" He reached towards Crip to search him, and when he reached, Pete went for his iron. Crip went for his. Only Ishmael and Guy got the drop first—Guy sparked Crip, Ishmael sparked Pete.

"So we closed the Hubba for the night," said Frank. "Told everyone the place was flooded."

"What happened to the bodies?" I asked.

"Black Charlie rolled 'em up in carpets and stuck 'em in the van like we planned. But Black Charlie kinda messed things up."

The plan was for Charlie and his woman Eugenia to dump the bodies in the Hudson in lower Manhattan, but instead, they left the bodies *and* the van just a few blocks away from the Hubba. When the cops rolled out the carpets and found Crip and Pete, Eugenia got picked up 'cause the van was in her name!

"Man, Frank, seems everytime I leave, something bad happens."

Bobby Monroe persisted with wild ideas that he could make us a ton of money if I ever gave the green light. The way he groaned about it, you'd think he was a senior citizen on a fixed income! But a thousand a week was more than he needed. Not to mention he got paid to do *nothing*.

I blamed that broad Alice, the one he couldn't get it up with at his party. He always had extra money until he got tied up with *her*. But Bobby couldn't get a handle on that lady.

Not that Alice was a lady. She was a big freak motherfucker with big, brown titties and a big ass. Probably had a big pussy too. And she loved the sniffing. She'd sniff all day and night and got Bobby on that. Turned him into a nervous wreck and planted ideas in his head.

So when Bobby came to me with a fabulous new supplier, I knew she had somethin' to do with it.

"Bobby! I told you not to fuck around with the drug business!"

"It's okay. You know this guy already. Joe Peters."

I knew Joe, all right. He was this white dude in Green Haven with Bobby and me. I didn't like him then, and I sure wouldn't speak to him out here.

"Joe Peters? Are you crazy? Joe Peters is a fuckin' tramp!"

Bobby turned defensive, like I was passing up the great deal of the '70s.

"But Joe's brother's got a lot of product coming from, uh, France or Japan or something. We can use this guy! But he wants a couple kilos from us up front. You know, to hold him over till his stuff gets here. We can do that, right?"

Bobby stood beaming, thinking he'd promoted himself from Smitty's man on shotgun to international heroin broker. What you have to understand is Bobby was the *man* in the joint. He had a sense of the universe because he'd been in for so long. He knew everybody, got the best jobs and could go from one side of the pen to another.

Nobody else was allowed that, but the officers liked Bobby, so he roamed free. And while he may have been the whole loaf in the joint, on the street, he was just a bun. Notice I didn't say crumb. Without me, that's *all* he would be, but the point is, all that shit from the joint didn't count out here.

Bobby couldn't accept that. He'd see Smitty pickin' up duffel bags with thirty or forty grand and think, "Why am I only getting a thousand a week?" That broad Alice asked him the same thing. Got it in his mind he could be doing exactly what I was doin', that the only thing he needed to be me was a connection, a supplier. And that's why Bobby jumped at the chance to do business with Joe Peters.

"Bobby? If Joe's brother's got this fabulous connection in Europe, why on earth would he need a couple kilos of our shit?" A professional asks these types of questions when faced with a new supplier. But Bobby wasn't a pro. He didn't know what the fuck he was doing.

Oh, shit.

"Bobby? Did you tell Joe that you and I were in the business?" Bobby put his hands in his pockets, then looked down and rocked on his feet, silent. "Well, you go back and tell Joe that *you*, not Nick, are in the drug business. Say Nick nothing. Don't confirm anything. You wanna fuck with Joe Peters, that's your business, but we don't fuck with guys we don't trust."

Fuckin' Bobby. It was just like Ishmael said at the jumu'ah. He was a child who needed to be taught. But obviously, that bitch took him to school too, and made him ripe for Joe Peters, informant for the Feds.

See, Bobby thought that all he needed to be me was a supplier, but didn't take into consideration that if everything started over from day one, the people at the top would be up there again, and the people at the bottom would still be down at the same place. He wanted the easy way out.

So when Joe promised Bobby an endless supply of powder in exchange for an eighth of a kilo up front, Bobby bit. That's how the law gets to you. They target the weakest in your pack, then offer his chance to shoot straight to the top.

On the way back from the Tombs, Bobby was downtrodden and depressed. I gave him the "I told you so" speech, and for the first time in his life, he snapped at me.

"Man! I'm *sick* of you fuckin' sayin' I told you!"

I peeled the Mercedes to the side of the road and let him have it.

"You listen here! One thing you got to learn is keep yo' motherfuckin' mouth shut. I run this shit. If you'd done what I told you, you wouldn't be in trouble now. I'm the one who got your black ass on bail. And I'll go back and get my motherfuckin' money back!"

Bobby just mumbled all the way home.

Stan Morgan rolled into the bar with these treacherous-looking guys.

"Look at Stan with his crew," said Frank. "We should take that nigger out." Wally and Guy agreed. They didn't like how he came into our bar in a group of three, not having the respect to enter one at a time.

But Stan and I were close. Real close.

"If you don't like him," I said, "fine, don't like him! But you can't take out Stan and his dudes just for that! If you tell 'em not to come in again and they do, *then* you got beef."

"All right," said Frank, "but Stan's a weak muthafucka."

I was surprised by that. I never assessed Stan as weak. At the same time, Stan did drop some weight—he was always a big, full-figured guy. Plus, he looked tattered, even though he wore good clothes. Just seemed lost without Reggie at his side.

For ten years Reggie and Stan were joined at the hip. First they were my lieutenants, then my partners, but after living large off my success, got in their heads they could do better on their own. But that didn't happen, 'cause months after leaving my protection, Reggie ended up dead in the Bronx, rotting on the 18th hole of the Mosholu Golf Course.

Everybody thought I was behind it, which wasn't true at all. I think one of two things happened to Reggie, the result of his messing with this attractive young girl. Scenario one was a typical love drama—her policeman father tells Reggie to stay away, Reggie won't listen, the father has two cops work him over.

But this beautiful bitch also had a boyfriend coming out of state prison, and he had a reputation as a very jealous dude. I'm thinking this broad set Reggie up, telling her man how Reggie was down with me. Then this guy and his confederates rolled out on Reggie. His body was broken up, so I figure they gave him a crescendo of beating to force out the location of my stash. Since Reggie didn't know—we'd split by then—they killed him.

However it happened, Stan seemed fucked up about it. Plus he was hung up on his woman problems.

"Yo, man," he asked, serious, "have you heard anything about Jackie?"

The rumor was that his wife Jackie had been fuckin' this dude. When a woman disses you like that, it affects your street rep. Especially if you accept it without takin' her to the curb. You gotta say, "Bitch, get out!"

"Stan, you got to do somethin' about this. You got to kill him, or her, or *both* of them. But you can't just sit there and not do nothin'." Stan nodded. He really respected my advice.

If only he'd taken it.

See, right around this time, a tough Italian named Ambrosio, an assistant U.S. Attorney for the Southern District, was letting people know he was gonna be the one to take me down. I couldn't blame him for trying. For a man in his position, it seemed a good career move.

But according to a dude at Jegazzy's, Ambrosio had just issued subpoenas for a big federal narcotics investigation, all names in the powder game he wanted brought before a grand jury.

Stan Morgan was rumored to be one of the names.

"Dude," said Ishmael, "we gotta take out Stan."

I thought Ishmael was jumping to conclusions for wanting Stan killed. Stan hadn't turned informer, and even if he was on the subpoena, all that meant was Ambrosio thought he could squeeze information out of him.

"I dunno," said Wally. "If Ambrosio zeroes in on Stan, he'll crack under the pressure."

"Stan's a weak link," said Jazz. "He's a threat to himself, *and* us."

Maybe that was true, but Stan was an old friend. Given our history, I didn't think he'd ever turn on us. He'd be fine just pleadin' the Fifth and taking a contempt.

"Well, he sure didn't do anything about his old lady cheatin' on him," said Frank. "I don't think he can cope with difficult situations."

"Not to mention he's back in the grave," said Ishmael.

"Stan?"

"Yeah, he's buyin' coke from me, heroin from Jazz, speedballing the two."

"Maybe you oughta hook up with him," said Frank. "Feel out your instincts on whether he'd crack or not. See how his failures might impact us."

"Coco can check out the subpoena in the meantime," said Guy. "You know, to see if Stan's a target."

"What's up, dudes?"

I took a seat at the Alabama Bar & Grill, Guy's spot in the Bronx. He drank a Coke while his half brother Coco eyeballed the Yankees game. You could tell there was blood between these two, although the real difference was the muscle.

Guy was lean and hungry. Coco had these broad shoulders from being in the Navy, and since he'd been with the Tuckahoe police, developed a little macho-cop strut, too.

'Cause you get that with a sidearm and a license to kill people.

All in all, Coco was a well-balanced guy. Sometimes got a little loud, but Guy kept him on a tight leash, even though Coco was the older brother by a few years. Who knew how that happened, but that's one thing I didn't know, and never asked Guy about. His childhood. From what little I heard, it seemed a typical story for any single-parent street kid. No father, but not much of a mother, either.

"We're just laying up here waiting for Gaps," said Guy. "He's gonna give Coco the money for that information."

"You heard about Stan?" I asked.

"Still waitin' to hear back," chimed in Guy. "It's just that Gaps has been late for the payments. He still owes Coco for all his investigative work."

Around the bottom of the eighth inning, Gaps showed up in his Mark IV and, as always, had West Indian Frank, this fierce Jamician dude, ridin' shotgun. Gaps stepped out of the car, handed the duffel bag to Coco—"Twenty G"—gave me some skin, then split back to Brooklyn.

That's all you got with Gaps. One underground dude.

But even if Gaps was late for the payment, the amount we owed Coco was only $10,000—$5,000 for Joe Beechum, $5,000 for Crip and Pete. The $5,000 for Stan Morgan was still pending.

"What's the story, Guy?" I asked, pulling him aside.

"Well, we were thinking Crip was the only informer. Since Coco found out Pete was one, too, I figured it was only fair to double the money."

"What about that other five grand?"

"That's for Stan."

"But Coco said he hadn't heard anything. We don't know if he's on the subpoena or not."

"Yeah, but, uh, Coco's gotta extend himself either way. We still need to pay him for that."

I drove up to see Stan at his small mansion in New Rochelle, the grand prize of all that money we used to make together. His two kids played with their mother Jackie in the front yard. Looked like a real happy home on the outside.

But I despised that woman for bringing Stan down. Underneath her suburban clothes, she was just a hustlin' lady, a street person like her mother. I saw that long ago—that's why I dumped her in the first place—only Jackie had this power over Stan he couldn't escape. If she hadn't come into his life, we'd probably still be partners.

The bitch waved hello and I went to the basement, where Stan shot stick by himself at the pool table. I took a cue and joined in the game. As I sunk the eight ball, I remembered Stan as just a scrawny seven-year-old, living at his grandmother's.

Me and his brother Winnie used to rob jewelry stores, so I'd see little Stan now and then. When I came home from Green Haven years later, I was kinda stunned to see him at six feet with real muscular shoulders. But it seemed he'd reverted back to that scrawny state.

It was hard to look at him.

Heroin had made him lax about life. He not only let Jackie cuckold him, but some people ran off with his money and he didn't do anything about it. He barely even broke the rack with his hit.

"Stan. Listen to me. You can't be doing that shit no more."

He looked at me from across the table and tears welled in his hollowed eyes. Somewhere inside, a part of him wanted to quit. He just didn't know where to find it.

He put down the cue and walked up the steps.

The next afternoon, December 10, 1975, Stan waited for me at a table in the Shalimar, ready to hear my plan to help him out of his situation.

"Yo, Stan!"

Stan looked up to see Solomon Glover pulling a rifle from his overcoat, firing the first of eight shots. When it was all over, the cops searched Stan and found a letter in his pocket. It was a letter from Stan's attorney, informing him that the government had just charged him to appear before the court on federal narcotics charges.

Poor Stan. He was a great guy, but underneath it all, just a fool. He didn't know that he didn't know. That's why he had to go.

By Any Means Necessary

GUY WAS REALLY EAGER to check out LA, so I touched base with my only connection in Hollywood, Maurice Downs. He used to buy weight from me when he dealt in Detroit, but left for Hollywood to get into the movie production scene. He did some acting, built a motion-picture promotional agency and produced a flick called *Sheba Baby* that starred Pam Grier.

Guy and I met him on the set of this all-black disco thriller.

"Nick! My man in Harlem!"

Maurice gave me a big hug and showed us around. I had to say, while I dug *Shaft* sticking it to the mob, *Disco 9000* looked like the dregs. But Maurice acted expensive, going on about the money he was making from his multiple contacts in the industry, so maybe he knew what he was doing.

Guy ate it up. He wanted to be a California man. As for me, I didn't like it. Something about LA made me think, this place is not cool. These movie people made me feel I should be strapped. And I wasn't. 'Cause I couldn't carry a weapon on the plane.

Maurice took us to a trailer and told me he was interested in receiving some weight on consignment. But in my mind, I was sayin', "If you're getting the kind of money you *say* you're getting, why do you need this powder?" When I said we could work something out, Guy brightened up.

"Yeah, Maurice! You could make a movie in Harlem about *us*!"

I wasn't sure if he was joking. Either way, I was glad to get the fuck out of there and back to the airport.

Ishmael and Frank lounged by the terminal, flipping through freak books they'd bought at the newsstand. I searched for *Roots* in my carry-on. I'd picked up a copy in Harlem and, bein' a fast reader, figured I'd get through it on the fourteen-hour flight to Japan.

Man, I can't wait for that fight.

That coming Friday, June 25, 1976, Ali was gonna face off at the Budokan Arena in Tokyo against Antonio Inoki, the top wrestler in Japan. A battle royale to prove once and for all that boxing was the greatest of all the martial arts.

Motherfucker! I left my book in the checked luggage. I asked the Pan Am lady if she could pull my bag, and she said it wouldn't be a problem. Shit was a lot easier in those days.

I was a very neat packer, so when I opened up the bag and saw my threads out of place, I was certain somebody'd gone through my stuff.

What if they planted some shit on me in Japan?

What if I couldn't get back into the States?

It was too risky. I booked a flight back home.

Man.

I was *really* lookin' forward to a good fight.

"Yo, man," said Smitty. "There's this chick outside. She ain't got the cash to come in, but she wants to talk to you. It's Son's sister."

"Who the fuck is Son?"

"He's got a good rep. Eddie Big Hands knows him. Her, too. She's cool. Think her name's Shamecca." I was glad I let her in. She walked across the dance floor of the Hubba like a ray of sunshine. Girl couldn't have been more than nineteen, and with light skin, a nice big butt packing that tight, red miniskirt, looked absolutely gorgeous.

"Just a club soda," she told the waitress, "with some grenadine and a squeeze of lemon."

That won't do.

"Château Mouton Rothschild," I told the waitress. She poured it with envy.

I asked Shamecca how I could help, and she said her brother was stuck in jail without collateral for his bail. I knew how that felt, but was too caught up in her deep browns to hear her sob story.

"It's just that Son's hooked up with Guy, Mr. Barnes, and Guy promised to pay the bail weeks ago."

Oh, hell. That was a mistake.

Seems Son had gotten pinched in service to Guy, and it was a Council rule to take care of the crew's legal bills. Wasn't just courtesy, it was good business. If a dealer was trapped in jail for more than a night or two, he might think he'd been abandoned. Might get real tempted to turn informer.

"How much is bail?"

"Ten grand."

Goddammit, Guy. He wouldn't waste but five minutes to call the bondsman and fix that up.

"Son doesn't have the money," she said, "but if you'd let me, I could pay it off by working here. I could do that!"

The go-go dancer shook that ass on the elevated table.

"You ever dance before?"

"No."

"Well, what do you do?"

"I'm studying at City College to be a registered nurse."

I didn't see how that would help in a place like this.

"Let me see what I can do."

"Would you?" she asked, putting her delicate hand on my forearm. "I'd do *anything* to help out my brother."

A few weeks later, we met at Tre Amici on the Upper East Side, an elegant Tuscan restaurant packed with top men from the five families of the Cosa Nostra. It was the perfect place for a first date. This wasn't just a restaurant. It was a dining emporium, a gourmet experience for mobsters.

On any given night, you'd see Vinnie Scungille shoveling a mound of ziti, Louie Gorgeous at the piano bar, or Tommy from Brooklyn sipping espresso with a turned-up, diamond-ringed pinky. But this evening, all the attention centered on me. Some gave a nod of recognition. Others just looked and stared. They'd gotten the message from Paulie, all right.

You come to Harlem, you get sparked.

I stare back. If they wanna make the silent statement, I'll make one, too. *I'm here. You gotta recognize that.* That's my message. But I'm also scanning the room. If something happens, I gotta know who to spark up first.

"Your table, Mr. Galante."

The maitre d' seated the bald-headed legend at the table to my right. I sized the old man up as he put his cigar on the ashtray, tucked the napkin into his collar and bored his eyes right into me.

At least I knew where my first bullet was goin'. Right through the glass of his horn-rims into his brown eye.

This guy was the last of the old-time Italian overlords. Recently released after twelve years in the Atlanta Penitentiary on narcotics conspiracy, he was the prime candidate to be *capo di tutti capi*, the boss of all bosses of the five families. Feared as a ruthless, violent motherfucker, he looked like he was gonna pull it off.

And his first order of business? To take me down. Back in the day, *he* was the one who controlled the distribution of heroin in New York City, and he hated the fact I had his old job. He let it be known he was gonna take back the streets of Harlem.

To me, this was a joke.

I guess Galante didn't realize the industry changed during all his years in the pen. Now that he was out, he didn't know *what* the fuck was happening! He didn't realize that old, all-powerful image the Italians used to have in Harlem wasn't going no more! But if the big man ever stepped foot over Lenox into my turf, I'd personally greet him with my message.

Everybody's the same size with a 9mm in the hand, motherfucker.

"I feel like we're in *The Godfather*."

Shamecca tickled my ear with a soft whisper. I turned my gaze from the old man to this lovely creature. Her brother Son sat across with his girlfriend, head buried in the menu, a bit intimidated by the scene.

Shamecca just dove right in.

"What's a *melanzane*?"

Galante practically coughed up his grappa.

"An eggplant," I answered, flat.

"That's what I want! I've never tried that before."

Shamecca had a real curiosity about her. I wasn't surprised she was a college girl. We got to talking about her poetry class, and while I could've bowled her over with the Shelley I memorized in the joint, seduction has its stages. I gave her a bite of *patti di pollo vivian*.

She licked her deep red lips at the taste.

As we finished our dinner, Matty Madonna stepped from the kitchen. He worked the crowd like a success story in his slim-cut suit from Armani. He gave the hugs and kisses on the cheek and all that Italian bullshit, but passed our table without a glance.

"Man," said Son, "that dude acts like we don't even *exist*."

But that's how we worked. No need to publicize our association. Besides, everybody in the room knew the score. With me movin' his goods, Madonna had millions of dollars, this fine new restaurant and a bright future.

The waitress came with our orders at our latest meeting spot, a private table at a midtown diner famous for cheesecake. With all those informants piling up, I figured this tourist spot was a safe haven, a place for public anonymity.

"You didn't miss a goddamn thing," said Frank, disappointed in his trip to Japan. The Ali match had been a fifteen-round draw, and while that sounds good on paper, this wrestler Inoki just chickened out. He lay on his back the entire fight and tried to take down Ali by kicking him in the shins.

Weird shit, man.

"Listen, guys," I said, moving on to business, "been doin' some thinkin'. Ain't no reason why the Italians oughta be one up on us. In *anything*. We gotta start followin' the path that they did. We gotta find ways to go legit."

The brothers were down with my plan till I got to specifics. Being a force in flake burgers didn't interest them, nor did the other tax shelters Bolden and Blake found through Goldman.

"I don't wanna invest in a nursing home," said Jazz.

That's not the point. The boys just weren't seeing the big picture.

"All right, then, I open the floor for a better suggestion."

"We oughta buy the Apollo Theater," said Guy. The brothers kind of laughed, though I wasn't sure it was a joke.

"Yo, Nick," interrupted Ishmael, serious, "that red Buick across the street. It's not lookin' so good."

"Get the fuck outta here," said Jazz. "You been sniffin' this morning?"

But I got the same vibes Ishmael did. It'd been happening a lot lately.

"Leave in twos," I said. "No contact for at least ten days."

Maybe I *was* gettin' paranoid, but I wasn't taking chances. Guy and I split for the Lincoln, and just as Smitty let me in, I heard, "Nick! Hey, Nick!" Bobby jumped out and Smitty went for his iron.

These two were like a pair of rottweilers—very loyal, very concerned for my welfare—so when they saw this white guy running toward me, they considered him a threat to my safety.

"Whoa! Nick, baby, it's me, Moon! Sally Moon!"

Moon was wiped out at only eleven in the morning. He gave me a hug and a sloppy kiss on the cheek and we laughed about Smitty almost poppin' his ass.

"Listen, Nick. I'm burnin' up! You know what I'm saying?"

Sally went on about how the heat was all over him, how he needed to get the fuck out of town. When he mentioned something about the Caymans, that was all I needed to hear.

"Hop in the Lincoln, Sally."

That evening we overlooked the white sand beach from the Royal Palms Hotel balcony. No bags, no clothes.

"I'll head out and get us some things in the morning," said Guy.

"I'll call some broads and fly 'em in," said Sally. "I don't wanna get the clap out here. You guys in?"

"Count me out, Sally." Grand Cayman seemed kind of special. I wanted Shamecca to see this place for herself.

"Tell her to bring that chick," said Guy. "The one with the one-inch nipples and naturally pink lips."

The next morning, the guys were into a big steak breakfast when Guy showed up wearing a nice pair of trim trunks. He got everyone else these baggy-ass Joe Fraziers.

"What the fuck you buy me these for?" I asked.

"Man, you got that big stomach, and I didn't know..."

I wouldn't call it a big stomach. A bit of a paunch, maybe, but that was it. But Guy is such a lean dude, I'm wondering if he's trying to show me up!

"What you sayin'?" asks Smitty, looking at his XXXLs. "We all fat muthafuckas or somethin'?"

By now it's a crisis situation. The girls are gonna arrive any minute, and I sure don't wanna be seen in this horrible getup.

"Here, Bobby," I say, giving him a hundred. "Get the concierge to remedy the problem."

It was solved within the hour.

Bobby and Smitty looked like beached whales in their Speedos. Me and Mecca sipped daiquiris by the beach.

Shamecca was first to the pool the next morning. The girl was young and had a lot of energy. She didn't feel like sunning, so we smoked local weed and saw Stingray City from the glass-bottom boat. Then we water-skied, went cave diving and shot underwater photography. Tourist shit, but wholesome fun.

At dinner, Shamecca ordered an exotic French wine, plus sautéed shrimp for the table. We danced salsa all night in the ballroom and she shook it better than any go-go girl in all our spots. And at sunrise? I walked her to the beach, where a local offered her a ride on a white stallion.

It was a perfect moment, choreographed entirely by me.

"I love horses!" she beamed, wrapping her tight body close. "It's so exciting to be with you!"

While Shamecca rode through the a.m., I split for the bank in George Town with the rocks she'd smuggled in her pussy. Sally gave me the idea—"You oughta keep some diamonds in a safe-deposit box down here. If you ever gotta split the States for good, you can start again with a little security."

It didn't sound bad. The Caymans were great. Not having to walk around with a gun really relaxed me.

With Plan B set, I met Shamecca at the casino, then took her to the craps table and taught her all the tricks. To me, shooting dice was as easy as breathing, but Shamecca had her eye on the sophisticates around the Baccarat table.

"I wanna learn *that*."

"All right, Mecca, but it's a fast game."

Even I didn't have a grip on the speed and accuracy involved. I let her give it a try, expecting she'd quit after a few minutes. Hours later, the crowd rooted from behind as she bet my money like a pro.

Damn, this girl gets off on high stakes.

We cashed in her chips—a few more grand to add to the box—and just for fun, she tested a twenty-dollar slot on the way out.

"Three cherries!"

Her eyes lit up as the cash dumped below and the bells started ringing, and all of a sudden...

Eureka!

"Now, I'm not talking about Caesar's Palace or the Sands. Just a small one. Just one casino. Something to get us started."

"What about the Italians?" asked Wally.

True, the Italians had a stranglehold on the gaming business, a fierce rep and a steamroller of legitimacy. But they'd gotten soft underneath their Brooks Brothers suits. They'd gotten rich and fat off legitimate money out in Vegas. And that left them with a soft underbelly we could pierce.

"The Italians are kicked back and relaxed. I don't think they're ready to go to war. They ain't used to sparking for anything they want."

But if we had to cut a swath of blood down the motherfuckin' Strip, that's just what we'd have to do. We'd have to move in and take over by any means necessary, like Malcolm said. By any means necessary. It would be worth putting our lives on the line to take Vegas. How many Italians would be willing to put their lives on the line to keep it?

"But even if we showed up with guns blazin', we got bigger issues. Like how do we get casino property? How do we get involved in that?"

"How do we?" asked Frank.

I didn't know. There was a lot of shit to consider. But I did know without clean money we couldn't open up a corner deli, let alone a casino.

"That's why we gotta make those investments! We're making too much to have cash just sitting around in safety-deposit boxes!"

"Then let's buy the Apollo," said Guy. "It's for sale at half a million and has great tax incentives as a historical landmark. You know, like a tax shelter."

The brothers perked up immediately. I had to say, it'd be a real feather in our cap to own the Apollo, the shining star of 125th Street. Guy had really done his homework, and if Jazz were here, he'd have jumped all over the idea.

Lately he'd convinced himself to be a super entrepreneur in the music business. Always going on about his gigs as a record producer, whatever the hell that meant. Maybe he was producing now, but he'd have to pay the $10,000 fine for a missed meeting.

Just as we adjourned, Jazz ran in, breathless with news.

"You're not gonna *believe* who just came to my door!"

It was Mikey Pugliese. Our man for synthetic, back from the dead.

"He showed up out of the blue! He promised to pay that fifty grand he owed and offered a batch of pure heroin on consignment."

"Don't sound right," said Ishmael.

"No doubt. And the thing is, I moved *twice* since that dude last saw me. I sure didn't leave a forwarding address. I think the government let him know where I live. I think he's a snitch."

"I know Pugliese," said Madonna. "He's a soldier of Galante. Get the old man's permission before you do the work. Otherwise, he's gonna have his reason to rally the troops for war."

"There ain't gonna be a conversation," I said. "I don't need Galante backin' my hand. I got Smith and Wesson backin' my hand."

In the middle of the night of July 29, 1976, we held hands in a circle in the basement of the Club Baron to invoke the solemn rite of termination. Each man spoke yes around the table. Each man felt the gravity of the stakes. If Galante wanted to rally the Mafia for a war against the Council, he'd have his reason within an hour.

Jazz and Guy strapped themselves with a .38 and a .380 from the arsenal. We intended for Jazz and his lieutenant, Scrap, to do the work, but Guy insisted he take over for Scrap as the triggerman—"If you're gonna be on the line, Jazz, I'm gonna be there with you."

That's what our oath was all about. One brother looking out for another.

Early that morning, Ishmael and I waited at the Baron while they removed our problem. We drank club soda and talked battle plans.

"So if we go to war," asked Ishmael, "where we gonna hit the mattresses?"

Good question. Joey Gallo talked a lot about this with me. We'd need a fortified compound for home base, somewhere the brothers could live for weeks on end while we did our raids.

"Jegazzy's. I'll have Solly bring all our firepower, turn the whole building into a goddamn fortress."

"Yeah," said Ishmael, "that sounds good. You know what else we oughta do? Get back to the jumu'ah. Every Friday. You know, for strength."

It was true. Once the money came in, other events took priority over our Friday jumu'ah. Ishmael was supposed to be the prime mover behind keeping that up, but he was always runnin' behind that coke at night.

Maybe the jumu'ah would give him a new high.

Back in the day, Ishmael used to be deep in the Nation of Islam— talked with Farrakhan, Elijah Muhammad, Malcolm X—and I think he fell from grace harder than he realized. Getting focused back on Islam could help him out, give him strength. Shit. Give us *all* strength.

Although right now, whatever the reason, I felt *all-powerful*.

Our unity was at a peak, a fever pitch. Black Nationalism rode strong among us. We were getting more money than we'd ever gotten before. We had the power of life and death over a lot of people. If we wanted to take a guy out, the muthafucka had to go, and that was known all over Harlem.

The whole fuckin' *city* sensed my power. Why else would so many people write so much about me? Gotta see *somethin'* in this drug-addict- turned-multimillionaire. Maybe it's 'cause I pulled together a group of ex-dope fiends and taught them to make a fortune off the shit!

We were the living embodiment of the whole Horatio Alger myth, the up-by-the-bootstraps stuff America was built on! Seemed to work for the Italians. I thought it odd during this *Godfather* craze how gangsters were suddenly symbols of the American Dream. Those dudes were killers, man! And they win Academy Awards off that shit?

Fuck it. That respect's been due to us a long time, and if it takes crime to get it, so be it.

Our time has come.

Galante put it on the wire he was gonna settle the score. I couldn't blame him. We'd thrown down the gauntlet all right. Guy and Jazz put ten holes in his dude, then dumped his burning body in front of the Columbia Medical Center. Yeah, we set his shit on fire! Guy had the gun so close to the guy's chest that when he shot him up, the shirt caught flame!

But nothing happened as the weeks went on. No retaliation. No Sicilian messages with dead fishes or horse heads or any of that bullshit. Nothin'. So I touched base with Madonna at the Rainbow Room to see what he knew.

"Madonna, you send the word to Galante. Tell him to come sparkin'!"

"Don't worry, Nick. I don't think he's gonna do anything against you guys."

"Well, why not?!"

"You're too well established among us for someone to move on you and me not know about it."

I couldn't believe it. After all that hype, Galante just lay on his back and took it.

Man, I was really looking forward to a good fight.

Bimbos

THE SEIZURE OF a large narcotics shipment by the DEA left Madonna dry for some time. Rather than wait for his importer to set up a new connection, Madonna decided to build his own. His contacts in Bangkok promised a steady pipeline of pure China White. The first package of 500 kilos was ready to roll. All he needed was cash to jump-start the operation—six million in total; he'd put up half, I'd put up half.

The price I could handle. I wasn't so sure about the cost.

"Matty, we don't have enough experience in this importing."

And while experience carries a dear old school, it's a fool who will learn in no other.

"It's gonna be fine, Nick. I got it all set."

Three men from his crew were to pick up the package from Thailand and smuggle it to the city. To me, this was just no good. Too many people were involved. Plus, Matty's guys were well past forty. If they took an importing bust, what was to keep them from turning informant? They'd die in prison otherwise.

"Listen, Matty, I've got this bright young kid who looks more Italian than Perry Como. His name is Chico Bob."

Chico Bob was a young Puerto Rican in Guy's crew. Not a guy you'd send to do a piece of work—kind of mild-mannered, but after the work was done, he'd get rid of the body just fine. Had a Clayton Powell look that passed for white, so he could rent an apartment or a car, do odds and ends without suspicion. Guy wanted to keep Bob doin' drops, but I said, "Look. Don't have Bob doin' shit that'll get him busted. We need him for bigger things."

This was one of those things.

"Matty, have Bob bring in the shit from Bangkok. If a hit comes, Bob'll take it. He's young and he'll stand."

But Madonna told me no. He had his goombahs.

"Italians don't turn," he said, striking the match and lighting our shots of Sambuca. "So you in? 'Cause with or without you, I'm doin' it."

We blew out the flames and toasted the Thai Connection.

The first step was a test run. Madonna's point man, a guy named Boriello, flew to Bangkok, put ten kilos of China White into two false-bottomed suitcases and handed them to two couriers bound for New York on August 17. Only the Feds had been trailing Boriello for some time, and at the layover in the Honolulu airport, DEA agents busted the couriers.

Chico Bob would've taken that bust. But Matty's guys? These two loyal Italians rolled over *immediately*. Under watch of the DEA, they flew to New York and gave the package to Boriello.

Bang! Boriello got busted with a hand-to-hand.

Once again, it should've stopped there.

Boriello was a trusted associate of Madonna's. He should've taken the bust like a man. He joined the sting operation instead. He put the package in the trunk of a rented Ford Granada and drove it to the drop-off spot in midtown Manhattan, right across the street from FAO Schwarz.

Madonna was still safe. Despite everybody turning, he had our foolproof system goin' for him. But it all fell apart, 'cause when Boriello passed the Granada key, Madonna's lieutenant didn't take it. *Madonna* took it. And the choppers came down and the police cars closed in. Caught Madonna red-handed.

Goddamn. How could such a smart and cultured guy get trapped on such an amateur mistake? Jesus, Madonna, why the fuck you take that key yourself?! How could you be so close to the goods? I dunno. Maybe you just couldn't step back from your thing.

Maybe you just liked the action too much.

Jazz had been hangin' with this Mexican at Torean's Social Club, and once they started sniffin', gettin' tight, the Mexican said his cousin in Spanish Harlem, Benito Cortina, had a lot of heroin to move.

"Cortina's top rate," said Jazz. "He can be our next Madonna!"

I doubted that, but with Madonna going away for thirty years in federal prison, somebody had to fill his shoes.

"Let's test the goods," I said.

I wasn't thrilled with the sample. Unlike Madonna's white powder from Marseilles—light, fluffy, beautiful—Cortina's Mexican Mud was dark brown, moist like taffy. But with nothing else out there, I dropped $250G to make the first buy.

"Great!" said Jazz, ecstatic. "I'll get the money to Cortina right away!"

The Council rule was that the brother who brought the connect controlled the package, but I had real concerns on this Mexican Mud. It was an incredible job to turn it into powder. You had to dry it, then grind the rock-hard strips in a blender. We'd need ten blenders to do the job, and since I had a blender of my own, I *knew* how much noise that would make.

Rather than have mills across the city, we'd have to confine it all to one, tightly secured area to reduce the risk of a bust. The brother in charge had to be on the ball, only Jazz had been fuckin' around, spending all his time in the recording studio and remodeling Jegazzy's.

He wanted to give our velvet lounge a glitzy, Studio 54 look, then take out the craps table and put in a sauna and massage parlor. All good changes, true, but Jazz was wasting too much effort on that shit. I wasn't convinced he'd keep proper focus on the connect.

"Sorry, Jazz. I'm gonna let Guy handle this one."

"But I found the connect! That's the rule! I oughta handle it!"

As it turned out, Jazz got his chance.

After two years of legal stalling, Guy finally went to trial on his bribery and phony license charge—acquitted on bribery, but sentenced to a year on criminal impersonation. A big blow, 'cause somebody'd have to take over his crew, plus the Cortina connect.

I was shocked at Guy's suggestion.

"Jazz?" I asked, sitting in the visiting room of the Bronx County Jail. But Guy gave a strong argument, shrewder than I'd expected.

"Thing is? We can *control* Jazz. Just gotta keep that tight rein on him. Make sure he don't get carried away with that extra power."

I walked past the growling, chained Dobermans and the Kawasaki bikes down the ramp of Kingdom Auto Leasing. The deafening roar of what sounded like a Formula One race nearly blew me back up. Inside the garage, three dudes from Guy's crew revved my Chevelle, my Citroën and Frank's Benz to the max as Coco fired an AK-47 against a wooden backboard.

The fuck these clowns doin'?

At Guy's suggestion, I'd put up the money for this Bronx garage the year before. A solid investment, 'cause if one of us got pinched with goods in the car, we could plead ignorance in court—"I don't know whose that is. I just *rented* the car."

Once Guy went away, this place became the unofficial headquarters of his crew—Chico Bob, Alpo, Kenny, Whop and J.J. I didn't mind that. It was good for the crew to hang out and get tight. What I did mind was Wally Fisher and his greaser friend Geronimo fucking up the engines of my rides.

"The fuck you touchin' my ride for, muthafucka?!"

I yanked Geronimo out of my Citroën by his wide collar. He was an Italian kid who tried hard to mask the white in him. Presented himself as a street hustler, but only did weird shit that wouldn't risk retaliation, like stealing hubcaps and shoplifting from JC Penney.

I didn't trust him a bit. If you dropped a dollar out of your pocket, he'd take it.

"Sorry," he squealed. "We were just testing out the guns!"

Solly'd just brought in a weapons shipment, and Geronimo got the bright idea of shooting the guns in the garage. That's why they were revving the cars, to mask the shots as backfires. Chico Bob shook his head. He wasn't sure what to think of this either.

"Yo, Nick," said Wally Fisher, slapping me on the back, "how's business?"

Mr. Barnes to you, motherfucker.

I didn't like Wally Fisher one bit, even if he was Guy's little brother. A scrawnier version of Guy, he seemed to think he had the same access to me that his brother did. Always asking about things he shouldn't.

"Check these out," he said, showing off his fleet. The brat was a car freak, and he babbled on about his dune buggy, his 1965 Plymouth Fury and his yellow Corvette Sting Ray.

"Hooked up Jazz with a Vette, too, but silver. Beautiful, right?"

I wondered where Wally Fisher got the cash for all these cars. He may have been struttin' around Guy's crew like he owned 'em, but Guy let it let it be known how he felt about his little brother fuckin' with powder. When Wally got busted for dealing, Guy took his car away from him. If it happened again, Guy warned, he'd kill him.

"Guy's ready for you on the phone," said Coco. Guy'd sent a message that I needed to come to Kingdom and wait for his call. I picked up the line.

"What's up?"

"Look, I got a little problem."

"Well, run it."

"My sister Vickie's been living with this guy Bimbo, and this muthafucka knocked her around and stole some money from my mother. I want something done. I want Bimbo taught a lesson in respect."

"I'll have Whop take care of it, immediately."

"No. Whop can't handle it."

"Well, I'll have Smitty take care of it."

"No. Smitty can't handle it. I want you to take care of this yourself. I want your personal signature on the situation."

"That's all you gotta say, bro."

Only one problem. When Guy hung up the phone, I still had no idea who this Bimbo was or where he lived.

"He's got a spot at 149th and Morris in the Bronx," said Wally Fisher, grabbing a .25 from the weapons box. "You want me to show you?"

Fuck that.

I ran to my car and took off. I didn't think twice about the consequences. Guy had been badly disrespected, and if I were in jail, I'd want him to do the same for me.

But as I was driving around, looking for this Bimbo, I realized I should've used another ride. I couldn't take care of *anything* in a white Mercedes. Figured some backup would be good, too.

I shot downtown to Bubba Jeans Emporium, Jazz's clothes store on 125th. Wally Rice was on the block with his wife's Chevy, so we got Jazz and hopped in.

"Yo," said Jazz, "Al and Eddie Big Hands are at the Sandwich Oasis; let's bring them too!"

It's a real party as the five of us rode uptown to hunt down Bimbo, but when we reached the spot, three black-and-whites pulled behind from nowhere. *This doesn't look good.* Five guys with loaded weapons packed in a station wagon with ten grand in the trunk?

We tossed our shit in the glove and Eddie copped the charge. I beat the rap easy, but damn, I should've known better than to be in a car with four dudes. The situation had conspiracy written all over it! All the same, I couldn't shake how the cops just closed in on us. It was like they knew we were coming, like someone tipped 'em off to my plan.

Like there was an informer in the ranks.

Guy had me looking out for Renee like a parole officer while he was in Riker's, so I went over to her pad on Fordham Road to see how she was doing.

The fuck is this?

Her door was slightly open, and that door was *never* unlocked. *Dammit.* I *told* Guy not to put his woman on the first floor, but that was his way of choosing shit. I put my nine in my hand and heard heavy breathing, so I pushed on in and saw Renee tied up on the floor with tape on her mouth. I locked up the apartment, untied her and calmed her down with a drink.

"Who did it, Renee? I'll do the work *immediately*."

But Renee didn't know the names. Either that or she didn't want to say.

"Should I just take him out? Or do we wait for Guy to get out of jail and let him take care of it?"

All of the evidence pointed to Wally Fisher, the only one who could've gotten in Guy's apartment with such a clean entry.

"Knock that muthafucka off and forget about it," said Ishmael. "We won't tell Guy a thing. His brother will be in the *ground* by the time he gets back."

"Now, we don't *know* it's his little brother," said Jazz. "Could've been that bitch! I mean Renee! She could've set that shit up herself and made it look like burglary. 'Cause I saw her last week with a new belt from Bloomingdale's!"

"But she probably stole that from the store," said Frank. "Girl's a little cross artist."

Ultimately, the choice was up to me.

Even if he didn't do the robbery, I had plenty of reasons for knocking off Wally Fisher. Behind that dumb grin lay a treacherous, untrustworthy muthafucka. And though I couldn't prove it, I figured he had something to do with my arrest up in the Bronx. He told me where to find Bimbo in the first place!

But goddamn, he was Guy's *brother*. I couldn't kill the brother of a brother.

"Here's what we'll do. We gonna give Guy his propers. We're not gonna say a fucking thing about his little brother. We'll let him do his bid and when he comes home, he'll take care of it."

Right then I made my biggest mistake. With the power of death over Wally Fisher, I chose to give him life.

Strike the King

THE COPS LISTENED ON earpieces and shot videotape inside the surveillance vans lining both sides of Sixth Avenue. My guests knocked on their windows, waved hello and walked past. I pulled up in the Mercedes, revealing my black suit with the white carnation for the cameras.

Thelma took my arm as the elevator brought us to the penthouse banquet hall of the Time & Life Building. She shimmered in a black cocktail dress, regal in a pearl necklace and a diamond bracelet. I nodded to the attendant, an undercover agent from the DEA, and told him to make sure nobody got in without an invite. Might as well make use of him while he was here.

The elevator door opened to a ten-by-twenty-foot flower arrangement, reading "Happy Birthday, Frank and Nicky" in white roses. The ceiling-to-floor windows gave a perfect panorama of the naked city. The waiters talked into the hidden mikes under their hors d'oeuvres trays while the guests danced away to the first of three disco bands.

We were all here, all out in the open. Each crew got their own table and all the brothers had different-colored suits—Brother was in purple, Wally was in blue and Jazz had on grey. It was a shame Guy was in the joint. He would've loved to be here tonight.

Frank James grabbed me and we shook hands for the cameras. Frank's cameraman made him center stage, mine made me center stage. I'd give Frank an album of my photos. He'd give me an album of his. Our gifts to each other.

One by one, the 200 guests paid their respects with greetings and envelopes stuffed with cash. As the evening closed, Smitty brought stacks of presents down to the Mercedes. I passed the agents, closed the door behind Tee, stepped into the car and let the tail follow me home.

It was October 15, 1976. What a happy forty-third.

A few hours before the snowfall on Christmas Eve, 1976, I handed out turkeys to the needy with Reverend Windham on the corner of 126th and St. Nicholas Ave. There were the usual onlookers—tabloid photographers and NYPD cops and DEA agents, but I didn't give a shit about them. This was my moment, my time to give something back to Harlem.

Now, I'm no fool. There was a real contradiction in what I was doing.

But all I can say is when people in the neighborhood asked for money—money for rent, money for college, money for surgery, money for someone who couldn't collect unemployment, money for someone whose car was about to be taken; the same one they needed to go to work—well, I didn't think twice about handing out stacks of hundreds to help out.

Yeah, I was flooding the streets of the city with powder, too, but if I wasn't doing it, someone else would, whether it be the Italians, the Hispanics, or the Country Boys. And you can be damn sure none of those guys would ever give a cent back to Harlem.

LEROY "NICKY" BARNES

The Hubba was doin' the hustle. That was the dance, man. Everybody was into it. Jazz did it in his white suit and Ishmael did it in his kaffiyeh. Frank James did it wrong and Bobby did it backwards with that big freak broad of his.

But oh, Shamecca. She just danced her little ass off. At my request, the deejay was playin' her favorite song—"I Love Music" by the O'Jays. We jived to the music and enjoyed ourselves to the hilt, shook it into the New Year of 1977.

It was year four of our reign. Long live the Council.

After three and a half years of legal stalling, it was time to face that old Rockefeller bust. Honestly, I don't know what the fuck they'd been looking for over that eight-month investigation, but even though the only drug they got me on was a joint, I was still uptight. Not because they had a legitimate case, but because I knew they would try to frame me.

The point against us was that we faced a Manhattan jury. These guys are not like the people in the Bronx. They may act sophisticated, but they still have that suburban mentality that if a guy is arrested, he obviously did it.

Given my rep in the papers, they would have handed me a conviction out of spite, so our strategy was to throw the case out of court before the trial even began. To do that, Breitbart called a suppression hearing to prove an illegal search and seizure took place at my Haven Avenue penthouse.

There's no jury present at a suppression hearing—only the judge, the defendant and the attorneys. But our case was special, so the prosecutors brought in Prince and Duke, the trusty cops from the NYPD K-9 unit.

On the morning of my arrest, the prosecutors claimed, Prince and Duke sniffed my vehicles in the garage and let off a distinctive bark, a sure sign that drugs had recently been in the trunk. Then they claimed the dogs gave off that same bark as they sniffed my penthouse, indicating the lingering scent of heroin in my pad. Thus, the barking of Prince and Duke linked the apartment to the cars in the garage to the overall conspiracy.

What a bunch of shit, man!

But the monkey show continued. Dead set to demonstrate the abilities of Prince and Duke, the prosecutors brought these different boxes to the courtroom, and when the dogs approached the box that had narcotics, they let off that special bark. Seemed pretty convincing, but now it was our turn.

Breitbart had the boxes cleared from the courtroom, then brought in his own box with his own goods. When he put that box in front of Prince and Duke, the dogs went up the wall with it! But when Breitbart lifted out the goods from inside? It was aspirin from the A&P!

Case dismissed!

I laughed so hard, I just had to go to the bathroom and relieve myself. The two cops taking a piss weren't too happy. They just looked at me with scorn as I washed my hands.

"Hmm," I said, "there's no more paper towels. I need a handkerchief." I reached into my right suit pocket and pulled out a roll of hundreds. "Nope, that's not a handkerchief." Then I looked in my left pocket and pulled out another roll of hundreds. "Nope. That's not a handkerchief either..."

I hit Jegazzy's to celebrate. I was home free, clear of all charges for the first time in four years!

"Yo, man," said Smitty, stopping me at the steel door, "I know you said to keep out the Italians, but Jazz told me to let this dude Louie in without a search. Just giving you the heads-up."

Since the Pugliese murder went down, I hadn't let Italians into our spots, knowing Galante might sneak in one of his men to do the job on me. So when I stepped into the club, packed on a Saturday night, I immediately hit the fifth floor to find out the situation.

"Yo, Jazz, what's this I'm hearin' on a guy named Louie?"

Jazz stepped up on his toes to get a little height on me. He'd worn his Afro a little higher over the past few months and, with a tweed jacket and diamond rings, sported an intellectual thug look.

"Louie D? Kind of a renegade Mafia guy. Out in California for a while, but now he's back. *Real* hooked up. Says he can get us anything from a Sherman tank to a ton of heroin. Wants to meet you, too."

"Look, Jazz, I don't wanna meet anybody. Above all, I don't wanna meet no white guys."

"Naw, this guy is cool! He can get us goods at the best, cheapest price. Got this big shipment of pure heroin and we can have it all. But right now, he's got preferred customers who need a couple kilos. His goods ain't in yet, so he wants me to advance him a kilo or two. We can do that, right?"

I was *stunned*.

"*What* did you say? Yeah, Jazz. What did you say?!" I didn't wait for his answer. "The fuck you thinkin', Jazz? He's got all of these goods but suddenly he needs a kilo from you? Why? Why?"

"Nothin' wrong with that, Nick! Louie told me he could wash some money as a sign of good faith. That's a good idea, right? We can change dollars with him. Told me he could take my money, go to the bank and uh, change it over to big bills tomorrow!"

"Jazz! Tomorrow's *Sunday*! Nobody's going to a motherfuckin' bank on a Sunday! Bank president ain't even goin' to the fuckin' bank on a Sunday! Fuckin' vaults are timed, asshole! Can't go any hour of the day and turn some dials and open up the vaults!"

"Well, Louie can do it. Wally Fisher vouched for him."

"Wally Fisher! Who the fuck is Wally Fisher to know *anybody*! The fuck could you listen to that moron!" My blood was up, but I managed to cool. Goddamn. Jazz was thinkin' *stupid*. "Look, forget about this shit. Don't even launder your fuckin' underwear with this dude, okay?"

But Jazz hadn't told the whole story. I could tell, because for the first time in his life, he was *silent*. I pressed him and he caved.

"Uh...I already gave Louie the money to wash."

Yeah, he had already put the shit in motion. He wasn't *asking* for my permission to deal with Louie. He'd already given him the money to launder!

I grabbed Jazz by his big medallion.

"What's the urgency to get your money washed on a Sunday? You tell me! What's your fuckin' urgency?"

But I already knew. Now that Jazz made a bit of money, bought a couple of cars and fluttered around his club like a moth, he didn't think he should be under my control. *That* was his urgency.

To prove his independence of me.

I felt something wrong even before I saw the chopper. I was driving in a Volvo sedan, a renter from Kingdom Auto, so I didn't expect any surveillance. But when the Datsun made the right turn behind me on Lenox and the Malibu pulled from the left to take his spot, I got bad vibes.

These guys are out to get me.

I parked the car in front of a local joint and dropped my shit with the bartender. "Hide this, man." I was Nicky Barnes. No way was he gonna refuse me. I got back in the Volvo, pulled off and headed east onto 138th. When I hit the red light, the Cutlass was right on my ass.

I gotta get the fuck out of here.

I ran the light, tried to blast by these motherfuckers, but it just wasn't happenin'. The cars closed in and the NYPD chopper pulled down, blinding me with the searchlight.

"You're under arrest!" blared the speaker from above.

I slammed on the brakes, awestruck. A damn chopper at Harlem rooftop level. That was really something.

My Kingdom for a Corvette

ON THE MORNING of March 16, 1977, the *New York Post* plastered the news on the front page—BIG SWEEP NETS 25. Or as the *Daily News* put it—A 200M DOPE RING IS SMASHED; GRAB THE KING AND 24 KNIGHTS. It was big drama. From dusk till dawn, a federal task force and NYPD narcotics detectives hit the streets with shotguns and riot gear, nailing Jazz, Guy, Chico Bob, Wally Fisher, Council middlemen and me.

They seized $300G in cash and a million in dope, and though they hadn't even scratched the surface, claimed we distributed a million dollars' worth of goods every month from the garage at Harlem River Motors. Seven of us were booked on narcotics conspiracy, the same thing that took down Vito Genovese and his family in the late '50s, but only I got the big one—heading a CCE, a continuing criminal enterprise.

"Not guilty, your honor."

The federal prosecutors wanted bail at $1.5 million, but the judge didn't think I'd flee the country, so he set it at $300G and sent me to the federal jail across the street, the Metropolitan Correctional Center. Of course, the federal prosecutors were just like Merola, ready to fight my bail attempts tooth and nail, so I had plenty of time to sit in my cell at MCC and prep for the trial.

The key was picking through the boxes of electronic surveillance tape to see what hard evidence the DEA had. They'd gone all out on surveillance, with taps on my phones and bugs at Harlem River Motors, but what really concerned me was the sixty recordings from their inside man, their federal informant. Wasn't Wally Fisher like I expected, but it might as well have been.

It was his fucking toady Geronimo.

It all started when Geronimo got busted on a flimflam operation selling nonexistent hot TVs to random names from the white pages. A nothing charge. A few months of easy time at most. But that motherfucker Geronimo had such a fragile ego, he desperately wanted *someone* to believe he was down with me. So he flipped, telling the DEA we were tight.

On a $200-a-week salary, more than he'd ever made in his life, Geronimo partnered with DEA special agent Louis Diaz, an Italian from Joey Gallo's old neighborhood, Red Hook, Brooklyn. Diaz was to pose as Louie D, a renegade mobster who bounced around from family to family with his freelance, dope-dealing operation. Geronimo was gonna be his nephew.

And this dynamic duo played Wally Fisher like a fool.

"My Uncle Louie's back in town," said Geronimo. "He's a big name on the Avenue, only he's dry at the moment. Think you can help him out with an eighth?"

"Yeah," said Wally Fisher, "bring him to me!"

The fuck were you thinkin'? You think major underworld figures go runnin' around, askin' for an *eighth* of a kilo!?

But Wally Fisher had that weak spot. He was so hung up on Guy's success, he'd do anything to one-up his brother, to land a major supplier of his own. So he hooked up Diaz with a steady supply of Jazz's dope, direct from a guy named Fat Stevie at Harlem River Motors.

When Diaz met with Wally Fisher to get the goods, he said he'd feel a lot more secure knowing Nicky Barnes's blessing was on the package. Wally told him not to worry, 'cause it all came from the same spaghetti. If that wasn't clear enough for the Nagra recorder strapped behind Diaz's back, Wally said, "I'll introduce you to Nick *personally*."

Moron. So concerned about impressing this big-time Louie D, he babbled on and on about his brother Guy bein' a major player and my right hand. He even rode shotgun in Louie D's Caddy and gave him a grand tour of the Hubba, Torean's, Bubba Jeans...all our spots!

It was all too easy for Diaz. Wally Fisher practically laid out the case for him. But as I waded through those boxes of surveillance tapes and listened to all of those rants, my confidence kind of bolstered. *Shit, man! I might wiggle my way out of this one!* Sure, Wally Fisher was throwin' around my name, but my voice wasn't on any of those fuckin' tapes! Diaz didn't even get to anybody on the Council!

And then I heard that tape.

Louie Diaz knew that Wally Fisher wasn't enough to bring me to court. What he needed was to penetrate my inner circle. And while I built the Council to be an iron fortress, Diaz unlocked it with the key to a Corvette.

Yeah, my kingdom for a fucking Vette.

When Jazz came down to Kingdom Auto one day to pick up his blue Datsun, Wally Fisher showed off his new yellow Corvette Sting Ray with a Saratoga top. That sealed the deal for Jazz.

"I gotta have one too."

Geronimo perked up. He'd been listening in the background, not saying a word, but arranged a sting with Diaz as soon as he got the chance.

"Yo, Wally," said Geronimo, "Uncle Louie can set up Jazz with a deal on a Vette."

"Yo, Jazz," said Wally, hours later, "I got this guy who can get you a new Vette for practically *free*."

"Oh yeah? Who is he?"

"A big-time connect on Pleasant Avenue. You oughta meet him. He's hooked up *everywhere*. He can get cars, launder money, anything you want!"

On the big night, Louie D rolled up to Jegazzy's in his black Lincoln Town Car, chauffeured by his partner, a DEA agent. Jazz told Smitty to let these guys in without a search, so the chauffeur walked right in with a blue Pan Am bag. Louie followed him with a Nagra.

"Looks okay to me," Diaz told Jazz, checking out the club. "This is nice here. You got a whiskey or something? Give me a cognac, a Martel and a little coke."

Jazz was out of Martel, so he handed over a Courvoisier.

"Here's to you, my brother," toasted Diaz, checking out the fourth floor casino. "You want to know something? You hooked up better than us. This looks more mob than what we got!"

"Put a gym up on the next floor," said Jazz, "guys can work out."

"Nice. This is fuckin' nice. Very, very nice."

"I got a bomb lease."

At the VIP lounge, Jazz got down to business, handing Diaz a leather bag with $50G in tens and twenties. "Take your time and count every stack." Louie handed Jazz a Pan Am bag in return, stuffed with $47G in unmarked hundreds.

"The money ain't dirty?" asked Jazz.

Point one for Diaz. He's got Jazz on money laundering. Now he's gotta work on the narcotics conspiracy. "I've shown good faith with your people. Your brother Wally? He's *my* brother. I love him like a brother. He been doin' certain things for me, and some things have worked out.

And some things haven't. The only thing I'm worried about, my brother, is *swag*. I was waiting for your package and then I went and bought a half a key from, ah, from Fat Stevie."

"Should have had 'em check with me, man."

Bang. Fifteen years, right there, for Jazz.

As for me? I'm still bulletproof. Diaz knew it too. He really wanted Jazz to say my name, to link Jazz's operation—the one he'd infiltrated—to mine. And Jazz hadn't said a thing about me, a feat given his big goddamn mouth.

"We the outlaws," Jazz rambled. "We should've been capitalists. What we doin' is the same thing the Rockefellers, the Vanderbilts…"

But right before Diaz headed for the door, Jazz just couldn't help himself.

"Yo, Diaz? What's this I hear about a hit on Nick?"

About two years before my arrest, the Feds took down Frank Lucas, king of the Country Boys, sending him away for life on narcotics conspiracy. But even though Frank was stuck in federal prison, word got around to the DEA that he was gonna put a hit on me.

I have no idea if this was true. Given Frank's little bullshit jealousies, I wouldn't be surprised if he told his prison bitch, "Yeah, I'd like to knock that motherfucker Nicky Barnes off."

If anyone was gonna get hit, it was Lucas. 'Cause a few months after his bust, the Country Boys got swept up, too. And the buzz on the wire was Frank flipped on 'em—all his brothers, cousins, whatever the fuck they were—to get a lesser sentence.

But Diaz has this insider information about Frank puttin' a hit on me, and he wants Geronimo to use it to get close to me, to catch me sayin' somethin' on tape. I wasn't about to listen to that motherfuckin' greaser Geronimo on anything, but Jazz?

I guess he wasn't as discerning with his company.

Man, it's just really ironic how it all turned out. Forget Frank Lucas or Carmine Galante takin' me down.

My own brother did that to me.

When I finally made it out of the joint, April 29, 1977, my first stop was to see Frank in Jersey. Ishmael lived close, so I played both of them the tape.

"Listen to this shit!" said Frank. "We gotta do him in."

I couldn't knock off Jazz just yet. Priorities changed after my arrest. My aim wasn't to punish Jazz. My aim was to beat the case. If I took care of Jazz now, I'd get scooped up off bail.

But Jazz needed to know what was coming.

I called the Council to an emergency meeting at Jegazzy's. Jazz had no idea what was coming when I hit the play button.

"*Yo, Diaz! What's this I hear about a hit on Nick?*"

I hit stop and the room was silent. Jazz was stunned. Tears and shit came to his eyes.

"I'm sorry," he said, "I just didn't—"

"Why did you mention my name?"

I spoke cool, but I was so pissed. If it weren't for Jazz and his big fuckin' mouth, the Feds would not have made the case! But now I'm connected in this goddamn conspiracy!

I pulled out my shit on Jazz, let him feel the iron right on his head. *Fuck the consequences.* "Why did you mention my name, *nigger*!?"

Frank knocked down my hand.

"Come on," he said. "You don't wanna do that, man."

You got lucky, Jazz. If Frank hadn't done that, I would've put two in your head. It's funny. When I brought you into this thing, I had no idea what your contribution would be. At least now I know. Havin' a big goddamn mouth. *That's* what you gave to the Council.

"Shoulda taken him out," said Guy.

"Don't worry. We'll get our chance soon enough. Just gotta pick the right time. We got bigger shit to worry about."

Although Guy had been in jail during the arrest, the prosecution still had enough evidence to charge him with conspiracy. He was as deep in this as I was. We needed to start planning our defense.

"What are we gonna do about Geronimo?" I asked.

Geronimo was currently in the FBI Witness Protection Program, secure in an anonymous location with a new identity, so our only chance of getting to him was through his family.

"Oughta take his mother hostage. Or at least threaten to kill her if her son says a goddamn word about us on the stand."

"Listen, Guy. We gotta think smart on this. Just stretch out to her like we did with Billings. Offer $50G from the treasury, double what the government's gonna give Geronimo for testifying."

Guy nodded. Now came the tricky part.

"Guy? I know that if you hadn't been in jail, your little brother wouldn't have gotten away with all that shit he was doin'. But he brought us down, man. There's just no arguing that."

"No doubt. If only I hadn't gotten that ID bust..."

"But I know he's your brother, too, so here's what we oughta do. We can have him take the stand and say he was lying the whole time. Have him say he just dropped my name, knowin' my rep from the papers, to gain a little cred with this Diaz."

"Yeah. Or we could just make him disappear."

"Like send him to the Bahamas?"

Guy didn't answer.

"Guy? That's your *brother.*"

"If I gotta play murder, I play murder."

Breitbart had gotten a call from Fred Ferretti, who was doing a feature on me for the *New York Times* magazine. Ferretti wanted me to pose for the cover in a photo shoot, but Breitbart told him to forget it, that the last thing we needed was more negative publicity in the months before trial.

A.M. Rosenthal, executive editor of the *Times*, called back with an offer we couldn't refuse. "I've got a mug shot of your client when he was arrested in the middle of the night for murder. He's got a number across his chest and he looks like he ate the victim's eyes out. And if I don't get a photo shoot with Nicky Barnes, I'm going to put *that* on the front page of the *New York Times* magazine section."

Since prospective jurors would be reading this magazine, I didn't want that mug shot plastered across the city. I wanted to present myself as someone a middle-class, Manhattanite juror could identify with.

On the day of the shoot, I chose exactly the right outfit. No fur coat or big diamond rings. No cigar in my hand and a fine, tailored suit like John Gotti would do. I wore a simple pale denim suit and a red, white and blue tie. That's what I wanted the jury to see, a clean-shaven American businessman. I stood in front of the camera and held my hands humbly before me.

Sunday rolls around. June 5, 1977. President Jimmy Carter is sitting on Air Force One, looking at the cover of his *New York Times* magazine. And something about my photo *really* rubs him wrong.

He thinks I look smug and arrogant.

How could he think that? Look at the picture! Do you see that red, white and blue tie? That suit isn't flashy. It's a wash-and-wear blue denim suit. See those stitches in there? That's machine stitched! Off the rack!

I know why Jimmy got angry. The same shit happened to Capone back in the day. The tabloids hyped him up as an American success story, a businessman of bootleg booze, and President Hoover didn't like this dirty Italian getting so much attention and respect.

Don't get me wrong, Jimmy. I know you did a lot for your sharecroppin' Negroes down on your peanut farm, but I believe the image of a well-dressed, successful African-American businessman just didn't sit right with you.

I guess the caption didn't help much either:

MISTER UNTOUCHABLE
This is Nicky Barnes.
The Police Say He May Be Harlem's Biggest Drug Dealer.
But Can They Prove It?

Well, that was like a big dare, and just like President Hoover went all out to "get Al Capone," President Carter was gonna "get Nicky Barnes" at any cost. He told his cabinet on Monday morning that my conspiracy trial was the most important case in the United States. He didn't want any citizen untouchable.

"If we can't put somebody like this away," he said, "there's something wrong with our system of justice."

True, I'd beat the rap time and again, but what Jimmy's not realizing is I'd been *framed* on those cases. That's the real problem with the justice system. Tryin' to fuck me over! And I hate to break it to the president, but he ain't the judicial system! That's not his job. That's why we got separation of powers!

But of course, the president wasn't asking me, so when Attorney General Griffin Bell came out of that cabinet meeting, he called up Robert Fiske, U.S. Attorney for the Southern District, and asked if he was sending in "the first team" to prosecute me. In other words, don't leave this to underlings; you gotta do this *yourself*.

The Council needed to look forward to the future. I had a lot of things I wanted us to do in our five-year plan. Like getting into importing. I was thinking we'd send someone to Vietnam for a year, just to live, just to get a feel for how we could best smuggle in powder. I was also ready to move on Vegas, to finally go legit through that route.

And I really wanted to fix up the Apollo Theater, make it the shining star it once was. When the Council bought it for Guy to manage, I knew it needed some work. The theater had fallen into disrepair over the years, but once we were through with the polish? It'd be our landmark, our lasting contribution to Harlem.

But as I talked about all these plans for the future of our brotherhood, Guy interrupted out of the blue with a past vendetta.

"I know who robbed Renee."

We all know too, dude.

"Ronnie Bell and Skeeter."

"Who the fuck are they?"

"Former friends of mine. Fucked me over on some powder a while back."

"Why the fuck would they do something as stupid as to rob your woman?"

"'Cause they thought they could get away with it. That's why people do that shit. But they're just a couple nobodies. I can knock them off and nobody gonna miss 'em."

"Guy? You can't be knockin' dudes off yourself, man. You're wanted for conspiracy! Contract it out."

"I gotta have the satisfaction of doin' it by my own hand. At least with Ronnie. He was a good friend, but he *betrayed* me."

Guy did it with a 9mm PPK. Made Ronnie get on the ground and beg for his life, then shot him in the head. Clean and ruthless.

Guy had turned into a true warrior. I was real proud of him.

When the great blackout hit New York City, July 13, 1977, I was watching television in the air-conditioned comfort of my Fort Lee penthouse. My first instinct was, good thing I'm in Jersey. But when I saw on the news that the Bronx was burning, I jumped into my Citroën and split for Wally Rice's house in Mount Vernon. His wife answered the door.

"Nick! What are you doing here?"

I was surprised she'd asked.

Three months before my conspiracy bust, Wally Rice got sentenced to six years in Sing Sing on some dope the cops planted in his trunk. Now that Natalie was all alone, and with all the looting and riots going on in the blackout, I had to make sure she was safe. That's how it worked in the Council. Brothers had to look out for each other's women.

"Hey, Natalie, I got an idea."

I put on the high beams of my Citroën and turned on the radio. Natalie and I joked around and listened to music while her kids played in the front yard. I sat in that lawn chair all night, just to make sure nothing bad happened. I thought that was a nice thing for me to do. Offer a little love under the circumstances.

"You know," said Natalie, as dawn broke, "I really miss Wally."

I was bleary-eyed from being up all day and night, but fuck it, I missed him, too.

"Wake the kids, Natalie."

I drove them all the way up to Sing Sing in Natalie's station wagon, one big, happy family.

"Sorry," the warden told me, "Mrs. Rice and her kids can go in, but you're not authorized to enter."

I couldn't believe it. Spent half my life tryin' to get out of prison, and now that I wanted in, they were keeping me out!

"Well, why not?" I asked. "I didn't drive up here just for nothin'!"

"You're not on the approved visitor list."

I checked it out for myself. Frank James was on the list. So were Gaps and Jazz. But I was nowhere to be found.

"I dunno, Natalie. Maybe Wally just made a mistake. You go on without me. Give Wally my love."

I watched them enter and waited outside on the grass. It was a nice summer day, so I passed right out, right there on the lawn of Sing Sing.

That's just how tired I was.

The United States of America Against Leroy Barnes

ON THE MORNING of September 26, 1977, I woke up at 6:30 sharp; showered, shaved and put on the exact same outfit I'd worn for the *New York Times* photo shoot. That's how I wanted the jury to see me then. That's how I wanted the jury to see now.

Murray Kempton, columnist for the *New York Post*, put it this way: "As Miles Davis taught a generation to dress like bankers in the '50s, Nicky Barnes is now teaching another generation of adventurous enterprisers how to dress as criminal defendants in the '70s."

I headed downtown in my white Mercedes, and like any successful businessman, left early enough to beat the rush-hour traffic. I didn't want to be late for trial.

I walked up the steps of the U.S. Courthouse at Foley Square. The line curled around the block. I told the powder people not to show, but a few legit friends waved hello. Some were women I'd been off with. Others just wanted to glimpse "Mr. Untouchable" in the flesh.

U.S. Marshals guarded the entrance to room 318, the largest courtroom in the building. The place had a real grandeur. Sunlight streamed through the high windows, lighting my path toward the long, black tables, arranged in an L before the judge's bench. This is where we sat, all fifteen defendants, and between us sat fifteen of the top criminal lawyers in the city—fourteen white, one black. I took my place at the far right, next to Breitbart and closest to the jury box.

"All rise for the Honorable Henry F. Werker."

The packed house—spectators and press, defense and prosecution—stood for Judge Werker, heavy in black robes and with a greased flip in his hair. It was all big drama and ritual, but really? Nothing but a show, 'cause Werker denied us justice right from the start.

"With respect to the selection of the jury. We have drawn a panel of 150 jurors and they will be numbered from 1 to 150. Their names will not be disclosed to counsel, nor will their street addresses."

"I object," said the defense counsel.

"You can object as much as you like," said the judge, "that is my ruling."

"Your Honor—"

"Sit down. I have made my ruling. I don't want to listen to any more."

With that, Werker ordered the first anonymous jury in the history of the United States. The judge said he'd let us know what county a juror lived in, but how was that gonna help? New York County stretches from Harlem to the Upper East Side down to Wall Street. There's a big difference in those neighborhoods!

Not knowing the names of the jurors meant we had no idea on their ethnicity. It's not easy to tell by looks alone if a guy is Italian or not, and having Italians on the jury had always been our ace in the hole!

That's why we won all our cases in voir dire!

The judge was killing us. He wasn't gonna give me a fair trial by a jury of my peers.

How can I be tried by a peer if I don't even know his name? I was gonna be tried by lottery numbers!

The prosecution gloated at their victory. They played dirty from the start, telling the judge that relatives of witnesses had been threatened with violence. I told Guy not to say anything to Geronimo's family, so I know that wasn't true, but Werker believed that shit.

That's why he made the jury anonymous!

"I will not have witnesses or families threatened," he told the jury pool. I almost fell out of my chair when he said it.

If I'm so bad that the judge has to protect the jury from violence, how they gonna think I'm innocent?!

On the last day of voir dire, we'd stacked the jury as best we could—eight women and four men, five blacks in total. The only ones who gave us concern were these two middle-aged women, housewife types who'd go whichever way the rest of the jury went.

With two preemptive strikes left, we had a choice. We could go with the jury as is or roll the dice, hoping for a black or a liberal. I scribbled a note to Breitbart on a yellow legal pad and handed it over—"Do it."

When I saw them fill the two empty seats in the juror box, I knew we'd just lost the lottery. The first was a thick guy from New Rochelle with a jacket that had "Bearcats" written on the back. Even though he was real friendly with the New Rochelle Police Department, he said he'd still be impartial when it came to me. I had my doubts.

The second was the Marlboro Man himself. This white guy took his seat in a ramrod position and proudly announced he was a bank executive from Westchester.

Muthafucka had Republican written all over him.

After the jury selection, Guy and I went to Forlini's. This Italian restaurant was everybody's spot to have lunch—from judges to prosecutors to defendants—during federal court. It was like Switzerland, a neutral ground to talk about the case. Judge Werker passed our booth with a nod and sat at his table.

"Man, I can't believe we got a Nazi on our jury."

"Don't worry," said Guy, under his breath. "We got this one in the *bag*, dude."

"What?"

"I had good eye contact with her."

"Who?"

"I know that broad, juror number two!"

It was the black woman who worked at a hospital. Guy not only knew what her name was, he knew where she *lived*.

The judge sequestered the jury to a downtown hotel, so there was no way to approach her directly, but Guy said he'd send a message through her family to name her price.

He got his answer the next evening.

"Seventy-five grand. She'll vote not guilty on all of us for seventy-five grand."

"We'll have Curt send her the money tonight," I said.

"No," said Guy. "Only through me. I know the family. I don't want anyone else to handle this."

"We oughta up it to $100G," said Ishmael, "then give her enough to pay off everybody on the jury."

"I don't think that's a good idea," said Guy.

"He's right," I said. "You never try and fix the whole jury. That's why Hoffa went to jail."

Even if we couldn't get a full acquittal, at least we'd fixed the lottery to ensure a hung jury. Those were good enough odds for me.

"Mr. Fiske, your opening statement?"

On September 29, 1977, U.S. Attorney Robert Fiske stepped before the jury in his dark suit and, in a soft voice, laid on the bullshit.

"The government charges in this case that these fifteen defendants who are on trial before you operated as part of a loosely knit but highly effective business organization headed by this man, Leroy Barnes, better known as Nicky."

Fiske pointed to a large, white poster propped on a stand. It had boxes and circles like a big flowchart, with each of our names printed inside. That was one thing we had going for us. Juries hate conspiracy cases. With a lot of who's who and who's where, they're time consuming and confusing.

"At the top of the organization is the man in charge, Leroy Barnes. The proof will show that this narcotics business was set up just like any other well-managed, big organization. The man at the top isn't out on the street selling heroin any more than the president of General Motors is on the floor of the showroom selling cars. He's an executive. He makes the big decisions and the big money. One basic thing makes his business a lot different from that of General Motors. The business he runs is a federal crime."

Then Breitbart took the ring like Ali. He came out swinging.

"Several years ago it became apparent to some police officers there was an uppity black man in Harlem. He had the nerve to earn a good living, he had the nerve to have a good deal of money and he had the nerve not to be afraid to answer back when someone spoke to him. So some cop said, 'Anybody with that much money must be a drug dealer. Let's go get him!' That is what this is all about."

In a strong opening move, the prosecution brought in none other than my doormen as their first witnesses. The first was from Stratford House in Hackensack. He testified he'd seen the occupant of Penthouse Two, rented to "Mr. Hobie Darling," at least sixty or seventy times, and that he'd say "Good morning, Mr. Darling" and "Good afternoon, Mr. Darling" whenever he saw him.

"Can you identify Mr. Darling in court?" asked the prosecution.

He pointed to me.

This continued with the doorman from Horizon House in Fort Lee, only this guy identified me as "Mr. Wallace Rice."

Then the prosecution brought in my tax return from 1975, when I declared $288,750 in miscellaneous income. It was their way to create an image of a man with something to hide—two false names and a lot of mysterious income.

This settled it for the Marlboro Man. He got red faced that he, a white bank executive from Westchester, wasn't doing as well as me, a black man from Harlem. He was dead set on sending us *all* away. He even gave Guy's attorney, Paul Goldberger, the finger after court adjourned!

"He gave you the international sign?" asked Judge Werker in his chamber.

"Yeah," said Goldberger.

"Well, I'm not gonna strike him."

"Well, he should be questioned, and we should question other jurors to see whether they saw this incident."

"I'm not gonna do that," said Werker. "If I start doing that, it will contaminate the whole jury."

Motherfucker did everything in his power to deny me justice.

The jury had been waiting to hear Geronimo ever since Breitbart set the stage in his opening statements—"We are going to prove to you that as he lay fornicating in the bed in his home with another woman, his wife was dying of asthma, induced from drugs that he supplied, and that he brought the other woman to the wake and *laughed* about it."

Geronimo didn't have a damn thing on me, but knew if he didn't come up with something good on the stand, the government wouldn't give him $25G for testimony. That's how it works.

Our argument was, "How can you believe this guy? He wants to get paid by the government! He'll say *anything*!" Of course, the prosecution argued, "How can you *not* believe this guy? If he doesn't tell the truth, he won't get the money!" The jury has got to sift through both arguments. Each can be equally convincing.

Geronimo told a tale about how he put a Nagra recorder in his back, strapped on a fake ankle cast, put a Kel transmitter inside his cane, then limped over to me at the Hubba and engaged me in narcotics talk. Fiske asked Geronimo if there was a tape recording that covered our conversation that night.

"Yes," said Geronimo.

I didn't worry, because once the tapes got played, the jury would know Geronimo was creating fantasies. That conversation never *happened*.

Only one problem. Fiske didn't want those tapes played. He wanted the jury to believe Geronimo on word alone. That's why the prosecution claimed there was a technical malfunction on not just one but *both* of Geronimo's recorders, at the exact moment of that conversation, preventing him from capturing my voice.

Breitbart jumped to object. "I think the jury and Your Honor and Mr. Fiske will see that this tape didn't malfunction...If we can't use the tapes, and Mr. Fiske doesn't play it, we can't show the lie!"

When the judge ruled against us, I got a real bad case of déjà vu. It wasn't the first time a judge wouldn't play a tape proving my innocence. The last time it happened, I got twenty years in Green Haven.

Only Breitbart wasn't giving up so easy. I knew he was a tough fighter, and by tooth and nail he got the judge to admit the evidence. As the 578 feet of tape rolled, the lawyers, the judge and the jury listened through multiple sets of white earphones. What did they hear? Barely audible voices, but a crystal-clear recording of "I Love Music" by the O'Jays, loudly playing in the background at the time of my "conversation" with Geronimo!

"That's Barnes," said Geronimo.

But all you heard was music. The jury sang along, the lawyers tapped their feet and Werker rocked back and forth in his swivel chair to the beat.

Geronimo gulped his glass of water on the stand.

"That's his nervous tick," said Guy. "Every time he fouls up, he takes a sip of water. So here's what we do. I know this chemist, and he can make a slow-acting poison. We can put it in that pitcher of water on the stand."

The next morning, Guy gave Chico Bob a Visine bottle wrapped in some plastic bags, but Bob came to me before doing the deed.

"I got it in my pocket, and if you want me to do it, I will. I'm a warrior. But even though Geronimo's a snitch, he saved my life once. Doesn't seem right for me to do it."

Chico Bob had a lot of heart. I always knew he wasn't the type to do work on somebody.

"Keep it in your pocket, Bob. Breitbart'll kill him on the stand for us."

As an employee of the DEA, Geronimo had to check in periodically with the DEA office in Manhattan to make updates. Each time the agents wrote up a report called a DEA-6. And in one DEA-6, Geronimo described a weekend with Wally Fisher, smoking angel dust in a Baltimore hotel room. To Breitbart, this sounded like a real think tank, so he hired a private investigator to check out the details.

"You *swore* that you were in Baltimore, Maryland," asked Breitbart on cross.

"Yes," swore Geronimo, under oath.

"Were you in Baltimore?"

"I was in Baltimore, Maryland."

Geronimo went on to say that when he returned to New York on Monday, he filed his DEA-6 at agency headquarters.

"And was it a fact, sir, that you had every opportunity to tell them what had happened during the weekend that had just passed?"

"Yes."

"You lied to the agents when you came back?"

"Lied? No. I did not lie, no."

"Were you so stoned that you wouldn't know the difference between Pennsylvania and Maryland?"

"No. I was not stoned, if that's the question."

"Do you know the difference between Pennsylvania and Maryland?"

"Yes."

Then Breitbart presented a hotel registration card from a Holiday Inn in the Poconos, the same weekend Geronimo claimed he was in Baltimore. It was signed in Geronimo's handwriting.

"Do you remember signing that card?"

"No, I don't remember signing this specific card, no."

"Was somebody else using your handwriting that day?"

As it turned out, Geronimo hadn't been to Baltimore at all that weekend. He and Wally were living it up in the Poconos, hanging behind their motel and breaking windows with a slingshot!

Mighty Whitey went in for the kill.

"Faced with the card, faced with your signature, knowing all that you now know, you still tell this jury that you were not lying about that trip?"

"Are you talking about *intentionally* lying?"

"Brazenly, pathologically, intentionally, psychopathically lying! That's exactly what I'm talking about."

Geronimo gulped his water.

"Yes."

But now that we'd established him as a liar, we had grounds to show that everything he told the DEA was, in fact, complete bullshit!

"If you are mistaken about this," asked Breitbart, "you might be mistaken about other things, right?"

"It is a possibility," said Geronimo."Yes."

I waited in line at the courthouse cafeteria during the lunch recess when Jimmy Breslin, the famous columnist for the *New York Daily News*, came to me with a question.

"I can't talk about the case, Jimmy. I mention anything about the case, the judge'll revoke my bail."

"I don't want to talk to you about the case. I want to tell you something and see what you think."

Breitbart gave the okay, so we sat with Breslin and listened to his story about Curtis, a twelve-year-old from Harlem sent to juvenile court on a charge for assaulting an old lady.

"I asked Curtis what he thought about Reggie Jackson, but the kid just shrugged. Didn't even show a sign of recognition. Then I asked if there was anybody he did admire.

"'Somebody real tough,' said Curtis.

"'Who's the toughest around here?' I asked.

"'Robby the toughest now. He stick up Nicky Barnes's bar.'

"'Well, if Robby's tough because he held up Nicky Barnes, then what do you think of Nicky Barnes? He must be something.'

"'Oh, he real tough and all that. But he's too fly. Buyin' all those cars and showin' that money around. I'm not goin' buy all those cars. One car'll do me. Then nobody'll know what I do. I won't be like Nicky. Too fly.'

"Do you think that's good," Breslin asked me, "that some kids examine you and decide that you're the standard?"

"That's not fair," I answered. "You're singling out one individual. It's the system that makes it this way. The kids don't have anybody to look up to because they don't see anybody around them making it. The kids look up to only what they can attain, what is realistic."

Not to mention that story about "Robby" was bullshit. *Nobody* stuck up my bars.

Once Agent Louie Diaz started buying from Harlem River Motors, the DEA had surveillance agents climb to the roof of the garage and drop a transmitter, then plant a bug inside the garage office. With the soul music blaring in the background, only about seven hours' worth of recordings were audible, but out of those seven, the prosecution jumped on a line from Bucky Beaver, a worker at the garage.

"Gotta pick up a kilo out of Nick's car," said Bucky.

Or that's what the DEA *claimed* he said. Bucky didn't say that at all! See, there was this dude at Harlem Rivers named Black Nick. Owned a couple of cabs and sold one that night, so all this cash was in his trunk. Some guys who worked at the garage were coming by to get their salary, and that's why Bucky said, "Gotta pick up a *payroll* out of Nicky's car, now."

To prove it, Breitbart brought the foremost audiology expert in the world to court. This guy had a special round-headed tape player, and when he put that tape from the bug on it, sure enough, it came out "payroll, payroll, payroll."

We knocked the prosecution out on that one. Just like the Geronimo tapes, any time the government brought up hard evidence, it couldn't pass the test!

But we had no control over the outright lies of others.

Agent Diaz took the stand to describe the night of March 11, 1977, his last buy from Fat Stevie, the event that clinched my arrest. He said Wally

Fisher escorted him into the garage of Harlem River Motors, and later that night asked, "Who the hell do you think was lookin' at you like a hawk as you walked in the garage? Nicky Barnes!"

The prosecution not only argued I was in the garage, they said I'd driven in with a black and white limo, that I was watching drugs bein' moved into the trunk of this limo!

I was so goddamn angry.

Understand this. I'm in the drug business. I sell drugs. But I'm not out in the combat zone selling stuff to people! People don't come to me and say, "Nick, I need twenty kilos" like they do in movies. They don't say, "Get a kilo out of Nick's car." 'Cause I'm not around it! I don't tell guys like Wally Fisher, "Yeah, go see Fat Stevie. I'll call Fat Stevie and tell him to give it to you, eh."

That's bullshit, man! Sure, the prosecution knew I was selling drugs. But knowing is not enough in a court of law! You've got to *prove* it. That's why they had to frame me in this motherfucking case! They had people get on the stand and tell lies, flat-out lies.

If they didn't frame me, they never could've fucking got to me.

"Nicky Barnes, Leroy Barnes, is not guilty and there is no conspiracy." With that, Breitbart launched into his closing statement, pacing back and forth in front of the jury, a fiery defense of my innocence.

"It has been said before that the title of the case is the United States of America against Leroy Barnes, et al. Well, I'm an American and I'm not against Mr. Barnes, but I have a vested interest. I'm an attorney. I'm an American and I love my country. I'm an American and I'm proud of the accomplishments of the American people. I'm proud of the majesty and greatness which are symbolized by the American people and the American flag...

"But I'm not blind. I love my country. I love America. But sometimes

LEROY "NICKY" BARNES

it makes a mistake. Sometimes its deeds have been deeds of which I'm not proud, and because I'm an American, I share in the responsibility and if I can do something to help, I help. I'm not proud of our historical relationship with the American Indians. I'm not proud of the way our country has treated blacks...

"As sure as God made little green apples, the integrity of our judicial process has, in fact, been invaded by the agents and the attorneys involved in this case...

"There was no way in the entire world that the results of this investigation would do anything except accuse Nicky Barnes. There was no way out once that car started rolling downhill; Nicky Barnes was going to be indicted, Nicky Barnes was going to be tried by a jury in this building...

"In contemporary society, I was trying to find an analogous situation, ladies and gentlemen. The only analogy I could come up with is that in the war on narcotics, the Nicky Barnes case is the My Lai Massacre. It's *obscene*...

"Are you angry? Are you the least bit annoyed? Are you offended? It's your system. I am proud to be a defense lawyer, but it is *your* system that is being invaded...

"Ladies and gentlemen, where law ends, there tyranny does begin. Ladies and gentlemen, Nicky Barnes is not guilty and there was no conspiracy here."

Imperial Destiny

MELLON WAS MY SISTER'S SON. He was nineteen and had been into powder for some time. I didn't groom him into anything. I hadn't even watched him grow up. His father Dutch, a hustler and an old partner of mine, dealt a little powder, and he got his son to do that with him.

Dutch died of a heart attack from freebasing too much cocaine, and when I heard Mellon got picked up on homicide, I helped him out with legal representation. He eventually beat the case, so he and I got tight after that.

"Look, dude," I tried to tell him, "if you need money, if you want to go back to school and stuff, I'll take care of you. I'll get you a place, get you a car, take care of your expenses. You could live on campus. You can just go for it from there."

But that's not what he wanted to do. He wanted to be in powder. He wanted to be the next Nicky Barnes.

I set him up with Guy and he earned a fierce rep as a dealer. He was a tough kid with a lot of strength. That's why I summoned him along with

Guy to my crib.

"If I should be convicted," I told them, "I want you two looking out for Shamecca. I want you to be her security."

Mecca was my jewel. She needed protection.

I dismissed Mellon, then told Guy the situation. "I've kept a few million at Mecca's for safekeeping. She's not gonna touch that. It's for the future survival of the Council. But I want you to have access to it. I want you to provide her with income in return."

I took Guy to Shamecca's penthouse in the Bronx. I had gotten her this penthouse in a big apartment building with a big garage. Not the high-rise Fifth Avenue type, but more like something out of a Katherine Hepburn movie, with push-out bay windows. It was beautiful.

Mecca loved it. She asked what she could do for me in return.

"Nothing," I told her. "I just want you to enjoy it."

She didn't need to do the things the other women did. Although she told me how much she wanted to be part of the powder life, part of all the glitter and glamour, I didn't want her near any of that.

"Remember that, Guy. Keep her away from it."

Shamecca opened the door and let us in. She didn't have on any makeup or perfume. She was as beautiful as I'd ever seen her.

"Shamecca. This is my brother. Treat him as you treat me."

Guy left soon after, so Mecca and were alone. She held my hand as we sipped Le Montrachet.

"Your nails look so, so nice, and that ring looks so, so good."

I had a nice diamond ring on. Paid a couple hundred thousand dollars for the stone.

"You smell good, too," she said, putting my hand to her face.

Our favorite group at that time was LTD. Jeffrey Osborne. We listened to that on the eight-track and smoked a lot of dust. Not just a little bit. We freaked and her body smelled really good, like an exotic spice from the Orient.

The next morning, I knotted my muted gold tie from Armani, stepped into my tailored, olive trousers and tucked in my russet brown shirt. I latched on my lizard-skin belt and slid on my tan leather ankle boots. I put on my wool sports coat with the grey and lavender weave, draped my suede coat with the sable collar over my shoulders and watched Mecca sleep through the lenses of my purple-tinted Playboy sunglasses.

I kissed her cheek and drove to court.

It was November 30, 1977, and after hearing forty witnesses over six weeks of testimony, the jury began deliberation. The papers gave me a fifty-fifty chance of walking free, based on the weak case by the prosecution. The government had a lot of innuendo and hearsay, but they didn't have evidence. They had to manufacture that. It only proved how well insulated I was from the powder.

I was really confident stepping into the courtroom. I'd prevailed in cases where the government had much more evidence, and even if the jury *wasn't* fixed, I knew I would walk.

I played dominoes and Tonk with the guys while we waited for our verdict, but by the end of the day, there was still no answer. It didn't surprise me. The jury had to wade through a lot of material.

The next day, I came to court an hour late. The traffic was brutal coming down from Washington Heights. But the prosecutors thought I tried to leave the country. They wanted to throw me in MCC to make sure I didn't get any ideas. "I got more motherfuckin' reason than anybody to be here," I said, furious.

There was still no verdict by the end of the evening.

I headed home in my Mercedes. This time, the cops tailed me in a fucking motorcade. Maybe I gave everyone a good scare that morning, but this was just inexcusable. I pulled to the side of the street and marched to the lead car, driven by none other than Agent Diaz. He went for his shit like I was gonna carjack him.

"Jesus Christ! You again!"

"Nicky, we're just following orders, man."

"Tell you what, I'm gonna make it easy for you guys. I'm gonna settle in for the night at the Sheraton with my old lady."

I hit the hotel parking lot and Diaz pulled beside.

"Nicky, why don't you do me a favor? Just park your car behind us and we'll watch it for tonight."

"Fine, suit yourself."

I walked past the four cops posted in the lobby and checked in for the night. I called the Hubba and ordered a freak, but by the time she fell asleep, I was staring at the ceiling.

I thought about this friend of mine Ponch who married this chick Lillian. Ponch was an intelligent guy, and Lillian was just so gorgeous. A big, fat, brown butt and big titties. As kids we'd hang on the corner and shoot up, but years later, well into the '70s, Ponch and Lil were still on that same corner.

Sometimes I'd see Ponch outside the spots, like the Gold Lounge or the Shalimar. He'd knock on my Mercedes and wave. I'd step out and give him a hug.

"Yo! What's up, Ponch! Where's Lil?"

"I'm gettin' a fix for her. What drugs you got, man?"

I'd slip him a hundred and say, "Go out there to the Market and buy yourself some. My guys'll be there."

I hooked those two up real good, especially when we had packages comin' from all over Latin America and Europe. Since each country had different ways of growing and refining powder, the Council decided the blood test was most reliable.

"Go look up Lil," I'd tell Curt.

He'd take a bag from the shipment, slice it with a knife, whack the sample and bring it to Lil. He could tell how good it was, just watching her reaction when she shot it.

In the early days, I'd even take the package myself. I'd go up to their apartment, run down but shabby chic, give 'em a couple hundred dollars and the sample. We'd sit and drink and talk for hours about old times. They'd get high, talk about how they were going to stop using.

"You think it's too late for us?" Ponch asked, strung out with big, swollen hands. That happens to some people when they use heroin. The chemicals in the drug cause the body to retain fluid. That's how it affected Ponch and Lil. They had these tiny veins the size of a piece of thread. They had to dig and dig under all that extra tissue to get to them.

"Naw, Ponch, it's never too late."

I hadn't seen Ponch or Lil in such a long time. They had to be dead by now. That shit just destroyed them.

I woke up tired the next morning. I got off the queen-sized bed and put on my trousers, slightly wrinkled from the day before. The freak was gone when I picked up the ringing telephone.

"It's Louie. I just wanted to check that you're all right."

In other words, he wanted to make sure I hadn't split for the Caymans or somethin'.

"Yeah, I'm okay."

"Look, I'm sorry to tell you this, but I got some good news and some bad news. Which do you want first?"

"I don't care."

The bad news came first. The cops towed my Mercedes, 'cause I owed hundreds in parking tickets. I was furious. This motherfuckin' Diaz not only infiltrated the Council, he *promised* to watch my car.

"Nick, I'm real sorry, but me and my partner fell asleep. Swear to God. When we woke up it was gone. I tried to break it out of the pound, but they wouldn't let me take it."

"Well, what's the good news?"

"The good news? *We'll* give you a ride to court."

By midafternoon, the jury still hadn't reached a verdict. I hoped they'd be done soon. I still had time to hurry home, pack my things, grab Mecca and have a moonlit dinner on the beach in Nassau. Or maybe Hawaii. I'd been to a few of those islands. I'd pick one and stay. Go snorkeling, scuba diving, horseback riding…

I'd definitely chill there for a few months, then come back and start over as a businessman. I might even pull out of narcotics. Or at least I wouldn't do it the *way* I'd been doing it.

I could step away from the Council and just be their supplier. Let them insulate me. A double insulation. That'd be good. But even then, I'd only do it if someone gave me *massive* amounts of heroin. Just ten, fifteen or twenty packages? Naw. Wouldn't happen…

Shortly after three o'clock, the forelady softly spoke the verdict. "Guilty." I barely heard the screams and sobs from the gallery. I don't recall anything coming into my mind. I was completely blank.

Murray Kempton put it a little more eloquently:

> *It is hopeless work to search for the single word that describes the face of imperial destiny in the moment of disaster. Say only this for Nicky Barnes: He looked the way Napoleon must have when he got into his coach and started on the road back from Moscow.*

The U.S. Marshals flanked our table, ready to block any attempts at escape, any attempts at entry.

Guy hadn't even got up out of his chair. His head was in his hands as he wept. I lifted my brother from his seat and embraced him without words.

"You know," someone remarked behind us, "these guys love each other."

As I prepared to leave, one of the defense lawyers rushed up and stuck out his hand.

"I always thought you were 100 percent, man."

"You know, kid," I said, "I never thought they were going to get me."

"Don't worry," Breitbart whispered in my ear, "we'll appeal it. You'll be out." But all lawyers say that. And the government wins 80 percent of appeals.

The marshals handcuffed and escorted me to the exit. I stopped before the door and turned to Guy. He could walk free. The jury was deadlocked on his verdict, as good as an acquittal.

"My coat," I said.

The marshals waited in silence as Guy ran to the defense table for my suede coat with the sable collar, then placed it on my shoulders.

And with that, I left the courtroom.

"We may not look upon him ever again," wrote Kempton, "and it will be a long time before we look upon his like. Nicky Barnes is a great man, and to say that is not to dispute Acton's conclusion that all great men are bad men."

Life

I KNOTTED THE HERMÈS without a mirror in the conference room, pulling off my prison blues and putting on the chalk-stripe Saint Laurent. Might as well get lynched in style.

It was January 19, 1978. Sentencing.

Breitbart told me to expect the worst at this sentencing, but that I had a very strong case on appeal since an anonymous jury was unconstitutional. That was good news, 'cause I was ready to get back out on the streets, to get it all rolling like I used to.

The five of us—Chico Bob, J.J., Wally Fisher, Jazz and me—were brought through the side door into Judge Werker's court again, just as crowded as before. The press, the people, all wanted to see what Nicky Barnes was gonna get. So did Nicky Barnes.

So we're all sitting there, trying to be respectful while the judge is talking, but fuckin' Jazz is waving to his fans, grinning ear to ear and playin' the movie star! Now, I'd been before enough judges in my life to know if they don't get their propers, they will boost up your sentence in that moment, so I looked over at Breitbart so he'd tell Jazz to cut the shit out!

Werker hit Jazz first.

"Do you have anything to say before sentencing, Mr. Hayden?"

"I'm not guilty of anything, of anything. There is no justice! My association with Mr. Barnes is the only thing I'm guilty of."

That got Jazz fifteen years on heroin distribution.

J.J. got hit hard, sentenced to twenty for being part of the Kingdom Auto Leasing crew, but Werker was nicer to the "youthful offenders," as he called them. Wally Fisher got eight and Chico Bob got six. I wished he'd thrown the book at Wally Fisher, but was real glad for Bob. He'd serve three, four years tops. Not bad at all, plus Guy would take care of him during his bid. Those were the rules.

When it came to me, I stood up straight and said, "I am innocent of all the charges!" I always said that. Loud, strong, committed.

Werker was ten feet away, but he got in my face. "You are a great danger to the community! Your trafficking affected the lives of thousands of people in your own neighborhood. You need to be punished for running the largest, most profitable and most venal drug ring in New York City. It is the judgment of the court that you be committed to the custody of the attorney general on the count of the indictment continuing criminal enterprise, life imprisonment without parole and fined $125,000!"

Life without parole. Even when you know it's coming, it still stings. I truly believed I might get off light like some of the others, but Werker gave me the single stiffest sentence in the history of Manhattan federal court.

I'm sure President Carter slept well that night, but then so did I, 'cause four hours after my sentencing, I was back at MCC, bangin' Shamecca in the visitors room.

When she came in to see me, the guard turned his chair so his back was to us, givin' us the green light. Thank God. I needed pussy now, 'cause in a real prison, you can get booze, weed and blow, but you cannot get pussy.

"I'm so sorry, baby," said Mecca. She slid right up and sat on my lap. I already had it out. I didn't say a word and we just started fucking, man.

At MCC, me, Jazz and the three others who got sentenced, we all got special treatment because of me. They called us "The Untouchables." We got special food made by the cooks, any packages we wanted, and they let us bang our girls in the visitors room. You couldn't lie down on a table and fuck, but you could definitely freak off.

I had a number of regular women coming to see me each week, but had to put my wives on separate shifts so I could get what I needed without provoking a catfight. Believe it. You do not want your women running into each other, especially when it's Shamecca versus Lady Tee.

So there I am with Shamecca and we're grooving. I'm out of my chair and I'm holding her and she's holding herself up on the back of another chair. And then we both start skeetin' at the same time. Her chair goes over with a crash and she falls over backwards.

She's "Oh, shit!" hitting the floor as I'm trying to pick her up, my pants down and my dick hanging out. Mecca got up and pulled her dress back down, but nobody in the room even blinked an eye. They knew the score. And the guard? Never even turned around.

"Anything we can do for you?" Ishmael asked. We sat at a table in the visitors room.

"Look at this shit." I waved around some letters a guard had given me earlier. "I'm getting fan mail. Can you believe that shit? People writing me. Here. Telling me how I'm a tough, righteous dude."

"And you are, inshallah."

"What you got?"

"Couple things, good and bad. I heard from Wally Rice in Sing Sing, and you're not gonna believe this. He was there in the visiting room with Natalie and who walks in? Robert Geronimo, visiting a friend. Wally is sure he can find out where they're keeping him."

"They got him in witness protection, but they can't help it if he's stupid."

"So we can do the work on him?"

"Well, there's no reason now. He hurt us bad, he hurt me bad, and we should've taken him out before. But at this point, there's no point..."

Ishmael couldn't believe what he was hearing.

"... unless we do it on GP."

"Yeah, we do that muthafucka on GP!" Ishmael said, relieved.

We'd simply do it on "general principle." Punishment for him, deterrence and intimidation to others. What you got if you crossed the Council. What you got if you crossed Nicky Barnes.

"And there's something else you should know."

This had to be the bad news.

"Frank had Rusty knocked off. Maybe a week ago."

"What?!" Rusty was a nice kid, a go-getter in charge of Frank's crew. True, he didn't take care of the table sometimes and wasn't always around when Frank needed him, but he had a real independent streak that didn't jive with Frank.

"Rusty went over Frank's head, went to Mikey Coco and told him Frank had sent him. Frank found out about it."

Mikey Coco was an old supplier I hooked up the Council with before I went in, and the fact Rusty went to him directly was a no-no. Never should've done that.

But murders were Council decisions, especially something like this! And I would *not* have allowed it—Rusty was Frank's brother-in-law! His wife's brother!

Apparently, Frank auditioned people for the contract and one dude did it by killing the next passerby in the street, so he got the job. Frank told his new hit squad that Rusty was not to be shot but ice-picked to death, and his left hand with its diamond rings delivered to him.

The next night they lured Rusty to an after-hours club on 112th and St. Nicholas. One dude grabbed him and one stabbed him with the pick, but Rusty broke free and reached for his piece. So Frank's other man, Sabu, shot him in the back with a .45. They took the rings, bagged his head, left the ice pick in his back and stuck the body in the back of a new Oldsmobile in Harlem.

Ishmael was impressed by Frank's brutality, something to keep the crews in line, enforce discipline.

Well, I wasn't impressed.

I didn't see the point of killing Rusty, and I damn sure didn't like this bloodthirsty Cro-Magnon shit. If you're going to do a guy, just do the job and get on with it! Don't pull this hand as a trophy shit! And why the fuck would you waste a brand new Oldsmobile by leaving a dead body in it?

"Tell Frank I want to see him."

It was time to enforce a little discipline myself.

"Dude, did you forget that Rusty was your *blood* when you killed him?"

"Shouldn't've gone to the connect."

"But killing him? He was at your fucking wedding! He is your family! And all this voodoo shit, ice picks and choppin' hands off?"

"Muthafucka had it comin'. Hey, every time I gave him powder, he messed it up."

I understood Frank's beef but was amazed by how cavalier he could be with his own wife's brother.

During my months at MCC, I was taken to the federal courthouse for different legal procedures, and every time, the assistant U.S. Attorneys asked, "Do you want to help yourself? Tendy says we could make a deal."

William Tendy was a deputy U.S. Attorney for the Southern District, and sent the message that if I cooperated within 120 days of my sentencing and turned on the Council and our suppliers, I could really help myself. But after that, there was no chance to get reduction in my sentence.

I would never rat out my brothers, so I told the prosecutors to go fuck themselves, each and every time. They were nothing but weasels anyhow, spending all this money prosecuting me, then begging for my cooperation.

Besides, I knew it was all bullshit. I had life without parole in the federal system, which meant no matter how much I cooperated, the government could not walk up to a federal judge and ask for relief in my case. There were only three ways to get out: my appeal because of the anonymous jury, a presidential pardon or escape.

Now, Breitbart said we had a good chance on appeal and we did, I knew that. I'd have to count on him and my own smarts to get myself out. I had done it before; I could do it again. That's what expensive lawyers are for.

In the meantime, I had to make sure everything was kept safe and that the Council continued to grow. When I came back out, I wanted to return to an empire.

Marion Federal Penitentiary, a supermax prison in Illinois, was the prison built to replace Alcatraz. As the highest security prison in the U.S.,

LEROY "NICKY" BARNES

the only "level-six" in the country, it had 400 inmates, mostly violent prisoners, politicals and high profiles, like me.

The first thing I noticed was how everything was white. The walls were white, the floors were white, the ceilings were white, the lights were white...the guards were white.

And in federal prison, they're especially nasty if you're black—I don't give a fuck who you are. They'd do more for a white guy who's a kidnapper or molester. Trust me, they don't accord nothin' to a black man in the federal prison system. So I was a little surprised when a polite, well-dressed case manager came to my cell.

"Leroy Barnes, my name is Ron Thompson. I'm a counselor here. You have a visitor. You definitely have a visitor."

It had to be Mecca. I knew it from this dude's smile. She told me she would come out right after I arrived, and damn I wanted to see her.

"But we have a problem. You are not eligible to have visitors yet."

When you go into prison you submit a list of visitors. And your list has to be approved by the Bureau of Prisons. They do a criminal investigation check to see if the people on your list should be allowed to visit. I hadn't even made up my list yet, let alone had it checked, so Shamecca had flown all the way out here for nothing.

But this dude Ron, he's standing outside my cell shaking his head.

"Look, I'm gonna give you this visit because anybody that pretty, you should be able to see."

I always remembered how Ron did that for me.

It was nice to see my girl Mecca, but Marion was not MCC. Visitors were allowed only a quick kiss and no hug, no touching, nothing. I just sat at the table, looking at her with all my sweet, dirty thoughts.

Everything in prison moves in cliques. My clique was the New York and DC dealers, mostly black. People knew me and took good care of me, so I quickly became their ringleader. In the joint I had an invincible reputation.

You'd have to have been a street person—either in state or federal prison—to understand some of this. It's kind of difficult for me to explain the type of dudes in prison. Including myself. These were some vicious motherfuckers. Most in there belonged in there. The big complaint in the joint was that they got more time than the white boys. But it was never a matter of innocence or guilt. I lived with them. We were all serious hard felons.

So what did I do in Marion? Worked. Made contacts. Spent as much time as I could in the law library. And I got fucked up. We had booze, smoke, blow, even crack coming into Marion!

But then everything changed.

I got called to the office of the assistant warden. He told me the U.S. Attorney's office wanted to know if I had reconsidered cooperating with the government.

"Time in don't scare me," I said, "'cause I got a very good shot on appeal; I ain't flipping. Tell those muthafuckas I'll see 'em on the outside."

He just nodded.

That night, four guards came to my cell.

"I'll be cool," I told them, so they put me in restraints and marched me what seemed like half a mile, deep down inside the complex.

And I knew I was going to "the Hole."

The Hole is solitary confinement—extreme segregation. The first forty-eight hours they keep you down "for investigation." You're in a "strip cell," six feet by eight feet, completely white like the rest of the joint except for a sick fluorescent ceiling light, which is never turned off.

The chair and bed are welded to the floor. There is a toilet. The bed has a thin mattress and a blanket, depending on the time of year. There is a Bible, they give you a Bible.They also give you a sandwich. And a coffee three times a day.

You are kept in your cell twenty-three hours a day. The other hour, you are taken out and allowed to exercise—only because it's the law.

You stop knowing if it is day or night, and you quickly lose track of time. The only things you can do in your cell are exercise, talk to other guys in solitary the next cell down—we'd even play games of chess by just shouting our moves—or think. Once you're there you just say, *Fuck it. Man, there ain't nothin' I can do about this 'cause I sure ain't gettin' out.*

You just give up, and that's kind of the idea.

But you are allowed one ten-minute monitored call a month. I talked to Breitbart, who explained the situation. I hadn't violated any rules to get into the Hole; they just decided to put me there.

Breitbart thought it was bullshit and so did I. They wanted me to flip, and this was the closest they could get to torture. Well, fuck them, I could do the time. And Breitbart said he would get into it with the Feds.

So I slept, read parts of the Bible, did my push-ups and sit-ups, shadowboxed, stretched, paced. And then I had fifteen more hours to go before sleep. And this was every day. You think a lot. You play out your life, your past. Every moment, every detail, anything and everything you can remember. Because that's all you have, and you're glad you even have that.

ACT TWO

THE RISE

1940-1973

A Sharp-Dressed Kid

YOU EVEN SAW dandelions growing through cracks in the cement. That's how clean Harlem was. There were guys to scrub the curbs and sanitation trucks to hose off the horse-drawn wagons. In the summertime, vendors delivered ice on these wagons, but others had cantaloupes, oranges and other fruits. No pesticides. You could almost become a vegetarian!

We'd ride in back of the fruit carts yelling, "Hey Sweeto! Sweet Watermelllon! Sweeto! Cheapo!" People shouted from their brownstone windows, "Bring me ten oranges and two watermelons. And plug it right there so I can look at it!" I'd cut a triangle in the watermelon with a pocketknife, stick it in and pull out the plug. If the plug was red, I'd yell, "Yes maaam! It's ripe!"

The vendor worked us from sunup to sundown, and at the end of the day, when we got to the big stable on 128th Street, he'd give a dollar to whoever helped him the most. It was fun. We really enjoyed it. At night, we'd sleep on the roofs. Never heard of a pervert or a molester in those days. We even woke up to the smell of buns bein' baked! We'd get the lopsided ones for free, and what we didn't eat, we'd feed the pigeons.

Man, Harlem was cool then. I enjoyed being out on the streets way more than being at home, a red brick building on Eighth and 115th between a vacant pawnshop and the Wellworth. That was Big Jake's bar, managed by Fat Herbie. Herbie wasn't fat, just a little chubby, but his partner Yack was just out of prison, so he had these real thick muscles.

These guys did a lot of business, so Big Jake bought the pawnshop to stock his inventory, then bought the ground floor of our building and made it into a passageway. This was a story and a half above ground, and part of it stuck right out under our living-room window.

Being a daredevil kid, you *know* I'm gonna jump down on that thing! Plus my building had these really big, jagged blocks of granite on the outside. I could put my foot on one of those, then slide down from the passageway onto the street. Mother *hated* that. She was always worried for my safety.

And I always worried about hers.

Dad used to run these poker games out of our apartment. He'd sell beer and a little weed, and though I didn't know what the smell was at the time, my mother yelled, "Don't smoke that shit in here, Leroy!" When the game was over, he'd smack her for back talk.

He was a big guy, real heavy-handed. Caused a whole lot of stress in the house with his loud mouth. But Mother kept on him. She'd say he was fuckin' around with this woman and that woman, and he'd smack her some more. When I ran to her aid? He knocked me down, too.

My friends used to call him a flatfoot hustler, the kind of guy who has a car, changes his clothes and has a place, but the money he makes is only for himself. Couldn't really call Dad lazy, though. Always had a bullshit part-time job with the transit authority. Juggled a little drugs, numbers action and poker on the side.

But with all those activities, Dad never had a dollar more than he needed and rarely put any money in our apartment.

We lived rent free, since Dad was the super, but as sis and me got a little older, Mother said it wasn't right to have everyone sleeping in one room—she and dad on the queen-size bed, sis on the bottom bunk and me in the top. She pressed Dad for a bigger place.

Dad resisted for the longest time, but when the owner of our building said he needed a super at 375 Manhattan Avenue, Mom insisted he take the job and move us in. I thought this place was gigantic, five stories and the tallest on the block. It had French windows, big wide doorways and an old-fashioned intercom with a bell. Our living room was as big as our old apartment! Plus, sis and I each had a room of our own. We thought this was really great.

On the roof, we saw ferries going up and down the Hudson. There was a white architect who lived in our building, and he'd show me the bridges through his telescope and explain how they were built. He and his wife didn't have kids, so they loved me.

Jackie Gomez was another story. They didn't like him at all. They told me that Jackie was trouble. He lived across the street with his grandma in a communal apartment, but was getting too big to sleep in the same bed with her. So he often spent the night at my house. He just loved it.

"You lucky to have a mother and a father and a big place," he told me. He had so much less than I had.

Jackie got me doin' all the little devilment things kids do. He'd find the back way into a grocery, and we'd steal empty beer and milk bottles, then return them for nickels. Only Jackie wanted more money as we got older, so our hustles got a little more elaborate.

One time we went downtown to the Times Square subway station and worked the shoeshine boxes. I kneeled in front of this drunk white guy, and he pulled out a big wad of money, starin' at me like he wanted somethin' besides a shine. I snatched up that money and took off with Jackie right behind. We didn't get fifty feet before the cops surrounded us!

It was my very first arrest, and I wasn't even ten years old.

By the time Mother came to pick us up, she was cryin' louder than Jackie. "Nicky! You've gotta be a good boy!" She was always saying that. But she never told my father I got pinched, 'cause he would've killed me. Anyway, she was sick of talkin' to that motherfucker.

"I don't know how you conned me into moving here!" he'd yell.

Dad hated our new place. He was pissed 'cause as the super in our last building he got $30 a month, but only got free rent here. This building was twice as big, too, so it took twice as long to mop the floors. He cut some corners, like not changing the water in the bucket, so by the time he mopped from the fifth floor down to our basement apartment?

"Don't bring that goddamn dirty water in here!" Mom yelled. "Forget it! Just don't mop in here! The kids will do it."

That's when Dad handed me a key to his utility closet, located under a deep, long stairwell. I opened it up and grabbed the mop, but as I wheeled out the pail, I saw a package under the shelf. It looked out of place, so I opened it up and peeked in.

I knew what they were from the street. The biggest boy in my gang, the Tiny Turks, would go to the pusher on the corner and buy a "number five cap" for a dollar. Three kids could get high off of that. I'd never tried one myself, but now that I was alone with caps in my hand?

I sniffed part of one. I wasn't strung out or anything.

I knew they didn't belong to my father—he was a lot of things, but not a junkie—so I figured he kept 'em for some street-corner hustlers. Stashing dope seemed the kind of thing he'd do to earn a little money.

Dad and I were the only ones with keys to that closet, but he never figured out who took those caps. He never thought I'd use 'em or sell 'em. But I did. I went to the older neighborhood guys, told 'em I had good stuff. It turned fast and was easy to sell.

And that's when I learned the value of heroin.

Jackie and I experimented with some caps after that, but I never thought I'd get too heavy into it. Got a little tired sometimes, but I'd just lie in my bed and sleep. Jackie didn't have that option. He didn't wanna

LEROY "NICKY" BARNES

lie on his grandmother's floor all high. Maybe that's why he got hooked first, 'cause he didn't have anywhere to go.

As twelve-year-olds at the bottom of the Turk pecking order, zip guns were the only firepower we were allowed to have. Turk Seniors didn't trust Tiny Turks to carry the real thing. We made them under supervision of the Young Turks, and when we attached the barrel to the model airplane launcher, they made us wrap it up with a lot of friction tape. Otherwise, the barrel might explode in your hand when you shot it.

Now that I had my first weapon, I was all excited to use it. I hid behind a garbage can in a raid on Sabre turf, but just as I aimed my zip, our leader yelled, "Retreat!" In other words, nobody was comin' out from behind the cans, so let's just go on home.

I was real disappointed. I hated goin' home.

My father was so petty, he moved us back to where we used to be. I can't explain how aggravated we were to move out of a big, spacious place so this motherfucker could get thirty extra dollars a month. He didn't think at all about the comfort of the family. The neighborhood was a lot worse when we came back, too. The corner building had turned into a boardinghouse, and a lot of people flopped in there, just went to the open bathroom and shot up.

Mom and Dad were already arguing when I came home. Probably about money, but whatever it was, Dad had his hand back to hit Mom. And I wasn't gonna let him.

"Don't you hit her!"

Dad just smiled, looked right down on me.

"Shut the fuck up or I'll kick yo' little ass!"

But like the Young Turks said, "Everybody's the same size with a gun in the hand." I pulled out my zip and shouted, "Back up, muthafucka!"

"No, Nicky," scolded my mother, "don't do that. That's your father."

Dad just hesitated. He didn't know what the fuck I was holding.

"What's that?"

"You come on, muthafucka, and you'll find out what it is, *bitch*!" That's just what I called him! A *bitch*! Man, I remember that so distinctly, callin' him a bitch. He was so mad.

"Man," Dad laughed, "that ain't no fuckin' gun! I'm gonna kick yo' nigger ass. I'm gonna *kill* you!" When he ran to me, I fired. Bam!!!

I thought that'd be the end of it. 'Cause I had a .32-caliber shell in the gun and didn't expect to just wound him. Only I hadn't taped that barrel strong enough. Muthafucka exploded and the bullet just bounced off Dad's leather jacket. *Aw, fuck.*

When he came at me, I jumped right out the window. Moms was screamin' like I was suicidal, but I landed right on Big Jake's passageway, shimmied down like Spiderman.

I hit the street with a real good feeling. Me looking up, Dad looking down, Dad knowin' he can't climb out and get me. I ran off in the night, woke up Jackie and slept on the floor of his grandma's. I liked that. Shit, that was great, 'cause we were two Tiny Turks. We were part of the gang.

The next night, I told the Turk Juniors, the older guys, what happened with my dad.

"I know that motherfucker," said Arthur Powell. "I'll pistol-whip that nigga."

You couldn't just call him Arthur. It was always Arthur Powell. Lot of people did that at the time, goin' by the first and last name. Arthur Powell was tall, slender and tough, about 19 or 20.

"I know him too," said Little King. "Muthafucka's always playin' poker. Chasin' cool."

Little King was a fast talker. He was a little bigger than me and parted his hair down the middle like Langston Hughes, real wavy with that pomade. That's how Little King looked.

"Yeah, that nigga work the night shift at the powerhouse on 132nd. There's some huge, loud motors there. You could shoot that mo-fo and no one would hear it. We'll get Big King and bring him along."

Big King? That was *serious*. The two Kings weren't related, but Big King was just a large dude. Six-three, six-four. Looked like a linebacker. Naturally big. We all went to go confront my dad, and Big King just stood there, fierce, while Little King held out his .32.

Dad was tryin' to tell 'em to be cool, but he was scared. This gun was for *real*. I felt so strong with my gang backin' me.

"Hold off, Li'l King."

If Arthur Powell hadn't stepped in, Dad would've been dead. As our war counselor—every gang had one to decide if a conflict would escalate into warfare—Arthur Powell had the last word on violence. He let Dad off with a warning. "If you put your hands on Nicky one more time, I'll blow your motherfuckin' brains out, nigga."

And Dad believed him. He never touched me again, but our family was fractured after that. If Dad was home, I was away. If he was away, I was home. I'd talk to my mother and she'd cry for me to come back, but Dad was just not going to have another dominant male in the house.

I was on my own, but the gang was behind me.

Pat was from the all-girls junior high school on West 118th, and I went over to her house to smoke some weed and snort powder with the Tigerettes, the girl gang on the West Side. They had me on the bed in no time.

Mae-Mae fisted the base of my dick, and all that pressure bulged to the head like a squeezed balloon. She sucked it like pulp on an extra-ripe mango seed. Then her cousin Ella got on, tryin' to empty the glass through the straw. It felt good, like every nerve in my dick communicated to every nerve in her.

That's how complete our union was. I was feeling each pore. I was not getting my dick sucked. I was fuckin' her *mouth*. She ran her teeth on it, and every tooth gave me an individual tease.

Pat let me try her pussy. The weed brought me toward orgasm, only the heroin kept me from havin' one. But the combination of the two drugs was when I eventually skeeted, the actual ejaculation *prolonged*. It was good, man. It was good. And that's how I lost my virginity. That's when I had my first high off heroin.

Jackie wanted to move out of his grandma's and buy a place of his own, so he'd been lookin' for a big score. After he shot up at this junkie den on St. Nicholas and 118th, he got the idea we should stick it up, take all the money and dope inside. He knocked like he was comin' to get a fix, but right as the dealer opened the door, I pushed on in with a .32.

"Everybody on the ground! Where the money?!"

My gun was drawn on all these people, only I was so excited about my first stickup, I forgot to close the fuckin' door behind me! A bad mistake, 'cause when this lady came out of the communal bathroom in the main hallway, she ran off screaming, a red alert to everyone in the building.

Jackie just ran out, leaving me holding the gun on all these people. But while the dope fiends were too high to rise against me, the hallway was filled with angry residents, all up in arms and ready to attack. I couldn't escape through the hall without killin' people, so I put my pistol in my belt and just jumped out the window, falling a full story and landing smack in the middle of a pitch-black alley. I ran to each end, trying to escape, but the alley was walled on both sides. I was trapped.

"He's gotta be down there!"

"Maybe he climbed the wall."

"Maybe he crawled in a window."

I *knew* those voices.

The King Cole Trio had responded to the call. They were black patrolmen who ran three deep, and if you saw them ridin' up in their patrol car? You'd scatter off hiding. They had a treacherous rep as ass kickers, sadists who'd fuck you up like Oliver Cromwell. They were that cruel.

Bumpy paid these guys to look the other way on a lot of things, but robbery? That was open season. You did *not* wanna get arrested by them for that street shit. Believe it. If they'd seen me, they'd shoot first, ask questions later.

I pressed flat against the brick, right underneath the window, fearing for my life as the three beams flashed on the opposite wall. I shimmied to the left, hoping to find a ledge, and by pure dumb luck found one. I slid open the window and crawled in on my hands and knees, but the room was as dark as the alley.

"Please. Please don't hurt me."

The fuck?!

"I got a gun!!!" I hissed. I was so agitated I couldn't see.

"I'm blind," he said, real calm.

"Where the fuckin' door?!"

"Let your eyes adjust to the darkness."

Don't know why that blind guy didn't take me down. He was a powerful presence, in total control of that room. He just knew the darkness.

When I settled down, I saw the strip of light under the door. Calm and collected, I stepped into the hall and walked right out of the building.

That's how I escaped, by keepin' it cool.

"That's a sharp-dressed kid," said Fat Herbie.

"He'll make us some real money one day," said Yack.

It was obvious who they were talkin' about. Jackie didn't spend his robbery money on clothes. He blew it all on dope. But I bought the latest threads from off the rack, leaving me the best-dressed teen on the West Side. I invested in a sharp impression and it paid in full, 'cause when Fat Herbie needed a new dealer at Big Jake's poolroom?

He didn't pick Jackie.

"Jackie, we can still get down together. Only thing different is I'll conduct the business, since I've got the source."

I couldn't understand why Jackie was so annoyed with that. It should've been cool. We were best friends since we were kids, and if the situation were reversed? I'd have been happy to get goods through him! Only Jackie thought that since he was older, *he* should've been picked. He wanted the source all for himself.

So he just disappeared off the screen.

When Jackie got killed on one of his robbery attempts, I remember thinking, "Damn, he should've stayed with me 'stead of fuckin' around with what we were doin' before."

'Cause I was doin' *great* with cashmere coats from Phil Kronfeld and velour hats for $35. Had custom-made alligators and lizards on my feet, made at the same spot Mantan Moreland went to! I was wearin' *all* that, just workin' for Fat Herbie and Yack.

They started me off at the poolroom on St. Nick's, right around the corner from Minton's Playhouse. This was *the* spot for bebop and jazz, and Bud Powell, Fats Navarro, Miles…lot of those guys used to come in and buy stuff before their gigs. They'd tell me what they wanted and I'd pass the joint, the half-six or whatever the case may be. It was all out in the open air, like a Turkish bazaar.

"Don't worry about a thing," said Fat Herbie. "Just take care of business." I did exactly that, so Herbie had me doin' everything—cuttin' stuff, makin' drops. He trusted me to handle the most important job in his operation.

I drove Herbie's slant-back Buick down Pleasant Avenue, practically blocked with oversized and double-parked Cadillacs and Thunderbirds. The lookouts had a steel gaze on me, the nigger who'd strayed too far

LEROY "NICKY" BARNES

east, but I kept my stride as I stepped from the Buick and entered the storefront bakery.

"Fat Herbie sent me," I said.

A grandpa in his undershirt raised his brow from behind the pastry counter. He whisked to the back room, leaving me free to soak in the scene outside the window.

Old men dealt pinochle on a card table and teenage hoods played dominoes outside the Pleasant Tavern, but the real action was at the diner, where the top guys on the Avenue wore sharkskin suits, sipped espresso and made the big deals.

One day, they're gonna be dealing with me.

"Here, kid," said the Italian, coming out with a small brown paper sack. I drove to the Wellworth and dropped it off, a two-kilo package.

"You did good," said Herbie.

From here on out, I was his face for the East Side Italians.

I'd go there every week to pick up our package, and before long, Big Frank Madonna, an enormous guy with a huge rep on the Avenue, got to know me as the kid who took care of business for Herbie.

"Nicky, meet my little brother Matty. He'll be takin' care of you."

He was about my size with jet-black hair. I remembered him from back in the day, when the Tiny Turks came over to Benjamin Franklin High on Pleasant Avenue to play basketball. For such a quiet guy, he was a real hothead on the court.

That temper ended up his downfall, 'cause only a few weeks after our meet, he got pissed and shot up Tank, a black dealer workin' for Fat Herbie.

"Tank was just clownin'!" I told Herbie.

Tank was a great guy who liked to mess with people, but when Matty came to the West Side to collect his money and Tank clowned him about it? Matty sparked him. Killed him on the spot.

"That's just the way it is, Nicky," said Herbie. "We don't go clownin' with no Italians."

One night I was coming back from Birdland, ready to make a few drops for Herbie. I walked west toward Eighth along 111th, a long block dimly lit by a street lamp. That's when I saw Bobby Monroe, comin' east with two huge white guys in sailor suits.

Damn! What has Bobby gotten himself into?

But as Bobby walked under the lamp, he touched his lapel, wipin' me in to play the Murphy. We'd all learned the Murphy growin' up, and as the game goes, we'd dress sharp, go downtown and ask a group of white guys, "You wanna meet some nice girls?" Then we'd show pictures of black women in different poses, light-skinned Dorothy Dandridge types.

"But if you wanna meet the girls, you gotta come uptown with us."

Now, I hadn't played in a *long* time, especially with Bobby. He was too impatient. If the scam wasn't workin', Bobby'd just break down and rob the dudes. But Bobby got lucky by seeing me, knowin' how I play, 'cause those two Navy cats were bigger than he.

"Hey, Bobby! You got somebody else!"

"These guys want to meet Lola and Gina!"

"Well, what building you takin' them to?

"248."

"Yeah, that's open. Kind of crowded up there now. If you're able to get in, make sure you guard their valuables, 'cause I had some trouble the last time, and I *sho'* wouldn't wanna go through that again. You know how Bumpy gets!"

This is so dumb. I can't believe anybody goes for this stuff.

"Wait a minute, Bobby! Why don't I come with you and see if I can work them in?"

The white boys got all excited, and by the time we were inside the building, they were salivating. Ripe for the con.

"Lemme go up and straighten things out," I said. I ran upstairs to

LEROY "NICKY" BARNES

the top floor, took off my hat and coat and put 'em on the stairwell post. I undid the first few buttons on my shirt top, rolled up my sleeves, came back down and primed the whiteys.

"Listen, don't give any of the girls money. They will suck you bone dry and ask for more. Just give the guy at the door whatever he asks for. That's it. And remember, don't give those girls a *thing*. Bobby, you collect their valuables."

The tricks had their minds on the girls from the pictures, so they didn't think anything about passin' their coats, wallets, watches, jewelry over to Bobby, who stuffed them in a plastic shopping bag. He even wrote their names on the bag with a felt-tip pen!

"Now you two fellas meet me on the fourth floor in about five minutes. I'll tell you the apartment!" I ran up the steps with the bag, and by the time the whiteys followed? I was jumpin' across the rooftops, all the way to meet Bobby at the spot. I handed him a bag with the names of two suckers written on it.

"Thanks, Nick! Let's split the loot."

"Naw, keep it, Bobby."

Bobby needed all the help he could get. He was livin' in this short con-game world—some Murphy here, a small robbery there. Half-steppin' it in a world of gettin' a little money and not gettin' a little money.

I was workin' for Herbie and making plenty, but Bobby followed the Murphy to its natural progression. He wanted to be a pimp. The hos were gonna take care of him. He learned that style from the older guys—"How you pimp is, well, you just take a ho and make her your woman! Keep your foot on her neck. Tell her she ain't got a man. Tell her *you* the man. Then you give her security."

So Bobby got himself a hustling woman, and one night, as we were speedballin' at this workin' girl hangout, he pulled that slick talk on her— "You ain't gonna be on the street corner not sharin' your money with your man!"

Only Bobby didn't have any control over this broad. She wouldn't give his bank to him. And when Bobby brought her to the bathroom, smacked her up and took her money, she walked right out of the bar and into the precinct.

The street gossip was, "Shit! This bitch is a prostitute. He can't go to jail for this!" But the issue wasn't whether or not she was a prostitute. The issue was whether Bobby robbed, raped and assaulted her. Bobby didn't have a good lawyer, so instead of copping out, he blew the trial and got thirty years.

He'd ask us to do different things when he was stuck in Dannemora, but shit, we were all strung out on dope! None of us did anything to help him. Bobby was really bitter about that, about all of us abandoning him. He had every right to be. Somebody should've been there for him, and nobody was.

There was just no excuse.

Kicking the Habit

I STILL TOOK CARE OF business for Fat Herbie, but it got hard to walk the line between using and dealing. I only sniffed heroin at first, but now I shot it up, mixed it with coke and did speedballs.

Don't know how I became overwhelmed, but I started to regress. Started doin' that dumb junkie shit. In 1950, when I was seventeen, I was arrested for possessing a hypodermic needle. At eighteen I was charged with possession of burglary tools. At nineteen I broke into some parked cars and got sentenced to three years in reformatory.

My first stop was city prison, the Tombs. I doubled up with a guy on murder and since his crime had seniority, he got the cot. I got the blanket and the floor. I lay there with the cold sweats, shaking and sick, praying for that heroin to get out of my system quick.

It was ten slow days of my stomach feeling as empty as it could possibly be. Food only aggravated my colon. I had to fart all the time if I got a meal down there. I felt less than anything I could conceivably imagine, the sense of being at the bottom of a pit and of myself. I vowed if I ever got out of this situation, I would never use heroin again.

But in March 1954, as soon as I got out on parole?

My first stop was Brother Brazie's in Harlem. Sold me $20 worth of junk and I cooked it up, right there at his house.

I was strung out and hustling with Big Sid when we decided to stick up a junkie joint. Sid knocked on the door while I waited with his brother out in the hall. When the door opened, we pushed from behind and threw down. Sid and his brother grabbed up all the money and dope, but I got to eyeballin' this well-dressed broad on the couch.

I stuck my gun in her face—"Get up!"—and checked out her ass. It was real fine, nice and big like my woman Nita's.

"Quit fuckin' around!" yelled Sid.

"You go on," I snapped, waving him off. He ran out and down the stairs, leaving the girl all to me. "Take off your clothes, bitch!" She was scared to death. Her fingers trembled as she unbuttoned her blouse…

I hurried out of the building and almost tripped over Sid. He was sitting on the front stoop and got this look of fear. 'Cause my arms were full of clothes and the cops were right in front of us, ticketing my double-parked Buick.

"Stay back!" hissed Sid. I hung back till the police finally left, then we took the ticket and peeled on out. Sid was furious. "Goddamn, Nick! You gonna get us busted! Fuckin' some ho, runnin' out with her goddamn clothes!"

"I didn't fuck no one!"

"What the hell you doin', then!?"

"Sid, you ain't *got* a woman! If you *had* a woman, you'd take this too!" A blouse from Bloomie's, shoes from Capezio…It was some nice downtown shit! Damn straight I took it!

We drove on uptown to my place in Washington Heights, got our fix and divided the score. After they split, I put my cash in the closet, broke down my goods, hit the streets with my girl Nita and turned all that stolen dope by morning. We made so much money that night, I was able to buy a little weight from Brazie along with my coke.

Couple weeks pass. Big Sid and his brother come knocking on my door, lookin' for a fix. They already shot up their goods from the robbery, but I still have powder left over from Brazie. I hand 'em a couple of sixes and take the last of their cash.

More money for the closet, more money to buy more dope.

Days later they come back, only this time they ain't got no money.

"Yeah, Nick, I know we split up everything from the stick-up, but since you got those clothes and all..."

Then Sid starts talkin' about all the things I've got—like that beat-up '49 Buick convertible I got downstairs is a fuckin' Cadillac. It wasn't even roadworthy when I bought it! He's not makin' direct accusations, just signifyin' stuff, but I can see where this is goin'. 'Cause we've been doin' some treacherous shit together, and now they view *me* as the target.

Once those motherfuckers left, I told Nita, "Look, we got a car, we got a good supplier in Brother Brazie and we got a little bit of money. So here's what we're gonna do."

We found a nice, quiet brownstone on Hart Street in Brooklyn and moved in that night. You needed a key to get in the lobby door, so nobody could just come in unannounced. Wasn't much, but with a safe house and ride and girl, I was ready for business.

I kept my stash in the closet, and every morning I broke down some of my goods into street bags. I'd ride around the West Side and stuff 'em in my hiding spots—five behind a loose brick, five under an abandoned stairwell. This way, I wouldn't have to carry bags on me during the deal.

Evenings and nights were for dealing, and we had our system down like clockwork. Nita dropped me off at 116th in the Buick. I walked down to 110th, took the money from my customers, got back in the Buick and picked up the goods from my hiding spots. Nita dropped me off at 116th and made the deliveries; I walked down to 110th and took more orders.

We'd do that all night till we sold everything, and when dawn broke, we'd stop by Brazie's, buy some coke, go home and speedball till we heard the bells. That'd keep us awake for another day, so we just went out and did the same thing all over again.

Nita and I got in a real groove doin' that.

We didn't see Big Sid till months later, when we ran into him and his brother up in Harlem.

"Keep your hands on your shit, Nita," I said.

"Nick and Nita! What y'all doin' all the way up here?"

"Sellin' some of Brazie's stuff. You wanna buy any?"

I gave them powder, they gave me money and that was the last I ever saw of them. Their star fell, but mine was on the rise. All their money went in their veins, but I saved enough to put gas in my car. I had a TV, a bedroom, a living room, a bathroom and a business.

I was good to go.

With our little operation booming, Nita and I got hitched. Sold bigger packages and turned $1600 a day. Our profit gave us plenty to crew up, so I hired a guy for security when we made the deals. In time, I found dealers I could trust to work the streets for us.

I wasn't selling a fraction of the volume I'd do later, but still kept the cut low and the quality high. I was an addict. I knew what addicts wanted.

By 1959 my goods were in such demand, customers started asking for that "Nicky Barnes thing." So I packaged my goods with black tape. This way, people would know whose goods they were buying, and my name wouldn't be spread out on the streets.

Should've worked out fine, only Nita ran into this broad she knew as a kid. They talked about old times, about being junkies and about Nita being married to me.

"Nicky Barnes? Think I can buy an eighth off him?"

I never forgave Nita for her mistake. Should've been sharp enough to realize her bitch friend was an informant. But Nita hooked her up and

LEROY "NICKY" BARNES

the cops knocked down our front door. Found a set of works, a bunch of sixteens and some money. As the handcuffs went on, I watched the rookie cop delicately count the cash on the table, a bit taken aback by all that green.

I'll have to remember that.

If you're used to big volumes, you count cash like paper. If not, you count it like money.

After ten days of the sweats and the chills, I was ready for my five years. I had no idea what was coming. Green Haven State Prison wasn't like reformatory or city jail. This was eighty miles from the city, 2000 prisoners and thirty-foot walls, maximum security. This was permanent, the real deal.

I was thrown in the west prison block, divided into four sections. Whites packed A and B sections, 'cause that's where the easy jobs were. I slaved in the mill in Section D, where the fucked-up jobs were. But I worked hard, did good time and moved up to the machine shop in Section C. By the time I made it to Section A, making American flags on the huge industrial looms, I'd reached the peak of the prison work ladder.

And that's where I recognized Matty Madonna, doin' twenty years on his murder charge. I thought he was nothin' but a thug for what he did to Tank, but I got to know him from just workin' in the shop every day. He seemed an okay guy.

We'd chat about our basketball games and growin' up in Harlem, but that was the extent of our conversation for almost a year. He knew I'd been hooked up with Herbie, but he was just feeling me out, tryin' to figure if I was a sharp guy or a clown like Tank.

But once he broke the ice on narcotics? All we spoke about was powder. We both had real ambitions in the game, so we each wanted to know how it worked on the other's side.

I'd tell him about the West Side—how you'd never sell to anybody you didn't know, how Saturday and Sunday were the best time for dealing. "'Cause narcos never work the weekends."

He'd tell me about that diner on Pleasant Avenue, a barometer for when a shipment was coming in from Europe. If it was packed with the old guard, you knew it was on its way. "If it's packed with little greasers, nothin's doin' for a while."

He even let me in on a few secrets of his family, how the Mafia was organized to deal narcotics, how I could learn from it.

"If you wanna be protected from the powder, you gotta treat it like you're the don. You want all the profit to flow up, and all the risks to flow down. Use your captains, your *capos*, to pick up the money and make the drops. Use your *soldati* for dealing, for the grunt work on the streets. You need at least three levels between you and the powder, 'cause each level is a layer of protection. You might have as many as fifty people working under you, so that's why you gotta be *organized*."

Madonna and I talked a lot about cutting choices. We agreed it didn't make sense to be ruthless and greedy with your cut. You cut for high quality and quick turnover, even if you don't make as much off each package. Low quality powder just drags the operation down.

Turns out we even wanted the same things out of life, too. Fast cars and good-lookin' broads.

"You know what I'd love to have, Nick? A restaurant. But I don't want no front, neither. Gotta be three-star food, three-star service."

We struck up a pretty good friendship, unusual in the joint, 'cause blacks didn't intermingle with whites in a meaningful way. Us hangin' in the yard brought enough stares, but when he waved me over to his table in the mess? That was unheard of.

"Guys, this is Nick. He's a friend of mine from the West Side."

Matty introduced me to his crew, all renegades in narcotics. He had a big voice among these guys 'cause of his brother Frank, so they welcomed me.

There was Marty Yamin, a judge from Baltimore in for first-degree murder. He taught me a good chess game—"Ruy Lopez, always open with the Ruy Lopez"—and the value of a European car. "You'll never go back to Cadillacs. I promise."

Next to him was Sammy Katz, an old-time gangster linked back to Waxey Gordon and Arnold Rothstein. I'd see him running around the yard and think, "Man, the fuck is he doin' that for? That is so stupid." He was the first dude I ever saw jogging. Sammy Katz! Damn, he was a great guy. I smoked like a chimney then, so he'd hook me up with Camels.

It felt good to be part their group. They were cons, sure, but they were a real cultured bunch. Guys on the outside hooked 'em up with the dailies, so we'd eat, shoot the breeze and talk national and international politics. Got the latest hardbacks, too. Most were potboiler spy novels, but we'd sit around and discuss them anyway. A gangster book club.

These guys seemed to have everything, especially Matty. The warden put a limit on the size of our packages, but somehow Matty had these extra-big boxes in his cell, with two or three hundred dollars' worth of goods inside. Italian stuff like salami and imported cheese. He got all this 'cause he had his families lookin' out for him—the Lucchese family, *and* the Madonnas.

Sharp Italian guys were always comin' up to visit Matty. Well-dressed, pinky rings, always in Cadillacs. And when the Madonnas showed up to the visiting room? A real family reunion. He'd get to see his mother, his brother Frank and his uncle Sammy. They even brought nephews with them! Seemed to be the case with all the Italians.

But blacks? I'd peek inside the visiting room and see one or two at *most*. And the women weren't well groomed or attractive in any sense of the word. Some at least tried to do a manicure, but barely seemed able to hitch a ride up to the joint. Maybe it's because their guys weren't successful on the outside. I'd say the majority of black dudes in prison come in for chump change.

But shit. I was makin' *real* bank, and I didn't get a visit or a package or even a fuckin' postcard.

I was just like Bobby Monroe. I didn't get nothin' from nobody.

"Have you learned anything, Mr. Barnes?"

"Yeah," I told the parole board. "That old life is behind me. I wanna build something real, something that'll last."

"We're glad to hear that, boy."

And that was that. After three long years in Green Haven, I was comin' home.

I stitched up my last American flag and told Madonna the news.

"Then talk to my brother Frank as soon as you get home. He's gonna take care of you, Nick. A half-kilo on consignment, a couple thousand to buy a car and rent a stash house. Gonna give you a surprise, too."

I was real touched by Matty stretchin' out his family to me. First time anyone had given me anything. In prison *or* on the outside.

On my last night in the joint, all these plans played through my head. Starting now, the fall of 1962, I was gonna be a serious contender. I'd stay clean this time, 'cause not bein' a junkie was good for business. When you're a user, you get the fix, work the goods yourself. You can't distance yourself from the product.

I'd have to find manpower, too—people to pick up the drugs and money, people to drop off drugs and money, dealers for the street and workers for the mill. But piece by piece, one way or another, I'd build that organization. Just like Madonna taught me.

I'd be so deep from the powder, the cops couldn't touch me.

My future was clear, but come tomorrow, I'd be back out on parole. It would be so easy to get sent back to state prison.

But Frank would have the goods waiting, and I didn't wanna blow my one chance at having a major supplier on the Avenue. I'd have to make sure Frank got his money. I'd have to flatfoot it on the street.

I had get strapped, and I had to whack that stuff off myself.

Cheats and Lies

GABBY EASED HIS Lewisburg-hardened bulk behind the steering wheel of the deep burgundy 1963 Oldsmobile Starfire. I rode shotgun as we drove fifteen blocks to our work car, a black 1956 Chrysler 300 Sedan. We felt comfortable about the scene after circling the block twice, so we parked a distance away and walked to the Chrysler.

A short drive put us in Central Park, heading uptown to Harlem. Gabby turned left at 118th and parked three car lengths into the block, so we could back out for a quick getaway down Fifth Avenue, if necessary.

We entered the corner building and walked to the end of the hallway, down the staircase and into the dark alley. We opened the backdoor and went in. The naked overhead bulb was busted. I looked over the rail and up the stairwell. Pitch-black, all the way to the top.

That shit ain't right.

I reached for the stiletto on my left inner thigh, popped it open and charged ahead in the darkness, an act of pure instinct. Nothing was going to stop me from picking up my money. Gabby pulled the Italian Beretta from the back of his waistband and with ham hands, screwed on his silencer, gifts to me from Frank Madonna.

The glass crunched under our feet and the stairs creaked on our way to the fifth floor. With one flight to go, that smell stopped me in my tracks. An unwashed dope fiend was waiting to get the jump on us.

Only now, I had the advantage.

"Nicky Barnes comin' up! Whoever the fuck is up there better show or I'll spark this whole motherfuckin' hallway!"

A voice croaked from above.

"Nick? It's Boy. Boy Best. I'm sick. Real sick."

He stepped into the faint beam of Gabby's flash and shivered violently, his unusual light-brown eyes—that all the girls liked, glowed in the half-light.

"You squattin' on Reenie?"

"No. Just tryin' to beg some from her." That was a lie. Boy didn't beg for nothin'. He'd just put a gun in your side and take it.

"You strapped?"

Boy held his hands up, "I ain't strapped."

"Yeah," smirked Gabby, "Yeah." He put his silencer to Boy's chest, let him feel the iron.

"Where Ralphie?" I asked.

"She here," Boy said.

"She holdin'?"

Boy waved and there was the sound of slight movement as the shadows became Ralphie, Ralphie Red Bone as she was known because of her black Cuban skin and shoulder length, frizzy reddish brown hair. A leather miniskirt clung tight to her bow hips.

"Pass me the piece," I told Boy, "left hand."

She stood there like an emaciated warrior as Boy's hand rose between her legs and up her skirt. He pulled the blue steel .25 automatic from her vaginal vise. The barrel was still moist with her pinkness when my hand encircled it. I almost felt my dick arch. Ralphie used to be a beautiful woman.

Gabby moved them up the next flight and made Boy knock on the door.

"Reenie," I said, "it's Gabby and Nicky Barnes."

"Boy and Ralphie out dere!" she whispered, looking through the peephole of the reinforced door.

"We got 'em. Open up."

She unlatched the deadbolts and let us in.

Half her apartment was a palace, the other half chaos. A pile of broken and worn-out furniture, partially covered with red sheets, had been shoved aside in a pile to make room for the new leather sofa, dinette set and black and white, stereo television.

Gabby put Boy and Ralphie on the loveseat. Little round balls of perspiration rolled down Boy's smooth face, like water on a newly waxed car.

I could've sparked him right there, but I had to help. I knew what it was like to be sick, to have that hard driving need to get that drug in your system.

"Put something in the cooker, Reenie," I said.

An old friend but my newest pusher, Irene didn't operate on the street, just sat in her pad and waited for the deal. Got to where she was too afraid to lose business to leave the house. But the baby in her stomach had been dead for weeks, and she still hadn't gone to the doctor to get it removed. Lots of times I told her, "Reenie, you go and take care of that. Your spot ain't goin' nowhere. You'll still have it when you come back," but she just wouldn't listen.

Irene passed a set of works to Ralphie and a small glassine bag of stuff. Boy watched as Ralphie cooked a hit, drawing up a third of the eyedropper for him.

"Fill it," Boy told her, but Irene reminded them that this was *my* shit and it was the best.

"Right Nick?"

"That's right. You can walk with that bag. Go slow, Boy."

Boy was silent as Ralphie tied his arm to force blood into his veins, and then she stuck him. The blood pushed its way into the dropper like a small mushroom cloud. She squeezed the bulb, forcing the blood and heroin into his vein.

Gabby and I watched, four eyeballs locked on Boy as he began booting the blood up and down. We both got dry throat—not wanting, but reliving the dope-fiend life. A fucked-up experience.

Boy's face turned into a sponge and absorbed all that perspiration. He was high and rambling.

"Remember we was in Riker's together? We used to work-out? Yeah, I always respected you. Even when I beat down Monkey Man for your dope I respected you...Nick, I left a thousand messages for you. I *tried* to see you, man. I tried to tell you it was just one of those things."

I put the word out—*If I catch you, Boy, I will kill you. If I catch your brother Sugar, or any muthafucka in your family, I'll kill them, too*—and set lots of traps, only Boy proved too slippery for all of them.

This time he wasn't getting away.

"Tell you what, Boy. I'm gonna give you half a spoon as a gift. If you can handle it, I'll also give you a $500 package to sell on the street. That ain't a gift. That's a *loan*. By next week, I'll want $500 in return."

Boy's eyes lit up from his stupor. "I'll have it to you tomorrow." He got up, gave me a hug and told me how much he loved me. Ralphie sat there, kind of rock-faced, but I could see the appreciation in her eyes as she took Boy's needle, hit herself and got mellow.

"Boy, I don't want no, 'Here's $450,' or whatever."

"Five hundred dollars, Nick. *Tomorrow*."

He did just that. So I gave him a little more to sell and a little more to use. He not only became my top pusher, he pulled out of the grave and kicked the habit entirely. But even then, everybody knew that Boy Best, the fiercest stickup man in Harlem, was still hooked—firmly under my thumb.

LEROY "NICKY" BARNES

One night when I was in my new 1964 Cadillac Fleetwood, Gabby went up to Irene's to check up on her. Rain beat down on the roof and windshield, and I just dozed off. I was that tired, running ragged trying to turn Frank Madonna's package on time.

I woke up to a knock on my window.

It was Steve Austin, flanked by a big group of guys. I knew his beef. He'd sent out the message that he didn't like me taking money from his territory and going back to the West Side with it. Lotta bullshit.

Now, I was familiar with the rules. If you were West Side, you couldn't sell East Side. It was like the Hatfields and McCoys. One doesn't come into another's territory without a throwdown.

I couldn't work East Side by myself, cause I'd be the outsider, and somebody would kill me. That's why I hooked up with Gabby. He grew up east of Lenox Avenue and had a rep as a tough-guy. His presence allowed me to operate there.

Only Steve Austin wasn't seein' it that way.

"Man," I told him, "I just came home. Wherever I can make some money is where I'm goin'. If you don't like that, you can kiss my motherfuckin' ass, *nigger*!"

"What?" he asked, shocked.

"That's right, and get the fuck away from my car before I get out of here and put my foot in your ass!"

Nobody talked like this to Steve Austin, the number-one dude in East Harlem. I was ready to pop him with my shit, but that pack of hard muthafuckas behind him got me thinking. *If I do that, I'll probably get shot up myself.* So I told him, "Steve, I'm gonna put my gun down, and then I'm gonna get out and kick your motherfuckin' ass!"

I took my shit out real easy. Figured they'd knock me off right then, but that was the risk I had to take. No way was Steve gonna block me out. My powder was comin' from Frank on consignment, and if I was gonna get him his money on time, I had to have that East Side business.

I put my gun in the glove, pushed open the car door and stepped into the rain. My new shoes, my new jacket…everything was getting wet. We all walked into the hallway of Steve's bar on the corner. I pulled off my jacket, hung it on the stairwell and got ready to duke.

Got a couple of good left hands on him and was ready to slip a right jab—Bam! He hit me across the nose but didn't break it. Steve's crew cheered.

The floor was all wet and I slipped forward as I snapped off a jab, but I grabbed Steve as I fell and backed him up against the wall. He tried to shake me off.

Damn. This dude is kind of a strong motherfucker.

But I was a strong motherfucker, too, fresh out the penitentiary. I kept him pinned. We struggled and I spun him around, hit him with a left on top of the head, countered with a right to the midsection. He doubled over and tried to protect himself. Thought I'd take his lights out with an uppercut, but he grabbed it. We were clinched and locked up.

This ain't gonna end.

Then I heard that hard pop, the sound of a stiletto locking into position. That was my warning—hearing that motherfucker when it opened. I tried to pull Steve around and get the blade away from me, but I slipped again and fell against the wall. Steve started throwing shit at my body and my head.

My nose opened up as Steve's man Blue came at me with the stiletto. It was long, black and had chrome handles.

Brother Jones hit Blue's arm with a karate chop and knocked the blade from his hand.

I was as stunned as Blue.

"No good," said Brother Jones, Steve Austin's top security. "That's how a fair one goes."

He was playing by the rules. By putting my shit in my glove, I'd called for a fair one—just two people and their hands. And if you pulled out your gun or your blade on a fair one? Everybody would call you a fuckin' punk.

Brother Jones wasn't gonna have that mark on his crew.

"It's all over," he said, stepping between me and Steve. "Forget about it." And that's how the fair one of the '60s ended.

LEROY "NICKY" BARNES

Nicky Barnes and Steve Austin. That was talked around for a long time. That was big.

That really earned my rep on the East Side.

"Heard about your little scuffle," said Big Frank Madonna, sipping his coffee in a Yonkers diner.

"Listen, Frank, if I gotta wipe that dude out to clear the lane, that's just what I'll do. I won't lose that East Side business."

Frank saw things from a different perspective.

"You're my investment. I don't want you killed over territory. So you take everybody you have on the East Side, pull 'em over to the other side of Lenox. That's technically West Side, right? You'll be in control there. Now, I'm gonna give you a real good deal on this next package, but I want you to keep your cut low. Make the goods stronger than what anybody can buy on the East Side."

When our next package hit the streets, all the East Side junkies left Steve Austin's dealers and traveled west to get my goods, just as Frank predicted—"See kid, junkies are like *any* customers. They don't care who's the meanest guy out there. All they care about is who's got the best powder. Capeesh?"

"You won't believe it," my dealers told me. "People will be sick, but they'll pass other dealers and wait for us to show! When we do, they all rush up to get it. They're standing in *lines* for it."

Good news, but all the same, I couldn't have junkies bunching up on the street, putting such attention on my dealers. That was too dangerous. To keep the heat from catching on, I'd have to maintain a steady flow of powder on the street. That meant pushers on a 24-7 rotation and a mill running at constant speed. To pull it off, I'd have to build the organization I'd envisioned in Green Haven.

It couldn't wait any longer.

The first thing I needed was a good lieutenant. Of all the names that came to mind, Reggie Isaacs seemed perfect for the job. Nobody suspected him as a powder player. We shot up together as kids, but Reggie kicked before I did, and the only addiction he had now was golf. He was looking to marry and needed some money, so he jumped at the chance to get in.

A few weeks later, me and Reggie were drinking at the Shalimar when this real muscular guy came right up to my face. *Who the fuck is this?* I almost pulled out my shit and popped him.

"Nick? It's me. Stan Morgan."

"Damn, Stan! What happened to you? You was just a scrawny kid when I last saw you."

It was real good to see Stan, healthy, strong and doin' okay for himself. As we talked, I started to size him up. Stan was just flatfootin' it, but seemed a sharp kid and an excellent choice to back up Reggie.

All I needed now was a woman, to do all the things Nita used to do. So when I saw this powder client of mine hangin' with this fine piece of ass, I introduced myself to her.

"Hello," she said. "I'm Sista."

I didn't see it as an obstacle that she was going with a client. He didn't either, 'cause when I told him I was taking her away, he said that was fine, long as I still gave him the goods.

I trusted my instincts that Sista was special, that she wouldn't fuck up my operation like Nita did. When she said she'd been working the mill for her man, I let her try out her skills. Well, that just sealed the deal.

"Yo, man," Stan told me. "You're not gonna believe what she's doin'."

The way I ran a mill was that we'd open the glassine bag, scoop up some powder with a measuring spoon, then dump it in. But Sista? She came up with the idea of using the bag *as* the spoon. That's the spoon-in-one! That was her invention!

It was revolutionary, like Henry Ford coming in. She tripled our output and reduced the time by 50 percent. With her running the mill with her sisters and cousins, Stan and Reggie doing drops and picking up the money and a crew of dealers on the streets, my operation was churning out powder as fast as Frank could give it to us.

Soon enough, guys on Pleasant Avenue started comin' to *me* for business. Everybody wanted me to take care of their package, 'cause they knew I'd take care of the money. My reputation was that overpowering.

But of all the times I got offered better quality powder, I was never as sure about the quality of the supplier. My freedom and safety were well protected with Frank. I wasn't willing to trade that off. I'd built exactly what I wanted—a loyal crew that kept me three deep from the powder, and nothing was gonna compromise my unique position.

I was Nicky Barnes, the most untouchable dealer in Harlem.

"Hey, man, you gotta be kidding!"

But it was no joke. It was January 29, 1965, when the cops arrested me on the Bronx street corner and dragged me back up to Reggie's apartment on a cold night. I wasn't the least bit concerned. Reggie never left goods lying around his pad. He was careful like me.

"We got 'em," said the arresting officer, calling his superior on Reggie's telephone. "Naw, chief, he's clean, but don't worry. We know where his goods are. We're gonna lock his ass up and do the job on him."

Man, that's bullshit. They got no idea where the fuckin' goods are.

Then they carted me to my mill on Davidson Avenue. *Shit.* The place was stocked—thousands of glassine bags, hundreds of boxes of rubber bands, a few dozen cans of milk sugar, a couple of scales and $500,000 worth of Frank Madonna's dope. I took a seat to compose myself.

"Hey, Nick!"

The package flew toward me and naturally, I caught it. Instincts.

"Nice catch," said the cop, taking back the half-kilo bag of heroin. And that's how they charged me on possession! Dirty motherfuckers.

I sat in the Bronx County Jail, wondering how the cops knew where that mill was. I knew I wasn't the one who led them there. The only reasonable explanation was Reggie or Stan got careless on a tapped phone and let the whereabouts slip.

But that got me thinking, "Well, shit! If there were taps on Reggie's phone, there's gotta be a recording of that dirty cop! All his talk on framing me has gotta be on there!"

Once I got out on bail, I tracked down my pal Marty Yamin from Green Haven, to see if he could help me get those tapes played. The good judge was free and back on the street. His felony blocked him from practicing law again, but he kept tabs on the right kind of lawyers for guys in my situation.

"Eddie Rosner," he told me. "That's your man."

Pockmarked, chubby and fresh out of law school, Rosner was the new kid on the block behind the Manhattan Criminal Courthouse at 100 Centre Street. This was Baxter Street, home to a notorious strip of crooked lawyers and bondsmen called the Baxter Street Bar. They kept offices above the bars and restaurants on the block, hangout spots for cops waiting to testify in court. The lawyers just walked down, bought a patrolman a drink, slipped him a few grand and got favorable testimony for their client.

My case needed a bit more attention. My arrest was the culmination of a lengthy investigation between the Bronx DA and the Federal Narcotics Bureau—too big to be handled over a payoff at Forlini's.

A cop can't tap a phone without probable cause that you, a suspected felon, are making calls that directly relate to your felony. He's got to record his observations in a sworn affidavit, and based on that, the state supreme court will approve or deny his tap.

Same deal for a search warrant. Only the affidavit on mine was a strange read. "He" didn't observe me doing anything that would warrant a search. "I/We" did.

"All right," the judge asked the officer on the stand, "what does this mean? 'I/We?' Did *you* make the observations on the defendant? Or did *we* make them? If it was *we*, then we need *we* to appear in court for questioning."

"Your Honor," waffled the cop, "the 'I/We' was to indicate that my fellow officers made the observation, then told me what they saw."

In other words, this cop hadn't seen a fuckin' thing! He made a sworn statement under oath when he asked for that warrant, but flat-out lied to get it.

The judge lost it. He adjourned court till the next day, but we'd already won. See, when the cops got the search warrant for my mill, the probable cause was based on perjurious testimony, making the warrant bunk, leaving me victim of an illegal search and seizure!

When the judge suppressed all the evidence the next morning, I figured I was home free. Only one problem. Like Rosner said, "the government cheats and lies all the time," and the Feds still hadn't taken the stand.

The agent from the narcotics bureau told the judge that while the city cops arrested me on an illegal search warrant, *his* arrest was, in fact, perfectly legal. Right before the bust, he claimed, he put his ear up to Reggie's apartment and heard me say, "Oh, yeah! I got some heroin! And I'm goin' to get the heroin now over at 1789 Davidson Avenue!"

And the judge believed this shit!

Although he'd suppressed the evidence from the mill, he readmitted it, 'cause the tapes were no longer a factor in my arrest.

I was really, *truly* fucked.

I could see those wiretap reels right in front of me on the prosecution table. If we could get them played, I'd be set. That talk on framing me had to be on there.

Only now, those tapes were inadmissible as evidence! There was no legal reason why we could listen to them.

"Isn't there some kind of way you could cross-examine the dude and force him to blurt that out?" I asked Rosner.

"Nick, if we start talking about those tapes, the DA will erase those motherfuckers clean. I'm sorry. There's nothing we can do."

When the jury found me guilty on possession, the tapes were sealed in a manila envelope and sent downtown to the file room of the NYPD Narcotics Division, at the Old Slip Precinct. But if I wanted to leave Green Haven early, before my sentence of fifteen to twenty ran out, the tapes had to come out before I did.

"If we go on appeal," Rosner told me in the visiting room, "and we don't have the tapes, the appellate court will uphold the lower court's ruling."

"Well, get the fucking tapes, Ed! Get 'em! Why can't you figure a way to get those fucking tapes? It's been two fucking years now!"

Eddie Rosner was starting to annoy me.

When I got sentenced on this thing, February 1966, Rosner was just a big fat Jew boy. Now he'd slimmed down and gotten custom-made shirts, custom suits, great haircut, nice glasses, manicured nails...Yeah, this motherfucker's changing, and I'm saying to myself, "How much time is he delegating to do what needs to be done?"

At the same time, I'm thinking, "What would be the best way for me to do my time? What can I do to help myself?" It was time for me to take control. It's just a matter of survival.

What do you do when you're drowning in the water? You thrash, man. You're trying to get to shore. It's self-preservation. At least with me, that's always how it's been. You have to do it for yourself.

I subscribed to thirty-seven different law journals and pored over them in the prison law library, searching for answers to my questions. How do I get the tapes played without having them destroyed? How do I get access to them without letting the prosecutors know what I want? What can I say to Rosner to encourage him to go this route or that route?

There had to be some way for me to get those motherfuckin' tapes, but every lead ended in roadblock.

My hopes began to fail.

LEROY "NICKY" BARNES

The Brotherhood

THE LAST EXPERIENCE I had with Frank James on the street was when he robbed Monkey Man, this little kid I used as a dealer. Monkey Man was just real soft. So soft he sold all his powder behind closed doors.

When you sell out of your apartment, the police will usually come up with an informer, hide behind him like a stickup man. You'll let the informer in and give him some drugs—not knowing his true intent— and that's when the cops bang down your door, give the informant some dope and money, lock you up and take you to jail.

Monkey Man must've been real lucky, or real careful, 'cause the cops never caught on to him. And while Monkey got away from that shit, he didn't get away from Frank James, man! Fucking Frank caught the coke guy coming to deliver to Monkey Man, stuck him up in the hallway, took his coke, made him knock on Monkey's door, pushed in, robbed everybody, tied 'em up and ran out the house…

And then he did it again!

Frank got to hitting Monkey regularly, just 'cause he could! He always managed to find somebody to get up there and open that goddamn door. Frank just ate that shit up, but I couldn't have it anymore.

I was going to kill that motherfucker.

I circulated on the wire that my guy was about to pick up a lotta cash from Monkey Man. Frank got the message, 'cause I was up there in the dark, strapped in with a sawed-off, listening to him creep up the steps.

I was so aggravated, I had to handle this personally.

Should've got the jump on him, but when Frank saw those lights out? "Uh-oh," he said, "this shit ain't right." Turned back around, walked down the steps.

Motherfucker had instincts just like mine.

Since then, we'd sent a couple death messages to one another—"I'm gonna kill you without a doubt, you or your black-ass friends"—but now that we were both doing time in Green Haven, we buried the hatchet. Unless a guy shot you or stabbed you in the back or pistol-whipped your woman, all that street shit is forgotten once you go behind the wall.

Besides, Frank was just doing his job. His hustle was to take a gun, stick it in your side and take your shit, and I respected him as a professional.

"Yo, Nick," Frank told me in the yard, "I want you to meet some guys." Frank had always been the lone wolf on the street, but now was hooked in tight with a crew of Black Muslims. He brought me over and gave me the introduction.

"I remember you," said this little dude Jazz, "back at Riker's reading that book! Yeah, that was it, 'cause I was sayin' to myself, 'This motherf—this dude gonna make some real money one day! He gotta be smart. Reading a book. *The Prince*.' Yeah, I knew you was gonna get some money."

As Muslims, these guys rejected stuff I'd learned as an altar boy at St. Mark's Methodist on 137th. They were saying you can't go and see a man with white skin and blue eyes and say he's your father. 'Cause he *ain't* your father. He can't be your father. If Jesus is your father, he's gotta be black!

Now, I never became a monk, shaved my head or wailed in Israel at the wall. That didn't happen. But I decided to convert to Islam. I was attracted by that sense of well-being, a sense of black pride.

On weekends in the yard, I'd stand with the Muslims in a circle—we used to call it the square—and read from *Muhammad Speaks!*, the paper of the prophet Elijah Muhammad, the one who came into the black community to raise us like Lazarus from the grave of irresponsibility.

We learned about all the achievements of Africa. In school I was taught that Alexander the Great was the one who brought culture to Egypt, but now I discovered when Alexander the Great came to Egypt, they already had pyramids! They already had the Sphinx! They already had underground tunnels, irrigation...all this shit before Europeans came.

How the fuck could Alexander have brought anything to Egypt? That was just a myth to tell you African people were ignorant. How the fuck can a person build a pyramid and not know geometry and algebra? How could they do that? With basic math? I don't think so.

I felt pride in being black, and I shaved my head. No more straightening that shit. I rejected that European sense of value. I wore the bald head while other brothers wore the natural means, the fro. I embraced the motherland. I embraced beauty as formulated in the natural physique of the motherland. I embraced Islam as the religion of the black man, ready-made for me.

No more substance abuse. No more eating pork. No calling each other motherfucker and nigger. If I call a black man a nigger, I think I'm a nigger, 'cause he's a reflection of me. What comes out of my mouth is a reflection of my brain, and when I use negativity, that means negativity is inside of me. One of the ways we stop or eradicate negativity is by not using negative terms. We talk to each other as brothers. We call each other Aki. This is something that binds us and lifts us. We greet each other with "As-Salaam-Alaikum," our way of saying, "You understand. We're strong."

That's what we were learning, and those moments when we were getting together out in the yard were kind of precious. All of us had our hustles in the street—Frank was a stickup man, Jazz was a flatfoot, I was a drug dealer. We all were felons, and nobody protested his innocence.

But while we all did whatever it was we did, this Islam had something, meant something. I can tell you that Islam brought us together.

We felt stronger with it than we did without it.

Matty Madonna and a lot of his gang were still in the joint at this time, but I made a point of not just hanging around with those guys. There were certain occasions, like when we were out in the yard all day, when we'd have lunch. They'd invite me over, I'd sit down, eat, then take my plate and go. 'Cause I knew I wasn't supposed to be hanging out with these dudes.

Islam was hitting its widest currency, and with Elijah Muhammad calling whites devils, there was a contradiction in trying to be a standout black and hanging out with a white guy. That closeness between black and white just wasn't in vogue.

Madonna and his guys heard our talk about Yacub, the mad scientist who created white people, but they weren't too threatened. "Probably right about Yacub," Matty told me, "but we're Italians. That don't include us." At the same time, none of his gang cared to stretch out to any of *us*.

Except for one.

Say a group of Muslims was playing basketball in the yard. Matty and his gang might have a pool on who's going to win the game, or who's going to score the most points, although they'd only watch from a distance. But

Joey Gallo? He'd be right there on the sideline, hollering and screaming, "You fuckin' bum! How could you miss that?!"

He was the kind of guy who'd come into the bar and, if it were a birthday party, grab the mike from the emcee and start singing. Matty would just hang back with a cigar—same influence, you know—talking to his group in hushed tones, like they were planning to take over Naples or something. Meanwhile Joey'd be out talking with everybody, hugging everybody. There was this dude Molino in the joint who was gay, and Joey gave him hugs!

Joey didn't give a shit what you were. You'd see him walk around the yard, stopping whenever he wanted and talking to whoever he wanted to—the Latinos, the Panthers, the Young Lords, the Westies. He sat at mess with the Muslims and complained the spaghetti needed pork sausage! Just to fuck with us a little.

But nobody fucked with him, man.

Joey Gallo got big motherfuckin' respect. Big respect. He had those high connections to organized crime families, and had the power and the reputation of those families behind him. All, of course, but one.

I knew from the papers about his war with the Profaci family. Joey and his brothers, the famous Gallo gang, had some beef with their don, so they just said, "Fuck it!" They kidnapped the don's top dudes! That escalated into the Gallo-Profaci war, and a few of the Profacis were in the joint, lookin' to fuck him up. But if any of those guys came up to Joe and gave him bullshit?

"Get the fuck out of here!" he'd say.

Joey made enough allies across the board in Green Haven to back him up, too.

The two of us got along well, especially with our taste for culture and fine women. And boy, Joey had some beautiful girls coming in to see him. *Beautiful* fucking women, like they'd just come off of the beach somewhere. As for the culture, both of us were really well read, so we'd talk politics, art and philosophy. He was into existentialists like Sartre and Camus. I was into black intellectuals like Harold Cruse.

We'd talk a lot about the Mafia, just like me and Madonna used to. Joey'd go on about the honor and loyalty among the original Italians who formed the Cosa Nostra. Those strong ties in their illegal operation came about through strong family traditions. That's why Joey was so bitter about being fucked over by the Profacis.

"But the Gallos? We're brothers! We *gotta* be loyal to each other. That's what keeps us strong. That's how we fight back those sonsabitches and stake our claim!"

One evening after lockup, when I was on duty as the water boy, the guard told me to bring a bucket to Gallo, "Pronto."

Joey had the guards at his beck and call. Partly from hooking 'em up with gifts from the outside, partly from all the dirt he had on 'em. Since all the guards loved to hang with the legendary Crazy Joe, Joey'd milk 'em for information, like which guard was sleeping with another guard's old lady. Nobody was sure exactly what he knew, so everybody let him be.

I walked to a lighted cell on the other end of A Block, where Joey put the final touches on his canvas, a crouched leopard ready to strike.

"Care for a game?" asked Joey.

Guys in the yard always wanted to take him on in chess and he got tired of it, so this was kind of a rare occasion. I poured the hot water into the funnel sticking out of the bars, overturned the bucket and sat on it.

Joey took white, 'cause he had the home-court advantage. He put his pawn in front of his queen. I reached through the bars and made my move.

"A Sicilian defense," he mumbled, grabbing his knight and plunking it down. I stared at the board in deep focus. In chess as in life, forethought wins.

"Nick, you coloreds oughta show the mob who's boss."

Didn't see that comin'.

Sounded like a fuckin' joke, so I kept my eye on the game and said, "Joe, I got no beef with the Italians."

"Lemme give you some," he said, stubbing his Camel and lighting another. "What gets me is Joey can hit Pleasant Avenue and get a *white* kilo. Good price. Great shit. But you? You get *black* kilos. Not so good a price. I dunno, but that wouldn't make Joey happy. Joey'd think he was taken advantage of."

He took out my bishop, a quick score but a rash move.

"Thing is, Nick, *you're* the guy with the advantage."

The game was getting interesting.

"You black guys got heart. You got *stugots* to hit the fuckin' streets. The mob? Nah. Ain't got the nerve to do that. Used to, before they got fat and lazy out in Vegas. Made a *fortune* off it too. A fuckin' gold rush.

"But ya know what happened? The Feds. Went after guys like Galante and the mob got spooked. Literally. That's why they got you guys to do their dirty work, to bust your ass and take the heat on the streets. That why they sit back and play dominoes out on the Avenue. To be safe."

Joey took my queen but exposed his king.

"But if someone took over the streets again? They'd have so much money, so much fuckin' power? The mob would cry in their Sambuca. They'd sit in their social clubs and ask, 'Why in the fuck did we let the niggers and the Gallos run away with our fortune?'"

Joey bored his pupils right into me, black as olives.

"You in Harlem? Me in Brooklyn? We ain't fat like the mob, Nick. We're two starving street dogs, and that gives us nerve to *burn*."

Joey Gallo. Crazy motherfucker. Did he really think I'd be a pawn in one of his war games?

"Checkmate, Joe."

Black wins.

I found the key to get out of Green Haven—*Katz v. the United States*, fresh from the Supreme Court. In this case, federal agents placed a listening device outside a telephone booth where Katz, a bookie, made his calls, and the Court ruled that was a physical infringement on Fourth Amendment rights.

Well, shit! That's what happened in my case! A federal agent claimed he listened in on my door, and an ear is a listening device! Even though a guy's a criminal, and he's under surveillance, the Feds can't just go puttin' ears on people's doors! That's a violation of the Constitution! That was our grounds for an appeal!

And we got that motherfucker granted.

Now dig this. The appellate court ordered the Bronx DA to let us hear the wiretap tapes, to find out what exactly it was that placed that federal agent at our door. We'd been so worried about asking for those tapes, but now? We didn't have to ask for anything! I'd been waiting four motherfucking years to hear those tapes. I couldn't wait to hear 'em at the hearing.

At the Bronx County Courthouse, the reel just spun on the player, three-quarters finished—no sound. Completely blank.

Man, my life is going down the fuckin' drain.

"If there was anything on those tapes to begin with," said Assistant DA James Randolph, "the sound must have *dissipated* over the passage of time."

You sly muthafucka.

This black dude Randolph had just a hell of a vocabulary, but whatever he said about dissipation was fuckin' bullshit. Somebody in the system erased those tapes *intentionally*.

"Might as well wrap it up," he said. "We knew nothing was on there."

"Wait a minute!" snapped Rosner. "Play it to the end. If you've got something more important to do, go do it. I'm sitting here."

Just before the tape ran out, some faint, garbled sounds came out of the speaker.

"Stop the tape!" said Rosner. "I want it sealed and sent to the Department of Criminal Investigation. I want that part of the tape enhanced by a technician. I wanna hear what's on it."

"We'll send the tapes down to DCI and see what that is," said Randolph.

"No," said Rosner, "I'll go down *with* you to DCI, and we'll *both* listen." I applauded Ed for that. He had the foresight to do what he was trained to do. Run down every lead.

"Your time to waste," said Randolph.

I waited in the Bronx County Jail for two days, expecting the worst when Rosner came to my cell. He tossed me the transcript with a smile. "Looks like they quit erasing one conversation too early." I scanned the typewritten words. It was all there, all that talk on framing me. Just as I remembered.

"Dude," said Rosner, "you're home free."

District Attorney Burton Roberts, nemesis of all illegal activity in the Bronx, well this motherfucker was so bold...

"You've got five years in already, Mr. Barnes, so I'll tell you what we'll do. We'll give you a plea of five to seven, you'll cop out and go back to Green Haven. You'll be eligible for parole at the next parole meeting. You'll be back on the street in thirty days."

If I didn't take the plea, Roberts threatened to take me back to court. This time, he claimed, they had additional information to sustain my original search and seizure, independent of the perjurious warrants.

I talked with Ed in the hall.

"Ed, if I step foot back in Green Haven, I might not get out in thirty days. I might never come out! I mean, no telling what these people might do when I'm back in there!"

"Don't take it, Nick. We've got 'em, man."

"Fuck it, Ed. Let's roll with it."

"No good," I told Roberts. "I'll go back to trial." That answer didn't suit him at all. He was pissed.

Before they carted me back to the Bronx County Jail, Assistant DA Randolph pulled me aside.

"Nick, I don't know how this is gonna end, but if you get out, we're gonna get you back in. Remember that, mutha*fucka*."

Yeah, all that street shit just came out of him.

A week later, the warden slid open my bars and grumbled, "bring your shit out." And that was it. No plea bargain. No more trials. No parole.

They just cut me loose.

Rosner's reputation doubled for pulling that Columbo shit on those tapes. His star began to rise. Two years later in 1972, his practice went to the ground after Bob Leuci, famous SIU detective, busted him in a sting operation. That was too bad. He was a really good lawyer.

Thanks, Ed. I still owe you one.

Nicky Barnes
Comes to Harlem

AFTER MY BUST IN '66, I hooked up with an old friend, Jimmy Terrell, on a partnership. I'd cut Reggie and Stan loose, 'cause I wasn't sure at the time which one of them alerted the cops to that mill.

Before I went in, I gave Jimmy about four packages to move in my absence. That way he'd have enough to pay my lawyer and provide a nest egg for my return. We also swore a loyalty oath—that he'd look out for Sista, me, and the operation we'd built together.

But once I was in Green Haven? Jimmy was nowhere to be seen. Sista asked him to ride her up to the joint a couple times, but he got his lieutenant Watusi to do the job for him. There were even times when Sista had to give Rosner money herself.

"So what the fuck happened, Jimmy?" I asked, rolling in the new 1970 brown Cadillac Fleetwood.

"Nick, it's been a long four years."

Jimmy laid on the sob story. His troubles started when Watusi got shot and killed over some bullshit at the Gold Lounge, a hangout on Seventh Avenue for the powder crew. Then his woman got knifed in a catfight at Small's Paradise. She died, too. Not to mention the IRS was moving in on the house he bought for his poor mother, Zula May.

"And there was the bust," said Jimmy.

The cops hit two of his mills simultaneously and fifteen people went under. Jimmy had to get 'em all out on bail and get lawyers for 'em, too.

"When all these problems came," he told me, "it just *drained* my resources. I didn't wanna take goods out on consignment, 'cause I had concerns turning that package on time."

In short, Jimmy was uptight and out of powder.

At least that's the reason he gave for not paying my lawyer bills or taking the time to bring Sista up to Green Haven. I was still pissed. I was dissatisfied with how Jimmy met his responsibilities, how he broke our oath of loyalty.

All the same, Jimmy did scrape enough to give me a solid welcome back present. I still had my same old ride when I came back home—a 1966 grey Lincoln with a black top, black tires with the three white stripes. It was the in thing at the time, but I appreciated this new Caddy, plus the $15G Jimmy put in the glove.

"And now that you're back? We can just rebuild our operation! Got a table and dealers ready to go."

"Jimmy, I'm out. Finished."

I really meant it. Islam changed me. All those ideas on Black Power weren't just coming out of Green Haven, either. It affected people in the street. It had a real resonance in Harlem. I saw myself being a strong force in that. I wanted to be down with all the positive things going on in the neighborhood.

But I had to live and pay the bills, so when Jimmy started on about Fat Jack's Broasted Chickens, my ears perked.

Fat Jack was a weight client of Jimmy's who owned this broasted chicken joint in Harlem. He was doing well enough, but could do much better if he put a little time into his business. That's what happens when you're in powder. You don't run your side operations with as much intensity, knowing you can fall back on that dope income.

I thought it was a good idea to get involved. We could turn Fat Jack's into a national franchise, like McDonald's. Wouldn't take much money to get that running, thirty or forty thousand would be plenty, and considering what I'd been making before, this was like pocket change.

Only problem was, I didn't have that money on hand.

"Listen," said Jimmy. "You don't have to get back in the street biz. I'll handle that for you. All I need is you to come with me to meet the suppliers. Tongues been waggin' since you got back, and I got a couple Italians on the Avenue ready to go."

Everyone thought I was buried up there in Green Haven, so when I came home, that was big fuckin' news among the powder community. Even Rosner got bombarded with calls.

"Tell Nicky that Paulie wants to see him."

"Tell Nicky that Tony wants to see him."

Rosner tried to hook me up, but I didn't wanna do business with anybody who'd come through a lawyer. Criminal lawyers aren't the best criminals, so my instincts weren't workin' the right way on it. With the Bronx DA out for revenge, you never knew *who* he might have turned informant.

I couldn't go back to Frank Madonna—he was in jail on a long bid by now—so if I had to get back in the game, even for just a month or so, I didn't mind being associated with the names Jimmy gave me. And despite our problems, I thought it was worth it in the short term to hang with him.

I touched base with Jimmy's suppliers, got different offers and got an idea what goods were available. I also got an idea of what really went down with Jimmy while I was in Green Haven.

He'd been on top of the craps more than the powder. He was deeply in debt to street people who had his IOUs, deeply in debt to the Italians. Couldn't get the powder like he used to. Still did a small weight business and still kept his appearances up, but between the craps, sniffin' coke and partyin', he just wasn't in tip-top shape for a hustle consistent with his image.

By the time I got home, people weren't even calling him Jimmy. He was *Goldfinger*. Riding around in a $35G, customized gold Cadillac limo with a Rolls-Royce grill, TV and a wet bar and tinted windows and curtains. Eight-track kicked in with Shirley Bassey every time you opened the car door.

Yeah, he was acting like a real clown. His rep suffered.

That's why all the suppliers asked me the same question: if they gave the package to Goldfinger, would I put my name on it? In other words, if Jimmy fucked up their powder, would I be responsible for the money?

"Yeah," I told them, "I will."

That hooked me in deeper than I would've liked. With my name on the package, I had to be on top of Jimmy and make sure he was turning the powder to my level of satisfaction.

It only took a month till I'd earned enough to move on the broasting, and by then I'd made inroads with the brothers involved in the nationalistic efforts—the Nation of Islam, the Liberation Army and the Black Panthers.

The Panthers had this spot on 120th and Seventh Avenue, a storefront where they'd sell clothes, advise brothers on problems and give positive reinforcement.

But if I came by to hang out or to talk, I'd park my ride four blocks up at the Gold Lounge, then walk down. My instincts told me not to park a brand new Cadillac in front of their operation. That didn't seem like the right thing to do.

Once I was there, I'd see the same guys two days in a row, and they'd have the same clothes, even the same shoes on. I heard them talk about community activism and different things they were doing, but listened with half an ear.

'Cause the other half of me was thinkin'—*I wonder if Jimmy made that drop for tomorrow. Did he pick up that Q?* I didn't envision that in the joint. I didn't realize how different I'd be from the Panthers. Thought we'd have a more mutual groove.

It's like being in a jazz joint. You'll see eight dudes playing the music; if they don't like what's going on, they'll peel off. Then you'll have just two or three of 'em up there, and they'll start kickin', cause that chemistry is right. Maybe it's just a flicker of the eye, a beat on the piano or a hit with the alto, but everybody knows, "Oh, shit! Yeah, he's gonna solo!"

I didn't feel that with the Panthers, or any the guys in the Black Power thing. But when I walked back to my car, changed into my new threads and hit the Gold Lounge?

Well, those guys in the drug movement just grabbed hold of me. They all had the latest cars, all had diamonds and jewelry. And there's just a big difference between clothes, cars and attractive women, and no cars, no clothes and no attractive women. Polar opposites.

Plus, if I'm thinking about paying tomorrow's bills, I'm thinking about the guys who I hooked up with in the powder game. I'm not thinking about that with the Black Power people. What could I do with them? I had a brand new Cadillac, money and a great place to live. They didn't have *anything* like that. So I naturally gravitated back to powder, seeking my own comfort level. That hustling field just drew me in more than anything else.

When I told Sista I was getting back in business, she didn't want anything to do with it. She wanted a different life. She wanted to just be a regular married couple, not wondering if I'm out late, or whether I'm dead or in jail. If I came in with a gun in my belt, she didn't want to think about me killing somebody. She was just tired of it.

"We'll stop now and get smart," she said. "We've got just enough money to start a business. Just pick something and I'll be there with you and we'll do it together."

She was a good woman. She took care of business the whole time I was in the joint. But no woman was gonna tell me what to do.

"Sista, you can go your own way. You can have everything you want. But this powder, I'm movin'."

And I did just that. Sista was truly disappointed when I went back in there. She always told me I could've been a leader in Black Power.

"But if you won't lead it," she asked, "then why you gotta wreck it?"

I met Melvin up at the Gold Lounge. He sold me some really good sniff coke. That was the nub of his business—cocaine. He was a neighborhood guy who had a loose-knit powder operation. I supplied him with a little weight, we got to be friends through that and before long, we were trading freaks, goin' to parties together and just hangin' out.

"Yo, Melvin! What's up, dude?"

We hugged and patted each other's backs. You see that a lot with guys from Harlem—hugging each other. Yeah, we're showing a little love, but that's not the real reason. What we're really doing is searching each other—feeling for that gun. You'll feel for his shit down the small of his back or give him a poke in the belly. If a guy's got a shoulder holster, you'll feel that, too. You'll go through the ritual even if he's your dude. It's just street instincts.

Only problem with Melvin was he *wasn't* strapped. He had that seat-belt syndrome. I don't have to wear it. It's not going to happen to me. He felt nobody he knew would set him up. He thought he was too well liked.

Personally, I liked Melvin. He was definitely my dude. But all the same..."Yo, Melvin! The fuck you doin' lookin' at my wife?"

His eyes were all over Frankie Lee. I'd taken her out for a little play at the Shalimar.

"Wife? Where's her ring, Nick? You think *everybody* is your wife!"

"Where's yours?"

"Janice is home with the baby, but my main woman Sandra? She's gone. That bitch left me for Jesus."

"I *know* that's rough. Sista's been high on the Lord lately."

"No, man. Jesus from 115th Street."

"That simple-ass nigger?!"

Jesus was a flamboyant dude who styled himself like a pimp—hair flowin' down to his shoulders, leather vest on bare skin. Melvin couldn't have felt good about that. I tried my best to cheer him up.

"Frankie Lee! Come over and meet Melvin Combs."

Frankie Lee waltzed over with a smile. Half Chinese and half Hawaiian, she was a fabulous, exotic creature. Absolutely gorgeous. Stunned Melvin silent.

"You know," he finally said, "I would stick my tongue in her pussy. Really. Far as I'm concerned, that girl is *different*."

He was right. She was a stand-up ho with a strut. So trustworthy, I even let her make my drops from time to time.

Melvin and I got to talkin' about business, and he said I could pick up some blow down at his shop in midtown Manhattan.

"I didn't know you had a front!"

"Front? I got a business, Nick! Pedigree dogs for Manhattan's elite. Shih tzus, Lhasa apsos..."

"You gotta *pet shop*?"

"Closed for remodeling, but you just walk right on in."

I showed the next day and saw Melvin painting the walls in his big, floppy hat, leather sneakers and blue bellbottoms. His baby, Sean John Combs, bumped into a big sack of money with his little, rolling walker.

"Damn, Melvin?! Why you down here by yourself with all that money? Someone could just stick you up, and you ain't even strapped!"

"I got a gun!"

"Where is it?"

"Trunk of my car."

"Trunk of your car? Fuck you gonna get to that? How's that gonna help you in a stickup?"

Melvin went to his car and came back with this little green airline bag. I almost fell over when he unzipped it and pulled out his shit. It was something you'd fire off in an emergency, like a flare gun.

"Melvin? What the fuck is that? A toy?"

"Check this out, Nick. You can put shot shells in there! You wanna fire it?"

"Shit, no! Might take my damn arm off. It's your gun. You fire it!"

We smoked up and laughed. Little Sean cried out at the top of his lungs.

Man, kid's gotta set of pipes.

A few weeks later I rolled over to Frankie's penthouse in Yonkers. We were ready to go out for the night, but when I opened her closet to get to my clothes, Melvin's little green bag was sitting right there!

"Frankie Lee! You call up Melvin right now!" Frankie handed me the phone. "Melvin," I joked, "come over now and get this shit. Don't start bringing your stuff over here like you're stayin' here!"

"Oh! That's where it was! Hey, man, check to make sure I got my $3,500 in there." I looked in the bag and saw that little gun, plus the money. Melvin was about two grand short.

"Frankie Lee? How much did Melvin have in there?"

"About fifteen hundred."

"Yo, Nick," said Melvin, "I'm telling you, she spent that fuckin' money!" And that's what got Frankie Lee kicked to the curb. I didn't care about her and Melvin. Shit. I made the introduction. Her services were available to those I chose to share them with. But she lied to me about that money. I couldn't have that. That made her ineligible to be in my rotation.

As for Melvin, he eventually paid the price for not bein' strapped. He wasn't careful. He expected higher things from the people he was hanging out with. He trusted the guys he did business with. And they were snakes.

I don't know what the deal was with him getting killed. I do know the guy who sparked him gave him coke parties, shit like that. I told Melvin that dude was a treacherous motherfucker who'd stab you in the back. But Melvin didn't listen. He thought there'd be honor among thieves.

I dunno, maybe Melvin was just too nice.

Reggie and Stan had done well for themselves. Both had mansions, wives and children, Cadillacs and Lincolns. They even had a partnership in a GM auto dealership in Yonkers. I was impressed.

"Business has been good," said Reggie.

Reggie and Stan set up a big street biz on the East Side. That was Reggie's doing. He was from 116th and Lenox and could swing East or West. As for how they got the goods, I figured some supplier stretched out to them, knowing they'd been hooked up with me.

"Now that you're back," said Stan, "he'd really like to meet you."

"Why would you wanna set me up with your supplier?" I asked, thinking I'd trained them better.

"He's getting out of the business," said Reggie, "but before he does, he wants to talk to you. Maybe he's got someone he wants you to meet."

I trusted my instincts that Reggie and Stan weren't trying to set me up on a sting. Even when I took the bust on our mill, I didn't think they ratted me out. It was a fuck-up. Pure and simple. All the same, I didn't wanna meet anybody without knowing names.

"Mikey Coco," said Reggie.

Damn. *Coco* was supplying them? He was a legend on the Avenue. Murad Nersesian, aka Murad the Arab. Born to Lebanese parents, Coco grew up in East Harlem and turned out more Italian than the Italians. Had a fierce rep—used to be a button man for Carlo Gambino, so I thought, "Fuck it. If he wants to talk, I'd like to meet him, too."

The next day, Coco cruised into Reggie and Stan's dealership in his Rolls-Royce. *Muthafucka still got some Arab in him*. He wore a short-sleeved shirt to show his tatts—two eagles and a tiger, plus a U.S. Army one from his paratrooper days.

"Take a hike," he told Reggie and Stan.

"I hear you're out of the business," I said.

"I might have a change of heart," he said, drumming his thick fingers on the used Cadillac. "I've got this powder. And this shit is coming in hand over fist. We want you to move it."

"Give me a sample and we'll talk."

I sent out his sample for the blood test and it turned out great, better than anything I'd gotten from Frank Madonna. So I started negotiating with my current supplier, just to see if he could top it. Soon after, Coco sent me a message. I was to meet him at a diner he owned on Central Park West.

"Look," he said, sipping his coffee, "we know who you went to see, because the guy you went to see for your better price? Well, he's buying from *us*. Now maybe you weren't satisfied with our offer, but this is what we'll do."

With that, Coco laid down the deal. On top of what he promised before, he'd give me all the powder he'd planned to give Reggie and Stan. What kind of reputation did I have that he'd do this for me? Coco dumped powder on me before I'd even turned a *bag* for him!

It takes more than the ability to promote yourself to get that.

I scrambled to get everything ready for the package, but realized it was too much for just one guy. Mikey wanted big turnover, and my resources were spread thin. I needed guys who could turn this powder quick.

Goldfinger was out. His negative little habits began to exhibit themselves and get on my nerves. Too leisurely on the job, more committed to fuckin' with the music biz and being the Berry Gordy of our time than being a solid dealer.

So I started doing the math on Reggie and Stan.

Three people just seemed better than one. If I'm alone, cops on surveillance only focus on me. But if three of us are there? That cut down my exposure by 66 percent!

Just looking at the numbers, that's got to be a good thing for me.

Plus, three people can move three times more than one person, and having Reggie and Stan gave me a wedge into East Side territory. True, Reggie's carelessness did send me upstate to Green Haven, but I could tell he'd progressed. He had a big house, a couple cars and a major East

Side operation.

I figured he'd be extra careful the second time around.

I laid out the plan for Reggie and Stan. We'd use their table to cut the goods and have their lieutenant, Curt Molette, make the pickups and drops. In turn, we'd split the profit three ways.

To me, it all seemed a great deal, but Reggie and Stan were pissed. As these two saw it, I took their supplier right from under their nose. As I saw it, I was doing them a *favor*. Coco had told them the score—"If you want my package, you gotta go to Nick!"—but I wasn't taking advantage of that fact. I was giving as good a deal as Coco.

They grumbled, but ended up agreeing to my terms. 'Cause it's all about who's got the best package, and nobody was giving out product of Coco's quality.

Of course, Reggie and Stan quieted down after learning the value of bein' with me. We'd be counting money in Stan's basement all night! The pool table was just covered with the stuff. We clocked off about $150G profit every ten days, and that was after splittin' it three ways! For months this went on, so when Stan and Reggie came out of the blue and said they wanted to retire?

"You two are outta yo' goddamn minds. How can you guys retire now?"

"Me and Stan are gonna work on the dealership," said Reggie.

"Just for a while," said Stan. "Till things cool. We've been picking up a lotta heat on the East Side."

But Stan was just being a worrywart, and he knew it. So I pressed him on the real reasons behind this semi-retirement bullshit.

"Is that what Lady Jasmine told y'all to do?"

Lady Jasmine was this spiritualist Stan's wife Jackie had been goin' to. She worked the cards and read rocks or leaves or some shit—anything she could use to be sufficiently mystical. She also gave you these oil baths. You had to wait until the water cooled, and then you'd get out the tub. She'd come from behind, wrap the towel around and dry your body off. Some ritualistic stuff.

Anyway, Jackie got it in her head that there had to be a reason for all her good fortune, why she and Stan had such phenomenal love together. They'd done well and he hadn't gotten busted and things were working out really well. Had two boys, living up in the suburbs, doing good, feeling good about everything. She felt there *had* to be some reason for this.

She figured they were blessed through Lady Jasmine.

Shit! Lady Jasmine didn't have no magical fucking powers. I did. I got Stan turning powder faster than he'd ever done before!

Stan tried to pass the good news, this blessed woman, on to me, and she got me in the oil bath, put me in a gown, read the cards and relayed all this bullshit—stuff Stan said to Jackie and Jackie, knowingly or unknowingly, passed on to Jasmine. But this blessed lady was rearranging and refining the information to show me the extent of her extra knowledge.

I thought she was a motherfuckin' con artist. They paid her, and I'd have been paying her too if I hired her. But Lady Jasmine didn't like how I called her out. She told Reggie and Stan something bad was going to happen to them, that someone in their lives would cause them misfortune.

"She told me you were bad luck," said Stan.

They were just lookin' for an excuse to leave me. Forget the fact I'd treated them as equals. They were still pissed I took their supplier. They wanted that source.

They just couldn't be without that power.

The Education of
Frank James

THE NIGHT I MET FRANK JAMES, I was strapped. I got his message he wanted a meet, so I told him to come to the Tiger Lounge on 116th. When he slid into the booth across from me, I could tell he wasn't a dope fiend anymore. I still didn't know if he was a cross artist.

"I'm not tryin' to set you up no more, Nick. I'm just tryin' to make some money. I ain't got no gun, either."

"I got mine. State your business."

Frank was looking for some powder to turn. He said he could move as much as I could give him, but I had doubts. I could tell Frank had turned from a hungry stickup man to a guy who spent half the night sniffin', sleepin' all day and not takin' care of anything.

That was my assessment, but at the moment, I was in a predicament. Not having Reggie and Stan on board left me solo. All the heat came directly towards me, and with my name ringin' really bad on the West Side—"You gotta get Nicky Barnes' package!"—my plan was to pack up shop, work the East Side till things cooled.

Frank could be my instrument to do that, to tiptoe through the East Side without a whole lot of antagonism. His name would be on the street, not mine, and I could just run all my powder through him, like I'd done with Reggie and Stan. I figured if I could push Frank to turn what Reggie and Stan turned, that'd be *great*. But he'd have to get off his ass and take care of business!

I had some product left from Mikey Coco, so I gave Frank a little of that, just to test him out and see how he'd do. I told him to cut the shit, get it on the street and see me in a couple of days.

"Yeah, yeah," he said.

But a week later?

"Man, I'm not makin' any money off the package."

"Frank? How the fuck could you not make money? There's no way on earth you could not make money off this! You cuttin' it weak?"

"No, man, I'm puttin' in what you told me."

"Well, how many halves are there to your spoon?"

"I dunno."

"How could you not know? What do you mean you don't know?"

"My people do it up there at the mill. They just let me know."

"How the fuck you gonna let *them* tell you what you got? *You're* supposed to tell them what you got!"

Frank still didn't understand, so I wrote it all out on a cocktail napkin, showed him how to calculate the number of halves in a spoon.

"Oh, yeah! That's division! I know that! We learned that at reformatory!"

What struck a bell was I remembered it from reformatory, too!

"Good, Frank! If you got that, you won't have a problem."

But he did. Frank gave me the same story the next week.

I figured something was wrong at the mill, something that required professional help.

"Just this *once*, Sista. Nobody but you can figure out what's happening."

"No, Nick, that's the devil's work."

The next afternoon, Sista drove her brand new Cadillac straight from the dealership to the Sandwich Oasis, Frank James's restaurant on 125th Street. We sat at the counter as Frank's man Cro, a fierce muthafucka, cut salami with a butcher knife.

"Frank? Cro is a *warrior*. Can't have him slicing meat! You got to get him out on the street!"

Frank shrugged as Sista laid down the situation.

"I've been thinking about your problem. So you've got this husband-and-wife team running your mill, right? Well, what you need to do is get rid of them—*all* of them. They're stealin' from you! You bring in all new girls, and when they come in to work? Make them bitches strip. Make them take their motherfuckin' clothes off. If they don't wanna strip, fuck 'em!"

And just like that? Frank's problem was solved for good.

Yeah, Sista was a fine woman. I really do miss her.

The great panic of '72 made it hard to find a fix. Junkies guzzled illegal meth to keep the sweats from coming on and snapped up any junk that hit the streets—even synthetic. Soon the streets were out of powder. Completely. The West Side was dry. The East Side was dry.

I was sitting on ten kilos of Coco's powder.

"Frank, I want your operation opening up everything we got. We gonna cut this shit weak, gonna dump it all at once and double the price. I'm telling you, man. We can take over the East Side with this. Just you and me."

"I doubt that. Anyway, if I get $100,000 out of this, I'm going to retire."

"Oh, yeah? Well, if you retire at $100,000, I'll give you $10,000. If you don't retire at $100,000, you give me $10,000."

"It's a deal!"

We shook on it, flooded the streets and watched the money roll in. I don't think Frank ever recovered from that.

He loved making money off garbage.

Frank and I were dry and out of powder when out of the blue came Latino, a Cuban dealer. The Cubans had been bringing in a lot of powder after the French Connection took a big bust by international agents. Since Castro spread his exiles all over the world, Cuban dealers like Latino had enough connects to get the opium, process it to powder and ship to Spanish Harlem.

They did their own thing, their way. I had a lot of respect for them.

This guy Latino used to supply Frank—gave him low-level stuff, maybe an eighth of a kilo—but when he heard the word on the street, told him, "You and Nicky Barnes together? You bring him to me, muchacho."

We made the trip to his Spanish Harlem villa to see what he had to offer. It was ten kilos of powerful heroin.

"I would never give this much to Frank," said Latino. "He's too slow. He takes too long to get me my money."

We all laughed, but of course, that was the truth of the matter.

At the same time, I didn't have history with the Cubans as I did with the Italians. I couldn't get all that powder on consignment, and Latino wanted $300G up front for the goods.

"Look, Frank. I'm going to put up this money and we'll go partners on this, but the first thing I want is my money back. I'll give us both $1000 a week to live on till I do, then we go fifty-fifty." But what I'm thinkin' is, "If Frank passes this test and gets my money back to me, we've got a bedrock foundation for a partnership."

"Yeah," said Frank. "That's cool."

I told Frank when our dealers got their money, he had to collect it that very night. I didn't want guys sitting on money until morning. When people start doing that, they get a little bit cavalier.

"So when the money's there, Frank, I want it scooped up immediately."

Frank ran round the clock getting the money. He brought it all over to his house, and he and his wife Beverly counted the bills, turned them the right way. But as this money was comin' in, more than Frank and Beverly had ever seen in their life, I noticed a difference in the vibe between the three of us.

"Yeah, Nick. You know, I'm doin' all this work, but all I'm getting is $1000 a week."

I'm sure Beverly started talking in his ear, even though she didn't know a damn thing about the powder business. But if I were Frank, given the position he was in—ridin' an old deuce and a quarter, livin' on the ground floor in some raggedy-ass apartment, takin' a little blow when he had a little money—I would've been satisfied with my $1000 a week. I would've made my satisfaction known by not beefin', and I wouldn't have let my woman say a motherfuckin' thing about it.

Nothin'.

True, Frank was movin'. He was doin' a lot of combat in the inner trenches. But that was Frank's job! That's what he had to do in order for this partnership to exist! And if you give your word to a co-worker as far as money is concerned, you're supposed to keep it. That honor binds you with other honorable people. If you don't have it, the two of you are separate.

"All right, Frank," I said, "fine."

I upped his salary to five grand a week, and he grinded up the five till I got my money back. But I really didn't like that. His inability to understand that he had an opportunity greater than chump change.

I put his flaw in my mental Rolodex, but unfortunately forgot to recall it at the proper time.

In the downtime of the panics, I bought this out-of-service Sunoco station on Myrtle Avenue in Brooklyn. Didn't take much to get it up and running—all the tanks were there—but I wanted more than a front. I wanted a business that operated at a profit.

I knew from doing powder that you've gotta give customers something special. Your product must rise above the rest. In this case, I had to beat the Exxon station a few blocks over with a competitive advantage, something they didn't have.

That's when I got the idea: Fill your tank with gas? Get a free exterior car wash!

This ended up easier said than done.

A top-of-the-line wash requires hard work and skill. You gotta know how to simonize cars, lay on the right kind of wax, spray tires the correct way with the steam gun...just a whole lotta shit you take for granted when you get your car cleaned.

Doing full drive-through service got to be so exhausting—I was putting ten or twelve-hour days on this—I brought in Frank as a partner at some ridiculously low number. I got him up to speed on the ins and outs of the business, and once I felt secure leaving things in his hands, we traded off six-hour shifts.

But one day I opened the storeroom door to get some wax and these egg boxes of mannite just fell out! The whole room was loaded down with it!

"Frank? The fuck you doing, man?"

"It's cool, Gaps brought that over this morning along with the money he owes."

"Don't you understand this thing is separate from our drug operation?"

"Yo! This spot is perfect for meets! I just wash the car, then take the money from the backseat."

I had to explain to Frank that this was a legitimate business, that running a business means dealing with employees who aren't pushers, and customers who aren't junkies.

"True, but these customers? I'd take them out in a heartbeat."

He had a point. The black customers weren't a problem, but this was a mixed neighborhood, with Italians, Irish and Latinos, all a pain in the ass from time to time. Which got me thinkin'...

"Frank! Listen, man. What if we didn't have to deal with customers at *all*? What if the car wash could be *automated*?"

This was a revolutionary idea. Put your money in a slot and drive on through. The car gets washed and waxed, the blowers dry it and by the time you get out, the car is clean. We wouldn't have to go through the whole hassle of dealing with customers! One service person could run it all.

"That's good, Nick! You know what else, man? We oughta rename this car wash, let the neighborhood know black people own the place."

"Sounds kind of cool. I figure we can do that."

About a week later, Frank had the painters out. He'd renamed the place the "Right On! Car Wash" on this wide red, green and black banner. The tricolor of Black Power.

"The fuck is this, Frank!? People in this neighborhood are not black people! Why would the whites come here? They don't wanna hear that black is beautiful shit!"

"What difference does that make?"

"It's gonna make a lot of difference! The Italians aren't going to come! The Irish won't either!"

I was right. Everybody made the U-turn out of the Right On! Car Wash and headed to the Exxon station.

Man, I was pissed. I'd busted my ass, thirteen hours a day, spraying tires, vacuuming cars, wondering if the next customer was a DEA agent...and Frank got this red, green and black shit!

Well, that got the attention of the cops, and before long, the NYPD came into the neighborhood and handed out flyers with our pictures, saying we were known narcotics traffickers circulating drugs to their children.

My legitimate business went down the tubes. Aw man, it was too bad. The automated wash was a great idea. I was talking about that in the '70s, when nobody was doing it. I wanted to go as far as we could— incorporate, take it national, sell stock, go public…

That's how big I thought it could be.

If only I hadn't listened to Frank James. He wasn't in any shape to deal in the real world. He didn't think about anything but the drug money.

The Seven Samurai

I WAS SURPRISED when the NYPD caught on to my partnership with Frank. I kept a low profile and told Frank to do the same, but it was just too hard to hide the shitload of money we were making on the East Side. Street gossip develops when a guy like Frank moves from a South Bronx ghetto to a Long Island high-rise.

You can't stop that.

Now that we were heavy on the cop radar, we could either split until things cooled or build up our partnership to withstand the heat. Ultimately, I was just looking to make money and stay out of jail, but if I were to build something with Frank, I wanted it to last. I didn't want to put in all this effort, like I'd done with Reggie and Stan, only to end up back at square one.

There were a lot of reasons to keep me from doing it. Frank left bad marks in the way he handled that thousand-a-week incident and ruined my car wash. He hadn't even paid me my $10G for losing the bet!

Still, I didn't expect him to be a Boy Scout. You got to let a few things slide with ex-dope-fiend heroin dealers. And despite all his bullshit, I never had chemistry with a partner like I did with Frank.

You know, you kind of draw people into your life. You kind of create that chemistry that draws people into your life, whether it's for something positive or something negative. Well, me and Frank, we've got a *positive* chemistry.

There's something coming from me, and there's something coming from him, and it's magnetic. It pulls us together. And we feel this shit happening.

Maybe it was 'cause we *were* ex-dope-fiend heroin dealers. Maybe it was that Frank and I turned to Islam in Green Haven. Wherever it came from, Frank and I had it. Even when we were enemies on the street, Frank matched me tit for tat and slipped clean from my traps. He always knew what I was thinking.

"Yo, Nick, maybe we oughta bring in someone to help us work the East Side."

"Like who?"

"Wally Rice. He wants to be part of what we're doin', and he don't even know *what* we're doin'. All he knows is we're making money and his goods don't sell against ours."

That's chemistry! Right there. Frank read my mind and picked the perfect dude to be down with us. Wally Rice. He was Frank's old partner, a bright guy, a good hustler and an excellent ally.

"But don't you and Wally got beef?"

When Frank got sent to Green Haven, Wally was supposed to look out for his old lady. He fucked her instead.

"Naw, we cool now. He gonna be the other best man at my wedding."

As Frank and I sat in Wally's real estate office on 125th Street, I let him know my feelings on the situation. I simply didn't wanna go through an experience like I did with Goldfinger. If something happened to where I got pinched, I needed someone to look out for me and my women.

"Wally, I'll do the same for you, bro, but if you wanna be part of this, you gotta promise not to go pullin' the kind of shit you did with Frank."

"I promise," he said, quiet and reserved. "I was very young then."

With Wally in, Frank and I looked for other guys to get in our thing. Who would be good guys to be with? Who could we count on to take care of us, to look out for our families? Who would watch our backs in a crisis situation?

"As-Salaam-Alaikum, Brother Barnes."

There he was, behind the register at the boutique on 125th and Seventh. My mind flashed back ten years before, to the fair one of the '60s.

"That night in the hallway! You took that blade from Blue!"

"Yeah, they were gonna take you out that night, but since you put your shit in the glove...well, you know how the rules go."

Right On! Sista always talked about how her friend Helen Jones sold some nice things here. Sam was her husband.

"Yo, Frank, guess who I ran into when I got your wedding present? Sam Jones!"

"You mean Ishmael Mohammed. Just changed his name. Yeah, he's an honorable dude with a strong operation. He'd be good to bring in this. I was thinkin' 'bout Gaps, too. He could be our presence in Brooklyn."

Why not? There was enough opportunity on the streets of New York to make us all filthy rich. Man, it was amazing how the pieces just fell in. When it came time for everybody to be there, everybody was there!

We all wore white tuxes with black leather lapels as Frank James tied the knot. It was a strong crew. All four guys had street smarts, just like I had. We were all ex-dope fiends. We'd been to reformatory and all came through state prison in the '60s. We'd all made that prison conversion to Islam—all of us. We shared those experiences and they flowed between us, linking us all together.

As the wedding bells rang, moments with Gallo flooded my thoughts. In all our talks on the chemistry between Catholicism and the Cosa Nostra, I never mentioned my belief that Islam could do the same thing for a Black Mafia.

But I always knew it.

And without even realizing, like I was guided by something in the back of my mind, I'd created it.

Yeah, the Italians had their thing, but now? We had ours.

"The Council," said Ishmael. "That's what we should call ourselves. I came up with it last night after my readings."

It was a good name. I called the first meeting of the Council to order.

"The first step is to divide territory."

Gaps got Brooklyn all to himself. Wally, Ishmael and Frank were all East Side guys, so they carved out the specific areas they wanted to work in. My operation would cover the West Side. I'd face a lot of heat moving back there, but with four guys flanking me, I considered myself bulletproof.

Once we settled the turf, I laid out the rules: "No Council member can infringe upon the street location of another without permission. As for the powder, we can each bring in our suppliers with Council approval, but a brother must sell that powder to other brothers at the same price he paid for it. He cannot make extra money off another brother."

"You know, I've got this Avenue connect that—"

"Let's hold off on that, Wally. I've got someone who'll work fine for all of us."

Matty Madonna was back on the streets and sent word he wanted to see me. Our face-to-face was still pending, but I was sure he didn't just wanna reminisce about old times. Whatever the case, I was the guy connected to organized crime. I was the guy through whom their benevolence flowed. None of the brothers could get the shit I was getting.

"We're a brotherhood in the true sense, and a democracy in the true sense, so each brother will be entitled to one vote. All homicides must be unanimous, but if any matter comes to light that I don't approve of, it only seems right that I have the power of ultimate veto."

The brothers recognized that, knowing mine was the guiding energy that brought our whole thing together.

"Now understand what I'm about to say. I don't care if a guy falls, it is *not* his responsibility to take care of himself. A Council brother must be supported by the other Council brothers."

This was the most important rule. It meant paying lawyers, providing for a brother's needs and the needs of his family. It meant paying a brother a visit in the joint, doing things that didn't have a dollar value.

"And we gotta look after each other's women. No matter what. Under no circumstances may a Council member have intimate relations with the wife or women of another member."

It was clear who was driving this thing. I was in command. I was in control. But each brother needed to know his duty to me, and to the brotherhood.

"No matter what happens to us as individuals, the Council will remain strong. I want us to close ranks and watch each other's backs. I want a circle that *nobody* can penetrate."

"I don't know, Frank. He gotta big mouth, and I wanna keep this under wraps, keep our name *off* the street."

"Yeah, but Jazz is real excited to be part of what we're doing. You can trust him, man. You know that. I'd like to sponsor him."

I was ambivalent. I didn't have history with Jazz like Frank did. They grew up together as East Side guys. I only knew him through the Muslim brotherhood in Green Haven. At the same time, those days gave me plenty of love for the guy. He had a lot of heart, which was why I got him out of state prison in the first place.

Months earlier, when Frank told me Jazz had strong grounds for an appeal, I checked into the matter and discovered the prosecutor who sent him to state prison was now a partner in my lawyer's firm.

I figured that gave Jazz a good shot, but since Jazz couldn't rub two dimes together, I paid all his legal bills to see it through. Matter of fact, I even sent over Ray Robin, the bondsman on Baxter Street, to get him out on bail in the meantime.

I sent Jazz a package on consignment to get his street legs moving again, and while his turnover wasn't as fast as I'd like, that was okay. He hustled hard, managed the package well and managed his people well. He'd only improve under my watch.

Plus, he'd made some inroads on the West Side. I could use another guy to flank me there. He was raw and close to the street, a good source of information for what was going on in the neighborhood.

All in all, Jazz fit the profile. He'd be a valuable addition to what we were doing. He was a bright guy and a good hustler, and even though he had a little guy's 'plex—always running his mouth—I could count on him to be loyal. 'Cause without me, Jazz would still be rotting in Green Haven. And he knew it.

"Man," said Jazz between puffs of Buddha, "they oughta have concerts and shit. You could even make an album. Curtis Mayfield at Green Haven. Yeah, I could probably hook that up with my entertainment connections."

Jazz loved to talk about the joint when he was high. How Attica would be a better place if they did this and that. But to me and Frank? That was a no-no. We *never* talked about the joint.

"Get the fuck out of here, Jazz! Quit talkin' about the joint!"

"You gotta admit. It's a good idea…"

Now that we'd voted Jazz into the Council, we threw him a private freak party at the Flash Inn, a big hustler hangout on 125th and St. Nicholas.

"Yo, Nick! There's this kid Guy outside. Said you're expecting him."

"Yeah, Smitty, let him in."

I'd been hearing a lot about Guy through my new woman Thelma. He was the main man of her girlfriend Olive MacDonald, and Olive had been twisting Tee's arm to set up a meet.

"She's really anxious to see Guy rise. She thinks the one thing he needs is a steady supplier like you."

I knew Olive well through Jimmy Terrell—she was running his mill for a while, so I knew it wasn't a setup. I also placed a lot of trust in Tee's instincts. If she thought Guy was sharp, I figured it was worth a meet.

"Mr. Barnes," he said, extending his hand, "I'm Guy Fisher."

It was a solid first impression, despite his blue Chuck Taylors. He dressed inexpensive, off-the-rack sharp, but his clothes were new and neatly pressed. Didn't look like he made too much money, but that was fine, 'cause a lotta people weren't making money with me in the picture. Mainly the streets were mine.

I invited him into my booth and offered him a drink.

"I don't really drink alcohol," he said, but when Frank laughed at his club soda, Guy didn't flinch. The kid was strapped with confidence. I respected that.

"Tee says you're looking for a chance," I said.

"That's right, I won't let you down."

I went through the drill with Guy—"You have a stash? A car?"

"I make my drops with an old VW Bug. Not much, but it does the trick."

"What kind of operation do you have?"

"Got a few guys dealin' for me. Can't pay them full time, so they keep their day jobs. Really loyal, though. That's what's important."

I liked Guy. He was an outgoing, friendly, good-looking kid, a young dude doing all the right things, just like me at his age. But I wasn't running some youth outreach program. I needed to know his turnover, how much I could make off him.

Guy told me he wanted big powder, more than I would've thought.

"And I'll turn it in five days."

"That's ambitious, Guy. Ten days is fine. Just don't give me excuses on this and that. I don't wanna hear anything. All I want is my money."

"Like I said, I'll get it to you in five."

As I talked through the details with Guy, Ishmael stepped into the booth and gave me the sign.

"Guy, you'll have to excuse me."

"The fuck else am I supposed to do at my freak party? Motherfuckin' ho oughta know the rules!"

I drove Jazz in silence to his West Harlem apartment, my mind caught up in our last moments at the Flash Inn—the girl screaming in the bathroom stall, Jazz pushin' up against her, yellin', "Bitch! Keep still…"

"Jazz, we don't party like that. If it happens again, you can't roll with us. Understood?"

He took a drag of his zing and handed it over. I refused. I'd had enough party for one night.

"I've been thinking, Nick. It don't seem quite right what we're doing. We just have six people in our thing."

Tempted to make it five.

"Why not, Jazz?"

"Got to make it seven. You know, for luck."

Relationships evolve, either up or down. Olive and Thelma were getting closer on a social level. Guy and I hung out more through them. Naturally, I started to consider him a candidate for the Council.

It wasn't a matter of me liking him, thinkin' he was a cool dude. His money was always correct and turned in properly. He never was late with anything. When he made drops, he was there on time. I gave him more packages to pick up and he never slowed down.

I had independent ways to determine what he was doing—Where did he operate? What was his crew like? My people knew what was going on the street; they checked my questions. I found out that Guy worked the South Bronx, and I wanted presence there, a hub we could build off of. Plus, Guy was a go-getter with a fresh face, a different face from the guys on the West or the East Side. Couple brothers knew enough about him to say he wasn't a snitch, wasn't wired and wouldn't be runnin' the flimflam with the powder. He had credentials and they were correct.

Wasn't quite Muslim like we were. His generation hadn't done that prison conversion in the '60s, but came up from the path of the Five Percenters. This was a splinter group of the Nation of Islam that had a rep for being a little irreverent to the older crew—they believed blacks were gods, that they were part of the 5 percent of people who knew the truth—but Guy's faith easily accommodated what we were about.

I made my case to the Council.

Any new member had to have a sponsor and be approved by unanimous vote. This was my system. Even if a dealer interested me, the Council might see something negative in him that I couldn't. A bad egg could be harmful to all of us, so it was best for everybody to pass judgment.

Frank James was the only one who had reservations.

"I'm telling you, Nick, he's not qualified, and I don't trust nobody in this business who don't drink, use drugs or smoke. We don't know how he gets his kicks. Maybe somethin's drivin' him we don't know about."

"Frank, that's not a good enough reason for me."

And nobody dared question my authority.

"It should be our oath of unity," said Ishmael, bleary-eyed from his all-nighter. "All seven of us should link hands in a circle. Each man can speak one word until the vow is complete."

"That's good, man. That's really, really good."

The atmosphere turned scared as we crossed our arms across our chests and held hands. That was important. Crossing arms before you linked hands. If you only linked hands, you'd only have solidarity in the group.

But this way? I embraced myself. I felt the power flow between the brotherhood and *me*, from my back up to my shoulders through my whole body. Of all my highs, I'd never had one as good as this. This was our circle. Nobody could penetrate us. This was my family.

Frank spoke first, then Wally, then Gaps, Ishmael, Jazz, Guy and finally, me.

"Treat...My...Brother...As...I...Treat...Myself."

High off of brotherhood, I launched into business.

"If we're all going to treat each other as equals, we *all* should have access to the source. I'm going to introduce us all to Madonna. We should all have access to the powder. We all need to share in the power."

It was the right decision. I knew I wouldn't regret it.

ACT THREE

REVENGE

1977-1998

Treat My Brother as
I Treat Myself

THE HOLE IS NONTIME. That you are learning nothing, doing nothing, is the worst. But even though I was stuck in solitary, I didn't feel alone, 'cause my brothers were backin' me on the outside. I knew that. And once I got outta the Hole, I wanted to help them any way I could, even from behind bars. Same for my women, Mecca and Tee. They were good to me. I wanted to help them, too.

Fuck, man, I was forty-five years old, halfway through my life. I had a lot to do. Move more powder, take the Council legit...

But here I was, a lion in a cage. I wanted out. I wanted to hunt. I wanted to fuck my women. I wanted to roar.

Took seven months till Breitbart managed to get me out on a court order, but when they finally released me into the general population at Marion, my status soared. Few had been in the Hole so long without breakin' or goin' nuts. But it only steeled me up, made me hungry to make some moves.

Marion was a great place to do it. Believe it.

Every time I went to prison I came out with better contacts in the powder game. You can associate with known felons without getting into trouble, and don't even have to worry about surveillance 'cause they can already see you! And in Marion? They didn't have any quarter-bag dealers. No, they only had the big boys. The biggest suppliers.

And here I was, the biggest distributor.

I had just finished another chess game in the yard when Herbie Sperling got up from his dominoes and came over. A tough Jew from the Avenue, Herbie grew up with the Italians and acted like he was one of them.

Along with Mikey Coco, he'd been one of the top three importers in the city, and, like me, was in for life on conspiracy, busted in a big shakedown on Pleasant Avenue in '73. I remember hearing that when the cops arrested him in a rented Benz and found two pistols in the glove and an axe under the seat, "You can be fucking sure I'll never rent no car from Avis again," Herbie told them.

He gave me a smile with his friendly, pudgy face, but I knew better. Before he went in, he got to the guy who ratted him out. Cops found the victim's torso in the back of a burning car. The only way they could identify the body was from the guy's teeth…in his stomach.

"Nicky, I have someone. Someone good who has product and needs to move it."

"Who you mean? I know 'em all."

"Mark Reiter. Call him 'Jew Boy,' like me. Late twenties. Small-time coke dealer—ran a chop shop and other work. I like him, so I hooked him up with my people in France, in Italy. He's gonna be bringing in a lot of product, but he wants someone reliable to move it."

"How you know him?"

"He was on Gotti's crew working under the Gambinos, but he ain't no more. Gotti had to kick him out on account of his selling dope, 'cause the family wanted it that way, but that was just a show thing. Still works for Gotti and Gotti's still in dope, but I figure you know people in Harlem who can take the shit."

I asked Herbie the only questions that matter: "How much he got? What can I do it on? Price?"

"I gotta talk to Mark, but the price'll be good and it won't have been too stepped on. And Nick, you know, I'm kinda hopin' my son, hey, his name's Nick too, I'm kinda hopin' he can help here as a middleman thing. He's turnin' twenty-one. Good kid but needs some direction in life."

"Lemme think about it, Herbie."

In November of 1978, Frank came to visit me. We sat down in the visitors room and talked face to face.

"And how are all of you doing? How's Guy?"

"He gettin' a lotta action off PCP and dust."

"Why no powder?"

"Ever since we stopped doin' business with Coco, Guy kinda been doin' his own thing."

"Coco was top shelf! Probably the best importer in New York! Why the fuck would you stop doing business with Coco?"

"Prices too high. Plus, he always stayed on our case for money."

"Was he not gettin' paid on time?!"

This didn't sound good. If Guy wasn't maintaining with my suppliers, then I sure as shit was not gettin' money, and neither would the Council. Took me *years* to build those relationships, and if these guys were fuckin' it up? That'd be the end of everything.

"But things are better, Nick, 'cause I got this dude Vinnie who gonna hook us up. He's good."

"Mikey Coco is not good, Frank. Mikey Coco is the best."

"Yeah? Well, Vinnie got a lawyer in Philly who can get you out of jail in three months. All he needs is a hundred G."

"Why the fuck don't the Council give it to him?!"

"Well, we weren't too sure of what we should do," Frank waffled.

"That's why I came to you, to get your decision. I mean, if you say it's a go-go thing, we'll, uh, we'll take care of it. But we didn't know if…"

"Gimme the lawyer's name."

"I don't have it."

"Then get it for me. I'll make sure you're not talkin' to a federal agent. And what about Breitbart? Council paid him, right?"

"We gonna get together on that. See, we're a little short on money since we got rid of Coco."

"Frank, Frank! You listen to me. The guy who's gonna get me outta here ain't some friend of Vinnie in Philly! It's Breitbart, you hear me? Council gotta get him paid! You guys gotta take care of this and take care of me! You tell 'em. You tell the brothers to get me fuckin' outta here!"

On April 23, 1979, the U.S Court of Appeals for the Second Circuit denied my appeal. Breitbart said we would go to the U. S. Supreme Court.

I didn't have many visitors at Marion, because it was a lot of work for anyone to come out to see me for such a short time. Still, people came. They started coming more and more 'cause of problems back home, decisions which had to be made, or they wanted to fill me in on situations.

Late in '79, Thelma, Frank's wife Beverly and Ishmael's wife Helen came to visit like three foxy browns. I could only see one visitor at a time, so as they strutted in, one after the other, the inmates were checkin' it out and shakin' their heads.

I saw Tee first. I couldn't touch her, but she was nice to look at. The silky thighs and wet pussy I had to imagine, but just to see that soft, feminine skin, that long hair?

Shit, at Marion, that was heterosexual sex!

After being in prison, you'd be surprised how satisfying it is just to sit near an attractive woman.

"I heard about this thing with Mecca, baby. The fuck you thinkin'?"

Thelma's mother just died, so I didn't want to be too hard, but she was doin' some stupid shit that needed correction. I'd recently gotten a letter from Shamecca. I'd told Guy to buy her a BMW and she'd been seen driving it around Harlem, so when she was parked in front of the restaurant El Mundial near 116th and Seventh, Tee knew it was hers and knew I bought it.

Well, Tee stormed in the restaurant and got into it with Mecca—screaming at each other, pushing and clawin' until the guys broke it up and scooted Mecca out. They left Tee-Bone alone. They knew they best not fuck with Tee-Bone.

Mecca left and drove down 116th, but Thelma ran out the restaurant, got into her Volvo and just rammed Mecca's BMW, a full-on collision. Pinned her against a parked car.

The two women get out of their cars and they're screamin' again and goin' at each other. And now there are two nice new wrecked cars in the middle of the street. So the police pull up, arrest both women and take 'em to the precinct.

"You wrecked the Volvo, you wrecked Mecca's car. They're both mine, woman!"

"I get it, okay. So look, I'm having problems with the dealers. They're slow with the money and say the dope's too weak to turn. People at the mill are getting lax, too. And I need more manita, baby. Where am I gonna get manita?"

I thought about it. Tee ran a great table, but dealing is a bitch. It's a lot harder for a woman, too, 'cause without havin' threat of enforcement to deal with bad customers on the retail side, she was going to have to team up.

"Hey, listen, here's what I want you to do; it's simple. On your next key or half-key, give half to Curt. He'll sell that as weight. Then give the other half to Ricky Miller." Ricky was one of my better dealers. "Ricky'll take that to the street, and he'll handle the milling and dealing and all that shit. You ain't gotta do a damn thing otherwise, hear me?"

"But I can mill and…"

"No! Don't, don't bother, baby. You just stay cool."

"But I wanna give it all to Ricky. You told me you get the real money by takin' it to the street!"

I understood her impulse for bigger profit, but she was just deceiving herself thinkin' she could do what I did.

"Listen, there's just too much shit you gotta consider in a street biz. You got to check the temperature on the street, you gotta calculate the cut, get the manita, run the mill, make the collections. Curt'll just sell that weight like Madonna did with me. He'll turn it over with no hassle, little risk."

"But I'll only make $20G per key that way! With Ricky I can clear $60,000, maybe even—"

"You wanna be in weight, baby, not hand to hand! That's how it's gonna be. You're a mother, Thelma. If you wanna fuck around with dealin', deal with our children! Spend your time dealin' with *them*!"

"Yeah, I know, I know. But after your birthday? I'm gonna stop sellin'. I'm getting out of it all, Nick. I'm going to get my GED, then do somethin' I want or start somethin'."

I just looked at her, blank.

"Yeah, I am!"

"We'll see about that."

Beverly James sat down and took her place, filling me in on Wally Rice's wife Natalie. I had heard about it, but Beverly had actually been there. While Wally was in prison he kept up trade through his wife. Only Natalie was not exactly Thelma. She ended up selling an eighth and forty pounds of Q to a DEA agent for $70,000.

"And I walked in on it!" said Beverly. "I went to visit her shop and the DEA was putting cuffs on Natalie! And then they pulled their guns on me and grabbed this baggie I had in my hand, but what's really funny? All that was in the baggie was a sandwich. I brought it over 'cause I thought

Natalie might be hungry."

That was my first laugh in a while. Beverly gettin' busted over a tuna fish sandwich.

"So, Nick, I wanna ask you somethin'."

"What's that, girl?"

"You know anything about who killed my brother?"

Damn you, Frank. I did not want to deal with this.

"Beverly, I heard about that and I'm so sorry. Rusty was a real good kid."

"Some people say it was Frank, but I can't believe that. I just can't. They got along fine. My brother was such a handsome, happy guy, it just really bothers me. But sometimes at night, I just lie in the bed and think—"

"Wasn't Frank," I lied. "He was real shook up about Rusty when he told me what happened. Rusty was his best guy, Beverly, his go-to guy. So no, it wasn't Frank."

"I know, I know. I just had to be sure. I had to ask you. You always tell it like it is. We love you, Nick. Everything you've done."

"You take care of Frank for me, girl."

Because that dude better start gettin' it together.

Helen Jones sat down, just as distressed as Beverly, but more worn out, like she'd been hittin' the pipe a little too heavy. We always got along real well, but I didn't have the history with Ishmael's wife like I did with Beverly.

Seemed a little strange, her comin' all the way out here to see me.

"Nick, I...I thought maybe you could talk to Ishmael."

"What's the problem?"

"It's that he's...he likes to rough me up before sex, Nick. That's what he does. At one time it was all right and all, I guess, but now there's more pain than pleasure. I tried to tell him, but...He can't figure out why I don't like it that way anymore. He thinks it means our relationship's suffering, and—"

"There's nothing I can do here, Helen. One man can't interfere in another man's private life."

I kept my real thoughts to myself. The irony was Ishmael, the one who revered Islam and preached the Koran, who told us we had to respect our women? A sexual deviant who took it out on the woman who loved him most. That's who he really was.

"I mean, it's not like it's savage brutality, but I...I just don't like it, and—"

"Helen? Never tell Ishmael you told me this. He would raise hell if he knew you'd said it to me."

Helen sighed, defeated. "Maybe he'll ease up. But I wanted to tell you anyway."

"You gotta talk to *him* about it. Be strong. But you gotta stick with him, too. You gotta help him and support him."

I had to say that, 'cause Ishmael really did need Helen, and she needed to be with him and put him in the right frame of mind for getting business done. That's all I cared about. When it came down to it, his woman was only important if she kept him happy and turning powder.

"I'm really grateful to you, Nick. And Ishmael, he really depends on you. I don't like him having to depend on anybody, but since it's you, I'm okay with it. You know what I think one of the problems is in all this? He and Frank are using a lot of blow. I think a lot of the violence comes from that. Those two have been really taking to the blow lately."

My tax attorneys, Bolden and Blake, finally came to visit me in Marion with that white dude Goldman in tow. Inside the lawyers' conference room, they explained that to protect my assets from government seizure and from a criminal tax liability, I needed to sign over my assets to Goldman and his wife. They'd hold the properties and the monies, then funnel it back when I got out or give it to whoever I appointed, like my children.

"It's the smart thing to do," said Bolden.

"You can shield your assets, avoid taxes and make some money at the same time," said Blake. "We're simply not legally allowed to own the assets ourselves."

Now, I had a lot of reservations about Goldman from the start, but I'd been working with Bolden and Blake for a long while, and they'd been doin' all the right things for me. So I trusted my instincts and started signing and initialing document after document.

We were all real excited about this.

On April 22, 1980, I sat in the law library reading the *New York Times* when I stumbled across an item in the B section. "Barnes Appeal: The Supreme Court refused to review the conviction of Leroy (Nicky) Barnes, said to be one of the major narcotics distributors in the New York area."

And that was it. Unless Breitbart could get me a new trial altogether, I would not be getting out through legal means.

There was no exit.

In the summer of '80, Ishmael came out to visit. He was all fucked up over the Natalie Rice situation.

"She's never been pinched. Council wonders if she gonna stand up under pressure. You know, they could use her to get to us. You think we should take her out?"

"Are you fuckin' nuts? How can the Council think about killing the wife of a member?! You and Frank, you two gotta quit basin' so much, man. You gettin' paranoid!"

I put aside Ishmael's crazy talk and got down to some real business.

"What's happenin' on the Apollo? I put $500G on that, and I know you put somethin' in, too. What's up with the money on that?"

Ishmael kind of shrugged.

"Things aren't working out the way we thought. Anyway, it's not in our hands. Don't worry, though. Guy's on top of everything."

I tried not to lose my patience, but the Council was getting stupid and lazy, a bad combination.

"Listen, man, you gotta monitor Guy! If he don't have the Apollo up and actually running as a front, then the IRS gonna be all over *you*. Understand me? And what happened with that lawyer Frank said could get me out for $100,000?"

"Frank said to let you know we're gonna put up ten grand and you put up the rest."

"What?! Frank can fuck himself. I'm the one in fuckin' federal prison. Treat me as you would treat yourself!"

I banged my fist on the table. Damn, I was so angry. I had to check myself so the guard didn't come over.

"I dunno, Nick, maybe things'd be better if you can find us someone with cheaper powder. I mean, we have everything ready, just no product."

I tried to simmer down. They were still my brothers and my only shot to get out of the joint. I had to work with them.

"I'm in touch with a guy, Herbie Sperling, here about a new connection."

Ishmael looked like he just found paradise.

"Yeah? That guy's big! How much he want?"

"He hasn't told me yet."

"This is great, man. Thank you, Nick, you always come through. Can you get us some details? This just what we need. We can do this on consignment, right? Aw, man. We get this? We can take care of you on everything."

Just like Frank, Ishmael was counting on me to provide the magic bullet supplier, someone who was gonna take care of them the way Madonna took care of all of us. And here I had this great source, Herbie's guy Mark Reiter. And with the prices Reiter was offering and quality of the goods Herbie said he had, the Council could make money. Big money.

But as I'm thinkin' 'bout all the Council's bullshit, I'm wondering why I should just hand over the Reiter connection when all they will do is fuck it up? I am *pissed* at the Council. They been fuckin' me over by not taking care of business! So I go to someone with more smarts, bigger balls and better instincts than all of them.

I summoned Thelma to Marion.

It was July 4, 1980 when I sat down with her. She always came to see me for Independence Day. But she looked bad, with two swollen black eyes. Not from a beating, but from a cosmetic surgeon on Fifth Avenue who removed the bags from under her eyes. I didn't get it. Tee was all of twenty-eight! She just had too much money on her hands. *My* money.

Well, if she wanted to spend it, I was gonna give her a chance to make it. See, Thelma was gonna deliver my nonverbal message to the Council: I got this new source. But I'm not givin' it to you. I'm givin' it to my woman. If you want access to it, you gotta go through her. 'Cause you've been fuckin' me over.

"He's gotta *good* package, Tee, stepped on but not stomped to death."

"What can I do with it?"

That was Thelma, always the pro.

"The powder's good, the real thing, so you could do a ten on it, but I don't want you cuttin' it at all. I want you handing it right over to your new customer."

"Who's that?"

"The Council."

Oh, my woman liked that.

But what she said next just tore me up.

"Baby, I saw your little bitch Shamecca with Guy at the basketball game. Guess they're real tight now, 'cause she had her hands up in his hair and that. I even think he got the BMW fixed for her."

I put it down to Tee talkin' smack, but as I replayed it in my mind, it kinda made sense. I could see Shamecca getting overinvolved with Guy based on the fact that I brought him and her together and told her, "This is my brother, treat him as you treat me." Of course that didn't include fuckin' him, but I could see how that language could lead to some intimacy.

The idea of it all just kind of blew my mind. I wouldn't have even wanted to sleep with any woman who Guy considered his woman. It's like fucking your brother's wife; it's not something you wanna do.

I had to find out whether or not he'd been banging Shamecca. I had to find out. The problem was I couldn't ask anyone on the Council about it. I couldn't accuse a fellow brother without proof. But I had ways of finding out, and if the truth came out that he was bangin' Mecca?

Well, he knew the oath. He knew the penalty for breaking it.

"What's this business I hear about you and Guy?"

I asked it kind of halfheartedly, 'cause I just wasn't sure.

Shamecca just opened her pretty little mouth in shock, denying it like it was the craziest thing she'd ever heard. I didn't interrogate her that forcefully about it for now.

I dunno, maybe I didn't really wanna know.

But I'd been doin' a lot of thinking about the Mecca situation. See, before I went to jail, I expected Guy to be an honorable dude, and set it up to where he'd be the one to provide for Shamecca. To remedy this, I needed to give Shamecca another source of income, means to support herself that had no ties to Guy.

That's why I decided to set her up with Reiter, too, just like I did Thelma.

"Mecca, I'm gonna set you up with a package."

"Can I take notes on all this?"

She just wanted to be the good student.

"You can't take notes on any of this, baby. This ain't Greek history. You just get that car key from Reiter when you meet with him, hand it to your brother and tell him to put a ten on the package. He'll know what to do from there."

The plan was for her brother Son to take Reiter's powder to the streets. But Son needed muscle, too. He was a good kid, but didn't have a rep for street toughness.

"I want Son to talk to my nephew. Mellon can make sure Son gets all the money ready for you to give to Reiter."

"I got it."

She nodded, so excited. In that moment, she was mine again, but in that moment I destroyed her, too. She was going from a City College student to hustlin' heroin. But she wanted it bad, and all I could think of was getting her away from Guy.

The Choice

IN DECEMBER 1980, everything at Marion stopped. An inmate stabbed the associate warden and the entire prison was put on lockdown, same as solitary except it happens to everybody. My cellblock got one hour a day in the yard. No law library, no visits, no speaking to other prisoners. I couldn't talk to Herbie about the meets with my girls. I couldn't investigate the Guy situation.

I couldn't do a goddamn thing.

After four months of lockdown, in April 1981, Breitbart got me transferred to Terre Haute, Indiana. Now, no federal pen is a breath of fresh air, but at Terre Haute I got easy access to the thing I'd been dying for—information.

On my very first day there I saw J.J. from Guy's crew, doing his time from our conviction. I asked him what the fuck was going on with the Council, but in the three years J.J. had been in prison, Guy never visited him either. But that was the least of it.

"Guy and his crew have been doing well, I hear, running weed the past two years. But with all the money he's making, he ain't given my woman a dime. Nothin'! Same deal with Chico Bob."

Chico Bob was back on the street on a "B minus number," which meant he got early parole. I loved Bob's loyalty, work ethic and education, but apparently, Guy considered these qualities weaknesses. He was supposed to have given Bob $500 a week that whole time he was in the joint, but when Bob came home, Guy didn't give him anything but a story. Worse, according to J.J., Guy had been fuckin' Bob's old lady while he was away!

"What about Guy and Shamecca? You heard anything about them?"

"Nuh-unh. Wouldn't be surprised, though. Guy ain't playin' on the up and up no more. He hoggin' up all that money he makin'! Just bought three Rolls. A Lear Jet, too."

Then J.J. gave me the only good news of the day.

"I'm working in the mailroom, see. And the officer who's my supervisor? He's a dude. Bent the rules a bit and gave me a key to the officer's room. There's a phone there—said I could use it to call my old lady—but I could deliver messages for you, man!"

I had a better idea.

With J.J. downstairs in receiving workin' on the case, I got Frank to mail in work shoes, honey, long johns, hand warmers—different things J.J.'s supervisor wanted. Since the mail came right to J.J., J.J. gave this shit right to him. In return, I got unlimited access to the telephone.

Now, I can find out things.

"You heard anything on Mecca and Guy?"

I got ahold of Eddie Big Hands on the line. I knew I could trust Eddie. We used to hustle back in the day.

"I dunno 'bout them, but I did see Tito Johnson at the Sandwich Oasis."

I knew Tito a long time. He was a dealer and a compulsive gambler. Years before he was at Riker's with me, and when I put up my bail, I took care of his too, so he could get out. That man owed me so many times.

"Well, what of it, Eddie?"

"Thelma was sitting next to him at the Flash Inn."

"What?!"

But I don't think it's a big thing, 'cause I know she be gettin' coke from him."

"Why Tee gotta go to a low-level muthafucka like Tito to get coke? Why can't she get coke from the Council?"

"I dunno, man. I dunno."

I hung up the phone and called Thelma right then at our penthouse on Haven Avenue.

"Are you gettin' overexotic with this dude Tito?"

She brushed it off immediately.

"I don't know what you're hearing, but nothing's happening. Just gettin' a little coke from him, that's all."

"Why can't you get your blow from the Council?"

"Tito's got *real* good coke, baby."

So I put all this in my mental Rolodex for a while. Thought about it. Man, she *couldn't* be fuckin' an underling. The idea of it all just made my stomach turn.

I called back Eddie Big Hands.

"Listen, dude, you need to be my eyes and ears in Harlem. I want you on Thelma like a parole officer."

I called my nephew Mellon to see what he knew on Mecca and Guy. Mellon said he hadn't heard anything about it, and since he was family, I didn't doubt his word.

"Only problem is Reiter's been cuttin' back on Mecca's packages. I think it's Son's fault. He too soft. He ain't got the muscle to hit the streets hard and get the paper on time."

I wasn't sure that was the case. Mellon was just pissed the package was comin' through Son and not him.

I kept calling around, asking lieutenants and middlemen the story, and found out the Council owed a lot of money to Reiter. I'm thinkin', "Why would they take out a package on consignment and not pay the supplier? What are they gonna do at the end of the day when they need more powder?" And sure enough, Reiter wouldn't give them any more goods unless they paid cash upfront.

Then I find out the Council made a couple big buys from Reiter, only these buys were *bad* buys. Before, if we didn't like the goods we could say, "Man, that ain't nothing. We ain't payin' 2 million for that shit." That's why you got to get your goods on consignment. That's why you got to keep a strong rep in business, so suppliers know you're reliable!

But the Council fucked up our spotless credit line, and now that they were stuck with the bunk goods?

It was too late. Lost all their money on garbage.

Kind of mind-boggling these guys could fuck up so much, all from letting our well-oiled machine break down, from not turning the package and payin' on time in the first place.

I had to figure a way to take control again, 'cause at the very least I *still* needed the Council to get me out of the joint. Our alternate plan was once Breitbart ran out of tricks, we were gonna have to do a jailbreak. I knew it could be done, but I'd have to have a support system to do it.

And right now, that support just wasn't there.

Eddie Big Hands was waiting in front of the Oasis when my Triple White rolled up. He thought Thelma was driving, but she was just riding shotgun.

LEROY "NICKY" BARNES

Tito was driving.

"Tito drivin' my white on white in white Benz?!"

It was just too outrageous to believe.

"Yeah," said Eddie. "He even rolled down the window and waved for me to come over. Thelma just smiled at me."

For three days I tried to catch Thelma at our penthouse, using every free moment to make my calls. When I finally reached her, all she had to say was, "Nicky, I been busy."

"I want you to get a flight here tonight!"

An hour later I called again to see what flight she got. A guy answered. I could hear my kids playing in the background.

"Who this?"

The voice on the other line copped a Jamaican accent. "I'm from da super of da buildin', mon. Jus' cleanin' da place. Paintin' an' cleanin'!"

I slammed the phone down. Tee's letting Tito live in my house! With my children!

When she showed to visit, I asked straight up what was happening.

"What do you want from Tito?"

I was mad as a motherfucker. I mean, I gave her fur coats, custom-made jewelry and imported leather jackets from Spain. I even had Louis Vuitton boots made for her!

"If you stay with him, that's your business, but you give me back *my* money, *my* car, *my* penthouse and the clothes you bought with *my* money. Then you and Tito can go and get on with it!"

My voice started shaking, so Thelma left the visitors room and went to the ladies' room, because I was about to bust her jaw right there.

J.J. handed over a large manila envelope that came to me in the mail. No return address. No note, no signature, nothin'. Only a blank piece of letterhead—*The Drug Enforcement Administration*—and two dozen pictures, color, of Guy eating with Shamecca, kissing Shamecca, holding Shamecca at a basketball game in Harlem.

And to think what I did for this Guy...

Man, I turned him on to get money. Did things for him I wish somebody in my life had done for me. I treated him like a brother. When I first saw this muthafucka he had on sneakers and was drivin' a Volkswagen. When I left him he had two Benzes and a BMW. That's a big difference. He didn't know what it was to have jewelry or a solid reputation in that powder game. He got all that through me.

And this is what he did; he banged my woman and then he styled about it on the street. He made it known, through this public demonstration of affection for Shamecca at these basketball games, that he had my woman. Fuckin' Guy. Had to have Shamecca. Just had to have her and had to make it known. Thing with Guy and Mecca is, I didn't have to hear about that! I doubt *she* wanted me to hear about it. But he wanted me to!

If Guy said, "Man, I wanna bang that!" I would have said okay. But not the way it happened. The way he was stylin' and profilin'. Like he just took all my shit. The king is dead. Long live the king. You know what I'm sayin'? And I'm thinking, "This faggot-ass muthafucka is letting people know that he has got a bone in my *woman*!" Three or four million women in New York. Why her? Because she was mine! I'm sayin' to myself, "What does that mean, nigger? That you do that to her?"

Well, look what I'm gonna do to you. Stupid muthafucka.

"I want you to lay down Guy in the ground. I want that nigga horizontal. Lay him down and I'll read about it. You don't have to tell me a motherfuckin' thing. I'll just read about it. I get the Amsterdam News."

I'm behind the glass as I'm talkin' to Frank. He's clean-shaven, has his jewelry on, but he's beginning to not look right. Fat. Not talking coherent and concerned with nonsense.

I'm real disappointed in how Frank's representing himself, how he and the brothers fucked up every chance I gave them to get their shit together. But if he did the work like I told him to? That was a start. We could cut the cancer and heal from there.

"Okay, man. Okay. I'll take care of it immediately."

"Good. I'll even give you a guy to warm up on. You know Tito Johnson?"

As the weeks pass, I'm not hearing a goddamn thing from Frank, so I pick up the phone and tell him I've been reading the *Amsterdam News* every day, but ain't reading a word about what I wanna read!

"Uh, yeah, Nick, umm, I've been thinking. Problem is the Council relies on Guy for a lot of things. We've all got that investment in the Apollo together, and the IRS is all over that now, so I don't think…"

Like dealing with a bunch of goddamn children.

"Frank, the only thing, the only motherfuckin' thing you have to worry about right now is doing what I told you."

Frank says he'll take care of it, again. But he doesn't.

I think some part of Frank wanted to knock out Guy for me, but maybe he either had too much history with Guy or just didn't hold our oath very sacred. At the same time, this is going into my fifth year in the joint. That was a big thing, 'cause Frank and them were beginnin' to realize, *this muthafucka ain't comin' out.* They believed I didn't have power anymore, and were makin' decisions based on that.

But I *know* the brothers are not as mentally sharp as I am!

And if I can't run this motherfucker no more, I sure can wreck it.

I mean, Guy is one thing, but to *not knock out a bum-ass nigger like Tito?!* Then I find out the real reason why Frank ain't layin' him down. Tito's supplying him and Ishmael with coke! Not even weight! Just personal sniff coke! Nothin' gonna happen to Tito as long as he's the one they going through! These guys would rather let Tito live than provide me honor and go without sniff coke!

But if they let Tito live, they're *certainly* gonna let Guy go. And I had to get Guy. I'd do anything to bring Guy down. Motherfucker tried to eat my heart out, like it says in African folklore—if you eat another warrior's heart his strength is yours. Well, I'm gonna *feast* on his! Got to make him pay! Got to make him pay...

So I started plottin'. How to do what I wanted to do.

On Monday, July 6, leaving the mess hall, I saw Ron Thompson, who'd left Marion and was now assistant warden at Terre Haute. His rep at the prison was a troubleshooter who took care of problems, so I knew arranging a call-out with him wouldn't arouse suspicion.

That afternoon I was interrupted while mopping the gym floor. The guards escorted me to the warden's offices, and a few minutes later, Ron called me in.

"What can I do for you, Nick?"

"Well, I been having some problems with my people. I mean my people on the outside. I want to speak to the U.S. Attorney's office, I want to speak to Bill Tendy, he's big up there, about maybe, about...doing some work."

I think Ron tried to hide it, but he was surprised. "That's fine. We can do it right now." He picked up the phone and dialed. It took a while until he could finally get Tendy on the line, but Ron briefly explained, then handed the phone over to me.

"Nick?" asked Tendy. "Okay, go ahead. Tell me what you have in mind."

When Tendy and his people had asked me to cooperate countless times, I'd told 'em to fuck themselves time and again. This must've been a nice moment for him.

"Well…. You mean specifically, right?"

"Well, no, just generally—the reason you want to get in touch with me."

"In general? There are a few friends of mine…former friends of mine that were just…that were supposed to be doing things for me, you know?"

"Yeah?"

"And they're doing things against me, really. And I have no way to reach out to get to 'em. And I want to get back at 'em."

"Um-hum."

"That's my primary reason."

"Yeah?"

"And I wanted to know what I could possibly do, you know? What it is you might want?"

"I understand. I can take care of this."

Exactly a week after my talk with Tendy, I got a call-out in the athletic room: "Barnes to visiting." When I got to the Terre Haute visitors room, a huge area, the guard said I'd been assigned a private room along the wall to speak to my lawyer.

In Marion you couldn't meet anybody in private. You couldn't conceal anything there or talk to anybody without people knowing. That's why I never would've cooperated in Marion. Still, I had to be careful.

I stepped inside the small room and closed the door. "Mr. Barnes?" A dark-haired man sat there in a suit. He spoke quietly. "I'm DEA Group Supervisor Larry Gallina. Last week you spoke to Bill Tendy. He asked me to come out to see you."

"You the one sent me the pictures?"

"No, but it was my idea."

"Yeah? Well, it worked."

"Look, Nick, we don't have a lot to offer here, you know that."

"I don't care." I just wanted retribution.

"Yeah, but Tendy wanted me to be very clear about this. What he can guarantee is your help will be brought to the attention of any court or agency, like the Bureau of Prisons, or the parole board, anyone that you request."

"Look, my only way out is for President Reagan to pardon me. I read the statute, I know it. And he'll just say no to that, no matter what I do and no matter what you say."

"You're right. We cannot promise anything in terms of reduction of your sentence. Our hands are tied on that."

"I understand, believe me. I know the law."

"And any statements you make will not be used against you."

Well, I knew that didn't matter; I was in for life without parole.

"And the government will make any accommodations to insure your safety and the safety of your family if we think that's necessary."

I nodded, that was fair. So I laid it down for him. In less than ninety minutes, I hit on almost everything. I told him about Frank and Ishmael and their suppliers. I described how Herbie Sperling hooked me up with Mark Reiter, how Reiter was giving packages to Thelma and Shamecca."

"Shamecca?"

"Beverly Ash, that's her real name."

Then I went back, telling him how the Council was buying and turning thirty kilos a month.

"What's the Council?"

Where've you been, man?

"That's my organization."

"We always called it the 'Nicky Barnes Organization.'"

I went on to tell him what we were moving now, and then I talked murders. That got his attention. They all want to hear about the murders.

I told him how we paid Coco to provide us information on informers, how Guy and Ishmael did the work on Black Crip and Pete, what got done to Joe Beechum at the Hubba and how Guy and Ishmael did the work on Galante's man Pugliese.

"This is very good, Nicky, but we need to cut this short. This is supposed to be a lawyer meeting, and I don't want to arouse suspicion. I'll report back to Tendy on all of this. We're going to want anything else you can learn on current deals on the outside, deals on the inside and anything else about the murders."

"Listen, though, I just wanna get Guy. You got to deal with those others yourself. I can't help you get anybody else but Guy."

"No good, Nicky. You can't cherry-pick your targets. If that means you won't cooperate, we understand. We want Guy Fisher, but we also want the rest of the Nicky Barnes Organiz—the Council, every one of them. We want Thelma Grant and Beverly Ash and their cohorts too. As well as all the suppliers you know and any others."

This was it. The reality.

"I gotta think about that."

"Then you think about it, but it's the only way we can do it."

Was I really gonna turn in *everyone*?

My women? That was an easy decision. They're cheating on me. Spending my money, living in my penthouses, driving my cars, pleading for my suppliers, asking my business advice...Meanwhile they fuckin' the only people I told them never to fuck! Top of that, they're lyin' to me 'bout it like I'm an idiot. *Fuck 'em.* I'd take 'em down, no problem.

Then I thought about my brothers.

Gaps. Wasn't sure what was goin' on with him. He just kinda checked out when I left and split for Brooklyn. But the only time we got in touch, I asked him to send me a package through J.J. in the mailroom. Nothin' much, just some naked pictures of chicks from some good magazines. I mean it ain't too much to ask! But Gaps pulled this bullshit attitude when I kept on him about it. Like I was being the boss again. That was a month ago, and I *still* hadn't got shit from that dude! *Nigger, shove those pictures up your motherfuckin' ass.*

And I thought about Frank and Ishmael. What those two did by fuckin' me over with the money and the lawyers happens all the time in prison between hustlin' partners, when one is in and one is out. It's like, "Man, you're in, I'm out and I'm going my own way."

I didn't wanna violate Frank and Ishmael on that basis alone. 'Cause shit happens. Not to mention what they say is true: there's just no honor among thieves. And you have to honor that street code of ethics. I was disappointed, real disappointed in those two, and if I were home, I'd have cut 'em loose for being disloyal. But that didn't seem enough to corroborate against 'em now. On a scale of one to ten, Frank and Ishmael were only fives.

But Guy? Him fuckin' Shamecca was above and beyond an act of disloyalty. This was an attempt to humiliate, dishonor and disrespect me. And there's a *big* motherfuckin' difference between disloyalty and disrespect. Had I been home, I would've killed Guy myself. But to hurt him now, I had to hurt Frank, the man who brought me into Islam, and Ishmael, the man who saved my life.

Ishmael's wife Helen came out of the blue to see me at Terre Haute. She looked bad. By now, she'd become a really run-down crackhead. Got strung out chasin' those rocks. *Man.* She and Ishmael were livin' so well when I was on the street. People even came in and vacuumed their stuff. Had a car, kids went to private school. Their youngest was about my youngest's age.

Damn, her mom and dad are gone.

Helen just looked at me, lost.

"Helen? Why'd you come all the way to see me?"

"I dunno, Nick. I dunno. I dunno how it is an operation as big as the Council comes to a halt just 'cause one guy goes down."

And then, I understood.

Once I went in, it all went downhill. The brothers realized they were kind of vulnerable, especially since Wally and Jazz got taken down, too. That cloak of invincibility was gone—the Council didn't feel it anymore—so they wanted to lie low. They did that and developed bad habits like drugs.

Ishmael and Frank and Guy started basing heavily. *Guy* was basin'! He'd never done anything before! Now, they weren't out trippin' like they were in the movies in Southern California. They didn't suddenly become guys you'd wanna run up against neither. Still pros, still cool, intact, strapped and ridin' deep in the cars. Day-to-day security is still there.

But all the people in the mills and on the street who trusted me and worked for all of us 'cause of *my* presence, *my* word, *my* laws? They weren't available to the Council now. 'Cause Guy, Ishmael and Frank weren't takin' care of business. They were tryin' to live our old life with no money comin' in.

Man, there was just no reason for any of this to have happened. Had the Council stayed on top of what they were doin', things would've been different. Had they only taken care of me in any kind of way.

Only Guy is fuckin' Mecca. Tito's fuckin' Thelma. Frank and Ishmael are basin'. Things weren't workin' out for anybody. There was nothing left. No unity, no discipline, no organization, no leadership. The whole fabric of our thing was wiped out.

None of it was worth saving.

Former Friends

"I CAN DO IT, THE COUNCIL."

It was four weeks later, mid-August, and I was with Gallina again.

"Okay, but just telling stories in a grand jury isn't going to be enough, it won't support indictments. We want you to help us build cases with corroborative evidence, information and specific acts."

Gallina told me the U.S. Attorneys needed deals in the making, current transactions, something to show my criminal enterprise was continuing.

"Don't worry, I've already made arrangements. We can do all of that."

I told Gallina it was going to be easy to set everybody up. "The Council's so far gone, they're just *dyin'* to find that magic bullet supplier." Like Joe Peters did to Bobby Monroe, the trick was to play on the Council's weakness. Offer a quick path that'd shoot them straight to the top.

And I knew just the man who'd get their tongues waggin'.

"Matty Madonna. He's in Lewisburg now, so you get the two of us in the same place. Find a way to get me into the general population of

Lewisburg, or bring him to Terre Haute."

"Great. I'll definitely tell Tendy. What about Herbie Sperling?"

"Yeah, he'd be good to get in on this, too. They moved him to Lewisburg, I think, so you just get us all in one place. I'll take it from there."

"I'll mention that to Tendy. Also, before I go, there's something else Tendy wanted me to tell you."

"Yeah?"

"After your federal trial in '77, the government learned Guy Fisher made contact during the trial with a female juror and bribed her so you'd all walk."

"Yeah, but she didn't do shit."

"Not true. Guy Fisher instructed the juror only to get himself off, not you or any of the others. That's why the jury returned no verdict on his charges only. The government just did not have enough evidence to prosecute him for jury tampering."

Reason enough to bring that nigger down.

On October 21, '81, two of my "lawyers" came to visit—Gallina and DEA Special Agent Stanley Morrissey. Morrissey was going to be the operations guy, so it was important that we meet.

"Here's what we're going to do," said Gallina. "We're going to impanel a federal grand jury for an 'investigation' into organized crime. We'll subpoena you, Sperling, Madonna and a couple other traffickers to Manhattan. No one'll suspect anything."

Morrissey went to the undercover operation: "At MCC, we want you to see your people, set up deals and make the arrangements. You'll wear a wire in these meetings."

"No wire."

"But we need to have them on tape saying—"

"No wire! You don't know what it's like in the joint, man. The guards check you every time you move!"

"Well, we can let the appropriate ones know—"

"How many of them you gotta tell?! And what about the one who was sick the day the memo went out, or the guy who didn't read it and he's, 'The fuck is this?' when I walk out of visitors, and everyone knows. Uh-unh. No wire."

"I'll ask Tendy, but I think we can live with that."

"Don't you worry, I remember shit. Just get me access to a private phone at MCC. I'll let you know the details of my meets."

The day after Joe Montana beat Cincinnati in the Super Bowl, I was taken to MCC, downtown Manhattan. I walked into the visitors room and there he was.

"You real lean, Nick! Looks good."

I wanted to kill him, to actually kill him right there with my bare hands. On the street, I could have, but here with the guards? Man, I knew I had to be chill if I was gonna pull anything on him, but I couldn't help but let out some of the anger.

"So, Guy? It's been *years* since the Council did anything about a lawyer for me. I've paid for everything."

"I know, I know. We gonna get that organized. I have a new connection for blow in Brazil. I'm gonna take care of everything from here on out. You don't have to worry about a thing."

Right. From here on out.

After our meet, I got on a private line with Special Agent Morrissey and described Guy's Brazil connection, only we both knew that was too vague to put a motherfucker away for life without parole.

"And Nick, I don't like telling you this, but I thought you'd want to know. While Guy was there meeting with you? Shamecca was waiting for him outside."

Got to get Guy. Just got to get Guy.

The federal grand jury in Manhattan was like a convention of suppliers and dealers. Herbie Sperling, Matty Madonna and me were all kept on the ninth floor. Frank Lucas was on the third floor.

But the rumor was that Lucas had been cooperating for some time, and if that were the case? Maybe he knew my situation. So when Herbie told me "Frank Lucas is talkin' shit about you, pal," I tried to play it cool.

"Frank Lucas? That stupid, country-ass, lyin' nigger? Don't *ever* listen to a goddamn thing he got to say."

"Yeah, yeah. But I got some things I wanna lay out for you. Why don't you meet me late tonight in the law library. It'll be a good place to talk since no one'll be there."

It was also a good place to get yourself snuffed, so as I made that long circuitous walk down to the library, I thought, "Shit, this might be a setup." If Frank Lucas told Herbie about my cooperation, Herbie was gonna have me killed, no doubt.

When I finally got there, the only person I could see was Herbie. That was a good sign. If it came down to hand-to-hand, I'd have the advantage. Even without a shiv.

"I've been thinkin', Nick. I still really want to get my son in there to do the meets, ya know, like we talked about? Work him in as the middle guy between Mark and your girls. That'll get him in good with Mark. I think we should do that. Makes it better for both sides."

"I got no problem doin' it that way."

"Then we'll do it at the Stage Deli like I used to. Always brought me good luck, that place."

The Stage Deli on 54th and Seventh was where Herbie used to operate, a spot where the pastrami sandwiches are too big to eat, not a place black dealers liked to go. As for the luck, I didn't exactly understand that, since Herbie was in the joint for life.

"I don't have to tell you how important it is we don't fuck this one up. It's my kid's first deal, you know. Wanna get him started off on the right foot."

"Absolutely, Herbie."

She's got to pay the price, I kept telling myself.

But I gotta admit, I was not prepared for the wave of emotion at seeing her actually walk into the visitors room. Nevertheless, I wanted to reach out and break her fuckin' jaw.

Shamecca gave me a hug and held it.

"Remember what they used to let us do here?" she whispered.

She was wearing a short skirt, and when I saw that she had no panties on? *Mecca is not making this easy.* I looked at the guard and he turned his chair right around.

Nicky Barnes still had some juice at MCC. Mecca turned around too, like she was gonna sit on my lap. I started fucking her hard and angry. So I got my hands under her shirt on her titties and just did what I wanted to her.

Betrayed her with a fuck.

"All right, baby, we got other business to take care of. We're gonna change how we do the Reiter thing."

She nodded, intent as ever.

"Reiter is still the supplier, but now you're gonna go through a middleman, a kid named Nick Sperling. You're gonna meet him at the Stage Deli, the one on 54th, this Thursday at noon. Bring a copy of *Life* magazine, you got that? That's how he'll know you."

She loved it, an eager fucking beaver.

"Give Son his weight, but for the other half, I got a new client, Bobby

Baker. Big, handsome black guy. Me and Bobby used to do business way back. He's gonna put you in some real money."

Yeah, I was her motherfucking mentor, lover, sugar daddy, and I was gonna fuckin' ruin her.

I unzipped again.

A week later I heard from DEA Agent Bobby Baker.

"I met with Shamecca, Nick. She gave me a list of prices. Man, I had no idea she was so beautiful. I kind of think she liked me. Said I was real tall and called me 'Highpockets.'"

"Go on. Then what?"

"I took the sample, paid for it, told her I'd get back to her about the buy."

I was thrilled. Shamecca on a sale to a federal agent.

Bye-bye, baby.

My other wife had it coming too.

Only she was going to be a lot harder. When I told her I was going to set her up with Nicky Sperling for the Reiter buys from now on, she refused.

She liked the action too much to go through a middleman.

I called to explain the situation to DEA agent Davey Smitts, the one who was gonna arrange the sting on Thelma.

"I can't just hook you up with her for a buy. Hooking Baker up with Mecca was easy 'cause Mecca don't know nothin' about hustlin'. Tee's different. She's too smart to deal with just anybody. Plus, she knows everyone I've done business with."

"So what do you think?"

"I can't make an introduction from you directly to her. We've got to hit her from a side angle. Here's what we're gonna do. There's a place, the Flash Inn on 125th and St. Nicholas." The Flash was a popular eating spot for hustlers—women liked to go and wear their latest shit and show off their newest car from their man.

"Go and buy a 'Get Well' card. Write on the inside, 'I heard you were sick. Touch base with me if there's anything I can do,' and write your telephone number. Give the card to the bartender at the Flash to give to Tee."

About a month later I told Smitts, "Maybe this ain't gonna work. She's gonna detect it. I know my woman."

But soon after Thelma visited me at MCC.

"Who is this guy Smitts? Do you know him at all? Got an out-of-town area code."

"Yeah, I know him."

"He's been tryin' to get to me. Wanted to know if there was anything he can do for me."

"He's a cool dude."

"But is he all right?"

"Yeah, he's on time. One of those dudes I'd see sometimes. His volume wasn't big enough to stay with us, so I dropped him. But he'd be good for what you're doing now. *Real* good."

"So what went down?" I asked Agent Smitts.

"I met Thelma to pay for the dope in advance."

"Good. Did she ask you to count the money in front of her?"

"Yeah! How'd you know?"

Damn. I trained her too well.

When we used to count money, we flipped through it fast, fluid. I always told Thelma, "When someone passes you money, make 'em count it. If they're uncomfortable countin' it, don't fuck with 'em, because they haven't been doin' it at that level."

"How'd you count it?"

"I kind of fumbled, so I just told her to count it herself. Then she took the money and said she'd get back to me later with the dope."

I thought it was all over, but obviously, greed made that bitch bite.

"I've been meeting her on a regular basis," Smitts continued. "She makes me meet her at all the hot places—Hannibal's Fish House, The Copper Hatch, Maxwell's Plum. I was surprised she was so public."

"Then you got her?"

"A lotta sales. A kilo all in. She told me that after you went to jail she took over the organization, and that since she wasn't flashy like you, she could do her own thing without being noticed. Said *she* ran the Council now."

Oh, Thelma. I didn't feel bad at all.

Frank James finally came too MCC for a visit.

"Man, it'd be real great to get that Madonna connect goin' again. I mean, the stuff I'm gettin' now is okay, but nothin' like Matty was givin' us. I dunno. Maybe you could arrange for him to give it to me—I mean *us*—on consignment."

And the very next day? Ishmael comes in with the same fuckin' story on how he'd love to get his hands on Matty's product again. Man, the brothers were just crawlin' back, hopin' to be the one with the source.

This time, I had no problem givin' it to 'em.

"Listen, Matty. Thought I might hook up some of my guys with your brother Frankie."

Matty's cell was right next to mine, so we talked low that night about it. I liked him a lot and didn't want to see him or his brother get jammed up, but fuck, this was my best chance to get to Guy.

"I dunno." Matty sounded cagey, like he knew something. "It's just that I heard things…"

About what?

"Tell me straight, Matty."

"The Council ain't got a good rep on the street no more. They got nothin'. I would hate to have Frankie supply your guys and there's a problem, and then he has to kill one of 'em 'cause it was bad business." *More likely that Frank and Ishmael would spark Frankie first.* "That would hurt our friendship. You understand."

Maybe Matty knew. Maybe he figured it out. He's a smart motherfucker (which is why he's been out some years and is now a capo in the Lucchese family, enjoying a table up at Rao's off Pleasant Avenue). But this was not good, because I was countin' on using him to deliver the Council to the Feds. By the time my stint at MCC was up, all I'd done was set up my women.

Guy was still untouched.

"Any of your people need powder?" Gigi Inglese, aka "Gigi the Whale" or just "Fat Gigi," wanted to know.

A major supplier on Pleasant Avenue and a fat fuck of a good guy, me and Gigi had a real camaraderie going at Terre Haute, just talkin' about the street—wise guys, black guys, women, parole, lawyers—shit cons talk about.

He was a perfect dude to bring in on this thing.

"Only person I know who's shoppin' right now is Frank James."

Just like Sperling, Gigi wanted to get his son, Patsy Inglese, involved as a middleman, so I set him up with Mecca. That was important, 'cause the Feds only had Mecca on one sale, the sample to Baker. But since she had a clean record, in order for her to spend the maximum time in prison, they needed to get her on *two* sales.

See, I didn't want her to walk away from prison in just a few years. I wanted her to know what's it's like to be down for serious time.

A few days later I called Frank at the Sandwich Oasis to follow up, and none other than Wally Rice answered, home free after his six-year bid.

"Damn, Wally! I hear you've been out like two weeks! How come you ain't even given me a 'Hi, dude!'?'"

"You know how it is, man…"

"Yeah, whatever." *You lucky I ain't goin' after you, too, nigger.* "Put Frank on."

He did.

"Yo, Nick, what's up? Everything's all right. I saw Patsy and told him I liked the sample he gave to Mecca, so I put up the money."

"Good, Frank, I'm glad."

Glad? I was fucking thrilled! I told the DEA where the meet would be and they got it on videotape. Bang! Frank James buying a quarter-kilo of heroin from Patsy!

In September 1982, Frank came to Terre Haute. Fat Gigi's shit had whetted the Council's appetite.

"We turned Patsy's goods. Just waitin' for the re-up."

Shit, man! I was real impressed with Frank for turning the package in the first place.

Looks like I'd rebuilt the Council just so I could destroy it.

"In the meantime, Nick, I need another source."

That's what I wanted to hear.

The only thing left for the DEA was to get Frank on a big buy. Something that would lock him up for good.

"Okay, I got somebody here. I'm pretty sure he'll move, but I'll have to finalize things with him. I'll just give him the phone number of the Oasis so you won't have to come all the way out here again to find out the details. Now, I'll arrange for you to get an eighth as a sample, but when you get a call and the caller tells you that '*The dude* told me to call about gettin' sandwiches for a party,' you'll know it's from him."

"Yeah, that's great."

"And if you're satisfied with the goods, you can come back and buy 'em. Now listen up. This guy keeps it real low, so he usually gets his old lady Nancy to transact his business. She'll probably be the one who calls."

I had to admit, I played this one beautifully.

Nick Allina and Nancy Burgstahler were two DEA agents who posed as a husband-and-wife team involved in the drug biz. And their specialty? The reverse. See, it's not so easy for a DEA agent to go to a guy who's selling and buy a large quantity of drugs.

So the DEA got the idea of going to a dealer and sayin', "We got these goods available, and you can have it for the right price." Now, if you're a street guy and you say, "I like that package. We want $25,000 for this package," they'll give you a sample. You'll take it, come back and say, "Yeah, I'll buy it." Then they can arrest you on a reverse. 'Cause that's conspiracy too.

A week later, I asked Nancy how it went.

"Frank told me he moved two to three kilos, or half a million, every ten days. Said he wanted to buy one kilo to start and then more each week. I told him a kilo would cost him $195,000, but he wanted to pay just half, with the rest on consignment. Told him that was cool, but then he said he had to go out and visit you before moving ahead."

"Then I'll handle him here."

"Oh, and do you know a guy named Wally Rice?"

"Yeah, sure."

"While I was talking to Frank, he came up and introduced himself, 'I'm Wally Rice, Frank's partner.' We got him on tape saying this."

"I don't believe it!"

Now, understand this. I didn't try and knock Wally off. But here he was, fresh out the joint, and he didn't trust Frank enough to let him have exclusive access to the supply. That's why he went right up to Nancy and introduced himself. Dumb-ass Wally. That was gonna hurt him. If he'd only said, "You know, Frank is takin' care of this, I'm gonna stay in the background," I couldn't have gotten to him!

Days later, Frank James came for his visit.

"Nancy got a great package at a great price, man. You sure did us good. Only thing is she wants $100G up front and, uh…well, I just bought my woman Ernestine a new Benz, you know, and I'm buildin' a disco upstairs at the sandwich shop, too. So you think you could get her source to give it to us *all* on consignment?"

"I dunno. I'll see what I can do," I told him.

"Man," gushed Frank, "you're really pulling it all back together!"

Then Frank got all penitent. "I know I haven't been takin' care of business like I should, but if you could just get us this package on consignment, I know we can make big money. Then I'll *really* be able to look out for you."

"Thanks, brother. I appreciate that."

Motherfucker.

Few days later I called Nancy.

"How'd it go down?"

"I don't know."

"What?!"

"I mean, I sort of made a play for Frank to try to close the deal, ya know?" That was good, 'cause Frank, like all of us, liked a freak. And Nancy was this really attractive white girl. Big breasts. Frank *loved* big breasts. "But Frank got all flustered and asked where the package came from, and I said, 'Marseilles.'"

"That's fine."

"But then he asks me, 'What can I do it on?'"

That's a favored expression among drug dealers. It means "How many times can you cut it on?" Kind of occupational jargon dealers use to detect who's legit and who ain't.

"Well, what'd you tell him?"

"I told him, 'You can do what you want to with it.'"

Now, that's an acceptable expression under some circumstances. If Madonna said that to me? I'd've thought it was legit. 'Cause he knows what I do with the package. But someone new like Nancy? No good. No *way* could Frank have fallen for something like that. It's like I told him and everyone else: "Trust your instincts. If your instincts tell you something is wrong, don't fuck with it."

But apparently Frank's instincts were too clouded by the basin'. I even heard later that Frank said, "I *knew* somethin' was wrong with that bitch!" Too late. He violated the basic rules of caution.

He arranged the buy anyway.

He'd pay the price of bein' stupid.

A Message

BILL TENDY WANTED ME in a secure location before the arrests went down, so on October 14, 1982, two guards came to my cell at Terre Haute and escorted me to a van and into the custody of two deputy U.S. Marshals. Then I was taken to a waiting plane, flown to New York City and driven downtown to the marshal station underneath the Federal Courthouse at Foley Square.

My new digs were a big improvement over Terre Haute, one of about five secure bedroom apartments for high-levels cooperating with the Feds. Here we could receive food, wear street clothes and watch our own TV, right there in the cell. But I didn't want to be here, not yet.

If it had been up to me, I would have stayed at Terre Haute and kept plotting to bring down Guy Fisher. I wasn't convinced the government had enough on him to put him away for life. Problem was, you really can't tell the Feds what you want and don't want when you're a felon serving a life term.

The day after my arrival, I was brought upstairs to a courthouse conference room where Bill Tendy sat at a large wooden table. He seemed tough, smart, fair. Plus, he had a big rep as the one who convicted Carmine Galante in '62 and turned Joe Valachi, the first Italian to break *omerta*, the code of silence in the Cosa Nostra.

"You know Howard Jacobs, your lawyer? He used to work with our office."

A middle-aged, white, Jewish guy with bushy hair and glasses, Jacobs looked like a straitlaced '50s throwback, not a bad quality for a lawyer representing a guy like me. They assigned him to me because in the process of cooperating, you have to tell what *you* did, too. If you want to convince the jury, you can't hold out on nothin', so you've got to confess it all. And if you're confessing shit, you'd best have a lawyer.

I didn't contact Breitbart.

As I saw it, the Justice Department and a defense lawyer, no matter who he is, are in opposition to each other. One's bent on prosecution, the other on acquittal. So I decided the safest thing was to stay on the side of the Justice Department. Breitbart's a good guy and a great lawyer, but I took Jacobs for the job.

"We have a problem, as you know," said Tendy. "We are going to arrest Frank James, Wally Rice, Beverly Ash, Thelma Grant and Mark Reiter. But we don't have anything on Guy Fisher, Samuel Jones and Thomas Forman."

"Look, I want *all* of them to get the same charge I did! Continuing Criminal Enterprise, Statute 848. They did the same things and we were all equal. Especially Guy."

"We know, but we're not sure we can get them on that. I don't know that it applies here."

"I think it applies if I show you how the Council really worked."

"Explain."

"All right, first, the law says a person has to be 'one of several leaders,' right? That's exactly what the Council was, seven number ones, all equal. Second, each one of us had 'at least five people' under him."

Shit, I *knew* CCE! I'd been reading my own case for years. I'd been to district courts, court of appeals twice and even denied by the Supreme Court.

"Third, the narcotics sales? We did this with Madonna's package, right after the Council was formed. We're doing it now when Nancy sells to Frank. That's your continuing part, right there. I source the supply, we all take our piece, cut it and sell.

"Fourth, as an enterprise we made more than $10 million a year. And five, we 'caused intentional killing' to make this enterprise work better. We all did it. All seven. All murders were voted on. All murders had to be unanimous."

"You're right," said Tendy. "I think we have a case."

"Mr. Barnes," said a young, Latin-looking guy, "I'm Benito Romano, I work under Bill Tendy. I read what you provided to Agents Gallina and Morrissey, but in order to get Guy and the rest, we're going to need you to confess to the murders committed by the Council. We need that to put it on them too."

"That's a problem," said my attorney, Jacobs. "If he confesses to those murders he has no immunity, he can be sentenced to a lot more years."

"The government will oppose that," said Romano.

"But a judge will deliver it."

I interrupted. "Right now, what do I care? I'm in for life without parole, so if I can put Guy and the rest of them away for life? I'll tell you 'bout *all* the Council murders."

That surprised the room.

"We can do this tomorrow, then," said Tendy. He walked me over to the marshals waiting at the door and told me straight up, "What you're doing? It's very important. We lost Joe, but we're going to get you out."

I knew just what he meant. After Joe Valachi got on national TV, testified day in and day out? Tendy hoped to get him his freedom, but never could. Valachi was left to die in prison. And then he told me something that really surprised me.

"Frank Lucas? He's already been released from prison into the Federal

Witness Protection Program."

Shit, if that clown was gettin' out? Maybe it'd all work out for me, too.

Days later, Agent Morrissey asked for a word.

"They picked up Frank and Wally at Wally's real estate office. They're at MCC with bails at $1 million. They got Thelma down in North Carolina and should have her back in New York by now."

"What about my kids?"

"Tito disappeared with them. We have agents trying to find them."

"Fuck, man! We gotta get them! People are gonna find out I'm behind this!"

"We're trying, we're searching every place we know."

This seriously worried me.

Why couldn't the government take care of business?

"Mark Reiter's on the lam, but we'll find him. We also picked up Shamecca. Apparently, she resisted, put up a real fight with the cops. The others were easy, she was not. Her bail is only $50,000, but she's going to be in a tight spot, you know."

"Brought it on herself."

The Feds now planned to put the heat on Mecca so she'd testify against Mark Reiter, all in an effort to make Reiter flip on John Gotti. Could've used Thelma for the same thing, but Tee would know how to take the heat.

The press was all over the story, with the *New York Post* reporting "Black Godfather Leroy Barnes, the biggest drug dealer in the country, has sung on his wife, hoping to get out of jail." Well, that was bullshit. Bill Tendy knew, the DEA knew, my lawyer knew—there was nothing, nothing the government could offer me!

I did it for revenge 'cause that's all I had.

On December 14, Benito Romano came to see me in my room, where we worked sometimes. In his late twenties, Romano was a young guy to be working such a big case, but he was outgoing, and all the other U.S. Attorneys liked him a lot. We had a good rapport; he was extremely sharp.

"Hey, man, I'll make you a sandwich, I got some tuna fish."

I didn't have knives or forks, but I could open the can and then use the lid to make the sandwich. I was trying to get the stuff out of the can when he said, "Nick, Shamecca was killed last night. I'm sorry."

"How?"

"Shot in the head, execution style, three times."

I *made* this happen.

She didn't know anything about the powder game until she met me. She wasn't in that life. She was so attractive, and...At least she wouldn't be behind bars. She was so delicate. But they said when they arrested her, she was the only one who fought against them.

I guess she would have stood on her own.

I just broke down. Romano sat there with me for the longest time until I took control over myself and realized what was happening.

This was a message from Reiter, from Gotti, from the mob. They're thinking, "Nicky Barnes can make a problem for us, but we can't reach him." So they were gonna kill all the people I hooked up with 'em. A reminder of what might happen if I started telling tales.

I could barely look at the *New York Post* the next day.

JAILED DRUG CZAR'S MOLL RUBBED OUT.

The story read that Shamecca, out on bail, was sitting at the Monarch Tavern in Washington Heights when a guy came from behind in a white ski mask, swearing in an Italian accent, shooting her in the neck and the back of the head with a .45. Witnesses thought it was a black man who wore the white mask to make it look like he was white.

They were right. And who arranged the job? My own flesh and blood. My nephew Mellon did that shit. Told his crew, "I'm going to do what I have to do," then hired a friend to kill Mecca.

I always knew Mellon wanted to model himself on my image—multiple sources of powder, get entrenched with the Italian suppliers. So when Reiter reached out to him and said if he did the work, Gotti and the Brooklyn crew would be endeared to him? Just like everyone else in my life, Mellon did anything for the source.

And that's the route he took.

On January 4, 1983, I went before a grand jury and laid out all the crimes the Council and I had committed from 1973 to the present. Then I stood before Judge Werker and pled guilty to trafficking narcotics and participating in the decisions to commit four murders. But the confessions alone didn't make a case. The government still did not have enough on Guy Fisher. I needed a break to bring down Guy.

And then, it just walked on in.

"You know a Walter Centano?" asked Romano.

"Chico Bob?"

"Right, he's cooperating."

"What? Bob got pinched?"

"Nope. Guy Fisher did him wrong and he wanted to get back."

Turns out Chico Bob went back to work for Guy and did a deal for him, but got fucked out of his share of $40G. He confronted Guy on the payment, but when Guy screamed and threatened him? Bob said, "Fuck this shit." Went right into the DEA office in Manhattan.

"Chico Bob knows where all the bodies are buried," Romano told me. "Literally."

Now, I knew who we killed. I voted on it with everyone else. Only I had no idea where the bodies were since I didn't do the work. I could testify about the murders, but had no evidence to back me up. But now that Chico Bob was on the case?

"He's an eyewitness on Guy's murder of Ronnie Bell. This is just what we needed to bring Guy down."

I could see in Romano's face this was for real. He was happy, Tendy was happy and man, I was happy.

Now we had a case.

First we went after the white collars. I had some real suspicions on those slick niggers, those very black-is-beautiful lawyers from Detroit who were gonna work with me so they could grow themselves. The U.S. Attorneys did some investigation, and as it turned out? Bolden and Blake not only swindled my money, they handed it all to this white dude Goldman, just to get tight with him and his many social contacts in the Detroit political scene!

So on January 19, 1983, U.S. Attorney General William French Smith announced he was suing these three in federal court for the $1.3 million in total they stole from me. True, the government was gonna seize it all as illegal drug profit, to pay my fines and tax liens, but for the first time in my life, I didn't care about money. I couldn't spend anything in the joint anyway.

As that was happening, the DEA executed search warrants on the addresses of two of our old mills, making vacuum sweeps and finding traces of heroin and quinine. Amazing that after all those years, there was still enough evidence to build the blocks of a conspiracy. And people had been living in these apartments for years! One woman was even using a quinine drum for a laundry hamper!

Bob helped out with that part of the investigation real good, telling the DEA about one worker he found dead at the mill, a guy who OD'd from not wearin' a surgical mask. Bob had gotten rid of that body, so he showed 'em the location. But the dude had decomposed, and all the investigators found was a finger.

Now dig this. They were able to take the fingerprint off that finger and identify it! Chemistry, man. All the pieces just came together, and once the puzzle was complete?

Time to roll.

On March 10, 1983, the DEA swept up Guy, Ishmael, Gaps and six others who worked in various capacities for the Council. When Guy was sitting at the offices of the DEA after the arrest, he was chatting it up with the agents like he was really somethin'. As the discussion turned to me, he just pointed out his hand and index finger like a gun and said, "If I gotta play murder, I play murder."

He had every intention of doing it. So did the rest of the brothers. They put out a million-dollar contract to kill me, so the judge raised each brother's bail from one to five million. One of their defense lawyers said it was ridiculous—"Probably next to Ronald Reagan, Nicky Barnes is the most protected man in this country"—but the danger wasn't to me. It was to my children. The hit was on them, too.

And the DEA still had not found Tito Johnson.

"Nicky Barnes, I'm Rudy Giuliani." He shook my hand inside the U.S. Attorney's office. Bill Tendy told me about this guy, the new U.S. Attorney for the Southern District. A real no-holds-barred, take-no-prisoners prosecutor chosen by Senator Al D'Amato to "battle the drug epidemic engulfing New York," Giuliani had a vicious rep as someone who knew how to railroad you.

I figured I was in deep shit. Thought I wasn't gonna get anything from this dude.

"I'm sure Benito told you, if you perform per the agreements we've made, I'm going to look out for you. I know you've helped us on a lot of cases, and we appreciate that."

"Just find my kids. Just get Tito and find my kids."

I was surprised at how gracious Rudy was. That was his style— respect to me! He was real good to me, just like the U.S. Marshals. They worked harder for me with those tin badges than the Council ever did with those Benzes.

Warm-ups

ON MARCH 16, 1983, I was brought in to testify at the Nicholas Sperling trial, my debut as a government witness. The trial itself was a footnote. All the attention was on me and why I'd turned informant. I wore a blue blazer, dark pants, white shirt and red tie—looking like a nice middle-class American. This time, people didn't interpret my look as smug.

One writer described me as "noticeably thinner and less brash than the beefy arrogant figure he had cut during his earlier trial." Yeah, well, you shuffle in my shoes. It was hard, man. Every newspaper callin' me a rat, a traitor, a turncoat? They just didn't understand.

On the witness stand, when asked about my cooperation, I said, "I made an attempt to kind of reevaluate myself because I realized that the whole life was shallow," that "the millions of dollars we made from thousands of pounds of heroin didn't outweigh the damage."

Did I really feel that way? At the time, probably not.

But I was truthful about my real reason for testifying: "I did it because the Council double-crossed me like everyone else did." Hell, it sure wasn't to fuck over Nicholas Sperling. I never even met the kid, but he helped me get to my women and the Council, so I had to put him away for fifteen.

Now that I had my warm-up, the next six months were devoted to my testimony against the Council. Going to trial, I had an advantage because I was telling the truth. Romano's job was to determine what the cross-examination would be to try and discredit me, so we had mock trials in empty federal courtrooms.

"Now, Nick," prepped Romano, "not only do you have to tell the truth, but to the jury, you must *look* like you're telling the truth. They must believe you, so always be committed in what you say."

I gave a nod.

"The defense'll try and catch you in some kind of minor perjury in hopes of undermining your entire testimony, so tell the full truth as you remember it. Do not make anything up. If you do not remember something, just say you don't remember."

Not only could I remember everything, I'd been thinking about nothing else for the past two years.

"Emphasize the Council, the equality of the Council, not you as a leader. Don't let your ego get in the way here. Everyone thinks of you as leading the 'Nicky Barnes Organization,' so we must convince them that was wrong, it was the Council of Seven. If anything, you were merely first among equals."

I felt like we had mock trials too many times. I was like a racehorse just jamming to get out of the goddamn gate.

And when I wasn't preparing for trial? Well, I had no visitors anymore. Shit, all my former visitors were in cells by now. I did talk a lot to the marshals, DEA agents and Romano. We'd go on about politics, psychology, philosophy, religion, art—things which had always interested me. So I started reading more about those subjects, tried to educate myself some.

I rarely spoke to the other prisoners. The guys in the cells near me were not Joey Gallos or Matty Madonnas. All they wanted was to talk about what great criminals they were.

Truth be told, I hated being around cons.

I sat in a conference room alone and waiting. I was nervous and trying to organize what to say. A few minutes later the door opened and my children ran in. *Thank God.* They were healthy and safe and free from Tito. I gave them both a big hug.

I may have been a very bad man in the eyes of many people, but while it lasted I tried to be a good, if not always attentive, father. I had a lot of fun with my kids before my '77 conviction.

Now I'd have to explain it all.

What could I say? That I had put their mother in prison, that I was in prison for life and that their lives were in danger because of what I had done?

"So you can choose any name you like. What names are you thinking about? What are your favorite names? Nobody ever gets to choose their own names. You must be excited."

Of course, they liked their old names. And they wanted to know why they had to change.

"Because you're going to go to live with another family in another part of the country while your mama and I are gone."

"Why can't we stay with Aunt Betty?"

"Well, it's hard for her to take care of you. Your new home is gonna be great, that's what I hear."

The marshals introduced me to the couple that would be the surrogate parents for my kids. They were certainly aware of the security concerns, so I guess that made them even better people for taking my kids on. In the little time I had, I told them as much as I could about the character of each child, or as much as I knew.

The rest of the time I talked and played a little with the kids, like we did when they visited the pen. In the future, they would be allowed to visit me twice a year. I was sure they would get the same with their mother.

"When can we go on another picnic?"

The last I had spent time with them for real was a picnic in a Bronx park years before, but they obviously still remembered it.

"I don't know, but you'll go on picnics in your new home. You be good and listen to what your new parents tell you, like they were mama and me, you understand? They're going to be your family for a time."

They half understood. Their lives had never been quite normal, and I had already been gone five years.

We had been a good family way back, if not a typical one. And for me, these moments were really all I had left in my life. That's when I really saw what I had done: to my life, to the people around me, to my children. I just wanted to go back. I wanted to go back and make a different turn.

And then the marshals took my kids away.

Did I miss the life myself? Sure I did. Shit, I still do. Not the crime, but the deals, the organizing, the managing and making the damn thing work. The rewards were good, too. The stacks of money, the Moët, the Jensen Healeys, the furs, the big nights at Studio 54, the trips to South America...the celebrity.

Everywhere I went, people hushed and looked. A restaurant owner would introduce himself and send out plates on the house. They loved having me in there; it gave the place real heat. And the women? I could walk into a bar, turn off the juke and ask who wanted to be mine tonight. All the ladies would raise hands.

I'm not trying to brag. That's just how it was.

And shit, I'll admit it, the drugs—blow, angel dust, weed and all the combinations?

Maybe I was the bad guy, but I lived large, I lived well.

But if my own sin had been pride, the sins of my brothers were envy, lust, greed, gluttony, sloth....

For these, we needed to pay for the rest of our lives.

Wrath

AN ESCORT OF federal marshals flanked my entrance to the courtroom on October 17, 1985. The place was packed, silent. I felt the stares as I stepped into the witness stand and settled in. I looked at Guy and the rest of my brothers. Straight at 'em, every one, right in the eye.

What goes around comes around, muthafuckas.

Romano started with simple questions to warm me up. I needed that. I had rehearsed with him sometimes even in this courtroom. You gotta be casual and calm in front of a jury. Don't act smug. Give them a cursory glance but that's all, don't look at 'em. You gotta be cool about what you say in front of them. That's the advice the prosecutors gave me.

I went through my past, my incarcerations, suppliers, running a table, number of kilos we turned, weight business versus street business, East Side versus West Side and other narcotics shit to get the jury up to speed. Then Romano asked, "What did Frank James say to you and what did you say to James during that conversation?"

This was a tricky part. Suppose I answered, "This whole Council thing was my idea, and I had the germ of it even before I met Frank. I got these guys together and we hooked up this Council." If it had been phrased that way going to the jury, they would have seen the other guys as working for me. The notion of equals was accurate, but I had to add some wrinkles in there. And it's not like they would be testifying to challenge me.

"Well, James told me that, he said that he had been talking with some black narcotics dealers from the East Side, and that they were concerned with, at least were interested in formulating, a black narcotics dealers' organization…And he asked me at that time if I was interested in getting down with them."

Then Romano asked about the rules and codes of what would become the Council.

"We decided that the Council would be, would operate on a democratic format." I could feel my heart pounding now. As I kept going I started getting emotional, remembering it all, remembering these guys when they were strong and good to each other, when we *were* a brotherhood. "We agreed that under no circumstance…" my voice was choking now, but I had to get out the words, "would any Council member become intimate with the wife or women of another Council member. So we agreed when we had our Council meetings we would join hands, and for each member—"

I stopped. The wave of emotion came over me. I just started tearing up. I bowed my head down, pulled out a red handkerchief and wiped my eyes. It took a minute to try to regain my voice.

"…And for each member we formulated an oath of brotherhood. We voted that we would never break that oath of brotherhood. We would join hands and each man would say a word. And those seven words were 'Treat my brother as I treat myself.'"

I got very upset. The defendants, they just stared at me.

I could see Romano thinking maybe he should recess. I nodded that I was okay. I steeled myself for the hardest part.

"Do you see any members of the Council here in the courtroom today?"

"Yes."

"Will you please pick them out?"

And then the emotion swept through me and passed, leaving only a cold vengeance. I looked into his eyes and pointed a hard finger at him. "Guy Fisher." I pointed at each of them, one by one, with the conviction of an angry, unmerciful God.

"Frank James. Wally Rice. Ishmael Mohammed. Thomas Foreman."

I was damning them all to hell.

I went through the four Council murders, but made sure to add, "Mr. James told me that he had his brother-in-law ice-picked to death." Poor Beverly was right there in the audience. Though Frank swore to her that he had nothing to do with it, at that moment, she knew the truth. Even if she's convinced herself otherwise, which I hear she has.

Before the day ended, Romano handed me the photo album Frank gave me after our party at the Time & Life Building. A birthday gift turned evidence. I opened it and sat there, just looking at those beautiful pictures of me and Tee, Frank and Bev. Everyone was so happy.

"He's been brainwashed!"

Suddenly this black guy tore down the center aisle of the courtroom, screaming. The marshals split ranks and moved in, converging on me and pulling this nut-job out of the courtroom.

"He don't know what he's talkin' about! He's been brainwashed!"

Bill Kunstler was famous as a radical lawyer. A tall guy with crazy hair, he was defending Guy Fisher, but had a hard time with his usual rhetoric in Judge Milton Pollack's court. See, Pollack was an old, cantankerous warhorse of a judge, and he didn't allow lawyers to blurt out "objection." He said, "If you want to object, raise your hand, then write your objections out in hand."

But even though Kunstler had to tone it down, he and I got into it, right from the start. "When you contacted the U.S. Attorney," he asked, "you told him, 'I have no way to reach out to get to them, and I want to get back at them.' Is that correct?"

"That is correct."

"So the only motivation for you to be in the courtroom today is *revenge*?"

"That is correct, Counselor..."

We only got more and more heated.

"Did you not have a number of meetings with Benito Romano, the Assistant United States Attorney that questioned you?"

"Yes, I did."

"And how many meetings did you have with him?"

"Several."

"Well, when you say several, how many do you mean, approximately?"

"If I had an approximate figure, Counselor, I would give it to you. I don't have an approximate figure."

"How many hours would you say you spent with him?"

"I haven't the slightest idea how many hours I spent with him, Counsel! I didn't count the hours!"

"I am not asking you to count them. Was it a great many?"

"A great many? What do you *mean* 'a great many'?!"

Motherfucker was tryin' to show I was brainwashed by the government!

At recess, the attorneys sat me down and scolded me for the outburst. Romano was mad. "It was a fair question he was asking you, Nick, but you've got to be cool in there. Don't let him bait you! Now, we talked about this. If you can't control yourself, you're going to blow it and these guys are going to walk!"

The next day I went in, cooled out and took it right to Kunstler when he tried to rattle me. First he asked about my drug use. I explained I mostly used morphine, cocaine and heroin. "That's what's sold on the streets of Harlem, where I come from." And that, yes, I still took drugs— "Presalin and Inderal for high blood pressure."

He asked how many women I'd had, a ballpark figure. "I think *many* would be an accurate method to describe it, Counselor." As for their behavior, I went on to say my women could have millions of men in New York, only "they don't have to have my friends or members of the Council."

Then he wanted to know about the money. I told him my most profitable years were '73 to '75, when I personally grossed about $5 million. "Wasn't it necessary," he asked, "to maintain a record of expenditures and of money received?"

"Maybe at IBM, but not with the Council of Brothers...We were making money hand over first, Counselor, money wasn't a problem."

And then the question everyone had to know: "In your entire career from the streets and gutters of Harlem to the position which you aspired to, have you ever personally killed a man?"

"No."

My testimony ended after three days, and towards the end, I got asked why I personally went after Bimbo when Guy Fisher asked me to. I thought about it and answered, "I'd go through hell for Guy in a pair of dynamite drawers."

And that was true.

The Shuffle

ON NOVEMBER 21, 1983, after testimony from over 100 witnesses and five days of deliberations, the sequestered jury of eight men and four women found all the Council defendants guilty. Guy, Frank, Wally and Ishmael were convicted on CCE, among other charges, and Gaps on narcotics conspiracy and racketeering.

Two months later they were sentenced.

Guy got forty years followed by life without parole. Frank got life without parole plus forty years. Wally got life without parole plus thirty-five years. Ishmael got life without parole plus sixteen years.

But it bothered me that none of them were found guilty of murder. I pleaded guilty to our homicides in order to bring them all down with me.

Now, only I would be sentenced for the Council's capital crimes.

My work for the government led to almost fifty indictments, and because of my cooperation, in 1985 Mike Wallace did a *60 Minutes* segment, "Should Nicky Barnes Be Freed?"

I thought it might help the next year, August 28, 1986, when it was time to be sentenced on my guilty plea of murder, racketeering and conspiracy. The prosecutors didn't want a sentence at all. In fact, the day before my appearance in court, Romano took me upstairs to see Giuliani again.

"I wrote a letter to Judge Pollack," Giuliani told me, "about all the work you've done for us. We're trying to get a reduction for you. I'm trying to do that. I made a commitment to you, and the U.S. Attorney's office will stick to that."

Giuliani didn't have to do that, but he did. Shit, he didn't have to see me and tell me himself, but he did. The man was straight up. So I stood there in court with Howard Jacobs next to me. I told the judge what he wanted to hear; only now, it was kind of true.

"I did a lot of wrong to a lot of people, society and to myself, and for that I am truly sorry. I embrace traditional values now. I mean positive, good, constructive values, the values that should be held in all communities. I'm not trying to say that I am number one American. I am just a guy that came from the street and made a sharp turn, that's all."

Judge Pollack talked about the Council trial. "I was impressed then with your demeanor, credibility and frankness of your testimony. I balanced the extreme seriousness of your offenses against the remarkable degree of public service you have since rendered."

I'm thinking this is good.

"Ten years," he said.

I thought I was gonna walk out free. Right then. I didn't think I would get any time at all.

My lawyer Jacobs calmed me down, told me to hang tough. He was going to talk to the attorney general about a presidential pardon.

In the late 1980s, Giuliani wanted to get to John Gotti, the Teflon Don, as much as Robert Fiske had wanted to get me, "Mr. Untouchable," a decade before. And the U.S. Attorney wanted to use me to do it. I had no problem, especially since it involved testifying against Mark Reiter.

Gotti was making a lot of his money selling heroin to Harlem, his plan to return the Mafia to greatness. And his point man for dope was still Mark Reiter. Though a major target, Reiter had eluded the Feds for years. Thelma got too scared to testify against him. Shamecca was dead.

I told the jury how I set Reiter up with Thelma and Mecca, how Reiter hired my nephew to kill Shamecca and her brother Son in order to send me a message. The prosecutor passed Shamecca's mug shot to the jury, and the jury gasped at how pretty she was. Nobody looks good in a mug shot. They didn't even see her with her good face.

The prosecutors credited my testimony for Reiter's guilty verdict, and said because of me, the Mafia's heroin days in Harlem had finally ended. I was just glad to knock off Mark with my testimony, give a little justice for Mecca.

Mark got two life terms plus sixty years because of me, and after that, Giuliani worked extra hard for my pardon.

"Rudy will get you a pardon after Election Day," the federal prosecutors told me. Giuliani even wrote a personal letter to President Reagan before he left office. He did everything he could.

But when Giuliani can't get it done, damn, it's hard to get done, 'cause that guy was connected up.

I bided my time in the witness security unit of Otisville. Didn't really talk much to the other prisoners, just worked out a lot, did my chores—cleaned the mess, separated the recyclable goods from the regular garbage, mopped up—then went to my cell and lay in the bunk. Now and then I'd think about Mecca, about our time in the Caymans. I really had everything I needed then.

I wonder if those diamonds are still in that deposit box.

In February 1992, I stood in front of Judge Milton Pollack. Again. He'd aged since we last met. Had a microphone 'cause he could barely talk above a whisper. Had on headphones so he could hear. This eighty-four-year-old muthafucka's sittin' up there with all this electronic shit, lookin' like some weird Game Boy character.

I awaited my sentence. Again.

After Giuliani couldn't get me a pardon in '88 and left the U.S. Attorney's office, he passed my case to his successor, Otto Obermaier. Realizing I was never getting a pardon, Obermaier changed tacks, going before the Rules Committee in Congress, asking that the law be amended so sentences could be reduced for guys who cooperate *after* they get to prison, not just before.

And goddamn, it worked. Congress changed the law, just for me, leaving me eligible for resentencing on my '77 and '86 convictions. Obermaier filed a request with Judge Pollack for my immediate release, delivering a thirty-three-page brief on how I "participated in sophisticated and dangerous undercover operations" even though my "life was necessarily in constant jeopardy," how I "provided the government with extremely valuable cooperation of historic proportions," and finally, how "recognition must be given to the extraordinary cooperation such as Barnes rendered."

Now, nine times out of ten when a federal prosecutor says he wants to put a man on the street, he does it. And apart from that, everyone knew Giuliani was the driving force for my release—Obermaier even said so in court as he begged the judge for my release. *Begged* him for it.

My lawyer, Howard Jacobs, got up and told Judge Pollack that I was a "terrible, horrible drug dealer back in the 1970s" but now had graduated cum laude in the prison education program, prepared other inmates for the GED, taught English and even won a national poetry competition.

Finally, it came down to me.

"I hope that Your Honor will consider that the person who stands here now is not the same person who was convicted in 1977. I think I made a conscious effort to change my life, to change myself, to change my values and to consciously construct a positive character to guide the rest of my life."

Judge Pollack nodded. "Six more years."

What the fuck is this magic number six?! I couldn't say that, because he could easily make it twelve, but why six more years?

Well, the judge must have seen my face, 'cause then he said to me, "Don't worry, you're a young man. You'll be out before you know it."

Young man? I'm fifty-nine years old!

Why did this happen? What was the problem? Publicity, man. That was the problem.

Senator Al D'Amato and Congressman Charles Schumer each had elections that year and wanted to show voters how tough they were on crime. So they both wrote letters "imploring" Judge Pollack not to release me.

Each got a pound of flesh out of that.

I waited out six more years in prison. And I have nothing to say about that except I've spent thirty years in the joint, and there's no such thing as a good day when you're in prison.

When I heard that Ishmael died of cancer while serving his bid I said to myself, *Dude, you might not get out of this motherfucker.*

But I did get out, in August 1998. I was sixty-four.

That first day out, I was going through the airport with the marshals. They were walking fast, telling me to keep up. I thought I was walking fast, but being in Otisville, you can't walk any distance without coming to a locked door. You don't ever stretch your legs out. You walk a kind of shuffle.

That's how I'd been walking all these years. I didn't even realize it till I was in the airport with the marshals. And I ran in the joint! Three or four times a week on the treadmill in Otisville. I guess I was used to goin' nowhere, 'cause these marshals? They were on the move!

So I just ran through the airport.

That was the most dramatic insight about how prison affected me. My movements were so much different than everyone else's. I didn't exactly know where I was movin' to, but that didn't matter. I was just overwhelmed to have my freedom. Overwhelmed to have the protection the marshals gave me and to know that, yo, I got a chance to make it legitimately.

Automated car washes, flake burger businesses, real estate...

Man, I felt so good about everything. About being alive. Freedom is something so uplifting.

Such a powerful feeling.

LEROY "NICKY" BARNES

Looking Back

I'VE THOUGHT A LOT ABOUT what happened. Years I've thought about it. If things had worked out the way I wanted, I would have never been in prison. Never in my wildest imagination could I have believed what was gonna happen, but there are a few things that all make sense when I look at it now.

I don't think I should have expected so much positivity out of an operation based on drug dealing and homicides. How can you find pluses in something that is so minus? It was fundamentally negative, so really, it was doomed from the beginning.

But there was one mistake of mine from way back, one mistake I didn't foresee in structuring the Council the way I did. It was the democratic aspect of it all. That was my downfall. I never should've treated those guys fairly. I should've treated them like dogs. That's what I should've done.

I could've done better as a solo entrepreneur, but I wanted to have a group of brothers to watch my back. And despite everything, the Council idea was still a good one, and it worked good for a while. Only it has to work all the time, and the guys just weren't as committed to the dollar as I was. I set anything aside if we were makin' money. The other shit just didn't count.

But they didn't have the mind-set for that.

I remember talking to Joey Gallo about *The Godfather*. All those biological family ties among the Italians that tightened up the Cosa Nostra. And I think that because of the fractures in so many African-American families, that had something to do with the inability of the Council members to bind together as a family when the father was gone.

The Council members were in foreign territory when it came to family loyalty. I'm talking about positive values. Unity, stayin' together. I don't know what kind of Oedipal bullshit was goin' on with these dudes in terms of me.

I don't know. But if you're gonna support the father, it's because of the tradition you were brought up in, it's not something you discover. And these guys just didn't have that.

Guy's dad left his mom. I heard him talk about his mother, but never his dad. Frank didn't have a mom and dad. Jazz? I never heard him say anything about a mother. Wally had a mom and no dad. Gaps had a mom and dad, but you would have never known. I never remember a Mother's Day when I heard anyone sayin', "I got to be at Mom's tomorrow."

I created a family with people who didn't understand family. And when I left, when "Dad" went away, it all fell apart, just disintegrated. They betrayed me, because they didn't understand what it was to have a family. And that was all I wanted.

But in chess, and in life, the man with forethought is the man who wins. I'm smarter than those guys were. That's why they're in the joint right now. When the game went against me, I changed tactics and knew they could never keep up.

But I still think about all of them.

My nephew Mellon got sentenced for the murders of Shamecca and her brother Son. He wanted to follow in my footsteps and got his wish.

Life in prison.

Thelma pleaded guilty to running a heroin ring. When she arrived for sentencing, she begged mercy from the court, brought up the fact she was five months pregnant by that motherfucker Tito. Got ten years and, as part of a secret plea agreement, turned over all my money, $10 million.

But there was more than that, I know, so all I wanna ask is, "The fuck you do with all my money?!" 'Cause I left you so much of that. Safe-deposit boxes full of it! Maybe it was that black belt in shoppin' you had.

Whatever.

Sista's alive, I think, although I haven't heard a thing about her. That's probably for the best, 'cause I wouldn't want her people to know she'd been married to me.

I didn't give Curt up. He's still out there makin' money. Didn't give Big Smitty up neither. But he's real sick now. Sorry to hear that, dude. I hope you get a chance to read this.

I never would've given Bobby Monroe up, no way. He ended up going to jail on his own on that Joe Peters thing. It was only gonna be five or six years on that, but Bobby caught a heart attack in a Riker's Island hospital. Too obsessed with sniffin' coke. That's what ended up killin' him. Just oversniffed and did some internal damage he was never able to recover from.

Ishmael's dead from cancer, and his wife Helen's dead too. You just knew neither of them were gonna make it.

Lot of guys are dead, man. Reggie Isaacs, Stan Morgan. Goldfinger. All of them killed. Man.

Couple of the guys are out. Gaps is out. Don't know what he's doin', but then again, he's probably more underground than I am! Jazz is out and in Harlem, fuckin' with some political activism.

Figures. A good avenue to run his mouth.

Frank James is doin' life in Otisville. Heard he's really gotten heavy into Islam since then, like an ancient Imam to the younger guys in the joint. Wally Rice is in Lewisburg doin' life, too.

You got yourself in that one, Wally. I never intended to give you up.

And Guy Fisher? There was some type of angst he had with his dad he superimposed on me. Some type of ill feeling he satisfied through trying to diminish me. So indirectly, he was striking back at the dad who left him. I dunno. I talk about Guy's contempt, envy or Oedipal animosity he eventually imposed on me, but really? I don't know the psychological mechanics that caused him to do the shit that he did.

Last I heard was he got a torrid affair goin' on with a homosexual. Some people? That's how they do their bid!

I remember this dude who came into the Wit Sec unit, used to be out on the floor with Guy, so he brought me some stories.

"How much time you facin'?" he asked Guy.

"Life," said Guy.

"Damn," he told him, "that's a lot of time for some pussy!"

Yeah, I'd like to see Guy die in jail. I'd like to see Frank and Wally get out. I kinda hope they do.

The Cake

❦ Cook Book

LILITH RUSHING

 RUTH VOSS

The Cake

Cook Book

CHILTON BOOKS—Publishers

A Division of Chilton Company

Philadelphia and New York

℞ Acknowledgments

We wish to thank the following for their help and encouragement in the preparation of this book:

Our sisters: Sybil Hancock, Coral Sanford, Vera Brannon and Ethel Brannon, for helping us to test the recipes and for letting us use their own favorite recipes.

Joanne Snider, the daughter of Ruth Voss; Emma Stephenson, her niece; Sue Breeden, Hilda Bracey and Fay Cantrell, nieces of Lilith Rushing. They also tested many recipes for us and gave some to us.

Our friend, Mrs. Alberta Bennight, who kindly gave us her mother's recipe, *Mrs. Alice Peet's Eggless Cake.*

The many other relatives and friends who have throughout the years given us their treasured recipes.

The J. C. Ferguson Publishing Company of Chicago, who allowed us to include the *Cocoa Coconut Cake, Half-A-Pound Cake* and *Whole Wheat Cake* from the "Modern Family Cook Book" by Meta Given, copyright 1953.

The Wichita Eagle and Beacon, who granted permission for the inclusion from their *Home Town News* by Frank Good, copyright 1961, of *Wacky Cake, Crazy Cake, Angel Delight Cake, Rhubarb Upside Down Cake* and *Green Apple Cake.*

Chilton Books for letting us include *Common Causes and Remedies in Cake Baking Failures* from "The Gold Cook Book" by Louis P. DeGouy, copyright 1947, 1948.

v

And last, but very far from least, Luther Rushing, husband of Lilith Rushing, cake-lover extraordinary, who has over the years courted dyspepsia by tasting every baked product that emanated from his wife's oven and continues to ask for more.

In compiling this book we made no attempt to include the many cakes that are native to various foreign countries, but chose to confine ourselves to those that can truly be said are home-made in America.

LILITH RUSHING
RUTH VOSS

WICHITA, KANSAS
March 1965

℞ Contents

Before You Begin

How to Use this Book 3
The Ingredients of a Cake 4
Basic Tools for Cake Baking 7
"How to"—A Glossary of Baking Terms and Procedures 8
Measurements and Equivalents 13
General Instructions 14
Time and Temperature Chart 16
A Cake on Which to Practice 17

Recipes

Chapter 1: Cakes for the Family 21
Chapter 2: Light as Air—Angel, Sponge and Chiffon 37
Chapter 3: Coffee Cakes 47
Chapter 4: Spiced and Spicy Cakes 55
Chapter 5: Fruit Cakes 64
Chapter 6: Cakes That Top Themselves and Somersault 73
Chapter 7: Budget-Minded Cakes 84
Chapter 8: Baked in the Refrigerator 89
Chapter 9: Pound Cakes 99
Chapter 10: Cupcakes 106
Chapter 11: Cakes for Party Giving and Party Going—At Home,
Church and Club 111

Chapter 12: Rare, Historical and Offbeat Cakes   133
Chapter 13: Transforming Commercial Mixes   150
Chapter 14: Fillings, Frostings, Icings, Toppings   157

*Common Causes and Remedies in
Cake Baking Failures*   179

Index   189

A fair lady once said, "Let them eat cake!"
    the history books record, there on the shelf,
We repeat, "Let them eat cake!"
    and homemaker dear, make it yourself!

Before
You Begin

HOW TO USE THIS BOOK

All measurements given are level, unless otherwise stated. We recommend the use of standard metal measuring cups with level tops and a set of standard measuring spoons.

"Butter" can be butter or margarine. However, natural butter gives the richest flavor and finest texture to cake and, if possible, its use is recommended. If country or dairy butter is a definite requirement, the fact is so stated in the recipe. The other recipes are adapted for the specific type of shortening listed. However, butter may be substituted in the following proportions:

1 cup butter equals ⅞ cup of solid or liquid oil or shortening (½ cup butter equals 8 tablespoons)

Thus, in replacing shortening with butter, use about one-eighth additional butter.

Sift all flour and confectioners sugar before measuring. If granulated sugar has "packed" in its box, that too should be sifted before measuring.

All the recipes in this book call for the use of standard SAS Double Action baking powder.

Fill baking pans about half full, but never more than two-thirds full, although loaf and tube pans may be filled a little higher.

Abbreviations Used

Tbsp. = tablespoon
tsp. = teaspoon
doz. = dozen
pkg. = package
lb. = pound
oz. = ounce

We have tried to catalogue these recipes so that the home baker can easily find the cake she wants to make. But many a kind overlaps another. Please consult the Index at back of the book which is cross-referenced.

All the cakes in this book have been tested and used over and over by homemakers.

3

THE INGREDIENTS OF A CAKE

The principal cake ingredients are flour, sugar, shortening, eggs, milk (or other liquid), baking powder (or other leavening), flavoring, and salt. Each has its own effect upon the success of the cake.

Flour

The flour absorbs and holds considerable moisture and aids in holding the other ingredients together. It also assists materially in building up and maintaining the skeletal structure of the cake.

There are various types of flour, each of which is preferable for a specific class of cakes. For instance, pound cake, fruit cake and cakes of the "heavier" type require a cake flour of higher gluten-protein content than do layer cakes, whereas angel food and sponge cakes need a cake flour of lower and softer gluten content.

The principal kinds of flour are bread flour, all-purpose, and cake flour. And although flour accounts for only a small percentage of the total cost of the cake, the wrong type of flour or an inferior grade can easily ruin the finished product. Therefore it is false economy for the cake baker to use anything but high quality flour of a type best suited for the specific recipe she is making.

Sugar

Sugar is a most important ingredient in cakes and should be used in exactly the correct proportions and should be carefully incorporated into the cake. As a whole, sugar serves the following important purposes in cake making: it adds sweetness; it aids in the creaming process; it creates a softening or spreading action in the batter; it imparts color to the crust; it retains moisture, thereby prolonging the cake's freshness; it forms the body of icings and fillings; it adds food value.

Excessive amounts of sugar tend to cause a thick, porous crust, coarse grain, and a soggy texture. They may make a cake rise well at first, but it will fall while baking. Insufficient sugar often means a low volume cake with a tough, coarse interior, and with inferior keeping qualities.

Sugar is usually creamed in with the shortening and eggs prior to addition of the other ingredients. In some cakes, part of the sugar is added with the flour.

Shortening

With the exception of angel food and some types of sponge cake, in which no shortening is used, the judicious use of shortening in nearly all cakes aids materially in the creation of the desired volume, grain and texture. The shortening, which is uniformly distributed throughout the mixed mass of cake ingredients, coats each tiny particle of batter, giving to the crumb of the finished product a long lasting softness. This means that the cake will retain its freshness for a longer period.

Butter, margarine, vegetable shortenings, liquid oils (corn and vegetable), and cream, are the principal shortening agents used in cakes. Each type has its purpose and the cake baker should follow recipe directions in the use of shortening.

Eggs

The primary function of eggs in cake is their effect on the eating qualities of the cake.

If whole eggs or yolks are used the cake has a pleasing golden color, giving it a definite appetite appeal. In such cakes as angel food, where only the egg whites are used, the snowy whiteness that results from the prolonged beating or whipping is especially desirable.

The beating of eggs forms a fluffy, foam-like mass which is much lighter and occupies a much larger volume than do unbeaten eggs. Thus, the air is incorporated and distributed throughout the cake batter and, when subjected to the heat of the oven, the expansion of this air exerts a definite leavening action on the cake.

In conjunction with the gluten of flour, eggs act as the supporting framework of a cake and therefore have a marked influence on the grain and texture of the cake. Eggs also impart a delicious flavor to the cake, and the nutritive value of eggs needs no explanation.

Milk

Milk helps to prolong the freshness of the cake, assists in promoting a desirable appearance, and helps to prevent greasiness. Milk also adds to the richness and flavor of the cake as well as to its food value.

Whole sweet milk, buttermilk or sour milk, dried milk, condensed and evaporated milk are used in different types of cakes. The kind called for in each recipe is planned to harmonize with the other ingredients.

Baking Powder

Baking powder is the principal leavening agent of cakes. While other ingredients can be considered the "body" of a cake, it is the action of baking powder that is mainly responsible for the conversion of the heavy mass of batter into a light, well-risen, appetizing cake. Thus, baking powder may be called the "soul" of a cake.

It is very important to use the exact amount of baking powder. Lack of volume, poor grain and texture, and impaired eating qualities are likely to result if either too little or too much baking powder is used. However, it is better to use too little than too much.

Since even the most carefully preserved baking powder can, and frequently does, deteriorate and lose its leavening action, it is suggested that a newly opened can, or one which has stood on the shelf for a time, be tested before using. To do this mix a teaspoon of the powder in one-third cup of hot water. If the powder bubbles vigorously it is in good condition; should it fail to bubble or do so only feebly, do not use it.

Flavoring

The proper use of flavoring can greatly enhance a cake, and the careless or improper use of flavoring can just as readily ruin the quality of what would otherwise have been a good cake.

Cake is made up largely of rich ingredients which in proper proportions and blended together in the cake create a naturally delicious flavor. This is further improved by the judicious use of flavoring.

Lemon and vanilla extract are the most commonly used flavorings, with vanilla probably the most popular. Vanilla blends exceptionally well with the shortening in cake, particularly with butter. Other popular flavorings are chocolate, cocoa, spices, brown sugar and molasses, almond extract, ginger, and orange.

In order to please the palate, the final flavor of the cake must represent a harmony of the individual flavors of which it is composed. The flavor should not be too strong but rather mildly tantalizing. If a predominant flavor is desired, it is often better to emphasize this flavor in the icing rather than in the cake itself. Harmonious flavorings make a taste-pleasing cake.

There are on the market many synthetic flavorings. It is heartily recommended that only pure extracts be used, for only these give the true essence of the desired flavor to the cake.

Salt

The main purpose of salt in cakes is its peculiar ability to bring out and intensify the inherent flavors of the cake and its ingredients. Without salt a cake would not *fall* flat but it would *taste* flat.

BASIC TOOLS FOR CAKE MAKING

1 set of mixing bowls of assorted sizes
2 nests of level measuring cups (1 for liquids; 1 for dry ingredients)
1 set of standard measuring spoons
3 spatulas of different sizes
1 rubber spatula
1 large slotted spoon (for separating eggs)
1 large wooden mixing spoon
1 rotary egg beater
1 long wire whisk (for beating egg whites)
1 short wire whisk (for whipping and general beating)
1 nut or spice grater
1 large flour sieve
1 large strainer
1 small strainer
1 lemon squeezer
1 paring knife
1 apple corer
1 wire cake rack (two-layer size)
1 wooden board (for chopping and for crushing crumbs)
1 oven thermometer
1 timer
1 10-inch cast iron skillet
1 2-quart double boiler
3 7-inch round layer cake pans

3 8-inch round layer cake pans
2 9-inch round layer cake pans
1 8-inch square baking pan
1 9-inch square baking pan
1 9-inch spring form pan
1 9-inch tube cake pan
1 10-inch tube cake pan
6 oblong loaf cake pans in assorted sizes from 7 to 15 inches
2 muffin tins
1 8-inch pie tin
1 9-inch pie tin
1 $15\frac{1}{2} \times 10\frac{1}{2} \times \frac{1}{2}$-inch jelly roll pan
1 large roll wax paper
1 large roll aluminum foil
1 box of wooden toothpicks (for testing)

"HOW TO"—A GLOSSARY OF BAKING TERMS AND PROCEDURES

Adding Flour and Liquid Alternately

This is important in order to keep the consistency of the batter as uniform as possible.

First, about one-fourth of the flour should be sifted and stirred in gently round and round with a wooden mixing spoon. Then the mixture should be beaten with a wire whisk until it is smooth. Next, about one-third of the liquid should be introduced in the same way. This procedure is then continued until all the flour and the liquid have been incorporated. Begin and end this process with an insertion of flour.

Adding Beaten Egg Whites

Use the "cut and fold" method. (See below.)

Beat the whites in a mixing bowl until they "peak" stiff and dry (stand up in sharp points) or "peak" stiff but not dry (stand up in softly rounded mounds) as called for in recipes. Use a long wire whisk.

Adding Beaten Whole Eggs

Beat the eggs with a rotary egg beater or short wire whisk until they are thick and light. Halfway beating only liquifies the eggs. So be sure the eggs are either unbeaten or *well* beaten.

Adding Whole Eggs (Unbeaten)

Drop the eggs, one at a time, right into the creamed sugar-shortening mixture and then beat *vigorously* with the wire whisk. Spirited beating is especially important when eggs are added unbeaten. The mixture should be lifted up while beating to enclose as much air as possible. Beating should be continued until each egg is thoroughly blended, then long enough thereafter to produce a light and smooth mixture.

To Beat (Use a Mixing Spoon or Wire Whisk)

Beating is a different motion from stirring. To beat, rapidly lift up the batter from the bottom of the bowl over and over. This blends the ingredients and introduces air into the mixture.

To Blanch Almonds (Remove Their Skins)

Cover the shelled nuts with boiling water, simmer for 1 minute on top of the stove, and then drain off the water. Rinse the almonds in cold water. Press the nuts between thumb and first and second fingers—the skins will slip off easily.

To Blend

This simply means to stir two or more ingredients together thoroughly.

To Brush

To spread a substance thinly over a surface with a small soft brush or with a piece of paper or cloth.

To Chill

To allow a mixture to become completely cold but not to freeze.

To Cream

The shortening or the sugar, or a mixture of both, is worked against the sides and bottom of a mixing bowl with the back of a spatula or wooden spoon until the mixture is smooth and plastic.

The shortening should be creamed separately first, then about 2 Tbsp. of sugar should be added and creaming continued. The remaining sugar is added in 3 or 4 portions with thorough creaming after each addition.

When all the sugar has been put in, the creaming is continued until the mixture is fluffy, light and creamy (not grainy or crumbly).

To Crumble

To break into small pieces with the fingers.

To Cut and Fold In

A rhythmic cutting down, lifting up, and folding over motion with a rubber spatula or wooden spoon. This motion keeps all the air bubbles in the feathery batter of angel and chiffon cakes. It should be done quickly, but carefully and thoroughly, until all the dry ingredients have disappeared.

To Cut In

Using two knives, to distribute a solid shortening throughout flour or other dry ingredients.

To Dot

To scatter small bits of something over a surface.

To Dust

To sprinkle lightly (usually flour or powdered sugar) over a surface.

To Flour

To cover with a light film of flour.

To Grease and Flour a Pan

Dip a piece of paper or cloth in shortening and spread evenly over the inside of a pan (the bottom more generously, the sides very lightly). Then dust some flour over it, shake the pan to spread the flour around, turn the pan upside down and knock out any excess flour.

To Knead

To stretch dough with the hands, folding it over and then pressing down on it with the heels of the palms. (Spread a large piece of wax paper on the table, or a clean dish towel, dust it very lightly with flour and stretch the dough on it.)

To Melt Chocolate

Do *not* do this over direct heat. Place the chocolate in the top of a double boiler over boiling water. Or place the chocolate in a small bowl that will fit into the top of a boiling tea kettle.

To Preheat

Set the oven to the required temperature and allow at least 10 to 15 minutes for it to warm up. If the oven has no caloric heat regulator, use an oven thermometer to indicate when the needed temperature has been reached, then lower the flame to maintain an even temperature and watch the thermometer while the cake is baking so as to raise or lower the oven flame if need be.

To Remove Cake from Pan

All cakes should be left in their baking pans for 3 to 5 minutes after removal from the oven. Then a knife or spatula should be run gently down between the side of the pan and the cake and run all around, easing lightly but firmly at corners of the pan. After that the pan can be turned over and a gentle shake will loosen the cake onto a plate or rack. Butter cakes should be left on a wire rack until they are completely cool.

An angel cake or sponge cake should be turned upside down in its pan as soon as it is removed from the oven. It should stand this way

(supported by the tube of the pan) for about 1 hour. It may then be removed from the pan.

To Scald

To heat to just below the boiling point.

To Separate Egg Yolks from Whites

The old standby is to crack the egg as near its middle as possible so the egg will break approximately in half. Hold the yolk in one half and let the whites fall into a bowl. The yolk can be passed from one half eggshell to the other until all the white is extracted. Then the yolk can be dropped into a cup or another bowl.

The yolk can also be separated by using a large slotted spoon. Place the spoon over a cup or bowl, break the egg into it, and the whites will run through the slots.

A third method is to puncture a small hole in one end of the egg and let the whites flow out into a bowl. (The yolk can be kept in the shell for several days if the hole is sealed with tape and the egg returned to the refrigerator.)

To Sift

To pass through a sieve.

To Simmer

To cook in liquid on top of a stove at just below boiling point.

To Sliver Almonds

With a sharp knife, cut each nut into several pieces, from the pointed end to the base. Spread the pieces on a baking sheet or pie tin and dry them in a 350° oven for 10 minutes. (Slivering should be done while almonds are still warm from blanching.)

"Spins a Thread"

This means that a syrup falls from a spoon in a threadlike stream about 3 to 4 inches long, rather than falling in droplets.

To Whip

To beat rapidly and continuously with a wire whisk, a rotary beater, or with a fork.

MEASUREMENTS AND EQUIVALENTS

1 pint	equals	2 cups
1 cup	"	16 Tbsp. or 8 fluid oz.
¾ cup	"	12 Tbsp. or 6 fluid oz.
⅔ cup	"	10 Tbsp. plus 2 tsp.
½ cup	"	8 Tbsp. or 4 fluid oz.
⅓ cup	"	5 Tbsp. plus 1 tsp.
¼ cup	"	4 Tbsp. or 2 fluid oz.
⅛ cup	"	2 Tbsp. or 1 fluid oz.
1 Tbsp.	"	3 tsp. or ½ fluid oz.

1 lb. all-purpose flour, sifted	equals	4 cups
1 lb. all-purpose flour, unsifted	"	3½ cups
1 lb. cake flour, sifted	"	4½ cups
1 lb. cake flour, unsifted	"	4 cups
1 lb. confectioners sugar, sifted	"	4 cups
1 lb. granulated sugar	"	2 cups
1 lb. brown sugar	"	2½ cups, firmly packed
1 lb. shortening (any kind)	"	2 cups
¼ lb. butter	"	1 stick, or ½ cup, or 8 Tbsp.
1 lb. chopped walnuts	"	4 cups
1 cup egg whites	"	whites of 8–10 eggs
1 cup egg yolks	"	yolks of 12–14 eggs
1 cup fresh whole eggs	"	5–6 eggs
1 oz. baking powder	"	2⅔ Tbsp.
1 oz. baking soda	"	2 Tbsp.
1 oz. cream of tartar	"	3 Tbsp.
1 cup lemon juice	"	4–6 lemons

℞ *General Instructions*

1) Set out and check all needed ingredients, pans, bowls, tools, etc. before you start to mix.

2) Allow shortening and eggs to stand at room temperature for at least a half hour before they are used.

3) Preheat the oven to the indicated temperature before the cake is inserted.

4) Before creaming shortening, pour boiling water into the mixing bowl to heat it. Drain and dry the bowl thoroughly. If shortening is placed in a warm bowl it will cream more readily.

5) Measure all ingredients accurately, as follows:

Liquids Use only standard level-topped measuring cups, but if a lipped measuring cup should be used, check the mark by lifting the cup to eye level.

Solid Shortening (*If Measured Sticks of Butter or Margarine Are Not Used*) Use metal measuring cups and fill them firmly with a rubber spatula. Level off the excess with the straight edge of a spatula or knife.

Flour Sift through a sieve. Then spoon into a measuring cup until it overflows. Remove the excess lightly with a straight-edge knife or a spatula. (Do not press down the flour or shake the cup to level it.)

Sugar or Powdered Ingredients Sift lightly through a sieve. Measure into a standard measuring cup or spoon and level off with a flat-edge knife or a spatula.

6) Fruits and nuts must be dredged with flour before they are added into a batter. This prevents them from falling to the bottom of a cake.

14

7) In separating eggs, if a bit of yolk drops into the whites, a cloth moistened in cold water and touched to the spilled yolk will pick it up.

8) When beating egg whites do not tap the beater on the edge of the bowl to clear it—the jar of the beater will make the whites lose their fluffiness. Tap the beater on your hand instead.

9) Egg whites for angel or sponge cake beat up lighter and more easily if they are at room temperature. They should be neither too warm nor too cold. Unless the kitchen is unusually warm, remove the eggs from the refrigerator and let them stand at room temperature for two or three hours before they are to be beaten.

10) When using heatproof glass pans, reduce the oven temperature 25° but use the same baking time called for in the recipe.

11) The sides of pans used for small cupcakes should be greased very little because heavy greasing tends to make the batter "turn in" at the top.

12) If directions are followed as to the oven temperature and the size of the pan, the cake should be done in the time specified. But to make sure, always test a cake before removing it from the oven in the following ways:

a) See if the cake has risen well and has a delicately brown crust.

b) If it is a butter cake, see if the cake has shrunk away slightly from the sides of the pan.

c) Press a finger lightly on the cake's surface—it should spring back and leave no imprint.

d) Insert a toothpick or wire tester into the center of the cake—it should come out clean and dry. If any batter clings to the tester the cake is not yet done.

13) If pans are new, butter them well and place them in a moderate oven for 15 minutes. Then wash them and they are ready for use. This treatment prevents cakes from burning in new pans.

14) For easy decoration of a child's birthday cake, press a cookie cutter in the shape of an animal lightly into the icing on top of the cake, to make an outline. Then the outline can be filled with tinted icing from a pastry tube, or with small colored candies, small jelly beans, or chocolate bits.

15) To store a cake, as soon as it is completely cooled, place it in a covered box (as airtight as possible). Set the cake on a large piece of wax paper inside the box; this makes for ease in handling.

Cakes can also be stored in the crisper drawer of the refrigerator where vegetables and fruits are normally stored.

Cakes can be made ahead of time and frozen un-iced in the freezing compartment of the refrigerator. (Frosted cakes can also be frozen, but icings have a more delicate flavor if they are served as soon as they are made.) Remove the cake from the freezer at least six hours before serving and allow it to defrost slowly at room temperature.

To keep a loaf or layer cake fresh after it has been cut, put a slice of fresh bread in the cake box with it, or an apple cut in half. These help to keep the cake moist.

Wrapping the cut cake in plastic wrap or aluminum foil and placing it low in the refrigerator is another easy way to keep cakes fresh and moist.

16) If baking at high altitudes the following adjustments should be made: The baking temperature should be raised about 25°. The leavening (baking powder, soda, or both) at 3500 feet should be decreased by about one-third, at 5000 feet by about one-half, and above 5000 feet by about two-thirds. It is also advisable to beat egg whites somewhat less; keep them soft and fluffy but do not beat them until they are dry.

17) In making applesauce cake, the applesauce is sometimes the only liquid used. But applesauce varies in liquid content, so often a little sweet milk or buttermilk is necessary. And too, sometimes a little more flour may be needed.

TIME AND TEMPERATURE CHART FOR CAKES

Type of Cake	Oven Temperature	Baking Time
Angel Food	350°	35–40 min.
Sponge	325°	60–65 min.
Jelly Roll	375°	12–15 min.
Cup Cakes	375°	15–18 min.
8–9-inch layers	350°	25–30 min.
9-inch square	350°	35–40 min.
13- × 9-inch sheet	350°	35–40 min.
Loaf	350°	55–60 min.
Fruit	300°–375°	1–2 hours

Slow Oven	250°–325°	Hot Oven	400°–450°
Moderate Oven	350°–375°	Very Hot Oven	450°–500°

A CAKE ON WHICH TO PRACTICE

¼ cup (½ stick) butter or
              margarine
1 egg
1½ cups cake flour, sifted
1 tsp. vanilla

⅔ cup granulated sugar
½ cup milk
2 tsp. baking powder
¼ tsp. salt

Remove the butter from the refrigerator and let it soften. Light the oven, set it to 350° and let it heat up (this takes 10 to 15 minutes).

Grease and flour an 8-inch square baking pan "grease and flour" is explained in the "How To" glossary (p. 8).

Place on the work table all the utensils, etc. that you'll need:

a mixing bowl
2 measuring cups
a measuring teaspoon
a large mixing spoon (wooden)
a wire whisk (or large fork)

a cereal bowl
a flour sieve
a wire cake rack
a spatula
toothpicks (for testing)

Put the softened butter and the sugar in the mixing bowl. Cream these together with the mixing spoon by pressing against the side of the bowl with the back of the spoon. Continue doing this until the butter and sugar are thoroughly combined and the mixture looks creamy (not lumpy or coarsely grained).

Break the egg into the cereal bowl and beat it well with the wire whisk or the large fork. Pour the beaten egg into the creamed butter-sugar mixture and stir it in thoroughly. Add in the vanilla and stir it in completely.

Sift together the flour and the baking powder and the salt through the sieve onto a piece of wax paper. Then sift them again into the mixing bowl on top of the creamed mixture. Now beat the mixture well with the mixing spoon or with a rotary beater or the wire whisk. Be sure all the flour is incorporated.

Pour the batter into the prepared pan and set the pan in the heated oven. Let the cake bake for about 35 minutes.

Test the cake then with the toothpick test (See p. 15) to see if it is done. If it is not, let it continue baking for ten minutes longer and then test it again.

Remove the pan from the oven and let the cake stand in the pan for about 5 minutes. Then gently ease the cake (using a knife or spatula to work around the edges) from the pan and place it on the cake rack until it is completely cool.

Meanwhile prepare the following Pink Frosting and when the cake is cool spread it on top of and on the sides of the cake. (Frosting directions can be found on p. 157).

Pink Frosting

½ stick butter or margarine	1 Tbsp. condensed milk
2 cups confectioners sugar, sifted	1 tsp. red cake coloring
⅛ tsp. salt	1 tsp. vanilla

Cream the butter in a mixing bowl with the sugar; add in a small amount of sugar at a time and make the mixture very smooth and creamy. Then add in the salt, the cake coloring, and the milk. Stir thoroughly with your mixing spoon until the frosting is completely smooth.

THREE SPECIAL WARNINGS

1. Do not open oven door during first half of time any cake is baking. This can cause it to fall.

2. In making yeast cakes, be sure to punch down the dough with your fist in between risings.

3. Always wash your beater well before beating egg whites. Rinse it in warm water.

Recipes

✥ Cakes for the Family
Chapter 1

MINTED CHOCOLATE CAKE

1 stick butter	1½ cups cake flour, sifted
1 cup granulated sugar	½ tsp. salt
2 egg yolks	1 tsp. baking soda
2 squares unsweetened choco- late	1 cup sour milk
	1 tsp. vanilla

Beat the butter, sugar and egg yolks until they are creamy. Melt the chocolate and add it to the egg mix.

Sift the flour, salt and soda together and add them into the egg mix alternately with the milk. Mix well, then add the vanilla and stir thoroughly again.

Bake in an 8-inch greased and floured square pan in a 350° oven for 30 to 40 minutes.

Frost with Uncooked Icing (See p. 175), adding ½ tsp. pure peppermint extract to the frosting mix.

LEMON CAKE

½ stick butter	1 tsp. baking powder
1 cup confectioners sugar, sifted	⅔ cup milk
	1 tsp. lemon extract
4 eggs, separated	1 cup granulated sugar
1 cup cake flour, sifted	1 tsp. vinegar

Cream the butter and the confectioners sugar together until they are smooth. Beat well yolks of 3 eggs, add them into the creamed mixture, and beat again.

Sift the flour with the baking powder and add it in alternately with the milk into the creamed mixture. Then put in the extract.

Pour this batter into two greased and floured 8-inch layer cake pans.

Now beat the whites of 4 eggs until they are stiff. Fold in the granulated sugar and the vinegar, and spread this mixture over the batter in the pans.

Bake for 25 minutes in a 350° oven. Put the layers together with Pineapple Egg Yolk Filling (See p. 159), which uses the fourth egg yolk.

THE ETHEL BRANNON CAKE

¾ cup boiling water
½ cup cocoa
1¾ cups cake flour, sifted
1¾ cups granulated sugar
1½ tsp. baking soda
1 tsp. salt

½ cup salad oil
7 egg yolks, unbeaten
2 tsp. vanilla
1 cup egg whites (8 large or 10 small eggs)
½ tsp. cream of tartar

Combine the water and the cocoa; let them cool. Sift the flour, the sugar, soda, and the salt together. Make a well in the flour mix and add the oil, the egg yolks, the cooled cocoa mixture, and the vanilla. Beat until smooth.

Beat the egg whites and cream of tartar together until they are very stiff. Pour the egg yolk mixture in a thin stream over the entire surface of the egg whites, gently cutting in until all is blended.

Pour the batter into an ungreased 10-inch tube pan. Bake in a preheated oven at 325° for 65 to 70 minutes. Invert the pan and let the cake cool.

PEANUT BUTTER CAKE

½ cup peanut butter
1 stick butter
1 cup brown sugar
½ cup granulated sugar
2 eggs, beaten

¾ tsp. vanilla
2½ cups all-purpose flour, sifted
3 tsp. baking powder
½ tsp. salt
1 cup milk

Cream the butter and the peanut butter together. Stir in the sugars and beat well. Add the beaten eggs and the vanilla.

Sift the flour with the baking powder and the salt. Add the flour mix into the batter alternately with the milk.

Pour the batter into a well greased and floured 13 × 9 × 2-inch pan. Bake in a 350° oven for 35 minutes. When the cake is cool, frost it with Uncooked Icing, (See p. 175).

IRISH APPLE CAKE

3 cups cake flour, sifted	1¾ cups applesauce
¾ cup granulated sugar	½ tsp. cinnamon
½ tsp. salt	¼ tsp. ground cloves
3 egg yolks	Grated rind of 1 lemon
2 sticks butter, softened	

Heat the oven to 350°. Grease and flour a square 9-inch pan.

Mix the flour, sugar and salt. Add in the egg yolks and the butter. Combine well. Divide the mixture into two parts. Press one portion into the greased pan.

Mix the applesauce, the cinnamon, the cloves, and the lemon rind; spread this on top of the dough in the pan. Spread the rest of the batter over the applesauce.

Bake for 40 to 50 minutes. Top with whipped cream or Lemon Sauce, (See p. 178). Serves 9.

CHOCOLATE FUDGE CAKE

2 cups cake flour, sifted	2 egg yolks, beaten
3 tsp. baking powder	3 squares unsweetened choco-late, melted
½ tsp. baking soda	
¼ tsp. salt	1¼ cups milk
½ cup shortening	1 tsp. vanilla
1 cup granulated sugar	2 egg whites, stiffly beaten

Sift the flour once; then measure it. Add the baking powder, the soda, and the salt, and sift three times.

Cream the shortening thoroughly, add in the sugar gradually, then cream them together until they are light and fluffy. Now add the egg yolks and the chocolate, then the flour and the milk alternately, a small amount at a time. Beat after each addition until the mixture is smooth. Add the vanilla and fold in the egg whites.

Bake in two greased and floured 9-inch layer cake pans in a 350° oven for 30 minutes. Put the layers together with Fudge Frosting, (See p. 163).

DELICIOUS HONEY CAKE

½ **stick butter**	½ **tsp. cinnamon**
¼ **cup shortening**	½ **tsp. salt**
1 **cup strained honey**	1 **tsp. baking soda**
1 **egg, well beaten**	½ **cup sour milk**
4 **cups cake flour, sifted**	

Cream together the butter with the shortening. Add in gradually the honey and the beaten egg and blend until the mixture is smooth.

Sift the flour with the cinnamon and the salt. Dissolve the soda in the sour milk. Add into the creamed mixture the flour mixture alternately with the milk. Blend together smoothly.

Bake in a greased and floured shallow 13 × 9-inch pan in a 350° oven for 50 minutes.

When the cake is cool serve it cut into slices or squares.

DELIGHT OATMEAL CAKE

1 **stick butter, softened**	1 **tsp. cinnamon**
½ **cup granulated sugar**	½ **tsp. nutmeg**
1 **cup brown sugar**	1 **tsp. baking soda**
1 **tsp. vanilla**	1 **cup milk**
1 **egg**	1 **cup rolled oats**
1½ **cups all-purpose flour,**	(**quick or oldfashioned**)
sifted	1 **tsp. baking soda**
½ **tsp. salt**	

Heat the oven to 325°. Beat the butter until it is creamy; add the sugars gradually and beat until they are thoroughly blended and smooth. Add in the vanilla and the egg; beat well.

Sift together the flour, salt, soda, and the spices and add them to the creamed mixture alternately with the milk. Stir in the oats.

Pour the batter into a greased and floured 9-inch square pan. Bake in the preheated oven for 40 to 45 minutes. Leave the cake in the pan. Frost it with Nutmeat Coconut Frosting, (See p. 165).

This cake can be served warm or cold.

WHITE BUTTER CAKE

1 stick country or dairy butter	½ cup water
1½ cups granulated sugar	½ cup milk
3 cups cake flour, sifted	1 tsp. vanilla
3 tsp. baking powder	8 drops of almond extract
¼ tsp. salt	4 egg whites

Cream the butter, add in the sugar and cream together until the mix is light.

Sift the flour with the baking powder and the salt. Add about 4 Tbsp. of flour to the creamed mixture, then add the remaining flour and the water and milk alternately. Mix well, but do not overbeat. Add in the extracts. Beat the egg whites until they are stiff and carefully fold them into the batter.

Pour the batter into two greased and floured 8-inch layer cake pans lined with lightly greased wax paper. Bake at 375° for from 25 to 30 minutes.

Ice the cake with a cooked icing of your choice.

CINNAMON PINEAPPLE CAKE

1 stick butter or margarine	2 large eggs
1 tsp. baking soda	2¼ cups cake flour, sifted
½ tsp. salt	½ cup milk
1 tsp. cinnamon	1 cup (8 oz. pkg.) creamed cottage cheese
1⅓ cups light brown sugar, firmly packed	¼ cup crushed pineapple, drained

Soften the butter or margarine and mix it with the soda, the salt, and the cinnamon. Gradually blend in the sugar. Beat in the eggs, one

at a time. Add in the flour alternately with the milk, beginning and ending with flour. Stir in the cottage cheese and the pineapple.

Turn the mixture into a well greased, lightly floured 9-inch square shallow pan. Bake in a preheated moderate oven at 350° for 50 minutes, or until a toothpick inserted in the center comes out clean.

Remove the cake from the oven and spread it with Cinnamon Pineapple Topping, (See p. 176). Broil until golden brown (about 20 minutes). Yield: 12 to 16 portions.

WHOLE WHEAT CAKE

1¼ cups all-purpose flour, sifted	½ cup shortening
	¾ cup granulated sugar
2¼ tsp. baking powder	2 eggs, beaten
½ tsp. salt	½ tsp. vanilla
¾ cup whole wheat flour	1 cup milk

Sift the white flour, measure it, and resift it 3 times with the baking powder and the salt. Then add in the whole wheat flour; stir it in thoroughly.

Cream the shortening with the sugar. Add the beaten eggs and beat the mixture until it is smooth. Put in the vanilla. Then add the flour mixture alternately with the milk into the creamed mixture.

Bake in two greased and floured 8-inch layer cake pans lined with lightly greased wax paper, in a 375° oven for about 25 minutes.

Cool the cake in the pans for 5 minutes; then turn it out to cool completely on a cake rack. Serve the cake plain or with your favorite icing or filling, or both.

(from Meta Given's THE MODERN FAMILY COOK BOOK)

DEPENDABLE CAKE

1 heaping Tbsp. butter (a little less than ¼ stick)	1½ cups all-purpose flour, sifted
1 cup granulated sugar	1 tsp. baking powder
1 egg	Pinch of salt
1 tsp. baking soda	1 tsp. vanilla
1 cup buttermilk	1 Tbsp. cocoa

Mix the butter and the sugar together thoroughly. Beat the egg and add it in. Dissolve the soda in the buttermilk; add this into the mixture.

Sift the flour, the baking powder, and the salt together and add them into the first mixture. Now put in the vanilla and the cocoa and mix the batter well.

Bake in a greased and floured 9-inch square pan in a 350° oven for about 30 minutes, or until a toothpick proves the cake is done. Top with One Minute Fudge Icing, (See p. 174).

JELLY ROLL CAKE

1 cup cake flour, sifted	3 eggs, well beaten
2 tsp. baking powder	6 Tbsp. hot water
1 cup granulated sugar	1 cup jelly

Sift the flour, sugar and baking powder together. Add in the eggs, then the hot water. Mix well.

Spread the batter about ¼ inch thick on a large lightly greased and floured jelly roll pan, 15½ × 10½ × 1-inch, that has been lined with lightly greased wax paper. Bake for 12 to 15 minutes in a 400° oven.

When the cake is done, turn it out while hot onto a large sheet of wax paper dusted with powdered sugar. Beat up the jelly with a fork and spread it on the cake quickly while the cake is warm. Trim off all the crust around the edges, and roll the cake by lifting up one end of the paper and gradually rolling the cake over and over.

Wrap the paper around the cake, then roll it in a clean cloth until it is cool. Before serving the cake, if desired, sprinkle powdered sugar over the cake.

LEMON MERINGUE CAKE

½ stick butter	1 tsp. lemon extract
½ cup granulated sugar	½ tsp. salt
3 egg yolks, beaten	1 tsp. vanilla
6 Tbsp. milk	1 tsp. baking powder
1 cup cake flour, sifted	

Cream the butter with the sugar thoroughly. Add in the rest of the ingredients and beat for three minutes.

Pour the batter into a shallow greased and floured 8-inch square pan, lined with lightly greased wax paper. Bake for 20 minutes in a moderate oven at 350°.

Finish the cake with Lemon Meringue Topping, (See p. 177).

APPLESAUCE CAKE, NO. 2 (with Walnuts)

2 cups all-purpose flour, sifted	**¼ tsp. ground cloves**
1 cup granulated sugar	**½ cup shortening**
½ tsp. salt	**1 egg (or 2 yolks, beaten)**
1 tsp. baking soda	**1 cup thick, smooth applesauce**
½ tsp. cinnamon	**1 cup chopped walnuts**
½ tsp. nutmeg	

Heat the oven to 350°.

Measure the flour, sugar, salt, soda, and the spices with the shortening into a bowl; beat with a spoon or electric mixer until the mix is fluffy. Add the egg and beat again. Stir in the applesauce, beating until the total mixture is smooth. Then stir in the walnuts.

Bake in a greased and floured 9 × 5 × 3-inch pan for 50 or 60 minutes. Let the cake stand in the pan for 10 minutes, then turn it out on a cake rack.

BLACK DEVIL'S CAKE (Sugarless)

½ cup shortening	**½ tsp. baking soda**
½ cup molasses	**½ tsp. salt**
2 eggs, well beaten	**1½ tsp. baking powder**
2 squares unsweetened chocolate, melted	**1 cup milk**
1¾ cups cake flour, sifted	**1 tsp. vanilla**

Cream the shortening with the molasses; add the eggs and the chocolate. Blend well.

Sift the flour, soda, salt, and baking powder together and stir them into the creamed mix alternately with the milk. Add the vanilla. Then pour the batter into two greased and floured 8-inch layer cake pans.

Bake at 350° for 20 minutes, or until the cake proves to be done when tested with a toothpick. Ice with your favorite icing.

ORANGE RAISIN CAKE

1 cup granulated sugar	1 whole orange
1 stick butter	1 cup raisins
2 cups all-purpose flour, sifted	1 tsp. soda
	1 cup buttermilk
Pinch of salt	1 egg

Cream together the sugar and the butter. Sift the flour twice with the salt, then stir it in with the sugar and butter.

Grind the orange and raisins through a food chopper (or chop up thoroughly by hand). Add all except 1 Tbsp. to the butter-flour mixture. Add the soda to the buttermilk and combine this into the mix. Stir in the egg. Blend well together with a spoon (do not use an electric beater).

Bake in a 10 × 6-inch greased and floured loaf pan at 350° for 45 to 50 minutes.

Ice with Creamy Smooth Icing, (See p. 172) to which the 1 Tbsp. of the ground orange-raisins should be added.

NUTTY APPLE CAKE

2 cups granulated sugar	1 tsp. baking soda
½ cup shortening	½ tsp. salt
2 eggs, separated	1 tsp. cinnamon
1 tsp. vanilla	1 tsp. nutmeg
2 cups all-purpose flour, sifted	4 cups chopped tart apples
	1 cup chopped pecan meats

Cream together the sugar and the shortening. Beat the egg yolks well and add them in. Add in the vanilla.

Sift the flour, soda, salt, and the spices together and combine them into the moist mixture. Fold in the apples and the pecan meats. Blend well. Now beat the egg white stiffly and fold them in.

Bake in a greased and floured 12 × 8 × 2-inch pan, at 300° for about 1 hour.

SWISS CHOCOLATE CAKE

2 cups cake flour, sifted	2 egg yolks
½ tsp. salt	1 cup milk
2½ tsp. baking powder	¾ cup unsweetened chocolate, grated
1 stick butter	
1¼ cups granulated sugar	2 egg whites, stiffly beaten
1 tsp. vanilla	

Sift together the flour, salt, and the baking powder. In a mixing bowl put the butter, sugar, and the vanilla, and beat in the egg yolks until the mixture is light and fluffy. Add in the flour mixture alternately with the milk. Beat the mixture until it is smooth, then add the chocolate, mixing it in thoroughly. Now fold in the egg whites.

Pour the batter into two greased and floured 8-inch layer cake pans. Bake for 25 minutes in a 375° oven. Take the layers out of the oven when they are done and let them set in the pans for 5 minutes before turning them out onto a cake rack.

Cool the cake thoroughly before frosting it with Uncooked Icing, (See p. 175).

DRIED APRICOT CAKE

1 cup dried apricots	1 tsp. vanilla
2 cups water	1¾ cups cake flour, sifted
6 Tbsp. granulated sugar	½ tsp. salt
½ cup shortening	1 tsp. baking powder
1 cup granulated sugar	½ tsp. baking soda
2 egg yolks	¼ cup water

Simmer the apricots with 2 cups of water and 6 Tbsp. of sugar for 30 minutes on top of the stove. Drain off the liquid and mash the fruit. Measure out ¼ cup of pulp.

Cream the shortening with 1 cup of sugar thoroughly; add in the egg yolks and the vanilla. Beat well.

Sift together the flour, salt, soda, and the baking powder, and add them alternately to the egg mixture with ¼ cup of water and the apricot pulp.

Bake in an 8-inch greased and floured square pan lined with lightly greased wax paper at 350° for 45 minutes.

SILVER WHITE CAKE

2½ cups cake flour, sifted

1⅓ cups granulated sugar

½ tsp. salt

2½ tsp. baking powder

1 stick butter, softened

1 tsp. vanilla

1 cup milk

3 egg whites

Heat oven to 350°. Grease and flour two 8-inch layer cake pans, or an oblong pan, 13 × 9 × 2 inches.

Sift the flour, sugar, salt, and the baking powder into a bowl. Add the butter, the vanilla, and ⅔ cup of the milk. Beat for 2 minutes. Add the balance of the milk and the egg whites. Beat 2 minutes more, vigorously. Pour the batter into the prepared pans.

Bake in layers for 30 to 35 minutes, the oblong cake about 35 minutes. Allow the cake to cool. Fill with your favorite lemon filling. Frost with a white icing. Sprinkle grated coconut on top.

MOTHER SANFORD'S SPECIAL CAKE

1½ cups soft brown sugar

½ cup shortening

2 eggs, beaten

½ cup molasses

½ cup milk

2 cups all-purpose flour, sifted

1½ tsp. baking powder

½ tsp. salt

1 tsp. cinnamon

½ tsp. ground cloves

½ tsp. allspice

¼ cup dates, chopped

½ cup seedless raisins

¼ cup chopped maraschino cherries

Cream the sugar and the shortening together thoroughly. Blend in the beaten eggs. Add the molasses and the milk and mix thoroughly.

Sift the flour with the baking powder, the salt, and the spices. Dredge the fruits with a little of the flour. Add the sifted flour and the floured fruits into the creamed molasses mixture and mix together well.

Bake in a greased and floured 9-inch tube pan at 350° for 55 minutes to 1 hour.

When the cake has cooled, frost with Snow White Frosting, (See p. 167).

GRANDMA'S MOLASSES CAKE

⅔ cup shortening	½ tsp. baking soda
¼ cup granulated sugar	¾ tsp. salt
¾ cup unsulphured molasses	1¼ tsp. baking powder
2 cups all-purpose flour,	2 eggs
sifted	½ cup milk

Cream the shortening with the sugar. Add in the molasses slowly; beat well.

Sift together the flour, soda, salt, and the baking powder; add one-half of this into the molasses mix. Now add in the eggs and beat again. Add in the rest of the dry ingredients alternately with the milk.

Bake in an 8-inch greased and floured square pan at 325° for about 1 hour.

MOLASSES LAYER CAKE

⅞ stick butter	1 tsp. vanilla
1 cup granulated sugar	2 cups all-purpose flour,
1 egg, beaten	sifted
3 Tbsp. molasses	¼ tsp. salt
1 tsp. baking soda	1 tsp. baking powder
¾ cup sour milk	

Cream the butter, the sugar and the egg together thoroughly. Add in the molasses and mix well. Dissolve the soda in the sour milk and add in the vanilla.

Sift the flour with the salt and the baking powder. Sift the flour mix into the creamed mixture alternately with the sour milk mix.

Divide the batter into two greased and floured 9-inch layer cake pans and bake in a 350° oven for 25 to 30 minutes.

Cool the layers and put them together with Peanut Brittle Filling, (See p. 159).

SPICED COFFEE LAYER CAKE

½ cup shortening
1 cup granulated sugar
2 eggs, separated
2 cups cake flour, sifted
2 tsp. baking powder

¼ tsp. salt
1 tsp. cinnamon
1 tsp. nutmeg
½ cup strong coffee

Cream the shortening; add in the sugar gradually. Cream them well together. Add in the egg yolks and beat well.

Sift the flour, baking powder, salt, and the spices together. Add these alternately with the coffee into the first mixture. Beat the egg whites stiffly and fold them in.

Bake in 2 greased and floured 9-inch layer cake pans in a 350° oven for 25 to 30 minutes.

Spread with Mocha Frosting, (See p. 164).

COCONUT GOLD CAKE

1⅞ cups cake flour, sifted
1¼ cups granulated sugar
¾ tsp. salt
3 tsp. baking powder
1 cup milk

1 tsp. lemon extract
1 tsp. vanilla
¾ stick butter
4 egg yolks

Sift the flour, sugar, salt, and the baking powder together in a bowl. Mix the milk and the flavorings in another bowl. Pour half of the milk mixture into the flour mix and beat well.

Cream together the butter and the egg yolks in a small bowl; beat about 2 minutes. Add the balance of the milk into the flour-milk mixture, then add in the egg yolk mix. Beat thoroughly.

Separate the batter into 2 greased and floured 8-inch layer cake pans. Bake at 350° for 25 to 30 minutes. When the layers have cooled, ice with Coconut Frosting, (See p. 161).

SURPRISE CAKE

1½ cups granulated sugar	2 Tbsp. cocoa
¾ cup shortening	½ tsp. nutmeg
3 eggs	½ tsp. cinnamon
1¾ cups cake flour, sifted	¾ cup sour milk
½ tsp. baking soda	½ tsp. lemon extract
½ tsp. salt	½ cup nut meats, chopped

Cream the sugar and the shortening together thoroughly. Stir in the eggs.

Sift the flour with the soda, salt, cocoa and spices, and add it to the creamed mixture alternately with the sour milk. Blend in the extract and the nuts. Beat thoroughly.

Bake at 350° in an 8-inch greased and floured square pan for 40 to 50 minutes. Frost with Surprise Frosting, (See p. 168).

QUICK CAKE

2½ cups cake flour, sifted	½ cup shortening, softened
1½ cups granulated sugar	1 cup milk
3 tsp. baking powder	2 eggs
1 tsp. salt	2 tsp. vanilla

Preheat the oven to 350°. Grease and flour two 9-inch layer cake pans.

Sift the flour, sugar, baking powder and the salt into a mixing bowl. Add the shortening and ¾ cup of milk. Beat until the flour is dampened. Then beat faster for 2 minutes. Add the eggs and vanilla and ¼ cup of milk and beat for 1 minute.

Pour the batter into the prepared pans. With a spatula cut through the batter several times to remove air bubbles.

Bake at 350° for 25 to 30 minutes. Cool the pans on a rack for 10 minutes. Then remove the layers from the pans and continue to cool them until they are cold. Frost to taste.

COCOA COCONUT CAKE

2 cups all-purpose flour, sifted

1½ tsp. baking soda

¼ tsp. salt

⅔ cup cocoa

⅔ cup shortening

1½ cups granulated sugar

2 eggs, beaten

1 tsp. vanilla

½ cup buttermilk

½ cup boiling water

Sift the flour, soda, salt, and the cocoa together 3 times.

Cream the shortening until it is soft. Add in the sugar and blend thoroughly. Add the beaten eggs and beat vigorously until the mixture is smooth and fluffy. Stir in the vanilla.

Now add in the flour mixture alternately with the buttermilk in 3 or 4 portions, beginning and ending with a flour insertion, and beating well after each addition. Add the boiling water all at once and stir until the batter is smooth.

Pour the batter into two greased and floured 8-inch layer cake pans. Bake in a 350° oven for 30 minutes or until the cake tests done. Turn the cake out on rack to cool.

Frost with Nutmeat Coconut Frosting, (See p. 165). Serves 10.

(From Meta Given's MODERN FAMILY COOK BOOK)

GRAHAM CRACKER CAKE

½ cup shortening

1 cup granulated sugar

3 eggs, separated

½ tsp. vanilla

¼ cup all-purpose flour, sifted

¼ tsp. salt

1½ tsp. baking powder

¾ cup milk

30 graham crackers, crushed fine

½ cup pecans, chopped

Cream the shortening with the sugar thoroughly. Add in the egg yolks and the vanilla and beat well.

Sift the flour with the salt and the baking powder. Add the sifted flour into the creamed mixture alternately with the milk and the crushed crumbs.

Beat the egg whites lightly and fold them into the batter. Lastly, add in the nuts.

Bake in two lightly greased and floured 8-inch layer cake pans, lined with lightly greased wax paper, for 25 minutes at 350°. Frost to taste.

BUTTERMILK CAKE

1 stick butter	½ tsp. baking soda
1 cup granulated sugar	½ cup buttermilk
1½ cups cake flour, sifted	½ tsp. vanilla
½ tsp. cream of tartar	3 egg whites
¼ tsp. salt	

Cream the butter; add the sugar gradually; cream continually.

Sift the flour with the cream of tartar, the salt, and the soda. Add it into the creamed mixture, a little at a time, alternately with the buttermilk. Then add in the vanilla.

Beat the egg whites stiffly and fold them into the batter.

Turn the batter into two greased and floured 8-inch layer cake pans or one medium-size loaf pan. Bake at 350° for 25 to 30 minutes (slightly longer if the loaf pan is used).

When the cake has cooled, frost with Creamy Smooth Icing, (See p. 172).

COCONUT JELLY CAKE

2 cups all-purpose flour, sifted	1⅜ sticks butter, softened
1¼ cups granulated sugar	2 eggs
3 tsp. baking powder	1 tsp. vanilla
¼ tsp. salt	¾ cup jelly
⅔ cup milk	1½ cups shredded coconut

Sift the flour before measuring, then resift it with the sugar, baking powder, and the salt. Make a hollow in the center of the flour mixture and add the milk, the butter, the eggs, and the vanilla. Beat well until the mixture is smooth.

Pour the batter into two greased and floured 9-inch layer cake pans. Bake about 20 minutes at 375°. Let the cake stand in the pans for five minutes before turning it out.

When the cake is cool, slice the layers horizontally with a sharp knife. Just before serving it, spread the cake layers with the jelly and sprinkle on each equal portions of the coconut. Then put the layers together.

Light as Air—Angel, Sponge and Chiffon
Chapter 2

FEATHERWEIGHT CAKE NO. 1

2½ cups cake flour, sifted
3½ tsp. baking powder
½ tsp. salt
1¾ cups granulated sugar
¾ cup shortening

1⅛ cups milk
1 tsp. almond or vanilla
               extract
⅔ cups egg whites, unbeaten
   (6 large or 8 small eggs)

Sift together the flour, baking powder, salt and sugar. Add the shortening and the milk. Beat for 2 minutes. Add the flavoring and the egg whites and beat for 2 minutes more.

Pour the batter into two 8-inch greased and floured layer cake pans and bake at 350° for 35 to 40 minutes.

Frost with Hula Frosting, (See p. 163).

YELLOW CHIFFON CAKE

2 eggs, separated
1½ cups granulated sugar
2½ cups cake flour, sifted
3 tsp. baking powder

1 tsp. salt
⅓ cup cooking oil
1 cup milk
1 tsp. vanilla

Heat oven to 350°; grease well and flour two round 9-inch layer cake pans, or an oblong pan, 13 × 9 × 2-inches.

Beat the egg whites until they are foamy. Gradually beat in ½ cup of sugar. Continue beating until the mixture is very stiff and glossy.

Sift the remaining sugar, the flour, baking powder and salt into another bowl. Add in the oil, half of the milk, and the vanilla. Beat for 1 minute with a mixer at medium speed or 150 vigorous strokes by hand. Add the remaining milk and the egg yolks. Beat for 1 more minute. Fold in the egg white meringue.

Pour the batter into the prepared pans. Bake the cake in the layer pans for 25 to 30 minutes, in the oblong pan, for 40 to 50 minutes. Frost with Chocolate Butter Icing, (See p. 171).

ORANGE SPONGE CAKE

2 egg yolks, unbeaten
¾ cup granulated sugar
¼ tsp. grated orange rind
4 Tbsp. orange juice
½ tsp. lemon juice

2 egg whites, stiffly beaten
1 cup cake flour, sifted
¼ tsp. baking soda
¼ tsp. salt

Grease and flour a 9-inch tube pan or deep round tin and line it with greased wax paper.

Put the egg yolks, the sugar, orange rind, orange juice and lemon juice in a mixing bowl and mix well. Fold in the beaten egg whites. Then after sifting the flour, baking soda and salt together four times, combine them in the mixing bowl with the other ingredients. Beat well.

Pour the batter into the pan and bake for 30 minutes at 375°.

The cake may be frosted or it may be sliced into layers and filled with orange marmalade or a cooked orange filling.

YELLOW ANGEL FOOD CAKE

1½ cups cake flour, sifted
½ tsp. salt
½ tsp. baking powder
5 eggs, separated

½ cup orange juice, pulp
    and grated rind combined
1½ cups granulated sugar
¾ tsp. cream of tartar
1 tsp. lemon extract

Sift the flour, salt and baking powder together. Beat the egg yolks until they are thick and lemon colored. Add the orange juice, the pulp and the grated rind. Beat until the mixture is light and fluffy. Gradually beat in the sugar. Fold in the dry ingredients.

Beat the egg whites with the cream of tartar until they are stiff but not dry. Fold them in the egg yolk batter and then add the lemon extract.

Bake in a 10-inch ungreased tube pan in a 325° oven for about 1 hour. Invert the pan until the cake is cool.

Ice with Orange Icing, (See p. 174).

CHIFFON CAKE

1 cup egg whites (8 large or 10 small eggs)
½ tsp. cream of tartar
2 cups cake flour, sifted
1½ cups granulated sugar, sifted
1 tsp. salt

3 tsp. baking powder
½ cup cooking oil
4 egg yolks
¾ cup water
1 tsp. vanilla
2 tsp. grated lemon rind

Preheat oven to 325°.

Beat the egg whites and cream of tartar together until very stiff peaks are formed. Sift the flour, sugar, salt and baking powder together in a large mixing bowl. Make a well in the center of the flour and add the oil, egg yolks and water. Beat with a wooden spoon until the mixture is smooth. Stir in the vanilla and the grated rind.

Gradually pour the egg yolk mixture over the beaten whites, folding in gently with a rubber spatula just until everything is blended. Do not stir.

Pour the batter into an ungreased 10-inch tube cake pan at once. Bake 1 hour at 325° or 50 minutes at 350°. Immediately turn the pan upside down to cool the cake. When it is cool, gently ease the cake from the sides of the pan with a knife. Lift out the cake and invert it on a plate.

FEATHERWEIGHT CAKE, NO. 2

½ cup shortening
1 cup granulated sugar
2 cups cake flour, sifted
2 tsp. baking powder

½ tsp. salt
⅔ cup milk
3 egg whites
1 tsp. vanilla

Cream together the shortening and the sugar. Mix and sift three times the flour, baking powder, and the salt; add these alternately with the milk into the first mixture.

Beat the egg whites stiffly and fold them in. Add the vanilla and turn the batter into two greased and floured 9-inch layer cake pans. Bake at 350° for 20 to 30 minutes.

Frost with Snow White Frosting, with coconut added, (See p. 167).

SYRUP ANGEL FOOD CAKE

¾ cup white syrup	¼ tsp. salt
1 cup egg whites (8 large or 10 small eggs)	¾ tsp. almond extract
	1 cup cake flour, sifted
1 tsp. cream of tartar	½ cup granulated sugar

Boil the syrup until it forms a soft ball in cold water. Beat the egg whites until they are frothy, then add to them the cream of tartar and the salt. Continue beating until the whites are stiff but not dry. Add the hot syrup, a little at a time, beating well after each addition. Add the almond extract.

Sift together the flour and the sugar. Fold this mix into the egg whites and the syrup mixture, blending lightly.

Bake in an ungreased 10-inch tube pan for 60 minutes as follows: first 15 minutes at 320°, then 45 minutes at 300°. When the cake is baked, remove the pan from the oven and invert it for 1 hour before removing the cake from the pan.

HOT MILK SPONGE CAKE

4 eggs	¼ stick butter
2 cups granulated sugar	2 cups all-purpose flour, sifted
½ tsp. salt	
2 tsp. vanilla	2 tsp. baking powder
1 cup milk	

Set the oven at 350°. Grease and flour a 13 × 9-inch pan. In a large mixing bowl beat the eggs with a rotary beater or electric mixer until they are very light. Beat in the sugar, salt and vanilla.

Heat the milk and melt the butter in it. Then beat the hot butter and milk into the egg mixture.

Sift together the flour and baking powder and beat them into the wet mixture very quickly.

Pour the batter immediately into the prepared pan. Bake for 25 to 30 minutes, or until the cake tests done when probed with a toothpick. Top with Broiled Icing, (See p. 169).

DARK CHOCOLATE ANGEL FOOD CAKE   *Very Good cake*

¾ cup all-purpose flour	¼ tsp. baking soda
4 Tbsp. cocoa	½ tsp. baking powder
1¼ cups egg whites (10 large or 13 small eggs)	1¼ cups granulated sugar, sifted
¼ tsp. salt	1 tsp. vanilla

Sift the flour once; measure it; add the cocoa and sift three more times. Beat the egg whites and the salt until they are foamy, add the soda and baking powder and beat until the eggs will just hold a peak, but are not dry. Fold in the sugar carefully, two tablespoons at a time. Fold in the vanilla. Sift a small amount of flour over the mixture and fold it in carefully; continue to add flour gradually until all the flour is incorporated.

Pour the batter into an ungreased 10-inch tube pan. Bake for one hour, the first 30 minutes at 275°, the next 15 minutes at 300° and the last 15 minutes at 325°. Remove the pan from the oven and invert it until the cake is cool. Then remove the cake from the pan.

EASY METHOD ANGEL FOOD CAKE

1 cup cake flour, sifted	1 cup egg whites (8 large or 10 small eggs)
1¼ cups granulated sugar	
½ tsp. salt	1 tsp. cream of tartar
	1 tsp. vanilla

Sift together four or five times the flour, sugar and one-half the salt. Beat the egg whites with the other half of the salt until they are frothy, then add in the cream of tartar; beat until the whites are light but not

dry. Fold the dry ingredients very carefully into the beaten egg whites. When the mixture is partly blended, add in the vanilla. (Be very careful when blending the dry ingredients with the eggs. Use the folding method.)

Bake in an ungreased 9-inch tube pan at 325° for 1 hour.

COFFEE ANGEL CAKE

1⅞ cups granulated sugar	2 Tbsp. water
1 Tbsp. instant coffee	2 tsp. cream of tartar
1½ cups cake flour, sifted	1 tsp. rum extract
½ tsp. salt	1 drop red food coloring
1½ cups egg whites (12 large or 15 small eggs)	

Sift 1 cup of sugar and the instant coffee with the flour four times.

Add the salt to the egg whites and beat until they are foamy. Beat in the water, the cream of tartar, the rum extract and the red food coloring. Continue beating until the egg white mixture is light and stiff but not dry. Then gradually beat in the remaining ⅞ cup of sugar. Using a wire whisk, carefully fold in the sifted sugar and flour. When the batter is thoroughly blended, pour it into an ungreased 10-inch tube pan.

Bake at 375° for 45 minutes. Invert the pan, letting it hang until the cake is cool. Remove the cake from the pan and frost it with Scotch Coffee Icing, (See p. 174).

THREE EGG SPONGE CAKE

1 cup cake flour, sifted	1 cup granulated sugar
1 tsp. baking powder	2 tsp. lemon juice
¼ tsp. salt	6 Tbsp. hot milk
3 eggs	

Sift the flour once, measure it, add the baking powder and the salt, and sift them together three times.

Beat the eggs until they are very thick and light and nearly white (5 to 7 min.). Add in the sugar gradually, beating constantly. Add the lemon juice. Fold in the flour mix, a small amount at a time. Add the milk, mixing quickly until the batter is blended.

Bake in an ungreased 9-inch tube pan at 350° for about 35 minutes. Remove the pan from the oven and invert it for 1 hour, or until the cake is cold.

CREOLE CHIFFON CAKE

¾ cup boiling water
½ cup cocoa
1 Tbsp. instant coffee
1½ cups cake flour, sifted
1¾ cups granulated sugar
4 tsp. baking powder
1 tsp. ground cloves

1 tsp. salt
½ cup cooking oil
7 egg yolks, unbeaten
1 tsp. vanilla
1 cup egg whites (8 large or 10 small)
½ tsp. cream of tartar

Heat the oven to 325°. Stir the water, the cocoa and the coffee together until the mix is smooth. Set it aside to cool.

Sift the flour, sugar, baking powder, cloves and salt into a bowl. Make a well and add the oil, the egg yolks, the cooled cocoa mix, and the vanilla. Beat with a spoon until the mixture is smooth.

Measure the egg whites and the cream of tartar into a large mixing bowl. Beat with an electric beater on high speed for 3 to 5 minutes, or by hand until the whites form very stiff peaks. Pour the egg yolk mixture gradually over the beaten egg whites, folding in just until blended. Do not stir.

Pour the batter into an ungreased 10 × 4-inch tube pan. Bake in the preheated oven for 55 minutes, then increase the oven temperature to 350° and bake 10 or 15 minutes longer. Turn the pan upside down with the tube over the neck of a funnel or bottle. Let it hang until the cake is cold.

Loosen the cake from the sides and tube of the pan with a spatula. Ice the cake with a fluffy white cooked icing flavored with 1 tsp. instant coffee. Decorate it if you wish with melted chocolate spooned over the icing at random.

SUGARLESS ANGEL CAKE

6 egg whites
Pinch of salt
½ tsp. instant coffee
½ tsp. cream of tartar

1 grain saccharin tablet, powdered
½ cup cake flour, sifted
1 tsp. vanilla
¼ tsp. almond extract

Beat the egg whites with the salt, the powdered coffee, the cream of tartar, and the saccharin, until they are high and stiff but not dry. Fold in the flour gradually. Then add in the vanilla and almond flavoring.

Bake in a slow oven at 300° for about 35 minutes in an ungreased 8-inch round pan.

This cake can be frosted with whipped non-fat milk sweetened with saccharin.

BURNT SUGAR CHIFFON CAKE

½ cup burnt sugar mixture made from	½ cup cooking oil
	7 egg yolks, unbeaten
1 cup granulated sugar	¼ cup cold water
½ cup boiling water	1 tsp. vanilla
2 cups cake flour, sifted	1 cup egg whites (8 large or 10 small eggs)
3 tsp. baking powder	
1 tsp. salt	½ tsp. cream of tartar
1½ cups granulated sugar	

First prepare the burnt sugar mixture by melting 1 cup of sugar in a heavy skillet until it is brown, then pouring in the boiling water. Set this aside.

Sift together the flour, baking powder, salt, and 1½ cups of sugar. Make a well in this and add the oil, the unbeaten egg yolks, one-half of the burnt sugar mixture, the cold water, and the vanilla. Beat well. (The rest of the burnt sugar mixture will be used in the icing.)

Whip the egg whites and cream of tartar together into very stiff peaks; gently fold them into the batter until they are blended. Do not stir.

Pour the batter into an ungreased 10 × 4-inch tube pan immediately, and bake for 65 minutes at 325°. Frost with Burnt Sugar Icing, (See p. 170).

LEMON LIGHT SPONGE CAKE NO. 1

6 eggs, separated	6 Tbsp. cold water
1½ cups granulated sugar	1 tsp. lemon extract
1½ cups cake flour, sifted	1 tsp. grated lemon rind
½ tsp. salt	1½ tsp. baking powder

LIGHT AS AIR—ANGEL, SPONGE AND CHIFFON 45

Beat the egg yolks until they are thick and lemon colored. Gradually beat in the sugar. Sift the flour and salt together and add them alternately with the water to the first mixture. Add the lemon extract and the rind.

Whip the egg whites until they are foamy; add the baking powder and continue whipping until stiff peaks are formed. Fold the whites into the egg yolk mixture.

Pour the batter into an ungreased 9-inch tube pan; bake at 325° for 50 to 60 minutes. When it is cool, cut the cake from the tube and sides of pan, lift out the cake by the tube, and invert it onto a plate.

LEMON LIGHT SPONGE CAKE NO. 2

1 cup cake flour, sifted	5 eggs, separated
1 cup granulated sugar, sifted	1½ Tbsp. lemon juice
1½ tsp. grated lemon rind	¼ tsp. salt
2 Tbsp. water	½ tsp. cream of tartar

Sift the flour once, measure it, and sift again four times.

Add ½ cup of sugar, the lemon rind, and the water to the egg yolks and beat with a rotary beater until they are very thick and light. Add the lemon juice gradually, beating constantly. Add the flour all at once, then stir until it is just blended.

Beat the egg whites and the salt with a rotary beater or whisk. When they become foamy, add the cream of tartar and beat until the mix is stiff enough to hold up in peaks but is not dry. Add the remaining ½ cup of sugar, about 2 Tbsp. at a time, beating well with the beater or whisk. Fold the egg white mix into the egg yolk mixture gently.

Turn the batter into an ungreased 9-inch tube pan. Cut gently through the batter with a knife, to remove air bubbles. Bake in a slow oven at 325° for 1 hour, or until the cake tests done when probed with a toothpick. Remove the pan from the oven and invert it for 1 hour, or until the cake is cold.

SUPREME ANGEL CAKE

1 cup cake flour, sifted	⅓ tsp. salt
1½ cups confectioners sugar, sifted	1 tsp. vanilla
1½ cups egg whites (12)	¼ tsp. almond extract
1½ tsp. cream of tartar	1 cup granulated sugar

Measure and sift together three times the flour and the confectioners sugar.

Measure into a large mixing bowl the egg whites, the cream of tartar, salt, vanilla, and the almond extract. Beat with a wire whisk until this mix is foamy. Gradually add in the granulated sugar, 2 Tbsp. at a time. Continue beating until the mixture holds stiff peaks. Sift gradually the flour-sugar mixture over the egg white mix. Fold in gently, just until the flour-sugar disappears.

Place the batter in an ungreased 10-inch tube pan, 4 inches deep. Gently cut through the batter with a knife. Bake at 350° for 35 to 40 minutes. When the cake tests done, invert it in the pan. Let it stand until it is cold. (If desired, a few drops of red food coloring may be added to the batter to tint it a delicate pink.)

CHERRY ANGEL FOOD CAKE

1 cup egg whites (8 large or 10 small eggs)	1½ cups granulated sugar
1 cup cake flour, sifted	½ tsp. almond extract
1 tsp. cream of tartar	¾ tsp. vanilla
¼ tsp. salt	⅓ cup maraschino cherries, sliced and chopped

Beat the egg whites until they are foamy. Sift the flour with the cream of tartar and the salt and add them into the eggs. Beat well. Fold in the sugar gradually. Add the flavorings.

Pour half of the batter into an ungreased 9-inch tube pan. Sprinkle on half the cherries, then add the remainder of the batter and drop the remaining cherries on top.

Bake for 50 minutes at 325° in a preheated oven. Invert the cake immediately and carefully on a cake rack. Allow the cake to hang until it cools and pulls away from the pan.

Coffee Cakes
Chapter 3

STREUSEL FILLED COFFEE CAKE

1½ cups all-purpose flour,
                         sifted
3 tsp. baking powder
¼ tsp. salt
¾ cup granulated sugar

¼ cup shortening
1 egg, well beaten
¼ cup milk
1 tsp. vanilla

Streusel Filling

½ cup brown sugar
2 Tbsp. flour
2 tsp. cinnamon

¼ stick butter, melted
½ cup chopped nuts

Make the filling first. Mix the sugar, flour, and cinnamon together. Blend in the butter and the nut meats. Set aside.

Sift the flour, baking powder, salt, and the sugar together. Cut in the shortening. Mix the egg with the milk and blend them in. Add the vanilla and beat just enough to mix well.

Pour half the batter into a 10 × 6-inch greased and floured loaf pan. Sprinkle on half the filling. Add the remaining batter and then the rest of the filling on top. Bake for 25 to 30 minutes at 375°.

COFFEE SPICE CAKE

2 sticks butter	3 tsp. baking powder
2 cups granulated sugar	1 tsp. cinnamon
4 egg yolks, beaten	¼ tsp. nutmeg
1 cup (4 oz.) bitter chocolate, grated	¼ tsp. ground cloves
2 cups cake flour, sifted	1 cup strong cold coffee
½ tsp. salt	4 egg whites, beaten
	½ cup almonds, chopped

Cream the butter, add the sugar, then cream them together. Add in the well-beaten egg yolks and the grated chocolate.

Measure the sifted flour, then sift it again with the salt, the baking powder and the spices. Add these dry ingredients to the moist mixture, alternately with the coffee. Fold in the stiffly beaten egg whites, and then the nuts.

Grease and flour two 8-inch square cake pans. Pour in the batter and bake at 350–375° for 45 minutes to an hour. Makes 2 cakes.

APPLE RAISIN COFFEE CAKE

1 cup all-purpose flour, sifted	¼ cup granulated sugar, plus 3 Tbsp. more
3 tsp. baking powder	1 cup whole bran cereal
½ tsp. salt	1 cup sweetened applesauce
1 tsp. cinnamon	1 egg
¼ tsp. ground cloves	¼ cup vegetable oil
¼ tsp. nutmeg	½ cup seedless raisins

Sift together the flour, baking powder, salt, ½ teaspoon cinnamon, the cloves, nutmeg, and ¼ cup of sugar.

Combine the bran cereal with the applesauce, the egg, the oil, and the raisins. Let the mixture stand until most of the moisture is taken up (about 5 minutes). Beat well. Add the sifted dry ingredients, stirring only until they are combined. Spread the batter into a greased and floured 8-inch square pan.

Combine 3 Tbsp. of sugar and ½ tsp. cinnamon; sprinkle this evenly over the batter.

Bake in a hot oven at 400° for about 35 minutes, or until the cake tests done by the toothpick test.

LEMON NUT COFFEE CAKE

**2¾ cups all-purpose flour,
sifted**
3 Tbsp. baking powder
½ tsp. baking soda
½ tsp. salt
½ cup chopped nutmeats
¼ cup shortening, softened

1½ cups granulated sugar
2 eggs
1½ tsp. grated lemon rind
¼ cup lemon juice
¾ cup milk
1½ cups bran flakes

Sift together the flour, baking powder, soda, and the salt. Combine in the nutmeats.

Cream the shortening with the sugar, then add the eggs and the lemon rind. Beat well. Stir in the lemon juice and the milk. Next add in the bran flakes. Then add the sifted dry ingredients, stirring only until they are combined.

Spread the batter in a greased and floured 10 × 6-inch loaf pan. Bake in a 350° oven for about 50 minutes. Cool before slicing.

GOLDEN SAFFRON COFFEE RING

**1 pkg. active dry yeast
or**
1 cake compressed yeast
½ cup warm water
⅓ cup milk
**3 cups all-purpose flour,
sifted**
6 eggs, slightly beaten

Pinch of saffron, ground
1½ sticks butter, melted
¼ cup granulated sugar
¾ tsp. salt
Sliced blanched almonds
**Sliced candied red and green
cherries**
Golden raisins

Dissolve the yeast in the warm water (lukewarm for the compressed yeast) in a large bowl. Stir in the milk, flour, eggs and saffron. Beat together with a wooden spoon for about 6 minutes, or until the dough is elastic. Stir in the melted butter. Cover the bowl with a towel and let the dough rise in a warm place away from drafts for 1 hour, or until it has doubled in size.

While the dough rises, grease heavily a fancy 10-cup mold and then flour it lightly.

When the dough has risen, beat into it the sugar and salt, then pour the dough into the prepared mold; let the dough rise again for 45 minutes, or until its size has doubled.

Bake in a hot 400° oven for 40 minutes, or until the cake is a rich golden brown. Cool the cake in the mold for 5 minutes; turn it out onto a cake rack and cool it completely.

When ready to serve it dribble Almond Glaze, (See p. 176) over the top of the cake, letting it run down the sides. Garnish the top with a wreath of almonds, red and green cherries and golden raisins.

If you prefer not to use saffron, yellow cake coloring may be used.

QUICK ORANGE STREUSEL CAKE

2 cups cake flour, sifted	1 egg, slightly beaten
½ cup granulated sugar	½ cup skim milk
2 tsp. baking powder	½ cup orange juice
¾ tsp. salt	⅓ cup cooking oil
1 Tbsp. grated orange rind	

Mix and sift the flour, sugar, baking powder and the salt into a bowl. Stir in the grated rind. Make a well and add the remaining ingredients. Mix only enough to dampen the flour (the batter will be lumpy).

Turn the batter into a greased and floured round 10-inch pan. Sprinkle with Streusel Topping, (See p. 178). Bake in a 375° oven for about 35 minutes.

FLUFFY COFFEE CAKE

1½ cakes quick yeast	½ stick butter
1 Tbsp. granulated sugar	½ cup granulated sugar
1 cup milk, scalded and cooled	¼ tsp. salt
4½ cups all-purpose flour, sifted	2 eggs, beaten

Dissolve the yeast and 1 Tbsp. of sugar in the lukewarm milk. Add in 1½ cups of flour. Beat this mix until it is smooth. Cover the bowl with a cloth and let it rise in a warm place until the dough has doubled in size (about 45 minutes).

Cream the butter, then add the sugar and the salt. Add this to the yeast mixture. Add in the eggs and the remaining flour. Knead lightly (see *Glossary*). Place the dough in a greased bowl, cover it with the cloth, and let the dough rise again until it has doubled in size (about 2 hours).

Roll the dough ½ inch thick and place it in 2 well-greased shallow pans, 13 × 9 × 2-inches deep. Let the dough stand and rise again until it has doubled in height.

Prick the top of the dough with a fork, brush with melted butter, and sprinkle on Honey Nut Topping, (See p. 177). Then let the dough rise once again for about an hour. Bake in a 400° oven for 20 minutes. This recipe makes 2 cakes.

BLUEBERRY COFFEE CAKE

3 Tbsp. shortening

½ cup granulated sugar

1 egg, beaten

2⅔ cups all-purpose flour,
            sifted

3 tsp. baking powder

1 tsp. salt

1 cup milk

¾ cup blueberries, (drained)
    either fresh, canned or
            frozen (thawed)

Cream the shortening with the sugar. Add the egg (beaten thick and light). Mix and sift the flour (except 3 Tbsp.) with the baking powder and the salt. Add the flour to the first mixture alternately with the milk. Sprinkle the remaining flour over the berries and fold them into the batter quickly.

Bake in a well greased and lightly floured shallow 10-inch square pan for 30 minutes in a 375° oven.

RAISED COFFEE CAKE

1 cup milk, scalded

1 cake yeast

¼ cup warm water

2 cups all-purpose flour,
            sifted (scant)

1 egg, lightly beaten

⅔ cup granulated sugar

¾ tsp. salt

4 Tbsp. shortening, melted

Sugar and cinnamon (to
            sprinkle on top)

Cool the milk. Soften the yeast in the warm water. Add the yeast and 1 cup of the flour into the milk. Beat well and let the mixture rise until it has doubled in size. Then add in the lightly beaten egg. Add the sugar, the salt and the shortening. Mix thoroughly. Add in the remaining flour and mix well. Cover the bowl with a cloth and let the dough rise until the quantity is almost double.

Pour the dough into a shallow well-greased pan, 10 × 6 × 2 inches. Cover this with the cloth and let the dough rise once again. When it has nearly doubled in size, sprinkle the dough thickly with sugar and cinnamon.

Bake for 20 minutes in a hot oven at 400°. Serve the cake while it is hot.

BRUNCH CAKE

1 cake active dry yeast	½ tsp. vanilla
¼ cup warm water (not hot)	2 cups all-purpose flour, sifted
¼ cup granulated sugar	½ cup brown sugar, firmly packed
⅝ stick butter, melted	½ cup flaked, shredded coconut
1½ tsp. salt	
⅓ cup scalded milk	1 cup pineapple tidbits, drained and cut up
1 egg, unbeaten	

Soften the yeast in the warm water.

Combine in a mixing bowl the sugar, ¼ stick of butter, the salt and the milk (cooled to lukewarm). Stir in the egg; add the vanilla and the softened yeast. Gradually add in the flour, beating well.

Cover the bowl with a cloth and let the dough rise in a warm place (about 85 to 90°) until the dough has doubled in size (for about 45 to 60 minutes).

Meanwhile, melt ⅜ stick of butter (3 Tbsp.) in a 9-inch round deep baking pan. Sprinkle in the brown sugar, the coconut and the pineapple tidbits. Spread the dough into this prepared dish, cover it again and let the dough rise again in a warm place until it has once more doubled in size.

Bake at 350° for 30 to 35 minutes. Remove the cake from the oven, let it cool for about 2 minutes, then invert it onto a rack or plate and sprinkle on some butter crumbled with a little powdered sugar.

BREAKFAST CRUMB CAKE

2 cups all-purpose flour, sifted	⅓ cup granulated sugar
1 tsp. salt	¾ stick butter
¼ tsp. baking soda	1 egg
2½ tsp. baking powder	¾ cup buttermilk

Sift together the flour, salt, soda, baking powder and the sugar. Cut in the butter until the mixture has the consistency of coarse meal.

Beat the egg lightly and add it to the milk; combine this mix quickly with the rest of the batter.

Pour the batter into a buttered and floured 9-inch square cake pan and cover it with Crumb Topping, (See p. 176).

Bake in a hot oven at 400° for 25 to 30 minutes. Makes 8 servings.

RIBBON COFFEE CAKE

2 Tbsp. shortening	2 tsp. baking powder
½ cup granulated sugar	¼ tsp. salt
1 egg, separated and beaten	¼ cup milk
¾ cup all-purpose flour, sifted	½ tsp. vanilla

For Filling

½ cup brown sugar	2 Tbsp. flour
2 tsp. cinnamon	2 Tbsp. melted shortening
1 cup walnut meats, chopped	

Cream the shortening with the sugar; add the beaten egg yolk. Sift the flour with the baking powder and the salt and add it to the egg mix alternately with the milk. Stir in the vanilla. Lastly, fold in the stiffly beaten egg white. Spread one-half of the mixture in a deep, greased and floured 8-inch pie tin.

Mix all the filling ingredients together thoroughly and spread one-half over the batter in the pie tin. Add the rest of the cake batter and top with the second half of the filling.

Bake in a moderate oven, 350–375°, for 45 to 60 minutes. Use the toothpick test to judge when the cake is done.

STRAWBERRY RIPPLE COFFEE CAKE

2 10-oz. pkgs. frozen sliced strawberries, thawed and drained
Juice of the strawberries
2 Tbsp. cornstarch
2 cups all-purpose flour, sifted
½ cup granulated sugar
½ tsp. salt

4 Tbsp. baking powder
½ tsp. cinnamon
¼ tsp. mace
1 Tbsp. grated orange rind
1 egg, beaten
1 cup milk
½ stick butter

Combine the strawberry juice and the cornstarch. Cook in a saucepan over moderate heat, stirring constantly until the mix thickens. Cool the mix. Gently stir in the strawberries.

Sift together the flour, sugar, salt, baking powder, and the spices; then stir in the orange rind. Combine the egg, milk and the butter and add them to the dry ingredients, mixing lightly.

Pour the batter into a greased and floured 9-inch square pan. Pour on the strawberry mixture. Bake 375° for 30 to 35 minutes.

QUICK COFFEE CAKE

2 cups all-purpose flour, sifted
¾ tsp. salt
2 tsp. baking powder
½ cup granulated sugar

⅓ cup shortening
1 egg, lightly beaten
¾ cup milk

For Topping

2 Tbsp. flour
½ tsp. cinnamon

¼ stick butter
4 Tbsp. granulated sugar

Sift the flour, salt, baking powder, and the sugar together. With two knives or a pastry blender cut in the shortening. Add the egg combined with the milk. Stir only until all the flour is dampened.

Spread the dough in a greased and floured 8 × 8 × 2-inch pan.

Mix the topping ingredients together and sprinkle them over the dough. Bake in a 400° oven for about 30 minutes.

Spiced and Spicy Cakes
Chapter 4

MOLASSES PEAR CAKE

½ cup boiling water
¼ cup shortening
½ cup molasses
1 egg, beaten
¼ cup granulated sugar
½ tsp. vanilla
1½ cups cake flour, sifted

⅛ tsp. salt
1 tsp. baking soda
¼ tsp. ground cloves
½ tsp. cinnamon
6 pear halves (canned or
                    fresh)
2 Tbsp. chopped nuts
6 maraschino cherries

Pour the boiling water over the shortening and the molasses. Mix the beaten egg, the sugar and the vanilla together thoroughly. Add this mix into the molasses mixture.

Sift together the flour, salt, soda and spices. Add these to the first mixture, beating until all the ingredients are blended.

Pour the batter into a greased and floured 9-inch pie plate, 4 inches deep. Arrange pear halves on top of the cake batter. Sprinkle on the chopped nuts.

Bake in a slow oven at 325° for 45 minutes. When the cake is cool, place a cherry into the hollow of each pear. Serves 5.

RAISIN NUT CAKE

1⅜ sticks butter
1 cup brown sugar
½ cup molasses
2 eggs, beaten
1 tsp. baking soda
1 cup sour milk

2½ cups all-purpose flour,
                    sifted
2 tsp. baking powder
½ tsp. cinnamon
½ tsp. ground cloves
1½ cups raisins
½ cup chopped walnuts

Cream the butter with the sugar, then add the molasses, and the eggs. Dissolve the soda in the milk and blend in.

Mix and sift the flour, baking powder, and the spices. Add the raisins and the walnuts to the flour mixture.

Combine the two mixtures and bake in three 9-inch greased and floured layer pans in a 375° oven for 25 minutes.

Cover with a favorite icing.

SOUR CREAM SPICE CAKE

1 stick butter
2 cups brown sugar
3 eggs, separated
2 cups all-purpose flour, sifted
¼ tsp. salt
½ tsp. baking soda

½ tsp. baking powder
1 tsp. ground cloves
½ tsp. allspice
½ tsp. cinnamon
1 cup light sour cream

Cream together the butter and sugar. Add the egg yolks and beat.

Sift together the flour, salt, soda, baking powder and the spices. Add these into the egg yolk mixture, alternately with the sour cream. Now, beat the egg whites stiffly and fold them in.

Bake in a greased and floured 9 × 5-inch loaf pan at 350° for 45 to 50 minutes.

SOFT GINGERBREAD (One-Hundred-Year-Old Recipe)

½ cup shortening
1 cup granulated sugar
1 cup molasses or sorghum
2 eggs
3 cups all-purpose flour, sifted
2 tsp. baking soda
½ tsp. salt

2 tsp. ginger
2 tsp. cinnamon
1 tsp. allspice
½ tsp. ground cloves
½ tsp. nutmeg
1 cup buttermilk

Cream the shortening; add in the sugar gradually; mix thoroughly. Add in the molasses. Beat the eggs well and add them into the creamed mixture.

Sift the flour with the soda, salt, and the spices. Sift a second time. Then add the flour alternately with the buttermilk into the molasses-egg mix. Beat hard to blend the batter thoroughly.

Pour the batter into a greased and floured 9-inch square pan and bake for 45 minutes in a 350° oven.

NUT SPICE CAKE

1 stick butter	1 tsp. baking soda
1 cup brown sugar	½ cup molasses
4 egg yolks	1 cup buttermilk
2½ cups cake flour, sifted	½ cup chopped walnut or
1½ tsp. baking powder	pecan meats
½ tsp. ground cloves	½ cup currants
½ tsp. nutmeg	1 cup chopped raisins
1 tsp. cinnamon	

Cream the butter and the sugar together. Beat the egg yolks and then beat them into the butter blend.

Mix and sift together several times the flour, baking powder, and the spices.

Add the soda and the molasses to the buttermilk.

Then add the sifted flour into the butter-egg mixture, alternately with the buttermilk mix. Lastly, add the nuts and fruits, lightly floured. Mix well.

Bake in a greased and floured 9-inch square pan at 350° for one hour.

GINGER CRUMB CAKE

½ stick butter	½ tsp. salt
½ cup granulated sugar	½ tsp. baking soda
1 egg	1 tsp. cinnamon
½ cup sweet or sour milk	1 tsp. ginger
½ cup molasses	1 cup fine, dry crumbs
¾ cup all-purpose flour, sifted	

Cream the butter and sugar together and beat in the egg.
Mix the milk with the molasses.

Sift the flour, salt and soda and the spices together and add them alternately with the molasses-milk into the creamed butter. Stir in the crumbs. Mix well.

Bake in a greased and floured 8-inch tube pan at 375° for 30 minutes.

SOUR CREAM CAKE

2 eggs, separated
1 cup granulated sugar
1 cup heavy sour cream
1½ cups cake flour, sifted
1 tsp. baking soda
1 tsp. baking powder

½ tsp. salt
½ tsp. nutmeg
½ tsp. cinnamon
½ cup chopped nut meats
1 cup raisins

Beat the egg yolks; add in the sugar and the sour cream and blend.

Sift the flour, soda, baking powder, salt and spices together and add them to the creamed blend. Add in the nuts and raisins, stirring sparingly.

Beat the egg whites stiffly and fold them into the batter.

Pour the batter into a greased and floured 9 × 5-inch loaf pan. Bake at 350° for 35 to 40 minutes.

MOLASSES GINGER CAKE

¼ cup shortening
¼ cup granulated sugar
1 egg
½ cup molasses
½ cup hot citrus fruit juice or
                    coffee
1¼ cups all-purpose flour,
               sifted

¼ tsp. salt
½ tsp. baking soda
½ tsp. cinnamon
½ tsp. ginger
¼ tsp. nutmeg
¼ tsp. ground cloves

Cream the shortening with the sugar until they are fluffy and light. Add in the egg and mix well.

Combine the molasses and the hot liquid.

Sift the flour with the salt, soda, and the spices. Add the flour mixture alternately with the molasses liquid into the creamed mixture. Blend thoroughly.

Pour the batter into a greased and floured 8-inch square pan. Bake at 350° for about 35 to 40 minutes.

Cool the cake for several minutes before removing it from the pan. Then slice the cake in half horizontally and fill and frost it with Sea Foam Frosting, (See p. 166).

SPICY PEAR CAKE

⅓ cup shortening

1 egg

¾ cup brown sugar

½ cup raisins

1 cup juice from canned pears

1¾ cups cake flour, sifted

1 tsp. baking soda

¾ tsp. salt

¼ tsp. nutmeg

¼ tsp. ground cloves

½ tsp. cinnamon

Measure the shortening, the egg, and the brown sugar into a large mixing bowl. Dust the raisins lightly with flour and add them in. Then add in the pear juice. Beat with a mixer at medium speed for 1 minute, or 100 vigorous strokes by hand.

Sift the flour, soda, salt and spices together and add them to the first mixture. Mix together at slow speed for one minute, or about 75 strokes by hand.

Pour the batter into an 8-inch greased and floured square pan and bake for 25 to 30 minutes in a 350° oven.

Frost with a favorite icing, or serve with whipped cream.

MOLASSES SPICE CAKE

2 sticks butter

¾ cup brown sugar

¼ cup granulated sugar

4 eggs, separated

½ cup molasses

1 tsp. vanilla

2 cups all-purpose flour, sifted

1 tsp. cinnamon

½ tsp. ground cloves

½ tsp. allspice

½ tsp. mace

¼ tsp. salt

½ tsp. baking powder

½ tsp. baking soda

¾ cup raisins, chopped

1 cup chopped nutmeats

5 Tbsp. milk

Cream the butter. Sift the sugars and add them gradually into the butter. Cream until the mix is smooth.

Beat in the egg yolks; stir in the molasses and the vanilla.

Sift the flour, then resift it with the spices, the salt, the baking powder and baking soda; add these gradually into the batter. Dust a little flour over the raisins and nut meats, then add them into the mixture. Stir in the milk and beat the batter until it is smooth. Finally, beat the egg whites stiffly and fold them in.

Bake in a greased and floured 9-inch tube pan at 350° for about 1 hour.

SPICED BANANA CAKE

⅔ cups shortening	½ tsp. mace
2½ cups cake flour, sifted	¼ tsp. nutmeg
½ tsp. salt	1¼ cups mashed bananas
1⅔ cups granulated sugar	⅔ cup buttermilk
1½ tsp. baking soda	2 large eggs
1½ tsp. cinnamon	⅔ cup chopped nuts

Cream the shortening and sift in the flour, the salt, sugar, soda, and the spices. Add in the bananas and half the buttermilk. Mix until all the flour is dampened. Beat vigorously for 2 minutes. Add in the remaining buttermilk and the eggs. Beat 2 minutes more. Fold in the nuts.

Bake in two greased and floured 8-inch layer cake pans lined with lightly greased wax paper for 30 to 35 minutes. Cool the cakes in the pans on a rack for 5 minutes, then turn them out on the rack and let them cool completely.

Frost with Candy Mountain Frosting (See p. 160), tinted pink. If desired, the frosting can be topped with an additional ½ cup of chopped nuts.

GINGERBREAD

2 sticks butter	2 tsp. baking soda
1 cup granulated sugar	2½ tsp. ginger
4 eggs	¼ tsp. nutmeg
1 cup molasses	¼ tsp. allspice
4 cups all-purpose flour, sifted	1 cup buttermilk
¼ tsp. salt	

Cream the butter with the sugar; add in the eggs, one at a time, beating after each. Stir in the molasses and beat again.

Sift the flour, salt, soda and the spices together. Add these to the molasses mixture alternately with the milk. Beat the batter smooth, then cover it with wax paper and keep it refrigerated until you are ready to use it, or freeze in individual portions for longer storage.

When gingerbread is wanted, pour out the needed quantity into a buttered and floured 8-inch square pan (fill it two-thirds full) and let the batter set until it reaches room temperature. Then bake it in a moderate oven at 325° for about 30 minutes.

This recipe makes 4 or 5 eight-inch square cakes.

Gingerbread can be served either warm or cold, but be sure that it is freshly made. Whipped cream is a delicious topping for gingerbread.

VELVET SPICE CAKE

1½ sticks butter
1½ cups granulated sugar
3 eggs, separated
2 cups cake flour, sifted
1 tsp. baking powder
1 tsp. baking soda

½ tsp. salt
1 tsp. nutmeg
1 tsp. cinnamon
½ tsp. ground cloves
⅞ cup buttermilk

Cream the butter with the sugar; beat in the egg yolks.

Sift together twice the flour, the baking powder, soda, salt and spices. Add them to the creamed mixture alternately with the milk. Beat the egg whites stiffly and fold them in.

Bake in a greased and floured 9-inch tube pan in a 350° oven for 1 hour. Frost with a chocolate or a white icing.

SPICY CHIFFON CAKE

2½ cups cake flour, sifted
1½ cups granulated sugar
1 tsp. salt
3 tsp. baking powder
½ tsp. allspice
½ tsp. cinnamon
½ tsp. nutmeg

¼ tsp. ground cloves
½ cup cooking oil
7 egg yolks, unbeaten
¾ cup cold water
1 cup egg whites (8 large or 10 small eggs)
½ tsp. cream of tartar

Sift the flour, the sugar, the salt, baking powder, and the spices into a mixing bowl. Make a well in this and add the cooking oil, the egg yolks and the water. Beat until the mixture is smooth.

Pour into a large bowl the egg whites and the cream of tartar. Whip until the whites are very stiff. Then pour the egg yolk mixture gradually over the whipped whites, folding in gently. Do not stir.

Pour the batter immediately into an ungreased 10-inch tube pan. Bake at 325° for 55 minutes, then increase the heat to 350° and bake for 10 to 15 minutes longer.

Turn the pan upside down until it is cold, then remove the cake from the pan.

SPICED PRUNE CAKE

1 stick butter	1½ tsp. baking soda
1 cup granulated sugar	½ tsp. cinnamon
2 eggs, well beaten	¼ tsp. ground cloves
1¼ cups chopped cooked prunes	¾ tsp. salt
	½ cup buttermilk
2 cups all-purpose flour, sifted	

Cream the butter, and add in the sugar. Cream until they are fluffy. Add in the eggs and beat well. Blend in the prunes.

Sift together the flour, soda, spices and salt. Add these into the creamed mixture in three portions, alternately with the buttermilk in two portions. Beat after each addition.

Turn the batter into a greased and floured shallow pan about 12 × 8 inches. Bake at 350° for 35 to 40 minutes.

CHOCOLATE SPICE CAKE

½ cup shortening	2 cups cake flour, sifted
1½ cups granulated sugar	2½ tsp. baking powder
⅔ cup milk	1 tsp. salt
2 squares unsweetened chocolate, melted	½ tsp. cinnamon
	¼ tsp. nutmeg
4 eggs, separated	¾ cup chopped nut meats

Cream the shortening with 1 cup of sugar and 2 Tbsp. of milk until the mix is fluffy. Add in the melted chocolate. Blend thoroughly.

Separate the eggs. Combine the yolks with the remaining milk.

Sift the flour, baking powder, salt and spices together. Add this flour mixture and the mixed milk alternately into the creamed shortening mix, beating well after each addition. Stir in the nuts.

Beat the egg whites stiffly and add in slowly the ½ cup of sugar, beating until the sugar is completely dissolved. Then fold the egg whites into the batter and blend thoroughly.

Pour the batter into two 8-inch greased and floured layer cake pans. Bake for 25 to 30 minutes in a 350° oven.

Frost this cake with a favorite icing, or serve it with whipped cream.

๕ Fruit Cakes
Chapter 5

Note: Many fruit cakes are cooked under steam in many different kinds of containers, but the secret of correctly baking a fruit cake in the oven is this: In the bottom of the oven place your broiler pan filled with boiling water. Keep it filled with boiling water while your cake is baking. You may remove the pan of water during the last fifteen minutes of baking time, and you will find that your cake is perfectly browned, moist and delicious.

AFFLUENT FRUIT CAKE

1 lb. butter
1 lb. granulated sugar
12 eggs, separated
2 tsp. cinnamon
1 tsp. ground cloves
1 tsp. allspice
1 lb. all-purpose flour, sifted
1 (½ pt.) glass plum jelly
5 lbs. white seedless raisins
1 lb. shredded citron

1 lb. candied cherries
1 lb. candied pineapple
1 lb. dates
½ lb. orange peel
½ lb. lemon peel
1 lb. black walnut meats, chopped
½ lb. pecan meats, chopped
1 cup pickled peach juice

Cream the butter and sugar together until they are light and fluffy. Beat the egg yolks well. Sift the spices into one-half of the flour. Beat the egg yolks, the jelly and the spiced flour into the creamed mix. Beat hard for several minutes. Now beat the egg whites stiffly and fold them into the batter.

Cut up all the fruits finely. Dredge them, along with the nuts, in the remaining flour. Then add the floured fruit and nuts into the batter. Mix in the peach juice and stir thoroughly.

This large cake (approximately 12 lbs.) can best be baked in two pans. Divide the batter carefully and pour it into two 10-inch tube pans that have been lined with greased heavy brown paper. Fit the paper into the pans smoothly.

Bake the cakes for 2½ hours in a slow 275° oven.

This cake can be stored for a long time if foil-wrapped, in either an airtight tin or the bottom of the refrigerator.

MOTHER-IN-LAW CAKE

2 cups all-purpose flour, sifted
½ tsp. salt
1 tsp. baking soda
½ tsp. baking powder
1½ tsp. cinnamon
1 tsp. allspice
1 tsp. nutmeg

½ cup shortening
1½ cups granulated sugar
3 eggs, unbeaten
1 cup prunes, cooked, drained, pitted and mashed
1 cup buttermilk

Sift together the flour, salt, soda, baking powder, and the spices. Put into another bowl the shortening and sugar and cream them together; add the unbeaten eggs. Beat thoroughly. Now add the prunes to this creamed mixture, and then add the flour mixture alternately with the milk. Blend together.

Pour the batter into two 9-inch layer cake pans that have been well greased and floured. Bake at 350° for about 35 minutes.

Remove the cake from the pans. Allow it to cool. Ice with Caramel Frosting, (p. 161).

TEXAS DARK FRUIT CAKE

1 cup shortening	2 lbs. dates, finely cut
2 cups brown sugar	2 lbs. figs, finely cut
8 cups all-purpose flour, sifted	2 cups pecan meats, chopped
4 tsp. cinnamon	1 cup walnut meats, chopped
2 tsp. allspice	1 cup almonds, chopped
2 tsp. nutmeg	1 cup molasses
2 tsp. salt	2 cups jam (any kind)
2 lbs. citron, finely cut	4 tsp. baking soda
2 lbs. raisins, finely chopped	3 cups buttermilk

Thoroughly cream the shortening with the sugar. Sift four cups of the flour with the spices and the salt. Blend the flour mix in with the shortening and sugar mixture.

Dredge the fruits and the nuts with the other four cups of flour and add them into the mixture. Then add in the molasses and the jam and stir well.

Dissolve the soda in the buttermilk and pour it slowly into the batter; stir continuously while doing so. Mix thoroughly.

Divide the batter into two well greased and lightly floured 10-inch tube pans. Bake at 275° for about three hours. Yield, 2 cakes.

MINCE MEAT FRUIT CAKE

1 (9 oz.) pkg. mince meat	1 egg, beaten
½ cup water	¾ cup all-purpose flour, sifted
1 cup chopped walnut meats	½ tsp. baking soda
1 cup (8 oz.) mixed candied fruit, chopped	½ tsp. salt
1 (15 oz.) can evaporated milk sweetened with 3 tsp. granulated sugar	

Break the mince meat into pieces and place it in a 2-quart saucepan. Add in the water and place over heat on top of the stove; stir until all the lumps are broken. Boil briskly for one minute. Remove the pan

from the heat and let the mix cool. When the meat has cooled, pour it into a mixing bowl and blend well. Add in the nuts, the candied fruit, the milk, and the egg. Sift the flour with the baking soda and the salt and stir it in until it is just blended.

Grease and flour and then line with wax paper and grease again either a 9-inch tube pan or a 9 × 5 × 3-inch loaf pan. Pour the batter into this. Bake in a moderate oven at 350° for 1 hour and 30 minutes, or until the center of the cake springs back when lightly touched and the top is golden brown. (If a glass baking pan is used reduce the heat to 325°.)

DELICIOUS FRUIT CAKE

¼ lb. mixed orange and lemon peel
¼ lb. citron
1 pkg. pitted dates
½ lb. candied cherries
½ lb. candied pineapple
2½ cups cake flour, sifted
1 small can moist coconut
1 lb. white raisins
1 lb. puffed raisins
2 sticks butter
1 cup granulated sugar

5 eggs
1 tsp. baking powder
1 tsp. salt
1 tsp. cinnamon
½ tsp. nutmeg
½ tsp. ground cloves
½ tsp. allspice
½ cup orange juice
1 (½ pt.) glass cherry or grape jelly
½ lb. whole almonds
½ lb. pecans, chopped

Shred the fruit peel, citron, dates, cherries and pineapple. Then dredge them with ½ cup of flour. Cut the coconut fine and add it in. Add in the raisins.

Cream the butter with the sugar. Add in the eggs and beat. Sift the remaining flour with the baking powder, the salt, and the spices. Then add the spiced flour mix to the creamed mix, alternately with the orange juice and the jelly. Combine in the fruits and the nuts. Mix thoroughly.

Turn the batter into a well-greased 10-inch tube pan lined with wax paper that has been lightly greased. Do not smooth the batter. Garnish the top with a few nuts, candied cherries or grated orange peel.

Bake at 300° for 3½ hours.

FAMOUS FRUIT CAKE

1 cup shortening
1½ cups brown sugar, firmly
                    packed
4 eggs
3 cups all-purpose flour, sifted
1 cup thinly sliced citron
1½ cups whole candied
                    cherries
1 cup chopped candied
                    pineapple

1 cup seedless raisins
1 cup chopped figs
3 cups coarsely chopped nuts
1 tsp. baking powder
2 tsp. salt
2 tsp. cinnamon
2 tsp. allspice
1 tsp. ground cloves
1 cup orange juice

Heat the oven to 275°; line two 9 × 5 × 3-inch greased and floured pans with lightly greased wax paper.

Combine the shortening, the sugar and the eggs. Beat for 2 minutes.

In a large bowl, combine 1 cup of the flour with the fruits and the nuts. Sift the remaining flour with the baking powder, the salt, and the spices. Stir the flour into the shortening mixture alternately with the orange juice. Pour the batter over the fruit mixture; blend well. Turn the batter into the prepared pans.

Bake the cakes for 2½ to 3 hours, or until tested done when a toothpick is inserted. Cool the cakes in the pans on a wire rack. Remove the cakes from the pans; peel off the paper. Wrap the cakes in a cloth dampened in wine or brandy, then cover them tightly with foil and store them for at least one week in a cool place.

Before serving, glaze the top of the cakes (See p. 176) and decorate them with a few nuts and candied fruits. Chill the cakes for easy slicing.

WHITE FRUIT CAKE NO. 1

1 cup shortening
1 cup granulated sugar
5 eggs
2 cups all-purpose flour, sifted
1 tsp. salt
1 tsp. baking soda
1½ tsp. baking powder
¼ cup unsweetened pineapple
                    juice
¼ lb. citron, finely cut
¼ lb. candied orange peel,
                    finely cut

2 cups almonds, blanched and
                    slivered
¼ lb. candied lemon peel,
                    finely cut
½ lb. candied cherries, sliced
¼ cup dates, chopped
¼ lb. dried apricots,
                    coarsely cut
¼ lb. pressed figs, finely cut
1½ cups pineapple tidbits,
                    cut up
¼ lb. moist coconut, shredded
½ lb. white raisins

Thoroughly cream the shortening with the sugar. Add in the eggs, one at a time, beating well after each. Reserve ½ cup of flour for dusting the fruits and nuts. Sift the remaining flour with the salt, the soda, and the baking powder, and add it to the egg mixture alternately with the pineapple juice, beating after each addition.

Dust the fruits, the coconut, and the nut meats with the half cup of flour. Add them in. Stir only until they are blended.

Pour the batter into a well greased and floured 9 × 5 × 3-inch loaf pan, lined with lightly greased wax paper. Decorate the top of the cake with glaced pineapple, almonds, cherries, dates or citron if desired.

Bake at 275° for 1½ hours, then at 300° for 1 more hour.

WHITE FRUIT CAKE NO. 2

2 sticks butter
2 cups granulated sugar
1 cup milk
1 tsp. lemon extract
2 tsp. baking powder
1 tsp. salt
2½ cups cake flour, sifted
1 lb. raisins

1 lb. citron, chopped
½ lb. candied pineapple, cut up
½ lb. candied cherries, cut up
1 lb. almonds, chopped
1 cup coconut, shredded
7 egg whites

Cream the butter and sugar together thoroughly; add the milk and the extract. Sift the baking powder and the salt with the flour and add them in. Dredge the fruits, the almonds, and the coconut in a little flour and blend them in. Lastly, beat the egg whites stiffly and fold them carefully into the batter.

Bake in a greased and floured 10-inch tube pan, lined with lightly greased wax paper, for about 2½ hours at 275°.

GRAHAM FLOUR FRUIT CAKE

1 stick butter
⅔ cup granulated sugar
½ cup molasses
1 cup all-purpose flour, sifted
1 cup graham flour
½ tsp. salt
½ tsp. baking soda
1 tsp. cream of tartar
1 tsp. ground cloves

1 tsp. cinnamon
1 tsp. nutmeg
1 cup raisins
½ cup currants
½ lb. citron, cut fine
½ cup milk
Grated rind of 1 lemon
2 eggs

Cream the butter with the sugar. Add the molasses and blend in.

Sift the flours together. Sift them again with the salt, the soda, cream of tartar, and the spices. Dredge the fruits and citron with a little flour. Add the spiced flour and the fruits to the creamed mixture alternately with the milk. Blend thoroughly, then add in the grated lemon rind. Now beat the eggs slightly and stir them into the batter. Beat the batter thoroughly.

Bake in a foil-lined loaf pan, 9 × 5 × 3-inches, or a foil-lined 9-inch angel food tube pan, in a 275° oven for about 3 hours, or until the cake tests done with the toothpick test.

EASY FRUIT CAKE

1 cup seedless raisins	¾ cup all-purpose flour, sifted
½ stick butter	½ tsp. baking powder
½ cup brown sugar	½ tsp. salt
1 egg	1 lb. candied fruit mix, sliced
1 Tbsp. grated orange rind	

Rinse the raisins in boiling water, then drain them thoroughly.

Cream the butter with the sugar until it is light and fluffy. Beat in the egg and add in the orange peel.

Sift together the flour, baking powder and salt; stir this flour mix into the creamed mixture. Stir together the raisins and the candied fruit and mix then into the batter.

Line a lightly greased 8 × 4 × 2-inch pan with foil. Pour the batter into the pan.

Bake in a slow oven at 275° for about 2 hours. This recipe makes about 2 lbs. of fruit cake.

DATE CAKE

1 (10 oz.) pkg. pitted dates	1 cup chopped nut meats
1 tsp. baking soda	1 tsp. vanilla
1 cup boiling water	1½ cups all-purpose flour,
1 Tbsp. shortening	sifted
1 cup granulated sugar	¼ tsp. salt
1 egg	

Cut the dates into small pieces. Sprinkle on the soda and pour the boiling water over them. Let this mixture cool.

Cream the shortening with the sugar. Add in the egg without separating it. Add in the nuts and the vanilla and beat. Then put in the dates and mix well. Finally, add in the flour and the salt.

Pour the batter into a 9-inch square greased and floured pan and bake at 325° for from 40 to 50 minutes.

CRANBERRY NUT CAKE

2 cups all-purpose flour, sifted	2 Tbsp. melted shortening
1 cup granulated sugar	1 egg, well beaten
1½ tsp. baking powder	2 cups fresh cranberries, chopped
½ tsp. baking soda	
1 tsp. salt	1 cup chopped nuts
Juice of one orange and its peel, grated	

Sift together the flour, sugar, baking powder, soda and salt.

Combine the orange juice, the grated rind, the melted shortening and enough lukewarm water to make the mixture equal to ¾ cup. Stir this liquid into the dry ingredients and stir in the beaten egg. Fold in the cranberries. Dust the nuts lightly with a little flour and fold them in.

Spoon the mixture into a greased and floured oblong loaf pan 12 × 8 × 2-inches and bake at 350° for 50 to 60 minutes. Let the cake cool and store it in the refrigerator to keep it moist.

PECAN CAKE

1 cup granulated sugar	½ tsp. cinnamon
1 stick butter or margarine	½ tsp. nutmeg
3 eggs	2 Tbsp. fruit juice
1 cup all-purpose flour, sifted	2 cups raisins
Pinch of salt	2 cups chopped pecans
½ tsp. baking powder	

Cream the sugar with the shortening. Add the eggs one at a time, stirring well after each.

Sift the flour with the salt, baking powder, and the spices. Add the flour, a little at a time, to the egg mixture, stirring in each addition thoroughly. Add the fruit juice. Flour the raisins and the pecans and stir them into the batter.

Bake in a well-greased and lightly floured 9-inch tube or loaf pan in a 350° oven for about 1 hour, 10 minutes.

Cakes That Top Themselves and Somersault

Chapter 6

PRUNE AND APRICOT UPSIDE DOWN CAKE

½ stick butter
½ cup brown sugar
½ tsp. lemon rind, grated
24 canned apricot halves
    (approx.)
30 cooked prune halves
    (approx.)
5 Tbsp. shortening

⅔ cup granulated sugar
1 egg, beaten
2¼ cups all-purpose flour,
    sifted
4 tsp. baking powder
½ tsp. salt
1 cup milk

Blend the butter with the brown sugar; add in the lemon rind; spread this mixture on the bottom of a cake pan 8 inches square by 2 inches deep. Arrange the apricot and prune halves to form a design on top of the sugar mixture in the pan.

Cream the shortening; add in the white sugar gradually; then add the beaten egg. Beat well. Sift the flour, baking powder, and the salt together and then add them alternately with the milk into the creamed sugar. Mix thoroughly.

Pour the batter carefully over the fruit in the pan. Bake for about 50 minutes at 350°. When done, let the cake cool a few minutes in the pan. Then loosen the sides of the cake with a spatula very gently and invert the cake onto a serving plate. Do this carefully as the fruit serves as the topping. This cake may be served warm, with or without whipped cream.

HANDY ANDY CAKE

2 cups cake flour, sifted	½ cup shortening
3 tsp. baking powder	¾ cup milk
1 tsp. salt	1 tsp. vanilla
1¼ cups granulated sugar	2 eggs

For Topping

2 egg whites	½ cup chopped walnut or
1 cup brown sugar	pecan meats

Sift the flour. Measure it; then sift it again with the baking powder, the salt, and the sugar into a large mixing bowl. Add in the shortening, the milk, and the vanilla. Beat for 2 minutes with an electric mixer at low speed or 150 strokes by hand. Add in the unbeaten eggs. Beat 1 minute longer.

Pour the batter into a 13 × 9 × 2-inch loaf pan which has been greased and floured.

Prepare the topping by beating the egg whites until they are stiff but not dry. Add the brown sugar gradually and beat until it is well combined. Spread this mix on top of the batter. Sprinkle on the nuts.

Bake the cake in a 350° oven for about 35 minutes. Allow the cake to cool before serving it.

TOPSY TURVY CAKE

⅞ stick butter	½ tsp. lemon extract
2 Tbsp. light cream	1½ cups granulated sugar
¾ cup brown sugar, packed	1½ cups cake flour, sifted
¾ cup coconut	1½ tsp. baking powder
¾ cup chopped nuts	½ tsp. salt
3 eggs	¾ cup milk
1 tsp. vanilla	

Prepare the frosting first as follows: Heat 5 Tbsp. of butter (⅝ stick) and the cream in a saucepan; stir in the brown sugar, the coconut and the nuts. Cook gently, stirring until everything is well blended. Then spread this mix evenly into an 8 × 12-inch baking pan and set the pan aside while making the cake.

To make the cake: Put the eggs, the vanilla, and the lemon extract into a mixing bowl and beat them lightly with a rotary beater. Add in the white sugar gradually and beat until the mix is fluffy. Sift the flour, the baking powder, and the salt together. Add these to the egg mixture and beat thoroughly. Heat the milk and 2 Tbsp. butter together just to boiling point. Add this gradually into the batter and beat slightly.

Pour the batter over the frosting in the pan and bake at 350° for 35 minutes. When the cake is done invert it on a rack to cool. Any frosting that sticks to the pan can be scraped out while hot and spread on the cake. Serves 12.

RHUBARB UPSIDE DOWN CAKE

1½ cups all-purpose flour, sifted	2 eggs, well beaten
¼ tsp. salt	1 cup granulated sugar
1½ tsp. baking powder	½ cup hot water
	1 tsp. vanilla

For Topping

4 cups sliced rhubarb	¼ stick butter, melted
½ tsp. cinnamon	1 cup granulated sugar

Place the sliced rhubarb in a well greased 9-inch square pan. Sprinkle on the cinnamon, the melted butter and 1 cup of sugar.

Sift the flour with the salt and the baking powder. Beat the eggs well and gradually add to them 1 cup of sugar. Stir in the hot water and the vanilla. Combine the egg mixture with the dry ingredients.

Bake at 350° for about 50 minutes. Remove the cake from the oven. Let it stand a few minutes, then turn it upside down onto a plate. Let it stand a few minutes longer before removing the pan. Serve this cake warm. (*Note:* This recipe requires no shortening.)

MAPLE UPSIDE DOWN CAKE

⅜ stick butter	½ tsp. vanilla
1 cup maple sugar	½ tsp. lemon extract
4 slices pineapple	1 cup cake flour, sifted
3 eggs, separated	¼ tsp. salt
1 cup granulated sugar	1½ tsp. baking powder
¼ cup water	

Melt the butter in a heavy 10-inch skillet. Remove the skillet from the heat, spread the maple sugar over the melted butter and cover it with the sliced pineapple.

Beat the egg yolks and add to them the sugar, water, vanilla and lemon extracts. Beat until the mixture is thick and lemon colored. Sift together the flour, the salt and the baking powder and add them into the egg mix. Beat for 3 minutes. Beat the egg whites stiff but not dry and fold them in.

Pour the batter over the pineapple and bake in the skillet at 350° for about 45 minutes. Let the cake cool for a few minutes in the skillet. Then loosen the sides of the cake with a spatula very thoroughly but carefully, in order to keep the bottom intact since it is the topping. Invert the cake on a serving plate. It may be served warm. Serves 8.

ORANGE CAKE

1½ cups granulated sugar	1 tsp. baking soda
Juice of 1 orange	¾ cup buttermilk
2 Tbsp. grated orange rind	2 cups all-purpose flour, sifted
1 cup raisins	1 tsp. vanilla
½ cup shortening	1 Tbsp. lemon juice
2 eggs, beaten	

Add one-half cup of sugar to the orange juice. Stir until the sugar is dissolved, then set the dish aside.

Pass the orange rind and raisins three times through a food chopper, or chop by hand very finely.

Cream together the shortening and 1 cup of sugar. Add in the eggs. Dissolve the soda in the buttermilk and add these into the egg mixture. Beat thoroughly into this mixture the raisin-rind mix. Next add in the sifted flour, the vanilla, and the lemon juice. Mix together well.

Turn the batter into a greased and floured 11 × 8-inch pan and bake for about 45 minutes in a 325° oven. Remove the cake from the oven, pour the orange juice over it immediately and let it stand until it is cool.

CHERRY UPSIDE DOWN CAKE

Make the cherry mixture first and set it aside to cool.

Cherry Mixture

**1 No. 2 can sour red cherries,
drained**
**¼ cup juice from the canned
cherries**

1 cup granulated sugar
¼ cup water
⅛ stick butter

Boil the cherry juice, the sugar, and the water together until the mixture spins a thread. Add the drained cherries and boil rapidly until the mixture again spins a thread. Melt the butter and pour it into the candied cherries.

Cake Batter

½ stick butter
½ cup granulated sugar
**1½ cups all-purpose flour,
sifted**
2 tsp. baking powder

¼ tsp. salt
½ cup milk
1 egg, well beaten
1 tsp. vanilla

Cream the butter and sugar together until they are fluffy. Sift together the flour, the baking powder, and the salt. Mix the flour and creamed mixtures together thoroughly; add in the milk gradually, then the egg and finally add the vanilla.

Pour the candied cherry mixture into a greased and floured 9-inch square pan. Spread the batter over the cherry mixture and bake in a 350° oven for about 45 minutes.

When the cake is removed from the oven, allow it to stand in the pan for 5 minutes. Then loosen the sides of the cake; turn it out carefully upside down onto a serving plate. If the fruit sticks to the pan, lift it off and place it on the cake. Allow the cake to cool and serve it with whipped cream.

APPLE TREAT CAKE

1 cup all-purpose flour, sifted	4 cups tart apples, peeled and sliced
1½ tsp. baking powder	
½ tsp. salt	1 tsp. cinnamon
½ cup granulated sugar	¼ tsp. nutmeg
½ stick butter	3 Tbsp. melted butter
1 egg, beaten	⅓ cup currant jelly
¼ cup milk	1 Tbsp. hot water

Sift together the flour, baking powder, salt and ¼ cup of sugar. Cut in the butter until the mixture resembles coarse cornmeal. Stir in the beaten egg and the milk. Spread the batter in a greased and floured 8-inch square baking dish. Arrange apple slices in parallel rows on top, slightly overlapping each other. Sprinkle on a mixture of the cinnamon, nutmeg, ¼ cup of sugar and the melted butter.

Bake in a hot oven at 400° for 35 minutes, or until the apples are tender.

Beat the jelly with enough of the hot water to make a syrup. Brush this over the warm cake as soon as it is taken from the oven. Serve the cake warm.

SYBIL HANCOCK'S COCONUT CAKE

1½ cups brown sugar	1 tsp. baking powder
1 egg	1 tsp. vanilla
1 tsp. baking soda	¼ stick butter
1 cup heavy sour cream	1 cup shredded coconut
1½ cups cake flour, sifted	

Place 1 cup of the brown sugar in a mixing bowl; add the egg and beat them together.

Dissolve the soda in the sour cream and add this into the sugar mixture. Sift the flour with the baking powder; add it in. Then add in the vanilla. Mix well.

Stir together the butter, the ½ cup of brown sugar and the coconut. Line an 8-inch square pan with this mix. Pour the batter over it.

Bake in a 325° oven for 35 to 40 minutes. Remove the pan from the oven and when the cake is cool to the touch, turn the cake upside down on a serving plate. The coconut becomes the topping.

DATE CRUMB CAKE

2 cups all-purpose flour, sifted	1 cup buttermilk
1 cup granulated sugar	2 eggs, beaten
1¼ sticks butter	1 cup (5 oz.) dates, chopped
⅓ cup brown sugar	½ cup nut meats, chopped
1 tsp. baking soda	1 tsp. vanilla

Mix the flour, sugar and the butter together until the mixture resembles coarse meal. Set aside one cup of this mixture and add the brown sugar to it. This is the topping.

Dissolve the soda in the buttermilk. Add this and the eggs to the remaining mixture. Mix well. Then add the dates and the nuts. Finally, add the vanilla.

Pour the batter into a greased and floured 13 × 9 × 2-inch pan. Cover it with the topping. Bake at 375° for about 30 to 35 minutes.

DUTCH APPLE BRAN CAKE

1½ cups all-purpose flour, sifted	½ cup shortening, softened
2 tsp. baking powder	½ cup granulated sugar
½ tsp. salt	1 egg
½ cup whole bran cereal	½ cup milk

Sift together the flour, baking powder and salt. Mix this in with the bran cereal.

Blend the shortening with the sugar; add the egg. Beat well. Add the sifted flour mix into the egg-sugar mixture alternately with the milk, mixing after each addition.

Place the batter in a greased and floured 9-inch square pan. Then prepare the topping as follows:

Topping

3 cups sliced, pared tart apples	2 tsp. cinnamon
½ cup brown sugar, (packed)	¼ stick butter

Arrange the apples on top of the batter. Combine the sugar and the cinnamon and sprinkle them over the apples. Dot the butter on top.

Bake the cake in a moderate oven at 375° for about 30 minutes.

QUICK ORANGE CAKE

1 stick butter, melted and hot	¼ tsp. salt
1 cup granulated sugar	¾ cup orange juice
2 eggs	Grated rind of 2 oranges
2 cups all-purpose flour, sifted	3 Tbsp. granulated sugar
4 tsp. baking powder	

Add the hot butter to 1 cup of sugar and beat thoroughly. Add the eggs one at a time, beating after each addition. Sift the flour, baking powder, and the salt together, and add them alternately with the orange juice to the first mixture. Blend in well; beat again.

Pour the batter into a greased and floured 8-inch square pan. Mix the orange rind with the 3 Tbsp. sugar and sprinkle on top. Bake for 50 minutes at 350°.

CHOCOLATE TOPSIDE CAKE

¼ stick butter, melted	2 tsp. baking powder
¾ cup granulated sugar	½ cup milk
1 cup cake flour, sifted	1 tsp. vanilla
Pinch of salt	¼ cup nut meats, chopped
2 Tbsp. cocoa	

For Topping

2 Tbsp. cocoa	½ cup granulated sugar
½ cup brown sugar	1 cup cold water

To make the batter, cream the butter and the sugar in a mixing bowl. Sift together the flour, salt, cocoa, and the baking powder. Add these to the first mixture. Blend well. Stir in the milk and the vanilla. Blend thoroughly. Add the nuts, then stir again. Pour the batter into a greased and floured 9-inch square heatproof glass pan.

Mix together the four topping ingredients and pour the mixture over the batter.

Bake for 40 minutes in a moderate 350° oven for 35 to 40 minutes. Serve this cake directly from the pan.

FRUIT SALAD CAKE (without Shortening)

1½ cups cake flour, sifted
½ tsp. salt
1 cup granulated sugar
1 tsp. baking soda
1 tsp. baking powder

2 cups cooked mixed fruit or berries, including about ¾ cup light syrup
1 egg
1 tsp. vanilla

For Topping

1 cup brown sugar
1 Tbsp. all-purpose flour

1 cup chopped nuts

Sift together the flour, salt, sugar, soda and baking powder. Add in the fruit and juice to these dry ingredients. Combine well.

Beat the egg and add it into the mixture. Lastly, stir in the vanilla. Mix well.

Pour the batter into a greased and floured 9-inch square pan.

Mix the brown sugar and the Tbsp. of flour together for the topping and sprinkle them over the batter in the pan. Finally, cover with the nuts.

Bake at 325° for about 55 minutes.

APPLESAUCE CAKE NO. 1 (Eggless)

½ cup shortening
1 cup granulated sugar
1 cup applesauce
1 cup raisins, chopped
2½ cups all-purpose flour, sifted

½ tsp. ground cloves
½ tsp. nutmeg
½ tsp. cinnamon
1 tsp. baking soda
½ tsp. salt

For Topping

2 Tbsp. brown sugar

1 tsp. cinnamon

Cream the shortening and the sugar together; add in the applesauce. Combine well.

Mix the raisins with ½ cup of the flour. Sift the remaining flour with the spices, the soda, and the salt, and add these dry ingredients into the liquid mixture. Beat well.

Pour the batter into a greased and floured 9-inch tube pan. Cover with the combined topping ingredients. (Sprinkle all over.) Bake at 300° to 325° for about 1 hour.

BANANA TEA CAKE

¼ cup shortening	¼ tsp. salt
¼ cup granulated sugar	2 cups cake flour, sifted
1 egg, beaten	1 cup milk
4 tsp. baking powder	1½ cups mashed bananas

For Topping

½ cup granulated sugar
blended with 2 tsp. cinnamon

Blend the sugar with the shortening and the beaten egg.

Sift the baking powder, salt and flour together. Add the flour to the first mixture, alternately with the milk. Mix the batter together well. Then fold in the bananas.

Pour the batter into a greased and floured 9-inch square pan. Sprinkle on the topping and bake for 30 minutes in a 400° oven.

FRESH APPLE CAKE

1 cup granulated sugar	½ tsp. salt
½ cup shortening	1 cup chopped pecan meats
2 eggs, beaten	1½ Tbsp. buttermilk
1 cup tart apples, ground or grated	1 tsp. vanilla
	3 Tbsp. granulated sugar
2 cups all-purpose flour, sifted	1 tsp. cinnamon
1 tsp. baking soda	

Cream 1 cup of sugar with the shortening. Add in the eggs and the apples. Mix well.

Sift the flour with the soda and the salt and add in the nuts. Mix the floured nuts into the egg-apple mix. Stir in the buttermilk and the vanilla. Combine well.

Pour the batter into a greased and floured 10 × 6 × 3-inch loaf pan. Sprinkle the top with a mixture of the 3 Tbsp. of sugar and the 1 tsp. of cinnamon. Bake for 1 hour in a 350° oven.

GRAPE UPSIDE DOWN CAKE

2 lbs. Concord grapes	**1⅓ cups granulated sugar**
¾ cup granulated sugar	**½ cup shortening**
2¼ cups cake flour, sifted	**1 cup milk**
2½ tsp. baking powder	**2 eggs**
1 tsp. salt	**1 tsp. vanilla**

Wash the grapes. Separate the skins from the pulp and save them. Cook the pulp until it is soft; sieve to remove the seeds. Add in the skins, stir in the ¾ cup of sugar and cook until the skins are tender (about 15 minutes). This makes about 2 cups of pulp.

Sift the flour, baking powder, salt, and the remaining 1⅓ cups of sugar together into a mixing bowl. Add in the shortening, ½ cup of milk, the eggs, and the vanilla. Beat for 2 minutes. Add the remaining milk; beat for 30 seconds.

Pour the batter into a well-greased and lightly floured 9 × 13-inch pan. Spread the grape pulp over it. Bake in a moderate oven at 350° for about 45 minutes. Serve the cake warm, with whipped cream. *Note:* The grape layer sinks to the bottom while the cake is baking and makes an upside down cake. Therefore turn the cake out upside down before serving it.

℘ Budget-Minded Cakes
Chapter 7

KANSAS SUNFLOWER CAKE

½ cup shortening	1 cup granulated sugar
2 cups cake flour, sifted	3 egg yolks
2½ tsp. baking powder	¾ cup milk
¼ tsp. salt	1 tsp. vanilla

Place the shortening in a mixing bowl; let it soften. Sift the flour, the baking powder, the salt, and the sugar together into a bowl. Add in the remaining ingredients, including the shortening. Beat vigorously until the batter is smooth.

Bake in 2 greased and floured 8-inch layer cake pans lined with lightly greased wax paper for 20 to 30 minutes in a preheated 350° oven.

Frost as desired.

(*Note:* This gold cake might be made at the same time Featherweight Cake No. 2 is made—to use up the leftover egg whites.)

ECONOMY CAKE

2 cups brown sugar	1 Tbsp. cold water
½ cup shortening	2½ cups cake flour, sifted
2½ Tbsp. cocoa	1 cup sour milk
½ cup hot water	1 tsp. vanilla
1 tsp. baking soda	

Cream together the sugar and the shortening.

Dissolve the cocoa in the hot water and add it to the creamed mixture. Blend thoroughly. Dissolve the soda in the cold water and add it to the mixture.

Then sift in the flour, adding it in alternately with the sour milk. Finally, add in the vanilla. Beat the batter until it is smooth.

Bake in a greased and floured 9-inch square pan at 350° for 40 to 45 minutes.

Ice with either a white or a chocolate icing.

SUNDAY SUPPER CAKE

1½ cups cake flour, sifted	½ cup milk
1½ tsp. baking powder	1 tsp. flavoring extract
¼ tsp. salt	1 (4 oz.) bar sweet chocolate, grated
1 cup granulated sugar	
½ stick butter	½ cup chopped nut meats
2 eggs	

Sift together the flour, the baking powder, and the salt.

Cream the sugar with the butter, then add the unbeaten eggs and blend well together. Add in the sifted dry ingredients alternately with the milk. Add the flavoring. Beat this batter for 2 or 3 minutes with a rotary beater or an electric mixer until it is light and very smooth.

Pour the batter into a greased and floured 8-inch square pan. Mix together the grated chocolate and the nuts and cover the batter evenly with them. Bake in a moderate oven at 350° for 35 to 40 minutes.

SUGARLESS ORANGE CAKE

2¼ cups cake flour, sifted	2 tsp. grated orange rind
2¼ tsp. baking powder	1 cup light corn syrup
¼ tsp. salt	2 eggs
½ cup shortening	½ cup orange juice

Sift the flour before measuring it, then sift it three times with the baking powder and the salt.

Cream the shortening with the orange rind. Add in the syrup very gradually, a tablespoonful at a time, beating hard after each addition to keep the mixture thick. Add in about one-fourth of the flour. Beat again until the mixture is smooth. Add the unbeaten eggs, one at a time, beating well after each. Then add in the remaining flour in thirds, alternating with the orange juice, and beat well after each addition.

Bake in two greased and floured 8-inch layer pans in a moderate oven at 375° for 30 minutes, or in a 9-inch square loaf pan for 40 minutes.

Top with Sugarless Orange Frosting, (See p. 168).

MRS. ALICE PEET'S EGGLESS CAKE

½ cup shortening	⅛ tsp. salt
1 cup granulated sugar	1 tsp. baking soda
1½ cups all-purpose flour, sifted	1 cup buttermilk
	1 tsp. vanilla
⅓ cup cocoa	

Cream the shortening and the sugar together carefully. Sift the flour, cocoa, salt and soda together about three times, then add them to the creamed mixture alternately with the buttermilk. Stir in the vanilla.

Bake in two 8-inch greased and floured layer cake pans at 325° for 25 to 30 minutes. Remove the layers from the pans and let them cool. Then put them together with Uncooked Icing, (See p. 175), and dot the top with chocolate chips.

PIN MONEY CAKE

1 cup granulated sugar	1 egg, well beaten
½ stick butter	½ tsp. baking soda
1¾ cups cake flour, sifted	1 cup buttermilk
½ tsp. baking powder	½ tsp. lemon extract

Cream together thoroughly the sugar and the butter. Sift the flour with the baking powder and add it to the creamed mixture. Add in the egg and stir.

Dissolve the soda in the buttermilk and pour it gradually into the first mixture. Add the lemon extract and beat the whole batter vigorously.

Bake in an 8-inch greased and floured tube pan in a 375° oven for 35 to 40 minutes.

Frost with Carrot Frosting, (See p. 161).

TWO EGG CAKE

2 cups cake flour, sifted
2½ tsp. baking powder
¾ cup granulated sugar
½ tsp. salt
½ cup shortening

¾ cup white corn syrup
½ cup milk
2 eggs, unbeaten
1½ tsp. vanilla

Sift the flour, the baking powder, the sugar, and the salt into a mixing bowl. Drop in the shortening, then pour in the corn syrup and ¼ cup of milk. Beat with a mixing spoon 150 strokes or for 1 minute. Add in the eggs and beat 250 strokes, or for almost 2 minutes. Add the remaining ¼ cup of milk and the vanilla. Beat 50 strokes, or for 20 seconds. Scrape the bowl and spoon often during the beatings.

Pour the batter into two 8-inch greased and floured layer cake pans lined with lightly greased wax paper. Bake in a 375° oven for 25 to 35 minutes, or until the cake tests done with a toothpick.

Cool the cake in the pans for 10 to 15 minutes on a wire rack before carefully removing it from the pans and taking off the paper.

Ice with Snow Peak Icing, (See p. 175).

EGGLESS CHOCOLATE CAKE

1½ cups all-purpose flour,
                    sifted
¾ cup granulated sugar
¼ tsp. salt
1 tsp. baking soda

¼ stick butter
1½ squares unsweetened
            chocolate, melted
1 cup milk
¼ tsp. vanilla

Sift together the flour, sugar, salt and soda. Cream the butter with the melted chocolate. Stir these two mixes into one batter. Add in the milk and the vanilla, then beat thoroughly.

Bake in one 9-inch greased and floured layer cake pan in a moderate 350° oven for 25 to 30 minutes, or until the cake springs back from

a light touch and shrinks slightly from the side of the pan. Turn it out on a cake rack and let it cool.

When the cake is cold, cut it horizontally in half. Put the two slices together with a boiled white icing or Chocolate Icing, (See p. 171).

EGGLESS, MILKLESS, BUTTERLESS CAKE

2 cups brown sugar	½ tsp. ground cloves
2 cups hot water	½ tsp. cinnamon
4 Tbsp. shortening	2 tsp. baking soda
1½ cups seedless raisins	1 Tbsp. lukewarm water
1 tsp. salt	3 cups all-purpose flour, sifted

Put into a saucepan the brown sugar, the hot water, the shortening, the raisins, the salt, and the spices. Boil these together for 5 minutes, stirring occasionally. Pour this mix into a mixing bowl and allow it to cool.

When the mixture is cold, dissolve the soda in the lukewarm water and add it in. Sift in the flour gradually, stirring and blending thoroughly.

Pour the batter into two small 8 × 4-inch greased and floured loaf pans and bake at 300° for 1¼ hours. Frost the cakes with Quick Caramel Frosting, (See p. 166).

BREAD CRUMB CAKE (No Shortening Required)

3 eggs	¼ tsp. cinnamon
1 cup granulated sugar	¼ tsp. salt
2 cups rolled crumbs from very dry toast	½ tsp. almond extract
	1 tsp. vanilla

Beat the eggs; add in the sugar; stir in the remaining ingredients. Combine well.

Pat the mixture evenly into a shallow 11 × 7-inch greased and floured loaf pan. Bake in a very moderate oven at 300° for about 30 minutes.

Ice to taste, or serve with whipped cream.

Eggs are the only leavening in the cake, giving it somewhat the texture and flavor of macaroons. (This is an excellent way to use up stale bread.)

℞ Baked in the Refrigerator
Chapter 8

RASPBERRY LOAF CAKE

1 pkg. (1 lb.) frozen rasp-
    berries, thawed

⅓ cup raspberry juice (from
    package)

1 (8 oz.) pkg. cream cheese,
    softened

1 (12 oz.) loaf pound cake

For Sauce

¾ cup raspberry juice
2 Tbsp. cornstarch

1 cup light sour cream

Drain the raspberries, reserving the liquid. Beat the cream cheese until it is fluffy and gradually add in the raspberry juice.

Slice the pound cake horizontally into 4 equal layers. On each of 3 layers spread 2 Tbsp. of the cream cheese mixture and top with one-third of the raspberries. Stack the layers, ending with the plain fourth layer. Chill the cake in the refrigerator until it has set. Also refrigerate the remaining cream cheese mixture (but do not let it stiffen).

After the cake has set, frost its top and sides with the reserved cream cheese mixture. Then chill the cake for several hours. Meanwhile prepare the raspberry sauce, as follows.

Combine the raspberry juice and the cornstarch in a small saucepan. Cook on top of stove over medium heat, stirring constantly until the mixture thickens and loses its cloudy quality. Remove the pan from the heat and allow the mixture to cool. Then gently fold it into the sour cream.

Serve slices of loaf topped with raspberry sauce. This recipe will serve 8.

Note: If the frozen raspberries do not yield enough juice, add some diluted raspberry sauce from the bottled variety that can be found in most grocery stores.

CHRISTMAS DAY CAKE

4 cups milk	¾ cup granulated sugar
2 envelopes unflavored gelatin	1 tsp. vanilla
2 egg yolks	2 egg whites, stiffly beaten
¼ tsp. salt	1½ cups heavy cream, whipped
¾ cup chopped maraschino cherries	1 12-oz. pkg. vanilla wafers
⅓ cup cherry juice	

Place 1 cup of milk in a small bowl and sprinkle in the gelatin. Allow it to soften.

In a double boiler, scald 3 cups of milk. Meanwhile beat the egg yolks with a fork. Pour the salt into the egg yolks, add them to the scalded milk and cook, stirring until the mixture coats a spoon. Allow the mixture to cool a few minutes; then add the cherries, the cherry juice, the sugar, and the vanilla extract. Stir until the sugar is dissolved.

Now refrigerate the mixture, stirring it occasionally, until it is completely cold and begins to thicken. Then fold in the beaten egg whites and half of the whipped cream.

Lightly butter a 9-inch spring form pan. Line the bottom and sides of the pan with vanilla wafers, pour in the filling and arrange more vanilla wafers on top. Refrigerate the cake for at least 12 hours.

At serving time, unmold the cake and frost it with the rest of the whipped cream.

UPSIDE DOWN ICE CREAM CAKE

1 can (1 lb. 14 oz.) fruit cocktail

1 quart vanilla or strawberry ice cream

1 baked round cake layer (white or gold, 8 or 9 inches in diameter)

Drain the fruit cocktail well. Spread the fruit in an 8 or 9-inch round pan. Spoon the ice cream over the fruit. Top with the cake layer. Wrap the pan in foil and freeze it in the refrigerator.

To serve, take off the foil and dip the pan in warm water until the cake can be loosened. Turn out upside down onto a serving plate. Makes 6 to 9 portions.

APRICOT-PINEAPPLE CHEESE CAKE

½ cup crushed pineapple, well drained (save the juice)

1½ cups canned apricot halves, well drained (save the juice)

1¼ tsp. salt

2 cups dry cottage cheese, lightly packed and sieved

¼ cup pineapple juice

¼ cup apricot juice

1 pkg. lemon flavored gelatin

¼ cup granulated sugar

1 cup heavy cream, whipped

½ cup finely crushed graham cracker crumbs

¼ stick butter, melted

3 Tbsp. finely chopped nuts

Place the pineapple in a medium size mixing bowl. Press the apricots through a sieve (there should be one cup of apricot pulp) and combine them with the pineapple. Add in the salt and cheese and blend thoroughly.

Bring the apricot and pineapple juices to a boil and dissolve the gelatin in them. Allow this liquid to cool slightly. Gradually add ⅔ cup of the cheese mixture to the gelatin mixture. Combine with the remaining cheese mixture. Blend thoroughly.

Blend the sugar lightly into the whipped cream. Carefully fold this into the cheese mixture.

Pile the batter lightly into a well greased 8-inch spring form pan. Chill the pan in the refrigerator for several hours or overnight. Unmold the cake onto a plate. Combine the crumbs with the butter and add

in the nuts. Sprinkle this blend over the top and sides of the chilled cheese cake. Serves 8.

UNBAKED FRUIT CAKE

1 lb. graham crackers
1 lb. dates, cut fine
1 lb. golden raisins
1 cup English walnuts,
          cut fine

1 lb. marshmallows, cut into
          bits
1 lb. red and green gumdrops,
          cut into bits
½ cup granulated sugar
1 cup heavy cream, whipped

Crush the crackers into crumbs. Mix in the chopped fruits, the nuts, the marshmallows and the gumdrops. Add in the sugar and the whipped cream, blending well.

Pack the mixture very tightly into two 9 × 5-inch loaf pans and wrap them snugly with aluminum foil. Let the pans stand in the refrigerator for about two weeks before using the cakes.

REFRIGERATOR FRUIT CAKE

1½ cups seedless raisins
1 cup prunes
1 cup pitted dates, cut up
1½ cups mixed candied fruits
          and peels, cut finely
1   stick butter or margarine
½ cup confectioners sugar
¼ cup light corn syrup

½ cup marmalade
1 tsp. cinnamon
1 tsp. ground cloves
½ tsp. salt
½ cup walnut meats, chopped
5 cups finely crushed graham
          cracker crumbs

Wash and drain the raisins. Pour boiling water over the prunes and let them stand for 5 minutes. Then drain, cool, slice and pit them. Combine all the fruits and peels.

Cream the butter with the sugar; blend in the syrup, the marmalade, spices, and the salt. Mix this in with the fruit; let it stand for 2 hours. Then blend in the walnuts and the crumbs.

Pack the mixture into a 9 × 5 × 3-inch loaf pan, which has been lined with wax paper. Chill the cake in the refrigerator for 48 hours or longer.

QUICK CHEESE CAKE

1¼ cups graham cracker crumbs	2 cups milk
1 stick butter or margarine, melted	1 (3¾ oz.) pkg. Pineapple Cream Instant Pudding powder
1 (8 oz.) pkg. cream cheese	

Make a graham cracker crust by combining the butter with the crumbs and pressing them firmly into the bottom of a 9-inch round layer cake pan. Set this in the refrigerator to chill until needed.

Stir the cream cheese until it is very soft. Gradually blend in ½ cup of milk until the mix is smooth and creamy. Add in the remaining milk and the pudding powder slowly. Beat slowly with an egg beater for 1 minute. (Do not overbeat). Pour this mixture onto the cooled cracker crust. Sprinkle some extra graham cracker crumbs over the top of the cake to make it extra crunchy. Then chill the cake in the refrigerator.

(To make Lemon Cheese Cake, use Lemon Instant Pudding powder instead of the Pineapple Cream.)

LEMONADE CHEESE CAKE

3 envelopes unflavored gelatin	1 (6 oz.) can frozen lemonade concentrate, unthawed
1 cup milk	¼ cup granulated sugar
2 eggs, separated	1 cup heavy cream, whipped
3 cups (24 oz.) creamed cottage cheese	

For Crust

1½ cups graham cracker crumbs	¾ stick butter or margarine, melted
3 Tbsp. confectioners sugar, sifted	

To make the crust, combine the crumbs, butter and confectioners sugar. Reserve ¼ cup for topping. Press the mixture firmly into the bottom of an 8 or 9-inch spring form pan and place it in the refrigerator to chill until needed.

Sprinkle the gelatin on the milk in a 2½-quart saucepan. Add in the egg yolks; stir well. Place the pan on top of the stove over low heat; stir

constantly until the gelatin dissolves and the mixture thickens slightly (2 or 3 minutes). Then remove the pan from the heat.

Sieve or beat the cottage cheese in the small bowl of an electric mixer at high speed for 3 or 4 minutes, or by hand with a rotary beater for about 4 minutes, vigorously. Stir the cottage cheese and the lemonade concentrate into the gelatin mixture. Wash the bowl and beaters (fat left on the beater will prevent egg whites from whipping).

Beat the egg whites until they are stiff. Gradually add the sugar and continue beating until the mixture is very stiff. Fold in the gelatin-cheese mix; then fold in the whipped cream.

Pour the cheese mix over the crust and top with the reserved crumbs. Chill the cake in the pan in the refrigerator for about 2 hours. Remove the rim of the spring form and slide the cake (still on the bottom of the pan) onto a serving plate. Makes 8 or 9 servings.

MARMALADE REFRIGERATOR CAKE

2 small pkgs. gingersnaps	**3 eggs, separated**
1 Tbsp. gelatin	**¼ cup orange marmalade**
2 Tbsp. cold water	**½ cup heavy cream**
1 stick salt-free butter	**1 tsp. marmalade**
¾ cup confectioners sugar	

Line a 7-inch spring form mold with the gingersnaps; crumble bits to fill the bottom completely.

Soften the gelatin in the cold water in a small pan and dissolve it by placing the pan in a bowl of hot water.

Cream the butter with ½ cup confectioners sugar until it is fluffy. Beat the egg yolks well and add them in. Fold in the liquid gelatin and the marmalade.

Beat the egg whites until they are fluffy; gradually add the remaining ¼ cup of sugar to the whites and beat until the mix is ropey (of a meringue-like consistency). Fold the egg whites into the first mixture. Pour the total mixture on top of the gingersnaps.

Chill the mold in the refrigerator for 24 hours. Remove the outer rim but not the base of the mold. Place the cake on the base onto a plate. Decorate the cake with the cream whipped with the 1 tsp. of marmalade and ring with half circles of gingersnaps.

PINEAPPLE DELIGHT CAKE

1 cup crushed pineapple	4 egg yolks, well beaten
½ cup pineapple juice	1 cup chopped pecan meats
1 pkg. lemon gelatin	4 egg whites
1½ cups granulated sugar	¾ lb. vanilla wafers
2 sticks butter	

Drain the crushed pineapple. Heat the pineapple juice to boiling point. Add in the gelatin and stir until it is dissolved. Set this aside to cool.

Cream the sugar with the butter; add in the egg yolks. Then add the pineapple, the gelatin mix and the nuts. Beat the egg whites until they are stiff and fold them into the creamed mixture. Crush the vanilla wafers. Put half the crumbs in a shallow pan about 11 × 7 inches. Pour on the fruit mixture. Spread the rest of the crumbs on top and pat down gently.

Refrigerate the cake for 24 hours.

CHOCOLATE REFRIGERATOR CAKE

¼ lb. sweet chocolate	¼ cup chopped walnuts
1 Tbsp. water	1 egg white, stiffly beaten
1 egg yolk	½ cup heavy cream
1 Tbsp. confectioners sugar	20 vanilla wafers, or 12 lady fingers

Melt the chocolate in a double boiler. Add the water and blend well. Remove the pan from the flame; add in the egg yolk. Beat vigorously. Add the sugar and walnuts. Blend. Fold in the egg white. Whip the cream until it is stiff and forms a peak and then fold it into the chocolate mixture.

Line a shallow refrigerator tray with one-half the vanilla wafers or lady fingers. Pour on the chocolate mixture. Cover with the remaining wafers. Chill the tray in the refrigerator for about 12 hours. Serves 6.

PINEAPPLE WHIPPED CHEESE CAKE

1½ cups fine graham cracker crumbs	1 (9 oz.) can crushed pine-apple
¾ stick melted butter or margarine	1 pkg. lemon gelatin
3 Tbsp. confectioners sugar, sifted	2 (8 oz.) pkgs. cream cheese
	¼ cup dry milk powder

Mix the crumbs with the butter and the sugar and press them firmly to line the bottom of a 9-inch square pan. Chill the pan in the refrigerator until it is needed.

Drain the pineapple; save the syrup. Mix the gelatin as directed on the package, using the pineapple syrup as part of the liquid. Do not chill it.

With an electric mixer at low speed, or with a rotary hand beater, gradually beat the gelatin mixture into the cream cheese in a large bowl. Chill the bowl in the refrigerator until the cheese mixture is very thick but not set.

With the mixer at high speed, or rapidly by hand, beat the dry milk powder into the cheese mixture. Keep beating until the cheese lumps disappear and the mixture doubles in volume. Then fold in the drained pineapple. Pour the total mixture over the crumbs in the chilled pan. Chill the pan in the refrigerator until the cake is firm (about 2 hours).

This recipe makes 8 or 9 servings.

VELVETY ICEBOX CAKE

1 Tbsp. gelatin	2 eggs
3 Tbsp. cold water	¾ cup orange juice
1 cup condensed milk	1 tsp. grated orange rind
1 cup water	2 dozen lady fingers or 1
2 Tbsp. cornstarch	medium sponge cake
1 cup granulated sugar	⅔ cup condensed milk
	(chilled for whipping)

Soften the gelatin in the cold water. Dilute the condensed milk with the cup of water. Scald 1¾ cups of this dilution in a double boiler. Mix the cornstarch with the sugar and add it to the scalded milk. Cook for 10 minutes, stirring constantly. Beat the eggs lightly and combine them with the remaining ¼ cup of diluted milk. Add this into the cornstarch mix. Cook a few minutes longer, stirring constantly. Remove the pan from the heat; stir in the softened gelatin. Add the orange juice and grated rind.

Line an 8-inch spring form pan with lady fingers or ½-inch fingers of sponge cake. Fill up the pan with alternate layers of the cooked mixture and fingers. Arrange fingers on top. Chill the cake for 3 or 4 hours in the refrigerator. Serve with the whipped condensed milk. (Con-

densed milk whips readily if very cold. Also chill the bowl in which it is whipped).

Garnish with cherries or sliced oranges. Serves 8 to 10.

CRANBERRY ORANGE CHEESE CAKE

2 Tbsp. unflavored gelatin	1 tsp. grated lemon rind
½ cup orange juice	1 tsp. lemon juice
2 eggs, separated	3 cups creamed cottage cheese, sieved
½ cup milk	
1 cup granulated sugar	1 cup heavy cream, whipped
½ tsp. salt	2 cups sweetened, cooked whole cranberries
2 Tbsp. grated orange rind	

For Crust

2½ cups graham cracker (or other favorite crumbs)	1⅛ sticks butter or margarine

Combine the crumbs and butter and press them firmly into the bottom of a 13 × 9-inch pan. Chill in the refrigerator until needed.

Soften the gelatin in the orange juice; put this aside.

Beat the egg yolks lightly in a saucepan. Add in the milk, ¾ cup of sugar, and the salt. Cook on top of the stove over low heat, stirring constantly until the mixture thickens. Add in the softened gelatin and stir until it has dissolved. Add in the orange rind, lemon rind, lemon juice, and the sieved cheese. Chill the mixture in the refrigerator until it is partially set.

Then fold in the whipped cream and the cranberries. Lastly, beat the egg whites until they are stiff but not dry and gradually add the remaining ¼ cup of sugar to them. Fold the egg whites into the cheese mixture.

Pour the mixture onto the crust in the pan and chill it in the refrigerator until it is completely set (about 3 hours).

MYSTERY FRUIT CAKE

1 pkg. honey spice cake mix	1½ cups seedless raisins
4 cups candied mixed fruit, cut up	1 cup dates, cut fine
	4½ cups pecans, chopped
½ cup red cherries, cut up	1 pkg. fluffy white frosting mix
½ cup green cherries, cut up	

Make the honey spice cake as directed on the package. Cool the cake and crumble it into a very large bowl. Add the mixed fruit, cherries, raisins, dates, and the nuts.

Prepare the fluffy white frosting as directed on the package, and mix it with the cake and the fruit.

Pack the mixture tightly into a foil-lined loaf pan, 9 × 5 × 2¾ inches. Or in an angel food tube pan. Cover the pan with foil and chill it in the refrigerator for at least 24 hours. Keep the cake refrigerated. To serve cut slices about ¼ inch thick.

CHOCOLATE WHIPPED CREAM CAKE

1 (4 oz.) bar German's sweet chocolate	1 tsp. unflavored gelatin
1 large pkg. (5 oz.) vanilla pudding mix	2 cups milk
	2 cups heavy cream, whipped
2 tsp. instant coffee	15 lady fingers, split

Break the chocolate into squares; set it aside. Combine the pudding mix powder, the coffee and the gelatin in a saucepan. Stir in the milk. Bring to a boil over medium heat, stirring constantly. Remove the pan from heat, add in the chocolate and stir until the mixture is smooth. Cool the mixture completely; then beat it until it is very smooth. Stir in 1½ cups of whipped cream.

Line an 8 × 4 × 3-inch loaf pan with wax paper. Let the paper extend beyond the pan's rim. Line the bottom and sides of the pan with lady finger halves. Alternately add two layers each of the pudding and the lady fingers. Chill the pan in the refrigerator for 2 or 3 hours until the cake is set. Remove the cake from the pan. Garnish the cake with the remaining whipped cream and a few toasted almonds or walnuts, if desired. Serves 6 to 8.

℞ Pound Cakes
Chapter 9

DE LUXE POUND CAKE

2 cups (1 lb.) country or
                dairy butter
2 cups (1 lb.) granulated
                    sugar
9 eggs
1 tsp. vanilla

½ tsp. mace
4 cups (1 lb.) all-purpose
                flour, sifted
½ tsp. salt
½ tsp. cream of tartar

Cream the butter and sugar together well. Beat in the eggs, one at a time; beat after each addition. Add in the vanilla and the mace.

Sift the flour before measuring it, then resift it with the salt and cream of tartar. Mix the flour into the creamed mixture until it is thoroughly blended.

Pour the batter into a greased and floured 10 × 4-inch tube pan lined with heavy wax paper that should also be lightly greased. Bake in a slow oven at 325° for about 1 hour.

(Pound cakes need no icing and can be stored for a long time if they are thoroughly sealed in aluminum foil and placed in the refrigerator).

HOLIDAY POUND CAKE

1 lb. country or dairy butter
2½ cups granulated sugar
1 Tbsp. vanilla
1 tsp. grated lemon rind
9 large eggs
1 cup chopped, candied red cherries
1 cup chopped, candied green cherries
1 cup chopped pecans
4½ cups all-purpose flour, sifted
1½ tsp. salt

Butter and flour the bottom of a 10 × 4-inch tube pan, and line it with lightly greased wax paper. Set it aside.

Cream the butter until it is fluffy and soft. Add the sugar gradually, beating thoroughly. Blend in the vanilla and the lemon rind. Add the eggs, one at a time, beating well after each.

Toss the cherries and nuts with 1 cup of the flour. Sift the remaining flour with the salt and fold it into the batter, ½ cup at a time, mixing until smooth. Lastly fold in the cherries and the nuts.

Bake for 1 hour and 45 minutes in a 325° oven. Cool the pan on a wire rack for at least 10 minutes before turning the cake out onto a platter.

This cake will keep several weeks if stored in a tightly covered container.

THRIFTY POUND CAKE

3 cups all-purpose flour, sifted
½ tsp. baking soda
½ tsp. baking powder
¾ tsp. salt
1 cup shortening
2 cups granulated sugar
4 eggs, unbeaten
1 tsp. lemon extract
1 tsp. vanilla
1 cup milk

Sift the flour, the soda, the baking power, and the salt together.

In another bowl cream the shortening with the sugar. Add in the unbeaten eggs, one at a time, then the extracts; now beat thoroughly. Then add in the flour mixture alternately with the milk.

Pour the batter into a greased and floured 9 × 5 × 3-inch loaf pan, lined with lightly greased wax paper, and bake in a 350° oven for about 1 hour and 10 minutes. Turn the cake out of the pan and remove the paper. Cool it on a rack.

MARBLE CAKE

1 stick butter
1½ cups granulated sugar
2 eggs
3 cups all-purpose flour, sifted
3½ tsp. baking powder

¼ tsp. salt
⅔ cup condensed milk
1½ tsp. vanilla
½ cup cocoa
2 Tbsp. condensed milk

Cream together the butter and sugar until they are light and fluffy. Beat in the 2 eggs vigorously. Mix the flour with the baking powder and the salt and add it alternately to the butter with the milk and the vanilla.

Put ⅓ of the batter into a second bowl. Add to this the cocoa and the 2 Tbsp. milk. Mix thoroughly.

Put the light and dark batters alternately by spoonsful into a greased and floured 9-inch tube pan. Bake in a 350° oven for about 1 hour, or until the cake shrinks from the sides of the pan. Invert the cake onto a cake rack and let it remain there in the pan until it is thoroughly cool. When the cake is cool, ice it with Fudge Frosting, (See p. 163).

HILDA BRACEY'S POUND CAKE

1 lb. granulated sugar (2 cups)
1 lb. country or dairy butter (room temperature)

1 lb. eggs (8 medium eggs)
1 lb. all-purpose flour, sifted (4 cups)

Cream together the sugar and butter.
Preheat the oven to 325°.
Add in the eggs and flour alternately, a small amount at a time, beating only enough to combine the ingredients completely.

Pour the batter into a greased and floured 11 × 7-inch loaf pan. Bake the cake for 1 hour.

Cool the cake in the pan for 10 minutes before turning it out onto a wire rack to finish cooling.

ICED SOUR CREAM POUND CAKE

2 sticks butter, softened
2½ cups granulated sugar
6 eggs
3 cups cake flour, sifted
½ tsp. baking soda

1 cup light sour cream
1 tsp. flavoring (vanilla, lemon or orange, or all three blended
Candied red cherries (for decorating)

Cream the butter with the sugar until they are light. Add the eggs, one at a time, beating thoroughly after each.

Sift the flour and soda 3 times and add them alternately with the sour cream into the first mixture, beating until the batter is quite smooth. Add the flavoring. Mix well.

Pour the batter into a 9-inch greased and floured tube pan, lined with lightly greased wax paper. Bake in a moderate oven at 350° for 1 hour and 20 minutes, or until a toothpick proves the cake is done.

Let the cake stand in the pan on a rack for about 5 minutes. Then turn it out and peel off the paper. Let the cake cool and then top it with a favorite icing, letting the icing run down the sides of the cake. Decorate with whole red cherries. Store the cake in an airtight box.

BASIC POUND CAKE

2 sticks country or dairy butter	2 cups cake flour, sifted
	½ tsp. salt
2 cups granulated sugar	2 tsp. vanilla
6 eggs	

Cream the butter and sugar together well.

Add the eggs, one at a time, alternately with tablespoons of flour. Combine well. Add in the salt and the vanilla.

Bake for about 50 minutes in a 9 × 5-inch greased and floured loaf pan in a preheated oven at 350°.

ENGLISH LEMON POUND CAKE

1 cup shortening	¼ tsp. yellow coloring
2 cups granulated sugar	½ tsp. salt
4 eggs	3 cups cake flour, sifted
1 Tbsp. lemon flavoring	¾ cup buttermilk
½ tsp. vanilla	1 tsp. baking soda
1 tsp. butter flavoring	1 Tbsp. vinegar

Cream the shortening with the sugar and add in the eggs one at a time. Mix well. Then add in the flavorings, the coloring, and the salt.

Sift the flour and add it in alternately with the buttermilk to the creamed mixture. Mix the soda and the vinegar in a small bowl and add them into the mixture. Blend well.

Bake in a 10 × 5-inch loaf pan that has been greased and lightly dusted with flour, in a slow oven at 325° for about 1 hour and 15 minutes, or until the toothpick test proves it done. Do not overbake.

CHOCOLATE LOAF CAKE

2 sticks margarine
2 cups granulated sugar
2½ cups cake flour, sifted
1 tsp. salt
1 tsp. baking soda

1 tsp. vanilla
4 eggs
1 cup buttermilk
3 (1 oz.) envelopes un-
   sweetened chocolate product
1 cup nuts, chopped

Cream together the margarine and the sugar. Sift the flour with the salt and soda and add it to the creamed mixture. Stir in the vanilla. Add one egg at a time, beating well after each addition. Add in the milk and mix thoroughly. Now add the chocolate product and blend; then stir in the nuts.

Bake in a lightly greased and floured 9 × 5-inch loaf pan lined with lightly greased wax paper at 350° for about 55 minutes.

Serve the cake plain or frosted with Butter Frosting, (See p. 160).

RAISIN WALNUT POUND CAKE

2¼ cups all-purpose flour,
                    sifted
1 cup chopped raisins
1½ tsp. cinnamon
¾ tsp. ground cloves
½ tsp. baking powder
¼ tsp. baking soda

¼ tsp. salt
1¼ sticks butter or margarine
1½ cups granulated sugar
3 eggs
¾ cup buttermilk
¾ cup chopped walnuts
2 Tbsp. grated orange peel

Preheat the oven to 350°. Lightly grease and flour a 9 × 5 × 3-inch loaf pan. Line the bottom of the pan with lightly greased wax paper.

Remove 2 Tbsp. of the flour and toss it with the raisins to coat them well. Sift the rest of the flour with the spices, the baking powder, salt, and the soda. Set this aside.

In a large bowl cream the sugar and butter together until they are light. Add in the eggs; beat again. Now beat the flour mixture into the creamed butter-egg mixture alternately with the buttermilk. Stir in the raisins, the walnuts and the orange peel.

Turn the batter into the prepared pan. Bake for 1 hour and 15 minutes, or until the cake tests done with a toothpick. Cool the cake in the pan on a wire rack for 10 minutes. Then turn it out, right side up, on the rack and let it cool completely. Sprinkle powdered sugar on top of the cake if desired.

SOUR CREAM CHOCOLATE CAKE

1 Tbsp. shortening	1 tsp. salt
1½ cups granulated sugar	2 squares unsweetened
1 cup light sour cream	chocolate
2 eggs	¾ cup boiling water, scant
2 cups cake flour, sifted	1 tsp. vanilla
1 tsp. baking soda	

Cream the shortening. Add a portion of the sugar, then add the cream and the rest of the sugar, mixing thoroughly. Beat the eggs and add them in.

Sift the flour; measure it. Add in the soda and the salt, and sift it again. Melt the chocolate and dilute it with the boiling water. Put the flour and the chocolate mix alternately into the batter. Mix thoroughly. Stir in the vanilla.

Pour the batter into a greased and floured 9 × 5-inch loaf pan. Bake in a 350° oven for about 35 to 40 minutes.

HALF-A-POUND CAKE

½ lb. cake flour	½ lb. butter, softened
(2¼ cups, sifted)	(2 sticks)
1 tsp. baking powder	½ lb. eggs (4 eggs)
¼ tsp. salt	2 tsp. rose water
¼ tsp. nutmeg	½ lb. granulated sugar
	(1 cup)

Sift the flour; resift it three times with the baking powder, the salt, and the nutmeg.

Cream the butter thoroughly; add in the flour mixture in three portions, mixing smooth after each addition.

Beat the eggs until they are thick and lemon colored. Add the flavorings and the sugar all at once and beat until the mixture is very light.

Combine the flour mixture and egg mixture, beating thoroughly.

Line a 9 × 5 × 3-inch pan with 4 thicknesses of smooth brown wrapping paper, the first (inmost) to be buttered. Pour in the batter, pushing it well into the corners of the pan. Then lay another piece of buttered brown paper across the top of the pan.

Bake in a 350° oven for ½ hour, then remove the paper from the top and bake one hour longer.

Cool the cake in the pan for 10 minutes before turning it out onto a wire cake rack to finish cooling.

(from Meta Given's MODERN FAMILY COOK BOOK)

SPICED LEMON POUND CAKE

4 cups all-purpose flour, sifted	2 cups granulated sugar
4 tsp. baking powder	6 eggs
1 tsp. ground mace	1 tsp. grated lemon rind
1 tsp. salt	1 cup milk
2 sticks butter or margarine	

Sift the flour, the baking powder, the mace and the salt together.

Cream the butter and gradually add in the sugar. Beat until the mixture is light and fluffy. Add in the eggs, one at a time, beating after each addition. Put in the grated lemon rind.

Now add in the flour mixture alternately with the milk. Beat the batter smooth. Pour the batter into a greased and floured 10 × 4-inch tube pan. Bake in a preheated oven at 325° for 1 hour and 15 minutes, or until the cake tests done with the toothpick test.

❧ Cupcakes
Chapter 10

QUICKLY MIXED CUPCAKES

2 cups cake flour, sifted
1⅓ cups ganulated sugar
¾ tsp. salt
½ cup shortening

1 cup milk
1 tsp. baking powder
2 eggs, beaten
1 tsp. vanilla

Combine the flour, sugar, salt, shortening, and ⅔ cup of milk. Beat two minutes by hand or in a mixer. Add the baking powder, the final ⅓ cup of milk, the eggs and the vanilla. Beat for two more minutes.

Fill greased and floured muffin tins one-half full. Bake in a hot oven at 400° for 20 minutes.

When the cupcakes are cool, cover them with your favorite icing. This recipe makes 16 cakes.

APPLESAUCE CUPCAKES

1 stick butter
1 cup granulated sugar
1 tsp. baking soda
1 cup applesauce
2 cups all-purpose flour, sifted
1 tsp. ground cloves

1 tsp. nutmeg
2 tsp. cinnamon
¼ cup buttermilk
½ cup chopped nutmeats
½ cup seeded raisins
2 Tbsp. brown sugar

106

Cream the butter and the white sugar together. Dissolve the soda in the applesauce and add them to the creamed mixture; blend well together.

Sift the flour with the cloves, the nutmeg and 1 tsp. of cinnamon and add to the batter along with the buttermilk. Beat all together smoothly. Add in the nutmeats and the raisins.

Grease and lightly flour muffin tins and fill them half full. Mix the brown sugar with the remaining tsp. of cinnamon and sprinkle on top. Bake in a 425° oven for about 20 minutes.

Makes about 20 cupcakes.

OATMEAL DATE CUPCAKES

1 cup all-purpose flour, sifted	½ cup chopped dates
¼ cup granulated sugar	3 Tbsp. cooking oil
3 tsp. baking powder	1 egg, beaten
½ tsp. salt	¾ cup milk
1 cup rolled oats, uncooked (quick or oldfashioned)	6 pitted dates, sliced in half lengthwise

Sift together the flour, sugar, baking powder and the salt. Stir in the oats and the chopped dates. Add the oil, the egg and the milk. Stir only until the dry ingredients are moistened.

Fill greased and floured muffin cups ⅔ full. Place ½ date on the batter in each muffin cup. Bake in a preheated hot oven, 425°, for about 15 minutes.

Frost the cakes with one-half the recipe for Orange Cream Frosting, (See p. 165). Makes 12 medium-sized cupcakes.

LOW CALORIE CUPCAKES

1 cup all-purpose flour, sifted	3 Tbsp. cooking oil
1 tsp. baking soda	2 eggs
½ tsp. salt	¾ cup buttermilk
½ tsp. nutmeg	1 cup rolled oats, uncooked (quick or oldfashioned)
1 tsp. cinnamon	¼ cup raisins
⅓ cup brown sugar	

Sift together the flour, soda, salt, and the spices into a bowl. Add the sugar, cooking oil, eggs, and about half the buttermilk. Beat until

the mixture is smooth. Fold in the remaining buttermilk, the oats, and the raisins. Mix gently.

Fill small paper baking cups or small greased and floured muffin cups one-half full. Bake in a 375° oven for 12 to 15 minutes. This recipe makes 20 small cakes.

Unfrosted these cupcakes equal 82 calories each.

SPICY CUPCAKES

1 stick butter	1 tsp. cinnamon
1 cup brown sugar	1 tsp. nutmeg
1 egg	1 tsp. ground cloves
1 cup sour milk	1 cup raisins
2 cups all-purpose flour, sifted	½ cup chopped nut meats
1 tsp. soda	

Blend the butter with the sugar. Add the egg and stir it in. Add in the sour milk.

Sift the flour, soda and spices together and add them to the creamed mixture. Finally, add the raisins and the nuts. Mix well.

Bake in greased and floured muffin tins for 15 minutes in a 350° oven. Place about 3 Tbsp. of batter in each muffin cup. When done, top cakes with Uncooked Icing, (See p. 175).

Yield, about 16 cupcakes.

VANILLA CUPCAKES

1 stick butter	½ tsp. salt
1 cup granulated sugar	1 tsp. baking powder
2 eggs	1 cup milk
2 cups all-purpose flour, sifted	1 tsp. vanilla

Cream together the sugar and the butter. Beat the eggs until they foam and add them to the first mixture.

Sift the flour, the salt and baking powder together and add it into the creamed mixture alternately with the milk. Stir thoroughly. Put in the vanilla and beat again.

Bake in greased and floured muffin tins for 15 to 20 minutes at 425°.

Makes about 20 medium-sized cakes. Top with a favorite icing if desired.

BUTTERMILK CUPCAKES

⅛ stick butter	1½ cups cake flour, sifted
1 cup granulated sugar	½ tsp. baking soda
1 egg, beaten	1 cup buttermilk
½ tsp. lemon extract	14 pecan halves

Cream the butter and the sugar together. Add in the beaten egg and the extract. Blend thoroughly. Sift into the batter the flour and the soda, adding in the milk alternately as you sift.

Pour the batter into greased and floured cupcake pans and bake in a 375° oven for 25 minutes. If the pans are filled about half full this batter will make 14 cupcakes.

Frost with Brown Sugar Icing, No. 2 (See p. 170) and place a pecan half on top of each cake.

PINK CUPCAKES

½ cup shortening	1 tsp. vanilla
1 cup granulated sugar	½ cup milk
2 cups cake flour, sifted	3 egg whites
½ tsp. salt	Red cake coloring
2 tsp. baking powder	

Cream the shortening thoroughly, then add in the sugar gradually; cream the mixture until it is light and fluffy.

Sift the flour, the salt, and the baking powder together. Mix the vanilla into the milk and add it alternately with the combined dry ingredients into the sugar mixture. Beat with a spoon after each addition until the mixture is smooth.

Beat the egg whites stiff but not dry and fold them carefully into the batter. Put enough red cake coloring into the batter to make the cake a delicate pink. Then divide the batter into 24 greased and lightly floured cupcake pans. (You can use small paper cups placed inside of muffin tins.) Bake for 20 to 30 minutes in a 375° oven.

When the cakes are cool, frost them with your favorite white icing.

SUNSHINE CUPCAKES

For these cakes use the same ingredients called for in the Pink Cup Cakes (See P. 109), except that, only ¼ cup of milk should be used. And instead of the egg whites, use 3 egg yolks beaten until thick and lemon-colored.

Frost with your favorite icing and color bright-red if desired.

✑ Cakes for Party Giving and Party Going—At Home, Church and Club
Chapter 11

ST. NICK'S CAKE

½ cup shortening
1½ cups granulated sugar
2 eggs
2 Tbsp. cocoa
2-oz. red food coloring
1 tsp. vanilla
1 cup buttermilk

1 tsp. salt
2½ cups cake flour, sifted
1 tsp. baking soda
1 tsp. vinegar
1 Tbsp. green food coloring
10 maraschino cherries, quartered

Cream the shortening and the sugar together smoothly. Add in the eggs. Make a paste of the cocoa and the red food coloring and beat it into the first mixture. Stir the vanilla into the buttermilk; mix the salt into the flour; add these alternately into the shortening mixture. Dissolve the soda in the vinegar and stir this gently into the batter.

Bake in two greased and floured 9-inch layer cake pans in a 350° oven for 30 minutes. Cool on a wire rack.

Frost with Uncooked Icing (See p. 175), tinted green with the green coloring. Decorate with the cherries.

CHILD'S RAINBOW BIRTHDAY CAKE

1⅜ sticks butter	3 egg whites, beaten stiffly
1½ cups granulated sugar	1 tsp. vanilla
1 cup milk or water	Green coloring
¼ tsp. salt	Pink coloring
3 cups cake flour, sifted	1 egg yolk
4 tsp. baking powder	

Cream the butter, add in the sugar gradually, and cream again. Add in the milk or water.

Sift the salt into 2½ cups of flour and fold it into the creamed mix. Beat thoroughly. Sift the baking powder into the remaining ½ cup of flour; fold this in now. Finally, cut and fold in the egg whites and the vanilla.

Divide the batter into three portions. To one portion add the green coloring. To another portion add the pink coloring. To the third portion add the egg yolk.

Bake in three greased and floured 8-inch layer cake pans in a moderately hot oven at 375° for 25 to 30 minutes. When the layers are cool, put them together with a white icing and decorate with colored jelly beans.

ST. PATRICK'S DAY CAKE

1½ cups granulated sugar	6 egg whites
¾ cup shortening	1 cup milk
3 cups cake flour, sifted	1 tsp. vanilla
½ tsp. salt	¼ tsp. almond extract
2½ tsp. baking powder	

Cream together the sugar and the shortening. Sift the flour once, then sift it again with the salt and the baking powder. Place the sugar and the shortening in a bowl and add the unbeaten egg whites and 4 Tbsp. of the milk. Beat together thoroughly. Add the extracts, then the flour, alternately with the remaining milk. Beat vigorously.

Bake in a 9-inch greased and floured tube pan for 45 to 50 minutes, in a 350° oven.

Frost with Basic Boiled Icing, (See p. 169), then cover with Green Tinted Coconut, (See p. 177).

CRYSTAL CAKE

2¼ cups cake flour, sifted	1 tsp. vanilla
1½ cups granulated sugar	1 cup milk
4 tsp. baking powder	1 tsp. orange extract
1 tsp. salt	4 egg whites, unbeaten
½ cup shortening	

Sift together the flour, sugar, baking powder and salt; add the shortening, the vanilla, ¾ cup of milk, and the orange extract. Beat well. Add in the egg whites, then ¼ cup of milk, and beat again.

Pour the batter into 2 greased and floured 8-inch layer cake pans. Bake in a moderate 350° oven until the cake tests done (about 30 to 35 minutes). Cool the cake, then remove it from the pans.

Spread between the layers and on top of the cake with Hula Frosting, (See p. 163).

JOANNE SNIDER'S BIRTHDAY CAKE

2 cups all-purpose flour, sifted	Grated rind of 1 orange
1 tsp. baking soda	2 eggs, separated
⅛ tsp. salt	1 tsp. vanilla
1 stick butter	⅔ cup buttermilk (or
1 cup granulated sugar	sour milk)

Sift, then measure the flour. Sift it three times with the soda and the salt.

Cream the butter until it is lemon colored; gradually add in the sugar, beating after each addition. Add the grated rind. Beat the egg yolks and add them in. Then add in the vanilla. Blend well. Next, add in the sifted dry ingredients alternately with the milk.

Beat the egg whites and fold them gently into the batter.

Turn the batter into a greased and floured 9-inch square pan lined with lightly greased wax paper. Bake at 350° for about 45 minutes.

When the cake is cool, frost it with Orange Coconut Frosting, (See p. 165).

BANANA NUT CAKE

3 cups cake flour, sifted	1 cup milk
¾ tsp. salt	1 tsp. vanilla
4 tsp. baking powder	3 bananas (more or less, according to size)
1½ sticks butter	
1½ cups granulated sugar	½ cup chopped nuts
3 eggs, separated	

Mix and sift the flour, salt, and the baking powder together three times. Cream the butter and add the sugar gradually; cream thoroughly. Then beat the egg yolks and add them to the creamed mixture. Beat this mixture until it is fluffy. Next add in the milk gradually, and the vanilla.

Beat the egg whites stiffly and fold them into the batter.

Bake in two greased and floured 9-inch or three 7-inch layer cake pans in a 375° oven for about 30 minutes. While the cake is baking, make Brown Sugar Icing No. 1, (See p. 169).

When the cake is cool, put slices of banana over the first layer, spread on icing, put on the next layer and cover with bananas and icing as before. Cover the top layer with bananas and the chopped nuts. Put the remainder of the icing on the sides of the cake.

POPPY SEED CAKE

½ cup shortening	¼ tsp. salt
1½ cups granulated sugar	1¼ cups milk
⅔ cup poppy seeds	1 tsp. almond extract
2 cups all-purpose flour, sifted	3 egg whites
3½ tsp. baking powder	

Cream the shortening with the sugar well; add in the poppy seeds. Stir well.

Sift the flour with the baking powder and the salt and add it to the creamed mixture alternately with the milk. Then add in the extract.

Beat the egg whites lightly and fold them into the batter.

Bake in two greased and floured 9-inch layer cake pans at 360° for 25 to 30 minutes.

When the cake has cooled, ice it with Vanilla Marshmallow Frosting, (See p. 168).

STRAWBERRY MERINGUE CAKE

2 cups cake flour, sifted	4 egg yolks, beaten
4 tsp. baking powder	¾ cup milk
¾ tsp. salt	1 tsp. vanilla
1 stick butter	4 egg whites, stiffly beaten
2 cups granulated sugar	1 qt. fresh strawberries

Sift the flour once and measure it; add the baking powder and salt and sift all together 3 times.

Cream the butter; add 1 cup of sugar gradually and cream together until the mix is light and fluffy. Add the egg yolks, then the sifted flour alternately with the milk, a small quantity at a time. Beat after each addition. Add the vanilla.

Bake in two 9-inch greased and floured layer cake pans in a 375° oven for 25 minutes. Allow the cake to cool.

Fold ½ cup of sugar slowly into the beaten egg whites. Place the two cake layers on a baking sheet, pile the egg white meringue on them and place them in a moderate oven to brown the meringue.

Prepare the berries (reserving a few as a garnish) by crushing them with ½ cup of sugar. Spread the berry mix gently on top of the meringue and put the layers together. Garnish the top of the cake with the whole berries. Serve at once.

MARASCHINO CHERRY CAKE

2¾ cups cake flour, sifted	⅔ cup milk
1¾ cups granulated sugar	16 maraschino cherries
1 tsp. salt	⅔ cup unbeaten egg whites (about five)
4 tsp. baking powder	
1¼ sticks butter	½ cup chopped nuts
⅓ cup juice (from cherries)	

Sift together the flour, sugar, salt, and baking powder into a bowl. Add the butter, the cherry juice, the milk and the cherries, cut into eighths. Beat vigorously for 2 minutes. Add the unbeaten egg whites and continue beating for about 3 minutes longer. Fold in the chopped nuts.

Pour the batter into two greased and floured 9-inch layer cake pans, and bake for 30 to 35 minutes at 350°.

When cake is cool frost with Snow White Frosting, (See p. 167) using cherry juice instead of water. Decorate with bright red cherries.

APPLE PRESERVE CAKE

¾ cup shortening	1 tsp. baking powder
1 cup granulated sugar	½ tsp. allspice
¼ cup light sour cream	1 tsp. cinnamon
½ cup apple preserves	½ tsp. nutmeg
3 eggs	½ cup chopped walnut meats
2 cups cake flour, sifted	½ cup seedless raisins
1 tsp. baking soda	

Cream the shortening and the sugar together until they are fluffy. Add the cream and apple preserves, mixing well. Add the eggs, 1 at a time.

Sift the flour, soda, baking powder and spices together three times; add them gradually into the liquid mixture. Roll the nuts and raisins in a little flour and fold them in.

Pour the batter into a greased and floured 8 × 4-inch loaf pan and bake at 350° for 50 minutes. Or bake in two 9-inch layer pans for 25 to 30 minutes.

Ice with Lemon Cream Butter Icing, (See p. 173).

CHOCOLATE BUTTER CAKE

3 squares unsweetened choco-late	1 stick butter
2¼ cups cake flour, sifted	1¼ cups granulated sugar
½ tsp. salt	3 eggs
3 tsp. baking powder	1 tsp. vanilla
	1¼ cups milk

Melt the chocolate and set it aside to cool. Sift the flour, salt and baking powder together. Cream the butter and sugar together and to them add one egg at a time, beating well after each addition. Stir in the vanilla. Now add the sifted dry ingredients alternately with the milk and the chocolate.

Pour the batter into two greased and floured 9-inch layer cake pans. Bake in a 350° oven for 30 to 35 minutes.

Cool the cake on cake rack and frost with Butter Frosting, (See p. 160), substituting 1 drop of peppermint flavoring for the vanilla called for in that recipe. If desired, tint the icing a pale pink with two drops of red cake coloring. Garnish with crushed peppermint stick candy.

SILVERY MOON CAKE

1¼ sticks butter	¾ tsp. salt
2 cups granulated sugar	1 cup milk
3 tsp. baking powder	5 egg whites
3 cups cake flour, sifted	

Cream the butter with the sugar.

Sift the baking powder with the flour and the salt and add it to the butter blend alternately with the milk.

Beat the egg whites, not too stiffly, then fold them into the batter.

Bake in two 9-inch greased and floured layer cake pans in a 375° oven for 20 to 35 minutes. Fill with Lemon Custard Filling, (See p. 159).

SPANISH LAYER CAKE

⅓ cup shortening	¼ tsp. ground cloves
1 cup granulated sugar	¼ tsp. salt
1⅞ cups cake flour, sifted	½ cup milk
3 tsp. baking powder	2 eggs, separated
1 tsp. cinnamon	½ cup raspberry jam

Cream together the shortening and the sugar. Mix and sift the flour, baking powder, spices and salt together; add these to the first mixture alternately with the milk.

Beat the egg whites stiffly and cut and fold them in. Blend in the egg yolks.

Bake in two well-greased and lightly floured 8-inch layer cake pans at 350° for 45 minutes.

When the cake has cooled, spread the raspberry jam between the layers and cover the top with a white frosting of your choice.

RUDDY DEVIL'S FOOD CAKE

2 cups cake flour, sifted	**2 eggs, unbeaten**
½ tsp. salt	**1 tsp. vanilla**
⅓ cup cocoa	**1½ tsp. red food coloring**
1 Tbsp. instant coffee	**½ cup buttermilk**
1½ cups granulated sugar	**1½ tsp. baking soda**
½ cup shortening	**¾ cup boiling water**

Sift together the flour, salt, cocoa and instant coffee and set aside. Gradually add the sugar to the shortening, creaming well. Beat in the eggs, one at a time. Add the vanilla and the food coloring. Add alternately and gradually the sifted dry ingredients and the buttermilk, beating smooth after each addition. Mix the soda into the boiling water and add them to the batter. Blend in.

Pour the thin batter into a greased and floured 9 × 5-inch pan lined with lightly greased wax paper and bake at 350° for 30 to 35 minutes, or until tested done with a toothpick.

Turn the cake out on a wire rack and peel off the wax paper. Frost when it is cool with Snow White Frosting, (See p. 167) or Chocolate Butter Icing, (See p. 171).

APPLE SURPRISE CAKE

2 cups chopped tart apples	**½ cup cooking oil**
1 cup granulated sugar	**1 egg, beaten**
1½ cups all-purpose flour, sifted	**1 tsp. lemon extract**
	½ cup chopped nuts
½ tsp. salt	**1 cup flaked coconut**
1 tsp. baking powder	

Chop the apples and pour the sugar over them. Let them stand until juice forms.

Sift the flour, salt and baking powder together and add them to the apple mixture. Add in the remaining ingredients.

Bake in a greased and floured 9-inch tube pan, at 350° for 30 minutes. This cake needs no icing but use one if you wish.

PRUNE CAKE

1½ cups all-purpose flour,
                    sifted
½ tsp. ground cloves
½ tsp. cinnamon
1 cup granulated sugar
½ cup shortening

2 eggs
1 tsp. baking soda
4 Tbsp. sour milk
1 cup cooked prunes,
                    chopped

Sift together the flour and the spices.

Cream the sugar with the shortening. Add in the eggs.

Dissolve the soda in the sour milk.

Add in the dry ingredients alternately with the sour milk mix into the sugar mixture. Lastly, add in the prunes.

Bake in two greased and floured 8-inch layer cake pans at 375° for 30 minutes. Fill the layers with Prune Nut Filling, (See p. 160).

COLONIAL FRUIT CAKE

3 cups cake flour, sifted
1½ tsp. baking powder
½ tsp. salt
1½ sticks butter
2 cups granulated sugar
4 eggs, separated
1 cup milk

½ tsp. vanilla
2 tsp. cinnamon
½ cup currants
½ cup chopped, moist citron
½ tsp. ground cloves
½ tsp. nutmeg

Measure the flour; sift it three times with the baking powder and salt. Cream the butter with the sugar well. Beat the egg yolks lightly and add them to the creamed mixture. Then add the sifted flour mixture alternately with the milk. Beat the egg whites stiffly and fold them in.

Divide the batter in half. Add the vanilla to one half; to the second half, add the fruit and the spices. Stir each gently. Bake each half in an 8-inch greased and floured square pan lined with lightly greased wax paper in a 350° oven, the white layer about 30 minutes, the dark layer 35 minutes. Cool the cake.

Put the spice layer on the bottom and spread with Snow White Frosting, (See p. 167). Add the white layer on top and cover the whole cake with the rest of the frosting.

RICH SOFT HONEY CAKE

½ stick butter or margarine	4 cups cake flour, sifted
¼ cup shortening	1 tsp. baking soda
1 cup strained honey	½ tsp. salt
1 egg, well beaten	½ tsp. cinnamon
½ cup buttermilk	

Cream together thoroughly the butter, shortening, honey, and the egg. Pour in the buttermilk; blend well. Sift the flour with the soda, salt and cinnamon and fold into the first mixture. Mix well and bake in a greased and floured pan, 13 × 9 × 2-inches, in a 350° oven for 50 minutes.

When cool the cake may be cut and served in square brownie-like pieces, or sliced in half to form a 2-layer cake and frosted with icing.

HOLIDAY CAKE

½ yeast cake	½ cup milk
½ cup lukewarm water	1 tsp. cinnamon
2½ cups all-purpose flour, sifted	¼ tsp. ground cloves
	¼ tsp. nutmeg
½ tsp. granulated sugar	1 tsp. salt
1 stick butter	1 cup chopped raisins
1 cup brown sugar	½ cup chopped figs or dates
1 egg, beaten	

Soften the yeast in the lukewarm water; add ½ cup of flour and the white sugar and beat well. Put this aside in a warm place to rise for about an hour.

Meantime, cream the butter and brown sugar, add the beaten egg and the milk. Sift together the flour, the spices and the salt. Then combine all the ingredients, including the yeast mixture, and mix well.

Pour the batter into a well-greased and lightly floured 9 or 10-inch tube pan. Cover it with a cloth and place it in a warm place to rise for 3 or 4 hours.

Bake for 1 hour in a moderate oven at 350°.

MIDNIGHT MALLOW CAKE

¼ lb. marshmallows (16)

3 squares unsweetened chocolate

¾ cup boiling water

2¼ cups cake flour, sifted

1½ tsp. baking soda

¼ tsp. salt

3 eggs, well beaten

1¼ cups light sour cream

1¼ cups granulated sugar

1 cup chopped nuts

Melt the marshmallows and the chocolate in a double boiler over hot water. Add the ¾ cup of boiling water; beat until smooth. Let this mixture cool.

Sift the flour, soda and salt together. Add in the marshmallow-chocolate mixture. Then put in the eggs, the cream and the sugar. Add the nuts last. Mix thoroughly.

Pour the batter into two greased and floured 9-inch layer cake pans. Bake in a 375° oven for 25 to 30 minutes. Cool the cake and frost it with Vanilla Marshmallow Frosting, (See p. 168).

CHEESY DUTCH APPLE CAKE

2 cups all-purpose flour, sifted

½ cup granulated sugar

1½ tsp. baking powder

1 tsp. salt

½ stick butter

1½ cups shredded cheddar cheese

1 egg, beaten

¾ cup milk

2 medium-sized tart apples

Sift together the flour, sugar, baking powder and salt. Cut in the butter until the mixture resembles coarse meal. Add the cheese and toss lightly to blend with the dry ingredients. Combine the egg and the milk; add

to the dry ingredients and stir until blended. Spread the batter evenly in a buttered and floured 9-inch square pan.

Pare, quarter and core the apples and cut them into 1/4-inch slices. Press the apple slices diagonally into the dough, with rounded edges up, about 1/2 inch apart. Bake for 35 minutes at 375°. Meanwhile prepare the glaze.

Glaze

3/4 cup granulated sugar	1/2 stick butter
1/2 tsp. cinnamon	1 Tbsp. lemon juice
1/3 cup water	

In a saucepan blend the sugar and the cinnamon. Add the water, butter, and lemon juice, and bring to a boil. Remove the pan from the heat and allow contents to cool slightly. Remove the cake from the oven. Pour the glaze over the cake, loosening the edges to let the glaze run down between the cake and the sides of the pan. Return the pan to the oven and bake 15 minutes or until the cake is well browned and the apples are soft. Serve this cake while warm, topped with Lemon Raisin Sauce, (See p. 178). Makes 9 to 12 servings.

SWEET BUTTERMILK CAKE

3 cups cake flour, sifted	1 tsp. vanilla
3/4 tsp. baking soda	1 tsp. lemon extract
2 tsp. baking powder	1 tsp. orange extract
1 stick butter	1 1/2 cups buttermilk
1 1/2 cups granulated sugar	2 eggs

Sift the flour, soda and baking powder together.

Cream the butter with the sugar. Add the vanilla, lemon and orange extracts. Add in the sifted dry ingredients alternately with the buttermilk. Beat in the eggs gently. Mix well.

Pour the batter into two 9-inch round layer cake pans (or a 13 × 9-inch loaf pan) which have been greased and floured.

Bake in a 350° oven for 25 to 30 minutes (40 minutes may be required for the loaf pan).

Remove the cake from the pans and cool it on a cake rack. When it is cool, frost with Butter Frosting (See p. 160), and decorate as desired.

DANISH WHITE CAKE

½ cup shortening, or 1 stick butter

1 tsp. vanilla

1⅓ cups granulated sugar

2½ cups cake flour, sifted

¼ tsp. salt

2½ tsp. baking powder

1 cup milk

3 egg whites

½ cup raspberry jam

¼ pint heavy cream

Cream the shortening with the vanilla. Add in the sugar gradually and continue creaming until it is well mixed.

Sift the flour before measuring; sift it again with the salt and the baking powder. Add the flour mix alternately with the milk into the creamed sugar mixture. Whip the egg whites well and fold them into the batter.

Bake in two greased and floured 8-inch layer cake pans lined with lightly greased wax paper, for 30 minutes, in a 350° oven.

Spread jam between the cake layers. Whip the cream and flavor it with ½ teaspoon of either vanilla or almond extract. Spread the cream all over the outer surface of the cake.

FUDGE NUT CAKE

1¾ cups cake flour, sifted

2 cups granulated sugar

2 tsp. baking powder

¼ ·tsp. baking soda

1 tsp. salt

¼ cup shortening, softened

1½ cups milk

1 tsp. vanilla

2 eggs

4 squares unsweetened chocolate, melted

1 cup nut meats, cut up fine

Heat the oven to 350°. Grease and flour two round 8 or 9-inch layer cake pans.

Sift the flour, sugar, baking powder, soda, and the salt into a bowl. Add in the shortening, the milk, and the vanilla. Beat for 2 minutes.

Put in the eggs and the melted chocolate. Beat for two more minutes. Dredge the nuts lightly with a little flour and add them in.

Bake for 35 to 40 minutes. Cool the cake and ice it with Honey Butter Icing, (See p. 173).

HONEY NUT CAKE

2 cups cake flour, sifted	½ cup honey
2 tsp. baking powder	3 eggs
½ tsp. salt	1 cup finely cut nut meats
1⅜ sticks butter	¼ cup milk
½ cup granulated sugar	1 tsp. vanilla

Sift the flour once, then measure it; add in the baking powder and salt and sift together three times.

Cream the butter; add the sugar gradually to it and cream thoroughly. Add in the honey, one-half at a time, beating after each addition. Add in ½ cup of the flour mix and beat until the whole mixture is smooth and well blended.

Beat the eggs until they are thick enough to pile up in the bowl; add them to the cake mixture and beat well. Add the nuts. Now add in the remaining flour in thirds, alternately with the milk in halves, beating well after each addition. Finally, add the vanilla.

Bake in a greased and floured 9-inch tube pan in a slow oven, 325°, for 1 hour and 5 minutes.

Frost with Honey Frosting, (See p. 163), or serve plain.

AMBER CAKE

⅓ cup shortening	¼ tsp. salt
1½ cups granulated sugar	¾ cup water
2½ cups cake flour, sifted	½ tsp. almond extract
4 tsp. baking powder	4 egg yolks, beaten

Cream the shortening with the sugar. Mix and sift the flour, baking powder, and the salt; add these alternately to the first mixture with the water and the extract. Fold in the beaten egg yolks.

Bake in a greased and floured sheet (shallow pan about 13 × 9 inches) for 35 minutes in a 350° oven. When the cake is cool, cut it in half and put it together with Mocha Frosting, (See p. 164).

MAPLE SNOW CAKE

2¾ cups cake flour, sifted	2 eggs, separated
½ tsp. salt	1 cup hot water
½ cup shortening	4 tsp. baking powder
1½ cups granulated sugar	½ tsp. maple flavoring

Lightly grease and flour two 9-inch cake pans and line them with lightly greased wax paper.

Sift the flour and salt together. Cream the shortening with the sugar until they are light and fluffy. Beat the egg yolks and add them to the creamed mixture. Add in the sifted dry ingredients alternately with the water. Beat the egg whites well and add the baking powder to them. Fold into the mixture. Add the flavoring.

Pour the batter into the pans and bake in a moderate oven at 350° for 30 to 35 minutes. Cool the cake and frost it with Maple Icing, (See p. 173).

FROSTED MOCHA CAKE

½ cup shortening	1 tsp. baking powder
1½ cups granulated sugar	1 tsp. baking soda
2 eggs	½ tsp. salt
⅔ cup buttermilk	1 tsp. cinnamon
½ cup cold strong coffee	½ cup cocoa
1¾ cups cake flour, sifted	1 tsp. vanilla

Cream the shortening with the sugar; beat the eggs well and add them in. Blend well. Put in half the buttermilk and the coffee.

Sift together the flour, baking powder, the soda, salt, cinnamon and cocoa; add one-half of this mix to the creamed ingredients. Beat well. Then add the remaining buttermilk and flour, also the vanilla, and beat thoroughly.

Bake in two lightly greased and floured 9-inch layer cake pans at 350° for 30 to 35 minutes.

When the cake is cool spread on Mocha Frosting, (See p. 164).

CHOCOLATE NOUGAT CAKE

3 oz. unsweetened chocolate,
cut very fine
½ cup boiling water
1¾ cups cake flour, sifted
1 cup granulated sugar
¾ tsp. salt
½ tsp. baking powder

¾ tsp. baking soda
½ cup shortening
½ cup dark corn syrup
⅓ cup sour milk
1 tsp. vanilla
2 eggs, unbeaten

Put the chocolate in a mixing bowl. Pour the boiling water slowly over it and stir until blended. Set aside to cool.

Sift the flour, sugar, salt, baking powder and soda into the chocolate mixture. Cream the shortening smoothly and add it in, then put in the corn syrup. Beat 200 strokes. Now add the milk, eggs and vanilla. Beat again thoroughly.

Bake in a 12 × 8 × 2-inch greased and floured pan in a 350° oven for 50 to 60 minutes.

Spread the top of the cake with Nougat Frosting, (See p. 164).

LARGE BIRTHDAY CAKE

3 cups all-purpose flour,
sifted
3½ tsp. baking powder
¾ tsp. salt
1½ cups granulated sugar

½ cup shortening (softened)
5 egg yolks, unbeaten
1½ tsp. vanilla
1¼ cups milk

Sift together the flour, baking powder and salt. In another bowl, cream together the sugar and shortening with the unbeaten egg yolks and the vanilla. Beat for 2 minutes. Add the flour mixture to the sugar mixture alternately with the milk. Beat only enough to blend.

Pour the batter into two deep 9-inch greased and floured layer cake pans. Bake at 350° for about 35 minutes. Remove the cake from the pans. Let it cool.

Ice with a boiled icing. Sprinkle with coconut and chopped maraschino cherries, if desired.

SUE BREEDEN'S CHOCOLATE CAKE

1 (4-oz.) pkg. German's sweet chocolate
½ cup boiling water
2 cups granulated sugar
1 cup shortening
3 egg yolks, unbeaten
½ tsp. vanilla

1 Tbsp. lemon juice
2½ cups cake flour, sifted
1 tsp. baking soda
¼ tsp. salt
1⅛ cups milk
3 egg whites, stiffly beaten

Melt the chocolate in the boiling water. Allow it to cool. Cream the sugar with the shortening until they are light and fluffy. Add the egg yolks, one at a time, beating after each addition. Add the vanilla and the melted chocolate. Mix until blended. Blend in the lemon juice.

Sift together the flour, soda and the salt. Add these sifted dry ingredients to the chocolate mixture alternately with the milk. Beat after each addition until the batter is smooth. Then fold in the egg whites.

Pour the batter into three 9-inch greased and floured layer pans lined with lightly greased wax paper. Bake in a 350° oven for 35 to 40 minutes. Let the cake cool.

Frost the cake top and between the layers with Coconut Pecan Frosting, (See p. 162), or with whipped cream.

WEDDING CAKE

(Cakes for a large wedding should be made by a caterer or professional baker, but for a small, informal home wedding or a family wedding at the church, the mother of the bride or a close relative often wishes to bake the cake for sentimental reasons.)

1½ sticks butter
2 cups granulated sugar
1 cup sweet milk
3½ cups cake flour, sifted
⅛ tsp. salt

2 tsp. baking powder (heaped)
6 egg whites, well beaten
1 tsp. lemon extract

Cream the butter with the sugar; add in the milk. Sift the flour three times with the salt and the baking powder, and then add it into the milk mixture. Fold in the egg whites lightly and quickly, then the flavoring.

This cake can be baked in layers in graduated size greased and floured pans so as to make tiers. It should be baked until the toothpick test proves it done in a 350° oven, for about 30 to 35 minutes.

Put the layers together with a white icing, and decorate as desired. Serves 10 to 12.

If a larger cake is needed, the recipe should be repeated before baking (not doubled or tripled) for greater ease in handling, and for better results.

BRIDAL SHOWER CAKE

½ cup shortening	½ tsp. salt
2 cups granulated sugar	½ cup milk
2½ cups cake flour, sifted	1 tsp. orange extract
3 tsp. baking powder	Whites of 8 eggs

Cream the shortening; add the sugar gradually, beating constantly. Mix and sift the flour with the baking powder and the salt; add it alternately to the first mixture with the milk and continue beating. Add in the extract. Beat the egg whites stiff and dry and cut and fold them in.

Fill a 9-inch tube pan, well greased and lightly floured, with the batter and bake for 50 minutes in a 350° oven. When the cake is cool, spread on a white icing.

BLACKBERRY JAM CAKE

3 cups cake flour, sifted plus	2 sticks butter
1 Tbsp. cake flour	2 cups granulated sugar
½ tsp. salt	1 tsp. baking soda
1 tsp. cinnamon	1 cup buttermilk
¼ tsp. ground cloves	6 eggs
¼ tsp. allspice	2 cups seedless blackberry jam

Stir together the flour, the salt, and the spices.

Cream the butter and sugar together well, then add in the sifted flour mix. Blend well. Stir the soda into the buttermilk; add into the mixture. Stir again. Add in the eggs, one at a time, mixing well after each. Lastly, add the blackberry jam. Mix it in thoroughly.

Bake in three greased and floured 8-inch layer cake pans for 25 to 30 minutes at 350°. Frost with a lemon, white or caramel icing.

VANILLA MARSHMALLOW CAKE

2 cups all-purpose flour, sifted

½ tsp. salt

2 tsp. baking powder

2 tsp. vanilla

1⅓ cups granulated sugar

⅔ cup shortening

3 large eggs

⅔ cup milk

Sift together the flour, salt, and the baking powder. Then blend the vanilla and the sugar into the shortening. Beat the eggs into the shortening mix, then stir in the flour mixture alternately with the milk. Beat the batter for ½ minute. Turn the batter into two well greased, lightly floured 9-inch layer cake pans.

Bake in a preheated moderate oven at 375° for 30 minutes, or until a toothpick inserted in the center comes out clean. Cool the cake on a wire rack. Spread the layers and the top of the cake with Vanilla Marshmallow Frosting, (See p. 168).

MARYLAND CAKE

2½ cups cake flour, sifted

1½ tsp. baking powder

½ tsp. salt

1 stick butter

1⅓ cups granulated sugar

1 tsp. vanilla

⅔ cup milk

4 egg whites

Measure the flour; sift it three times with the baking powder and the salt. Cream the butter with the sugar until they are smooth. Stir in the vanilla. Add the sifted dry ingredients alternately with the milk

into the butter mix. Beat the egg whites stiffly and fold them in to the batter.

Bake in two greased and floured 8-inch layer cake pans lined with lightly greased wax paper at 375° for about 25 minutes. Let the cake cool.

Frost with Tutti Frutti Icing, (See p. 175).

BLACK WALNUT CAKE

½ cup shortening
1 cup granulated sugar
1¾ cups cake flour, sifted
2½ tsp. baking powder
¼ tsp. salt

½ cup coffee
½ cup milk
3 egg whites
¾ cup black walnut meats, chopped

Cream the shortening with the sugar. Sift the flour before measuring, then sift the flour, baking powder and salt together and add them alternately with the coffee and the milk into the creamed mixture. Beat the egg whites stiffly and fold them in. Add in the nuts.

Pour the batter into two greased and floured 7-inch layer pans (or a medium size loaf pan) lined with lightly greased wax paper. Bake at 350°, the layers for 30 minutes, as a loaf for 45 minutes.

Allow the cake to cool and frost it with a favorite icing.

VANILLA WAFER CAKE

1 stick margarine
1 cup granulated sugar
2 eggs
⅔ cup milk
½ tsp. salt
1 tsp. baking powder

1 tsp. vanilla
½ cup shredded coconut
2½ cups crumbled vanilla wafers
½ cup chopped nuts
Flour

Cream the margarine with the sugar. Mix together thoroughly the eggs and the milk. Sift in the salt and the baking powder. Blend all these ingredients in a mixing bowl. Stir into this mixture the vanilla, the coconut, and the vanilla wafers. Very lightly dust the nuts with flour and stir them in last.

Bake in a 350° oven in a 9 × 5-inch greased and floured loaf pan for 1 hour. Frost with Brown Sugar Icing No. 2, (See p. 170).

MAJESTIC CAKE

¾ cup shortening
1½ cups granulated sugar
4 eggs
3 cups all-purpose flour,
    sifted

3 tsp. baking powder
1½ tsp. salt
¾ cup milk
2 tsp. vanilla

For Filling

⅓ cups chopped candied
    cherries

½ cup chopped raisins
½ cup chopped nuts

Cream the shortening and the sugar together. Beat the eggs well and mix them well into the shortening mix. Mix and sift the flour, baking powder and the salt; add them alternately with the milk into the creamed mixture. Add in the vanilla, then beat thoroughly.

Bake in 3 greased and floured 9-inch layer cake pans in a 400° oven for 25 minutes. Mix the filling, and when the cake is cool, spread it between the layers of the cake. Then spread the sides and the top of the cake with Ornamental Frosting, (See p. 166).

CORAL SANFORD'S COMPANY CAKE

2½ cups unsweetened apple-
    sauce
3 tsp. baking soda
2 cups granulated sugar
2 sticks butter
4 cups all-purpose flour,
    sifted
½ tsp. nutmeg
½ tsp. cinnamon

½ tsp. ground cloves
¼ tsp. allspice
¼ tsp. salt
2 tsp. baking powder
1 lb. raisins
1 lb. currants
1 lb. English walnut meats,
    chopped

Drain the applesauce as dry as possible. Add the soda to it. Cream together thoroughly the sugar and the butter. Add in the applesauce and stir thoroughly.

Sift the flour, then sift it again with the spices, the salt and the baking powder. Blend it into the applesauce mixture. Coat the fruit and the nuts with a little flour and add them into the batter. If there appears to be too much flour, thin to cake batter consistency with a little buttermilk or sour milk.

Bake in a 350° oven in a greased and floured 13 × 9-inch loaf pan for 55 to 60 minutes.

Frost with Brown Sugar Icing, No. 2, (See p. 170).

❧ Rare, Historical and Offbeat Cakes
Chapter 12

APPLE LAYER CAKE

½ cup shortening
2 cups granulated sugar
3 egg yolks
3 cups all-purpose flour, sifted

2 tsp. baking powder
¼ tsp. salt
1 cup milk
3 egg whites

Cream the shortening with the sugar in a mixing bowl. Beat the egg yolks well and stir them in. Sift the flour with the baking powder and salt; add into the creamed mixture alternately with the milk. Lastly, beat the egg whites stiffly and fold them in.

Bake in three 8-inch greased and floured layer cake pans at 325° for 30 minutes. Fill the layers with the following special filling.

Special Filling for Apple Layer Cake

1½ cups applesauce
1 cup confectioners sugar
(more or less according to the liquid content of the applesauce)

1 tsp. lemon juice
1 tsp. cinnamon

Add the juice and cinnamon to the applesauce in a small bowl; beat in the sugar until the mixture attains a thick custard-like consistency.

TOOTHLESS NELL'S CAKE

(Toothless Nell lies buried in Boot Hill at Dodge City, Kansas. Wyatt Earp, Bat Masterson and other law men of that day probably tried to keep her in bounds. We are told she liked this cake. How she ate it without teeth history doesn't record.)

3 Tbsp. granulated sugar	¼ tsp. cinnamon
¾ stick butter	½ tsp. salt
1 cup dark molasses	1 tsp. baking soda
2 cups all-purpose flour, sifted	1 egg, unbeaten
	4 Tbsp. warm water
¼ tsp. ground cloves	

Cream the sugar and butter together thoroughly. Mix in the molasses. Stir together.

Sift together the flour, spices, salt, and the baking soda.

Break the egg into the sugar and butter mixture and stir it in. Now add in the water gradually and stir it in.

Blend in gradually the sifted flour mix and beat until the batter is quite smooth.

Bake in a 9-inch greased and floured pan for 25 to 30 minutes at 325°. (If desired, when the cake is cool cover it with your favorite icing.)

POTATO FUDGE CAKE

2 sticks butter	½ tsp. salt
2 cups granulated sugar	½ tsp. allspice
4 eggs, separated	½ tsp. cinnamon
1 cup raw potatoes, grated	½ tsp. ground cloves
Grated rind of 1 lemon	½ cup milk
2½ cups all-purpose flour, sifted	3 squares unsweetened chocolate
3 tsp. baking powder	½ cup chopped almonds

Cream the butter; add the sugar gradually and continue blending. Beat the egg yolks well and add them to the creamed mixture along with the grated potato and the lemon rind. Sift the flour once, then measure it. Sift it again with the baking powder, the salt, and the spices.

Add the milk and the sifted dry ingredients alternately to the potato mix. Then melt the chocolate and add it in. Finally, dust the almonds with a little flour and mix them in. Beat the egg whites stiffly and fold them into the batter.

Bake the cake slowly for 1 hour in a 9 × 5-inch greased and floured loaf pan at 325°.

Cover the cake when it is cool with a fluffy white or a chocolate icing.

TOMATO SOUP SPICE CAKE

1 stick butter	½ tsp. cinnamon
1½ cups granulated sugar	½ tsp. ground cloves
2 eggs	1 tsp. baking powder
1 tsp. baking soda	1 can condensed tomato soup
2 Tbsp. water	½ cup nut meats, chopped
2½ cups cake flour, sifted	½ cup raisins
½ tsp. nutmeg	

Cream the butter with the sugar until they are light and fluffy. Beat the eggs well and add them in. Dissolve the soda in the water and stir it into the egg mixture.

Sift 2 cups of flour with the spices and the baking powder. Add this to the mixture alternately with the tomato soup.

Roll the nuts and raisins in the remaining half cup of flour and add them to the batter.

Bake at 350° in a square 9-inch greased and floured pan for one hour.

SALAD DRESSING CAKE

1½ cups granulated sugar	1 tsp. vanilla
1 cup creamy salad dressing	2 tsp. baking soda
2 cups all-purpose flour, sifted	1 cup warm water
3 Tbsp. cocoa	½ tsp. salt

Mix together all the ingredients and beat hard for two minutes.

Bake in an oblong 13 × 9 × 2-inch greased and floured pan at 350° for 30 minutes.

STRAWBERRY POP CAKE

2 cups granulated sugar	1 cup strawberry soda pop
¾ cup shortening	5 egg whites, beaten stiff but not dry
3 cups cake flour, sifted	
2 tsp. baking powder	1 tsp. vanilla
1 tsp. salt	½ tsp. almond extract

Cream the sugar with the shortening.

Sift the flour with the baking powder and salt; add it into the creamed mix, alternately with the soda pop. Fold in the beaten egg whites. Add in the extracts. Stir the total batter gently.

Bake in two greased and floured 9-inch layer cake pans at 350° for 40 minutes.

Frost the cake with Yummy Pale Pink Icing, (See p. 175).

CHOPPED PEANUT CAKE

2 cups cake flour, sifted	⅔ cup milk
1⅓ cups granulated sugar	1 tsp. vanilla
¾ tsp. salt	¼ cup milk (separately)
2½ tsp. baking powder	2 eggs
½ cup shortening, softened	1½ cups shelled raw peanuts

Sift the flour, sugar, salt, and baking powder together in a mixing bowl. Add the shortening; cream together; add in the ⅔ cup of milk and the vanilla. Beat for two minutes, then add the ¼ cup of milk. Beat together again. Add the eggs and beat for two minutes more.

Run the peanuts through a food grinder (or chop them very fine) and then mix them into the batter. Pour the mixture into two deep 8-inch layer cake pans that have been greased and floured. Put pans in a 350° preheated oven and bake for 25 to 30 minutes.

Remove the cake from the pans; allow it to cool; then ice with Peanut Butter Icing, (See p. 174).

(This cake should be allowed to stand about two days before it is eaten, in order to heighten the flavor of the peanuts.)

FIG CAKE

1½ cups granulated sugar	1 tsp. lemon extract
1¼ sticks butter	1 tsp. cinnamon
1 cup milk	1 tsp. nutmeg
3 cups cake flour, sifted	1½ cups finely cut figs
½ tsp. salt	(10 oz. pkg.)
4 tsp. baking powder	1 Tbsp. molasses
4 egg whites, beaten	

Cream the sugar with the butter. Add the milk. Sift the flour, salt and baking powder together. Add one-half of the flour mixture to the first ingredients, then add in the well-beaten egg whites. Blend in. Now blend in the rest of the flour and the lemon extract.

To about ⅔ of the mixture add the cinnamon, the nutmeg, the figs (floured lightly first) and the molasses. Using an 8-inch greased and floured round tube pan for the baking, alternately spoon into it the dark and light mixtures, as for marble cake.

Bake at 350° for about 55 minutes.

APPLE JAM CAKE (This Recipe Is over 50 Years Old)

½ stick butter	2 cups all-purpose flour, sifted
1 cup granulated sugar	
2 eggs	¼ tsp. salt
1 cup milk	2 tsp. baking powder
	1 tsp. vanilla

Cream the butter; add in the sugar gradually. Cream together well. Beat the eggs and add them in. Then add the milk.

Sift together the flour, salt and baking powder. Add these to the creamed mixture and also add the vanilla.

Bake in two greased and floured 9-inch layer cake pans at 375° for about 20 minutes. Set the cake aside to cool and prepare the filling.

Filling

3 large red apples	juice of 1 lemon with grated rind
1 cup granulated sugar	

Core the apples, then grate them (the skin as well as the pulp). Add in the juice and lemon rind, then the sugar. Simmer slowly in a saucepan on top of the stove for about 20 minutes, stirring constantly to prevent the mixture from sticking. When it is done it should be a nice clear red color. Cool this filling. When the cake is also cool, spread the filling between the layers and frost the surface of the cake with a white frosting.

DOUBLE BUTTERSCOTCH CAKE

⅔ cup butterscotch morsels	¼ tsp. baking powder
¼ cup water	1¼ cups granulated sugar
2¼ cups cake flour, sifted	1 stick butter
1 tsp. salt	3 eggs
1 tsp. baking soda	1 cup buttermilk or sour milk

Melt the butterscotch morsels with the water in a saucepan; set aside to cool.

Sift the flour with the salt, soda, and baking powder; set aside.

Add the sugar gradually to the butter, creaming well. Blend in the eggs one at a time; beat vigorously after adding each. Now add in the melted butterscotch and mix well. Then add in the dry ingredients alternately with the milk. Beat well.

Turn the batter into two 9-inch layer cake pans, well greased and floured. Bake at 375° for 25 to 35 minutes. Let the cake cool.

Spread Butterscotch Filling, (See p. 158) between layers and on top to within ½ inch of edge of cake. Frost the sides and top edge of the cake with Sea Foam Frosting, (See p. 166), or with whipped cream.

SPUD AND SPICE CAKE

1¾ cups granulated sugar	3 eggs, unbeaten
1 cup cold cooked mashed potatoes	1 tsp. baking soda
	1 cup buttermilk
¾ cup shortening	2 cups plus 2 Tbsp. all-purpose flour, sifted
1 tsp. cinnamon	
½ tsp. nutmeg	¾ cups chopped walnuts
½ tsp. salt	

Combine in a mixing bowl the sugar, potatoes, shortening, spices and salt. Cream for 4 minutes. Add in the eggs; blend well.

Combine the soda and the buttermilk. Add them alternately with 2 cups of flour to the creamed mixture. Coat the nuts with 2 Tbsp. flour; stir them into the batter.

Turn the batter into a greased and floured 13 × 9 × 2-inch pan. Bake at 350° for 50 to 60 minutes. Frost with Quick Caramel Frosting, (See p. 166).

BLACK BEAR'S CAKE*

¾ cup dark molasses
1 stick butter
1 Tbsp. honey
1 egg, well beaten
½ cup warm black coffee

1¾ cups all-purpose flour, sifted
1 tsp. baking soda
½ cup black walnut meats, chopped

Stir together in a mixing bowl the molasses, butter, honey, and the egg. Add in the coffee, then the flour sifted in with the soda. Beat vigorously. Mix in the nuts thoroughly.

Pour the batter into a 9-inch greased and floured tube cake pan and bake in a 350° oven for 50 to 55 minutes.

* *The Story of Black Bear's Cake:* When the American people began moving from the east to the southwest and westward, they went in covered wagons and on horseback. The women sweetened the cakes they made with molasses and honey, as sugar was a rarity. This molasses cake was cooked over campfires and in fireplaces.

By the time, some hundred years later, when this recipe reached our family, it was called Black Bear's Cake. And the recipe came with a legendary tale of how the cake got its name.

A pioneer family living in a log cabin was visited regularly by a shaggy black bear with a crippled foot. When he came to the edge of the clearing begging for food, they would put out their scraps. Often the woman would give him a piece of stale molasses cake. She noticed the bear came quickly the moment the aroma of the cake, baking in the fireplace, filled the air. The husband coming home one day found his wife baking the cake. He cried out, "Oh, you're baking Black Bear's cake!"—L.R. and R.V.

APPLE CIDER CAKE

2½ cups cake flour, sifted	1½ cups granulated sugar
2 tsp. baking powder	¾ cup shortening
¼ tsp. baking soda	¾ cup sweet apple cider
1 tsp. salt	3 eggs, unbeaten
1 tsp. cinnamon	Crab apple jelly

Sift together the flour, baking powder, soda, salt, cinnamon and sugar. Place the shortening in a mixing bowl and cream it until it is soft. Sift in the dry ingredients. Add the cider and mix until all the flour is dampened. Beat 2 minutes in a mixer at low speed or by hand for 5 minutes. Add in the eggs and beat one minute more.

Pour the batter into two well greased and floured 8-inch layer cake pans. Bake for 35 to 40 minutes at 350°. When the cake is done, let it cool. Slice the layers in half; spread crab apple jelly over one slice, cover with a second slice; spread lightly with Basic Boiled Icing, (See p. 169), tinted yellow. Repeat until all slices are used. Cover the sides of the cake with the remaining icing.

CHOPPED APPLE CAKE

4 cups chopped tart apples	2 cups all-purpose flour, sifted, plus
1 cup water (from cooked apple peelings)	1 Tbsp. flour
2 cups brown sugar	1 tsp. baking soda
½ cup shortening	¼ tsp. salt
	1 tsp. baking powder

Wash the apples thoroughly; dry them with a soft cloth; peel them. Put the peelings in cold water, bring them to a boil and let them simmer for 10 minutes. Drain off the water and save it; discard the peelings. Chop up the apples.

Cream the sugar with the shortening. Sift in the flour, the soda, salt, and baking powder. Blend thoroughly. Put in the water and stir again. Then add in the chopped apples. Blend together well.

Bake in a 9 × 5-inch greased and floured loaf pan at 350° for about 50 to 55 minutes or until the cake tests done (when a toothpick inserted in the center comes out dry).

SWEET POTATO CAKE

½ cup shortening	¼ tsp. baking soda
1 cup granulated sugar	2 tsp. baking powder
2 eggs	½ tsp. cinnamon
1 cup mashed cooked sweet potatoes	½ tsp. nutmeg
	¼ tsp. ground cloves
2 cups all-purpose flour, sifted	½ cup milk
½ tsp. salt	½ cup chopped nuts

Cream the shortening. Add in the sugar gradually and continue to cream. Add the eggs, one at a time, beating well after each. Add in the sweet potatoes. Mix well. Sift together the flour, salt, soda, baking powder, and the spices. Add them alternately with the milk to the creamed mixture, beginning and ending with the dry ingredients. Add in the nuts. Mix well.

Bake in a greased and floured 9 × 9 × 2-inch square pan in a 350° oven for 45 to 50 minutes. Top with a caramel icing, if desired.

VERA BRANNON'S ORANGE JUICE DATE CAKE

2 sticks butter	1⅓ cups buttermilk
2 cups granulated sugar	1 (10 oz.) pkg. pitted dates, chopped
4 eggs	
4 cups all-purpose flour, sifted	1 cup pecan meats, chopped
1 tsp. salt	2 Tbsp. grated orange rind
1 tsp. baking soda	1 tsp. vanilla

Cream together the butter and the sugar. Beat the eggs and add them in. Then sift the flour, the salt and the soda together and add them in alternately with the buttermilk. Now put in the dates, the nuts, the orange rind, and the vanilla. Combine well together.

Pour the batter into a lightly greased and floured 12-inch tube pan. Bake in a slow oven, 300 to 325°, for 1½ hours, or until the cake is firm to the touch.

While the cake is baking, mix for the topping:

1⅓ cups fresh orange juice	2 cups granulated sugar
1 Tbsp. grated orange rind	

Mix these ingredients well together until the sugar is dissolved. Let the mixture set until the cake is baked.

As soon as the cake is taken from the oven, stir the topping mixture again and pour it over the hot cake in the pan. As you pour slowly, punch holes in the cake with a long-tined fork or a toothpick. The cake will gradually absorb the juice. Let the cake stand in the pan 5 hours or longer.

This recipe makes a large cake but it will keep moist for days. Store it in the refrigerator covered with aluminum foil.

CARROT EGGLESS CAKE

1 cup brown sugar	2 tsp. cinnamon
1¼ cups water	1 tsp. salt
⅓ cup shortening	1 tsp. baking soda
½ cup chopped raisins	2 tsp. water
1 cup grated raw carrots	2 cups all-purpose flour, sifted
½ tsp. nutmeg	2½ tsp. baking powder
½ tsp. ground cloves	½ cup chopped walnut meats

Mix the brown sugar, the water, shortening, raisins, carrots and the spices in a saucepan and boil for 3 minutes. Cool this mixture to luke-warm.

Mix together the salt, the soda, and 2 Tbsp. of water. Add these into the brown sugar mixture.

Sift the flour and the baking powder together and blend them in to the mix. Fold in the nuts.

Bake in a greased and floured 8 × 4 × 2½-inch pan at 350° for 1 hour. Frost with Lemon Cream Butter Icing, (See p. 173).

MILKY WAY CAKE

8 Milky Way bars	1½ cups buttermilk
2½ sticks butter	2½ cups cake flour, sifted
2 cups granulated sugar	½ tsp. salt
4 eggs, well beaten	2 tsp. vanilla
½ tsp. baking soda	1 cup chopped nuts

Melt the Milky Way bars in a double boiler with 1 stick of butter. Set the pan aside to cool.

Cream the sugar and the remaining butter together smoothly. Add in the eggs. Then dissolve the soda in the buttermilk and add them in. Sift the flour with the salt and mix it into the batter. Stir thoroughly. Add the vanilla, nuts, and melted bars. Beat everything together well.

Bake the cake in a greased and floured 9-inch tube pan for 1 hour or more at 325°, until it tests done by the toothpick test.

Frost with Chocolate Chip Nut Icing, (See p. 171).

GREEN APPLE CAKE

1 cup brown sugar, packed	1 cup cold coffee
⅔ cup shortening	1 tsp. baking soda in ¼ cup cold water
2 eggs	
1 cup all-purpose flour, sifted	¼ cup breakfast cereal bran
1 cup whole wheat flour	1 cup raisins
½ tsp. salt	1 cup chopped nuts
2 tsp. pumpkin pie spice	2 green apples, peeled and coarsely chopped

Cream the sugar and the shortening in a large mixing bowl. Beat the eggs and add them to the mixture. Sift together the flours, salt and spice and add them to the batter alternately with the coffee and soda-and-water. Now stir the bran in well.

Dust the raisins and nuts lightly with flour and add them to the batter; then put in the chopped apples. Mix the total batter thoroughly.

Bake as a loaf cake in a greased and floured 11 × 4½-inch pan at 350° for about 50 to 55 minutes.

CRAZY CAKE

1½ cups all-purpose flour, sifted	4 Tbsp. cocoa
1 cup granulated sugar	5 Tbsp. melted shortening
½ tsp. salt	1 Tbsp. vinegar
1 tsp. baking soda	1 tsp. vanilla
1 tsp. baking powder	1 cup water

Measure all the ingredients into a mixing bowl. Beat them together for 2 or 3 minutes. Pour the batter into a greased and floured 9-inch tube pan and bake for 35 to 40 minutes at 350°.

SALT PORK CAKE

2 cups boiling water	1 tsp. baking powder
1 lb. ground salt pork	1 tsp. nutmeg
4 cups granulated sugar	1 tsp. cinnamon
½ cup molasses	1 tsp. ground cloves
1 egg, beaten	1 (15 oz.) pkg. seedless raisins
6 cups all-purpose flour, sifted	

Pour the water over the pork and let it stand until it is lukewarm. Stir in the sugar, the molasses and the egg.

Sift the flour, the baking powder, and the spices together. Add them into the pork mixture. Then flour the raisins lightly and add them in. Mix the total combination thoroughly.

Turn the batter into two greased and floured loaf pans, about 9 × 5 inches, lined with lightly greased wax paper. Bake in a 300° oven for 2 hours.

This recipe makes 2 cakes.

PUMPKIN CAKE

½ cup shortening	4 tsp. baking powder
1 tsp. maple extract	⅛ tsp. salt
1¼ cups brown sugar	1 tsp. cinnamon
2 eggs	¼ tsp. ground cloves
1 cup cooked, strained pumpkin	¼ tsp. allspice
3 cups cake flour, sifted	¼ tsp. nutmeg
¼ tsp. baking soda	¾ cup milk
	1 cup chopped walnuts

Cream the shortening and add in the maple extract. Add in the sugar gradually, creaming constantly until the mixture is light and fluffy.

Beat the eggs until they are light and add them in slowly to the creamed mixture. Continue beating. Now stir in the pumpkin.

Sift together the flour, soda, baking powder, the salt, and the spices, and add them alternately with the milk into the creamed mixture, stirring after each addition. Lastly, fold in the nuts.

Turn the batter into three greased and floured 8-inch layer cake pans lined with lightly greased wax paper. Bake in a moderate oven at 350° for 25 minutes. Ice as desired.

HOT POTATO CAKE

2 cups all-purpose flour, sifted
½ tsp. salt
2 tsp. baking powder
1 tsp. cinnamon
½ tsp. nutmeg
½ tsp. ground cloves
1 stick butter
2 cups granulated sugar
1 cup plain hot mashed potatoes

3 squares unsweetened chocolate, melted
1½ tsp. baking soda
¼ cup water
4 eggs, separated
½ cup milk
½ cup chopped nuts
1 tsp. vanilla

Sift together the flour, the salt, baking powder, and the spices. Set this aside.

Cream the butter with the sugar, then add in the hot mashed potatoes and the melted chocolate. Dissolve the soda in the water and add this into the mix. Beat thoroughly. Then beat the egg yolks and mix them in. Now put in the dry ingredients and the milk alternately. Continue beating. Beat the egg whites; fold them in. Lastly, add the nuts and the vanilla.

Bake in two 9-inch greased and floured layer cake pans at 375° for about 30 to 40 minutes. Ice the cake with either a white or a chocolate icing.

OVERNIGHT CAKE

2 cups granulated sugar
2 cups water
¾ cup shortening, melted
1 cup raisins
1 tsp. cinnamon

1 tsp. ground cloves
1 tsp. nutmeg
2 tsp. baking soda
3 cups all-purpose flour, sifted

Simmer the sugar, water, shortening, raisins, and the spices together in a saucepan for 10 minutes on top of the stove. Let the mixture stand overnight in the pan.

Next morning, simmer for 10 more minutes. Then let the mix cool.

When the mixture is lukewarm, sift the soda into the flour and add them into the cooked mixture. Stir together well.

Bake in an 8 × 4-inch greased and floured loaf pan at 350° for 45 to 50 minutes, or until the cake tests done with the toothpick test.

SCOTCH OATMEAL CAKE

1¾ cups uncooked oatmeal

1½ cups all-purpose flour, sifted

1 cup brown sugar

1 tsp. baking soda

½ tsp. salt

¾ cup buttermilk

1¼ sticks butter

For Filling

½ cup chopped nuts

1 lb. dates, chopped

¾ cup water

1 tsp. vanilla

Mix the cake ingredients together thoroughly until they are crumbly.

Cook the date filling ingredients (except the vanilla) in a saucepan on top of the stove over low heat until it thickens. Remove the pan from the fire; add in the vanilla.

Spread one-half of the cake mixture in a 9-inch square pan, that has been greased and floured. Add a layer of date filling and top with the remaining batter. Bake at 350° for about 35 minutes. Cut the cake into squares while it is warm but serve it cold.

EMMA STEPHENSON'S FRESH COCONUT CAKE

1 stick butter or margarine

1½ cups granulated sugar

1 tsp. vanilla

2 cups cake flour, sifted

2 tsp. baking powder

¼ tsp. baking soda

½ tsp. salt

½ cup buttermilk

1 medium-sized coconut to yield

½ cup coconut milk

1¼ cups grated fresh coconut meat

4 egg whites, stiffly beaten

(*To prepare the fresh coconut:* Pierce the eyes of the coconut with an ice pick. Drain off the milk into a clean container. Crack the shell all over with heavy blows of a hammer or mallet. Remove the outer shell and pare off the dark inner skin. Grate the white meat—leftover pieces can be wrapped in foil and stored in the refrigerator for later use.)

Cream the butter until it is fluffy. Add the sugar in 4 parts, creaming after each addition. Add in the vanilla. Sift the flour, the baking powder, the soda, and the salt together and add them alternately to the creamed mixture with the buttermilk and the coconut milk. Add in ¼ cup of the grated coconut. Then fold in the egg whites, gently but thoroughly. Pour the batter into two greased and floured 8-inch layer cake pans.

Bake in a 350° oven for 35 minutes. Cool the layers on a cake rack and then frost them with Butter Frosting (See p. 160). After the cake is frosted, sprinkle all over it generously with the remaining cup of grated fresh coconut meat.

ICEBOX GINGER CAKE

2 sticks butter	2 tsp. ginger
1 cup granulated sugar	¼ tsp. cinnamon
4 eggs	¼ tsp. allspice
1 cup molasses	¼ tsp. salt
2 tsp. baking soda	½ cup raisins
1 cup buttermilk	½ cup chopped nut meats
4 cups all-purpose flour	

Cream the butter with the sugar. Add the eggs, one at a time, beating well after each addition. Add in the molasses and beat well. Stir the soda into the milk and add them into the mixture.

Sift the flour with the spices and the salt. Then add it into the batter. Dust the raisins and nuts lightly with flour and fold them in gently.

Put the batter in a covered bowl and place it in the refrigerator. This batter will keep for a month and can be baked in muffin pans as needed. To bake, bring the batter to room temperature, pour lightly greased and floured muffin tins ¾ full, and bake in a 350° oven for 20 to 25 minutes.

WACKY CAKE

1 tsp. baking soda	⅓ cup cocoa
1 cup water	1 tsp. vanilla
1½ cups all-purpose flour, sifted	1 tsp. vinegar
1 cup granulated sugar	½ cup melted butter or cooking oil

Dissolve the soda in the water. Sift the flour, sugar and cocoa together into an 8-inch square pan. Make 3 holes in the mixture.

Into the first hole pour the vanilla and the vinegar.

Into the second hole put the soda-water.

Into the third hole pour the melted butter or oil.

Beat for 1 minute at medium speed.

Bake in the same pan for 30 minutes at 350°.

OLDFASHIONED LEMON CAKE

1 stick butter	4½ cups cake flour, sifted
1½ cups granulated sugar	2 tsp. baking powder
4 eggs, separated	¼ tsp. salt
1 tsp. lemon extract	¾ cup milk
½ tsp. grated lemon rind	

Cream the butter and sugar together until they are creamy.

Separate the yolks from the whites of the eggs and beat each separately. Beat the egg yolks until they are pale and thick and add them into the creamed mixture. Add in the lemon extract and the rind, and then add the dry ingredients alternately with the milk. Lastly, fold in the stiffly beaten egg whites.

Bake in two greased and floured 9-inch layer cake pans in a 375° oven for 20 to 30 minutes. Put the layers together with a lemon filling.

CAMPFIRE CAKE

2 sticks butter	¼ cup milk or ¾ Tbsp. powdered milk
1 cup granulated sugar	2 cups all-purpose flour
4 eggs, unbeaten	1 tsp. baking powder
1 tsp. vanilla	1 tsp. salt

Mix all the ingredients in the pan in which you will cook it. Any shallow pan or aluminum skillet will do. Melt the butter before adding it in.

Stir the batter with a fork in a circular motion for 10 minutes.

Bake in any kind of a camp or covered oven for 1 hour, and don't let it smoke. If the oven smokes, it is too near the fire.

Serves 10.

ROSY APPLESAUCE CAKE

1 cup granulated sugar

½ cup shortening, softened

2 Tbsp. unsweetened pine-
apple juice

¾ cup unsweetened apple-
sauce

1 tsp. red food coloring

2 cups all-purpose flour,
sifted

1½ tsp. baking powder

¼ tsp. salt

1 tsp. baking soda

1 egg, well beaten

½ cup milk

½ cup shredded coconut

Cream together the sugar and the shortening. Add the pineapple juice and stir it in. Stir in the applesauce and the coloring.

Sift the flour, measure it, and sift it again with the baking powder, the salt, and the soda. Add the egg to the batter; then blend in the flour mixture alternately with the milk. Last of all, fold in the coconut. Beat for about 30 seconds by hand.

Bake in a 9-inch tube pan for 35 minutes at 325–350°. When the cake is cool, cover it with Snow Peak Icing, (See page 175), and spread shredded coconut generously over the top.

❧ Transforming Commercial Mixes
Chapter 13

LEMON GELATIN CAKE

1 pkg. white cake mix	4 whole eggs
1 pkg. lemon gelatin powder	1 tsp. lemon extract
¾ cup cooking oil	1½ cups confectioners sugar
¾ cup water	6 Tbsp. fresh lemon juice

Mix the cake mix directly from the package with the gelatin powder, the cooking oil and the water. Add the eggs, one at a time, and beat after each. Add in the lemon extract.

Pour the mixture into a greased and floured 13 × 9-inch oblong pan. Bake at 350° for from 30 to 40 minutes. While the cake is baking mix the confectioners sugar with the lemon juice.

When the cake is done, remove it from the oven and immediately poke holes in it with a toothpick while slowly pouring the sugar-lemon juice combination over the cake. The hot cake will soon absorb this topping.

Cover the pan with aluminum foil and when it has cooled set it in the refrigerator for 24 hours before cutting it into squares and serving it.

150

This cake may be served right from the pan (a glass baking pan is ideal for this cake).

PRUNE COFFEE CAKE

½ stick butter, melted

¼ cup brown sugar, packed

3 Tbsp. corn syrup

1 egg, beaten

½ cup pitted, cooked prunes, cut up

½ cup liquid from cooked prunes

2½ cups packaged dry biscuit mix

½ tsp. cinnamon

⅓ cup granulated sugar

½ cup chopped walnuts

9 whole cooked prunes, pitted

Into the melted butter stir the brown sugar and the corn syrup. Set this aside.

Combine the egg, half a cup of cut prunes, the prune liquid, the biscuit mix, the cinnamon and the white sugar. Stir until blended.

Spread the mixture in a 9-inch square greased and floured pan. Sprinkle on the walnuts and arrange the whole prunes on top. Spoon the brown sugar mixture over all.

Bake in a hot oven at 400° for 30 minutes. Serve warm.

LEMON GINGERBREAD CAKE

½ stick butter

½ cup brown sugar

1 lemon

1 pkg. gingerbread mix

Melt the butter in a 9-inch square cake pan. Blend in the brown sugar until it is melted and smooth. Spread evenly in the pan. Cut the lemon into nine very thin slices, then quarter them. Arrange the lemon sections evenly over the sugar-butter in the pan.

Prepare the gingerbread mix according to directions on the package. Pour the batter very carefully over the lemon slices.

Bake at 350° for 30 minutes. When the cake is done, invert the pan on a serving plate.

CHERRY DREAM CAKE

1 lb. frozen cherries, thawed
and drained. (Save the juice)
⅓ cup granulated sugar
¼ tsp. salt
¼ tsp. almond flavoring

3 Tbsp. cornstarch
1 small pkg. white cake mix
2 cups heavy cream
2 Tbsp. granulated sugar
½ tsp. vanilla

Cook the cherries, the sugar, salt, and the almond flavoring in a saucepan until they come to a boil. Put the cherry juice and the cornstarch in a shaker and mix them well; then add this liquid to the cherries and cook until the mixture is very thick. As this cooks, mix the cake as directed on the package.

Grease and lightly flour a 2-quart casserole with butter; place the cherry mixture in the casserole; pour the cake batter over it, covering all the cherries. Do not stir.

Bake at 350° for 35 to 40 minutes. When done, invert the pan onto a cake plate that has an upturned edge. Some of the cherries will fall but can be replaced when the cake has cooled.

After the cake has cooled, whip the cream and flavor it with the 2 Tbsp. sugar and the vanilla. Frost the cake with the whipped cream. (A few uncooked cherries may be withheld to garnish.)

LEMON SPECIAL CAKE

1 box lemon cake mix
            (1 lb. 3½ oz.)
½ cup granulated sugar
¾ cup cooking oil
¼ tsp. salt

1 cup apricot nectar
4 eggs
2 cups confectioners sugar
Juice of 2 lemons

Combine the cake mix, the granulated sugar, the oil, the salt and the apricot nectar together. Add the eggs, one at a time. Mix well.

Bake in a 13 × 9 × 2-inch greased and floured pan for 30 to 35 minutes at 325°. When the cake is still warm, pour the following glaze over it.

Glaze: Mix the confectioners sugar with the lemon juice.

RAISIN COFFEE CAKE

1 cup golden seedless raisins
2⅓ cups packaged biscuit
           mix powder
⅓ cup granulated sugar

1 egg
⅔ cup milk
¼ stick butter, melted

For Topping

⅓ cup biscuit mix powder
3 Tbsp. granulated sugar

¼ stick butter

Combine the raisins, the biscuit mix, and the sugar. Beat the egg lightly and combine it with the milk and the melted butter. Add the egg mix into the dry mixture, blending in well. Turn the batter into a greased and floured 9-inch square pan.

Blend the topping ingredients until they are crumbly and sprinkle them over the batter.

Bake in a moderately hot oven at 375° for 30 to 40 minutes. This cake should be served warm.

LEMON POUND CAKE

1 pkg. lemon cake mix
    (or any yellow cake mix)
1 pkg. lemon gelatin powder
⅔ cup cold water

⅔ cup cooking oil
4 eggs
Grated rind of 1 lemon

Put together all the ingredients, except the rind, and beat thoroughly in a mixer or by hand. Then add in the rind.

Pour into a greased and floured 13 × 9 × 2-inch pan and bake at 350° for from 45 minutes to 1 hour.

EASY-DOES-IT CAKE

1 pkg. white cake mix
1 pkg. chocolate pudding mix

2 eggs, unbeaten
2 cups milk

Mix all the ingredients together thoroughly. Bake in two 9-inch greased and floured round pans for 40 to 45 minutes at 350°. Frost with a favorite icing.

To vary this recipe try a lemon pudding mix instead of the chocolate pudding.

DATE BAR FRUIT CAKE

1 pkg. date bar mix	1 tsp. cinnamon
⅔ cup hot water	¼ tsp. nutmeg
3 eggs	¼ tsp. allspice
¼ cup all-purpose flour	1 cup chopped nuts
½ tsp. salt	1 cup candied fruit, chopped
¾ tsp. baking powder	1 cup raisins
2 Tbsp. light molasses	

Heat the oven to 325°. Grease and flour a 9 × 5 × 3-inch loaf pan.

Combine the envelope of date filling from the mix package with the hot water in a large bowl. Add to this the crumbly mix from the package, the eggs, flour, salt, baking powder, molasses and spices. Blend well. Dust the nuts and fruit very lightly with flour and fold them in thoroughly. Pour the batter into the prepared pan.

Bake about 1 hour and 20 minutes, or until the cake tests done when probed with a toothpick. Cool the cake thoroughly. Wrap it tightly in wax paper and refrigerate it.

ANGEL DELIGHT CAKE

One angel food cake (made from a mix, if desired) cut into three equal layers.

Combine in a large mixing bowl:

1 pkg. frozen strawberries, thawed	1 egg white
¾ cup granulated sugar	1 tsp. lemon juice

Beat these four ingredients 5 to 10 minutes with an electric beater at high speed or with a hand beater vigorously for 12 minutes.

Ice between the layers and on top and sides of the cake with the strawberry mix.

EASY CHEESE CAKE

1 pkg. frozen slice-and-bake sugar cookies	2 eggs, beaten
	1 stick butter or margarine
1½ lbs. cream cheese	¼ tsp. salt
1 cup granulated sugar	1 tsp. vanilla

Line 2 greased and floured 8-inch round pans with slices of the frozen sugar cookies.

Blend the cheese with the sugar thoroughly. Add in the beaten eggs, the softened butter or margarine, the salt, and the vanilla, blending all thoroughly. Pour half of the mixture into each pan.

Bake for 25 minutes in a 400° preheated oven. Garnish with fresh strawberries or other fruit. Each cake serves 8.

STRAWBERRY SPECIAL CAKE

1 pkg. white cake mix (one that calls for no eggs)	½ cup water
	½ cup cooking oil
1 pkg. strawberry gelatin powder	½ pkg. frozen strawberries, thawed
3 Tbsp. all-purpose flour	3 eggs

Beat together all the ingredients, except the eggs.

Add in one egg at a time and beat after each addition.

Bake at 350° in three 8-inch greased and floured layer cake pans until the cake is firm when touched lightly (about 30 minutes).

Ice this cake with Frozen Strawberry Icing, (See p. 173).

EASY APPLE GINGER CAKE

¼ stick butter	2 Tbsp. grated orange rind
4 cups tart apples, peeled and sliced	2 Tbsp. orange juice
	1 pkg. gingerbread mix
1 cup granulated sugar	

Melt the butter in a 9-inch square baking pan. Arrange apple slices on the butter and sprinkle the sugar and orange rind over them. Dribble the orange juice over the apples and the rind and simmer in pan on top of the stove over low heat for 5 minutes.

Prepare the gingerbread batter as directed on the package; pour it evenly over the apple mix.

Bake at 350° for 30 minutes, or until the cake begins to shrink from sides of pan. Cool cake 5 minutes. Remove from pan and invert onto plate.

Serve with sweetened whipped cream.

BISCUIT COFFEE CAKE

2 cans refrigerator (not frozen) biscuits	**¾ cup (packaged) cinnamon-sugar mixture**
½ stick butter, melted	**Raisins and nuts**

Grease lightly and flour a ring mold or small tube-type pan.

Dip the biscuit slices in the melted butter and then in the cinnamon-sugar mix. Place one layer of the biscuits in the pan and sprinkle on nuts and raisins. Place a second layer of biscuits over the first and sprinkle on a few more raisins and nuts.

Bake in a 400° oven for 15 minutes, or until the cake is browned and the biscuits are done.

Serves 6.

❧ Fillings, Frostings, Icings, Toppings
Chapter 14

HOW TO FROST A CAKE

Painstaking care puts the artistic touch on a homemade cake—use artistry in frosting a cake.

To frost a cake is surprisingly easy. The rules to follow are:

Be sure the cake is cool. Brush off any crumbs.

To frost a two-layer cake: put one layer top side down on a plate. Heap about one-fourth of the frosting in the center of the layer and spread it evenly with a spatula or a knife almost to the cake's edge. Cover this with the second layer, keeping the top side up. Spread frosting on the sides of the cake. Put the balance of the frosting on top of the cake and spread it until the whole is evenly covered.

To frost an oblong cake: put the cake top side up on a cake plate or pan. Spread the frosting with a knife or spatula on the sides of the cake first; then heap the remaining frosting on top of the cake and spread it evenly all over.

You may then decorate either cake with nuts, sprinkles, candy pieces, or with a design in frosting drawn with a pastry tube.

BUTTERSCOTCH FILLING

½ cup granulated sugar
1 Tbsp. cornstarch
½ cup evaporated milk
⅓ cup water
⅓ cup butterscotch morsels
(crushed)

1 egg yolk, beaten
¼ stick butter
1 cup shredded, chopped
coconut
1 cup pecan or walnut meats,
chopped

Put the sugar and cornstarch in a saucepan; stir in the milk, then the water, butterscotch morsels and the egg yolk. Cook over medium heat, stirring constantly until the mixture thickens. Remove the pan from the heat, add in the butter, coconut and nut meats. Blend well. Set the pan aside to cool before the filling is used.

EGG YOLK FILLING

4 egg yolks
¾ cup granulated sugar
2½ Tbsp. cornstarch

¼ tsp. salt
1½ cups milk, scalded
1 tsp. vanilla

Beat the egg yolks; gradually add in the sugar, cornstarch and salt. Pour the scalded milk over this mixture. Cook in a double boiler over boiling water, stirring constantly until the filling has thickened. When it is cool, add in the vanilla, or any other preferred flavoring.

LEMON FILLING

1 cup granulated sugar
3 Tbsp. cornstarch
2 eggs
1 cup water

Juice of 2 large lemons
Grated rind of 1 lemon
¼ stick butter, melted

Mix thoroughly the sugar with the cornstarch. Beat the eggs with a rotary beater and stir them into the water. Add the lemon juice and the rind into the eggs-and-water. Now combine in the sugar mix.

Soften the butter in the top of a double boiler. Combine in the original mixture and stir to mix thoroughly. Place the pan over boiling water and, stirring constantly, cook the mixture until the filling is thick and smooth. Cool to lukewarm before spreading the filling on cake.

LEMON CUSTARD FILLING

1 cup granulated sugar	**1 Tbsp. all-purpose flour**
⅛ stick butter	**1 cup milk**
5 egg yolks	**Grated rind and juice**
	of 2 lemons

Cream together the sugar and butter. Add in the egg yolks and the flour, blending thoroughly. Then add in the milk. Stir the mixture. Now add the grated rind and the lemon juice. Cook in a double boiler over boiling water, stirring occasionally until the filling is thick enough to spread on the cake as thickly as you wish.

PEANUT BRITTLE FILLING

1 cup peanut brittle	**1 cup heavy cream**

Whip the cream until it is stiff. Run the peanut brittle through a food chopper or roll it by hand until it is thoroughly crumbled. Fold the brittle into the whipped cream and spread the mixture between cake layers.

If desired, this filling can also be used as a topping.

PINEAPPLE EGG YOLK FILLING

1 cup granulated sugar	**¼ cup milk**
¼ stick butter	**1 egg yolk, well beaten**
½ tsp. salt	**2 Tbsp. unsweetened pine-**
¼ tsp. grated lemon peel	**apple juice**

Measure all the ingredients, except the pineapple juice, into a saucepan. Stir them together thoroughly. Put the pan on top of the stove and cook over a low flame until the mixture when tested in cold water will form a soft ball.

Stir in the pineapple juice and cook about one-half minute longer. Remove the pan from the stove and beat the mixture until it is smooth.

PRUNE NUT FILLING

1 egg, beaten	½ cup chopped prunes
½ cup granulated sugar	½ cup chopped nuts
½ cup milk	

Boil together the egg, the sugar, the milk, and the prunes until the mixture is thick enough to spread, stirring frequently to avoid sticking. Allow the mixture to cool to lukewarm; then add in the nuts.

Spread between the layers and on top of the cake.

RAISIN FILLING

1 cup granulated sugar	1 cup raisins
4 Tbsp. water	1 egg white, well beaten

Boil the water and sugar until they spin a thread. Add the raisins and pour the mix slowly over the beaten egg white. Mix gently.

Spread on the cake and between the layers.

BUTTER FROSTING *Very Good*

¾ cup milk	1 stick butter
3½ Tbsp. all-purpose flour	½ tsp. vanilla
¾ cup granulated sugar	½ tsp. salt

Cook the milk and flour in a saucepan until the mixture thickens. It should look like a paste. Then when this has cooled add in the other ingredients. Beat until they are foamy. (If desired, any other flavoring may be substituted for the vanilla.)

CANDY MOUNTAIN FROSTING

¾ cup granulated sugar	3 egg whites
6 Tbsp. white corn syrup	½ cup chopped nuts
3 Tbsp. water	

Mix the sugar, corn syrup and water together thoroughly in a saucepan. Then boil them rapidly on top of the stove until the mixture spins a long thread. Beat the egg whites to stand up in very stiff peaks. Pour the cooked syrup mix slowly over the egg whites, stirring rapidly as you do so. Add in a few drops of red food coloring and any desired flavoring, either almond, vanilla, pineapple, mint or clove. Fold the total mixture together gently.

Decorate the frosted cake with the chopped nuts.

CARAMEL FROSTING

2 egg whites
1½ cups brown sugar
Pinch of salt

5 Tbsp. water
½ tsp. maple flavoring

Combine all the ingredients, except the flavoring, in the top of a double boiler. Beat 1 minute with a rotary mixer. Place the pan over boiling water; beat constantly until the frosting peaks. Remove the pan from the fire. Add the maple flavoring and beat about 2 minutes longer.

CARROT FROSTING

1 Tbsp. light molasses
1 cup granulated sugar
⅛ stick butter, melted
¼ cup milk

1 tsp. vanilla
½ tsp. cinnamon
½ cup grated raw carrots

Cook the first four ingredients together until the mixture forms a solid ball when tested in cold water.

Remove the pan from the fire; stir the mixture until its texture becomes grainy. Then add in the vanilla, the cinnamon, and the carrots.

COCOA FROSTING

Using the Creamy Smooth Icing recipe, (See p. 172) add 3 tablespoons of cocoa to the sugar and sift together.

Combine the egg whites, granulated sugar, salt, water, and the syrup in the top of a double boiler. Mix thoroughly with a beater over boiling water.

Add in the vanilla and the powdered sugar and continue beating until the frosting is thick enough for spreading.

Frost the cake on top and between its layers. Then dust all over the cake heavily with the coconut.

COCONUT FROSTING

2 egg whites	2 tsp. corn syrup
1½ cups granulated sugar	1½ tsp. vanilla
¼ tsp. salt	1½ Tbsp. confectioners sugar
⅓ cup water	1 (7 oz.) box shredded coconut

COCONUT PECAN FROSTING

1 cup evaporated milk	1 tsp. vanilla
1 cup granulated sugar	1 can tender, flaked coconut
½ stick margarine	1 cup chopped pecan meats
3 egg yolks	

Combine the milk, sugar and margarine in a saucepan. Add the egg yolks and the vanilla. Cook over medium heat until the mixture thickens (about 12 minutes). Stir it constantly. Remove the pan from the heat; add the coconut and the chopped nuts. Beat the frosting until it is cool and thick enough to spread. (Do not frost the sides of the cake when using this frosting.)

CREAM CHEESE FROSTING

1 3-oz. pkg. cream cheese	2½ cups confectioners sugar, sifted
1 Tbsp. milk	½ tsp. vanilla

Soften the cheese with the milk. Gradually blend in the sugar. Add the vanilla. Mix well until the frosting is smooth.

FUDGE FROSTING

2 squares unsweetened chocolate	⅔ cup milk
2 cups granulated sugar	¼ stick butter
2 Tbsp. corn syrup	1 tsp. vanilla

Cut the chocolate into small pieces. Then cook the sugar, the chocolate, the corn syrup, and the milk together. Stir constantly until the sugar is dissolved. Then stir the mixture occasionally to prevent it burning. Cook until the syrup forms a soft ball when tested in cold water.

Remove the pan from the fire. Add in the butter and cool the mixture to lukewarm. Add in the vanilla and beat steadily until the frosting is creamy and of the right consistency for spreading.

HONEY FROSTING

¼ stick butter	Pinch of salt
2 Tbsp. honey	1 egg white, unbeaten
2⅓ cups confectioners sugar	

Cream the butter and the honey together, then add in ⅓ cup of sugar and the salt. Cream again.

Add the egg white alternately with the balance of the sugar, beating well as you add them. When the mixture is smooth, it is ready for use.

HULA FROSTING

2 egg whites, unbeaten	1 tsp. light corn syrup
5 Tbsp. pineapple syrup (from the can)	½ tsp. vanilla
	½ tsp. orange extract
1½ cups granulated sugar	½ cup crushed pineapple, drained
⅛ tsp. salt	

Mix the egg whites, the pineapple syrup, the sugar, the salt, and the corn syrup together thoroughly in a double boiler. Set the pan over boiling water and beat the mixture constantly with a rotary beater until it will hold a peak.

Remove the pan from the hot water and add in the vanilla and the orange extract. Beat again. Then let the mixture cool. When it is cold, fold in the pineapple.

Frost the top and between the layers of the cake.

MAPLE FROSTING

1 cup maple sugar	⅛ tsp. cream of tartar
½ cup boiling water	1 egg white, beaten

Boil the sugar, water and cream of tartar together until they spin a thread from a spoon. Pour this blend slowly in a stream on the beaten egg white and continue beating until the frosting is thick enough to spread on a cake. (If desired, add a cup of chopped English walnut meats to this frosting.)

MOCHA FROSTING

⅔ cup granulated sugar	3 Tbsp. strong coffee
½ cup light corn syrup	⅛ tsp. salt
2 egg whites	1 tsp. vanilla
1 cup chocolate chips	

Combine the above ingredients, except the vanilla, in a double boiler over rapidly boiling water. Beat with a rotary beater for about 7 or 8 minutes, or until the frosting holds its shape. Remove the pan from the boiling water. Add in the vanilla. Let the frosting cool before spreading it on cooled cake layers. Dot the top of the cake generously with extra chips before the frosting has hardened.

NOUGAT FROSTING

1 egg white, unbeaten	¼ tsp. cream of tartar
1 Tbsp. water	Pinch of salt
1 Tbsp. honey	¼ tsp. vanilla
½ cup granulated sugar	⅓ cup chopped, blanched and toasted almonds

Put the above ingredients, except the almonds and the vanilla, in a double boiler and mix them well. Place over rapidly boiling water and beat constantly with a rotary beater until the mixture holds a peak. Remove the pan from the fire, add in the vanilla and the almonds. Then beat until the frosting is of the right consistency to spread over a cake.

NUTMEAT COCONUT FROSTING

½ stick butter
½ cup brown sugar
3 Tbsp. half and half cream

½ cup chopped nutmeats
¾ cup flaked or shredded coconut

Combine the above ingredients. Blend well. Spread the mixture evenly over the top of the cake.

Place the cake under the broiler (set for low heat) until the frosting becomes bubbly. Serve immediately.

ORANGE FROSTING

Use the Creamy Smooth Icing recipe (p. 172) but omit the vanilla and the cream. Substitute 1 Tbsp. grated orange peel and 2 Tbsp. orange juice.

ORANGE COCONUT FROSTING

3 Tbsp. butter
2 cups confectioners sugar

¼ cup orange juice
¾ cup grated coconut

Cream the butter until it is very smooth. Add the sugar gradually, alternating with a little of the orange juice occasionally, until all the sugar and juice have been creamed in.

Beat the frosting until it is smooth. Then gently beat in the coconut.

ORANGE CREAM FROSTING

1 stick butter
4 Tbsp. cake flour
½ tsp. salt

½ cup orange juice
3 cups confectioners sugar
1 Tbsp. grated orange rind

Melt the butter in a saucepan. Remove the pan from the heat. Blend in the flour and the salt slowly. Stir in the orange juice. Place the pan back over the heat; bring it to a boil, stirring constantly. Again remove the pan from the heat.

Now stir in the powdered sugar and the orange rind. Place the saucepan in a pan of cold water and beat the mixture until it is of a spreading consistency. Add more powdered sugar if necessary.

ORNAMENTAL FROSTING

2 egg whites	1 tsp. lemon juice
1 cup confectioners sugar	Few drops of coloring, if desired

Beat the egg whites until they are frothy, but not stiff. Measure and sift the powdered sugar; sprinkle 2 tsp. over the egg whites and whip them about 5 minutes with a wire whisk. Continue beating in sugar, adding a little at a time, until you have exhausted the cup of sugar. Add in the lemon juice and beat until the frosting will stand up in peaks.

(*Note:* This frosting can be used in a pastry tube to decorate cakes that have already been carefully iced.)

QUICK CARAMEL FROSTING

½ stick butter	3 Tbsp. milk
¾ cup brown sugar	2 cups confectioners sugar

Melt the butter in a saucepan; stir in the brown sugar. Cook over low heat for 2 minutes, stirring frequently. Add in the milk. Bring the mixture to a full boil, take it off the heat, and let it cool to lukewarm.

Then add the confectioners sugar and beat the mixture until the frosting is of spreading consistency.

SEA FOAM FROSTING

⅓ cup granulated sugar	1 Tbsp. corn syrup
⅓ cup brown sugar	1 egg white
⅓ cup water	¼ tsp. cream of tartar

In a saucepan slowly cook together the first four ingredients until the mixture forms a soft ball in cold water.

Beat the egg white with the cream of tartar until they are stiff.

Add the cooked syrup mixture to the egg white, beating constantly. Continue beating until the frosting is thick enough to spread.

SNOW WHITE FROSTING

2 egg whites	**Pinch of salt**
1½ cups granulated sugar	**⅓ cup cold water**
1½ tsp. light corn syrup	**1 tsp. vanilla**

Combine the egg whites, the sugar, the syrup, the salt and the water in the top of a double boiler. Beat for 1 minute with an electric or rotary beater. Place the pan over boiling water and beat constantly until the frosting forms peaks (7–8 minutes). Remove the pan from the boiling water. Add in the vanilla and beat the frosting until it is of a spreading consistency (about 2 minutes).

Frosts the top and sides of two 9-inch layer cakes or one 10-inch tube cake.

(For a smaller quantity of frosting, use half the ingredients and cook about 4 minutes.)

STRAWBERRY FROSTING

2 eggs whites, unbeaten	**⅔ cup frozen strawberries,**
1 cup granulated sugar	**thawed and drained**
	Pinch of salt

Combine all the ingredients in the top of a double boiler. Beat for 1 minute with an electric mixer or rotary beater. Place the pan over boiling water; beat the mixture constantly until the frosting forms peaks. Remove the pan from the boiling water. (Pour the mix into a mixing bowl, if you wish.) Beat the frosting until it is of a spreading consistency (about 2 minutes).

Spread the frosting on the cake and garnish the top with whole strawberries.

SUGARLESS ORANGE FROSTING

2 egg whites	2 Tbsp. orange juice
1½ cups light corn syrup	½ tsp. grated orange peel
⅛ tsp. salt	

Combine the unbeaten egg whites, the corn syrup, and the salt in the top of a double boiler and beat with a rotary beater until they are well mixed. Set the pan over rapidly boiling water and beat continually while the mixture cooks. Cook for seven minutes, or until the frosting will stand in peaks. Remove the pan from the boiling water. Add in the orange juice and the peel and beat until the frosting is thick enough to spread.

SURPRISE FROSTING

¾ stick butter, softened	2 Tbsp. cocoa
3 cups confectioners sugar	1 tsp. cinnamon
½ cup nut meats, chopped	2 Tbsp. hot coffee
2 Tbsp. light cream	

Place all the ingredients in a bowl and mix well until the frosting is very creamy and smooth. Spread the frosting on the cake and decorate it with a few extra nut meats.

VANILLA MARSHMALLOW FROSTING

2 egg whites	¼ cup water
1½ cups granulated sugar	1½ tsp. pure vanilla extract
⅛ tsp. salt	12 marshmallows (regular size)
1 Tbsp. light corn syrup	

Combine the first 5 ingredients in the top of a double boiler. Set the pan over rapidly boiling water. Beat the mix with a rotary beater at full speed for 7 minutes, or until the frosting stands in stiff peaks. Remove the pan from the range and put in the vanilla.

Cut the marshmallows into small pieces. Add them in and beat until the marshmallows have melted.

Spread the frosting between the cake layers and over the top and sides of cake.

BASIC BOILED ICING

2 egg whites, unbeaten
1½ cups granulated sugar
¼ tsp. salt
⅓ cup water

2 tsp. light corn syrup
1 tsp. vanilla
½ tsp. almond extract

Combine the egg whites, sugar, salt, water, and the corn syrup in the top of a double boiler. Beat for about 1 minute, or until the ingredients are thoroughly mixed. Then place the pan over boiling water and beat constantly with a sturdy rotary beater, or at high speed of an electric beater, for 7 minutes.

Remove the pan from the boiling water, and pour the mixture at once into a large bowl. Add the extracts and beat again until the icing is thick enough to spread.

Makes 4½ cups of frosting, enough to cover a large cake.

BROILED ICING

6 Tbsp. butter or margarine
¾ cup brown sugar
¾ Tbsp. heavy cream or
    condensed milk

½ cup chopped pecan or
            walnut meats
½ cup shredded coconut

Melt the butter in a saucepan; mix in the remainder of the ingredients. Blend them together smoothly. Spread over the top of a warm cake.

Place the cake about 3 inches below the broiler coils (set for low heat) and broil until the mixture bubbles and browns.

Serve the cake while the icing is still warm.

BROWN SUGAR ICING, NO. 1

1 stick butter
1 cup brown sugar

¼ cup milk
(Enough powdered sugar to
    make the right consistency)

Melt the butter and the brown sugar in a pan and bring to a boil. Add in the milk and boil for two minutes, stirring frequently. Set the pan off the stove and cool the mixture. Beat in the powdered sugar, enough to make the right consistency for spreading. (This is one of the easiest to make icings.)

BROWN SUGAR ICING, NO. 2

¾ stick butter

2 cups brown sugar

½ cup light cream

1 cup confectioners sugar

Place the butter, brown sugar and cream in a saucepan. Set on stove over a low flame. Stir occasionally. When the mixture reaches a rolling boil, remove the pan from the heat.

Add in the powdered sugar and beat well until the icing is creamy.

BURNT SUGAR ICING

3 or 4 Tbsp. burnt sugar mixture, made from 1 cup granulated sugar (as directed)

2 cups confectioners sugar, sifted

¼ cup shortening

1 tsp. vanilla

About 2 Tbsp. cream

To make burnt sugar mixture melt 1 cup of sugar in a heavy skillet over low heat until it is medium brown; stir constantly. Remove the skillet from the heat and stir in ½ cup of boiling water. Mix well; if any lumps remain, return the skillet to the heat and melt them. Cool the mixture before using.

Cream together the confectioners sugar, and the shortening; stir in the burnt sugar mixture. Add in the vanilla, and stir in the cream. Beat until the mixture is of spreading consistency.

BUTTERMILK ICING

1 cup granulated sugar

½ cup buttermilk

½ stick margarine

½ tsp. baking soda

Few drops vanilla

Cook the first four ingredients until a soft ball forms when dropped in cold water. Remove from heat. Add the vanilla and beat until the icing is creamy.

CHOCOLATE ICING

2 squares unsweetened chocolate
¼ stick butter
2 Tbsp. hot water

1 cup confectioners sugar
Pinch of salt
¼ tsp. vanilla

Melt the chocolate in the top of a double boiler. Remove the pan from the hot water. Stir in the butter and 2 Tbsp. of hot water. Blend in the sugar. Beat with a spoon until the mixture is smooth. Then add in the salt and the vanilla.

CHOCOLATE BUTTER ICING

⅓ cup soft butter (about ⅝ stick)
3 cups sifted confectioners sugar

3 Tbsp. heavy cream (scant)
1½ tsp. vanilla
3 squares (3 oz.) unsweetened chocolate, melted and cooled

Blend the butter with the sugar. Add in the cream and the vanilla. Stir until the mix is smooth. Blend in the melted chocolate. (For extra richness add 1 egg yolk.)

CHOCOLATE CHIP NUT ICING

2 cups granulated sugar
1 stick butter
1 (13 oz.) can evaporated milk

1 (6 oz.) pkg. chocolate chips
½ cup chopped nuts

Cook the sugar with the butter and the milk until they reach the soft ball stage. (To test, drop a few drops of the mixture into a cup of cold water and roll them between the thumb and first finger.)

Add the chocolate chips and beat until the icing reaches a consistency for spreading. Just before icing the cake, fold in the nuts.

CREAM CHEESE ICING

**1 (3 oz.) pkg. cream cheese,
softened**

**2½ cups confectioners sugar
1 tsp. vanilla**

¼ cup light cream

Beat the cheese and the cream together vigorously with an electric mixer or by hand until they are smoothly blended.

Add in the sugar and the extract and beat again for about 2 minutes, or until the icing is fluffy.

CREAMY SMOOTH ICING

**½ stick margarine or butter
2 cups confectioners sugar,
sifted**

**⅛ tsp. salt
1 tsp. vanilla
2 Tbsp. heavy cream**

Cream the butter with 1½ cups of the sugar and the salt. Add in the remaining sugar alternately with the vanilla and the cream. Mix well until the icing is smooth and creamy.

Makes enough icing for two 8-inch layers or 2 dozen cupcakes.

EASY JELLY ICING

**½ cup tart jelly
1 egg white, unbeaten**

⅛ tsp. salt

Place the ingredients in a double boiler over boiling water and cook, beating constantly until the jelly is melted. Remove the pan from heat and continue beating until the mixture will hold its shape.

EGG YOLK ICING

**3 egg yolks
½ cup granulated sugar**

**⅛ stick butter or margarine
Juice of one lemon**

Cook the ingredients in a double boiler until they are thick. This is an economical and delicious icing.

FROZEN STRAWBERRY ICING

1 lb. confectioners sugar
1 stick margarine

½ pkg. frozen strawberries, thawed (drain slightly)

Beat the ingredients together and spread between the layers and on top of cake.

HONEY BUTTER ICING

2 sticks butter
½ cup honey
2 cups confectioners sugar

4 egg whites, stiffly beaten
2 squares unsweetened chocolate, melted

Cream together the butter, the honey, and the sugar. Then gradually beat in the egg whites. Pour into this the melted chocolate. Blend well. Spread over the top and the sides of the cake and between the layers.

LEMON CREAM BUTTER ICING

2 cups sifted confectioners sugar
2 Tbsp. lemon juice

Grated rind of one lemon
½ stick butter, softened

Blend together the sugar, lemon juice and lemon rind. Add the softened butter and stir it in thoroughly. When the mixture is velvety smooth, spread it over the top and the sides of the cake.

MAPLE ICING

1 stick butter
4 cups confectioners sugar, sifted

6 Tbsp. milk
1 tsp. maple flavoring

Cream the butter; add in the sugar gradually. Add the milk and the flavoring. Beat until the icing is smooth.

ONE MINUTE FUDGE ICING

2 Tbsp. cocoa
1 cup granulated sugar
½ stick butter
¼ tsp. salt

¼ cup light cream
¼ tsp. vanilla
1 Tbsp. white syrup

Cook the ingredients together over low heat for one minute; stir constantly. Then beat steadily until the icing is very smooth.

ORANGE ICING

¼ stick butter
1 (1 lb.) box confectioners
                    sugar

1 tsp. lemon extract
Juice, rind, and pulp of 1
                    orange

Blend the butter with the sugar. Stir in the lemon extract, the orange juice, rind and pulp. Stir steadily until the mixture is quite smooth.

PEANUT BUTTER ICING

2 cups light brown sugar
6 Tbsp. heavy cream
⅜ stick butter

1 Tbsp. peanut butter
1 cup confectioners sugar
½ tsp. vanilla

Stir the brown sugar, the cream and the butters together in a saucepan over low heat. As soon as the mixture starts to boil, remove the pan from the heat and stir in the powdered sugar. Beat until the mixture is thick and smooth. Then stir in the vanilla.

SCOTCH COFFEE ICING

½ stick butter
½ cup brown sugar

3 cups confectioners sugar
¼ cup very strong coffee

Cream the butter; add the brown sugar and continue creaming. Then add the powdered sugar alternately with the coffee. Beat until the icing is of a consistency for spreading.

Pile thickly on the top and the sides of the cake; make deep swirls with the bottom of a large silver spoon as a decoration.

SNOW PEAK ICING

¾ cup white corn syrup

2 egg whites

Pinch of salt

1 tsp. vanilla

Heat the syrup to the boiling point. Meanwhile beat the egg whites with a hand or electric beater until they are stiff but not dry. Add the salt. Then slowly pour the syrup over the beaten egg whites, while continuing to beat, until the icing is fluffy and will stand in peaks from the beater. Fold in the vanilla.

Ices top of two 8 or 9-inch layers.

TUTTI FRUTTI ICING

12 maraschino cherries,
    drained and chopped

½ cup chopped figs, moist

½ cup pecans, chopped

Double the recipe for Snow White Frosting (p. 167).

Remove one-third of the finished icing and stir in the above ingredients. Spread this combination between the cake layers.

Spread the remaining plain icing on the top and sides of the cake.

UNCOOKED ICING

¼ stick butter, softened

3 cups confectioners sugar

4½ Tbsp. evaporated milk

1½ tsp. vanilla

Blend all the ingredients together by stirring slowly until the mixture holds its shape. Then beat until the icing is velvety smooth.

YUMMY PINK ICING

1½ cups granulated sugar

¼ tsp. cream of tartar

2 large or 3 small egg whites

5 Tbsp. cold water

1 tsp. vanilla

1 tsp. almond extract

Red food coloring

Mix together the sugar, cream of tartar, the egg whites and the cold water in a double boiler. Place the pan over boiling water. Beat constantly for several minutes with a rotary beater until the mixture has thickened.

Remove the pan from the fire and add in the vanilla and the almond extract. Blend well. Tint the icing pale pink with 3 or 4 drops of the red food coloring, and spread the icing at once on the cooled cake.

ALMOND GLAZE (For Fruit or Coffee Cakes)

1 cup confectioners sugar	⅛ tsp. almond extract
1 Tbsp. water	

Blend the ingredients together in a small bowl.

Dribble over the cake before serving, allowing the glaze to run down the sides of the cake. Decorate with a few whole almonds.

CINNAMON PINEAPPLE TOPPING

½ stick butter or margarine, melted	½ cup crushed pineapple, well-drained
⅔ cup light brown sugar firmly packed	⅓ cup flaked coconut
	1 Tbsp. pineapple juice
	¼ tsp. ground cinnamon

Combine all the ingredients thoroughly. Spread over the top of baked and cooled cake.

CRUMB TOPPING

½ cup brown sugar	1¼ tsp. cinnamon
2 Tbsp. all-purpose flour	¼ stick butter, softened

Blend together the sugar, the flour and the cinnamon. Cut in the soft butter until the mixture is crumbly.

GLAZE (For Fruit or Loaf Cake)

2 Tbsp. brown sugar	2 Tbsp. water
1 Tbsp. corn syrup	

Combine the ingredients in a saucepan and place over low heat. Bring to a boil and simmer for two minutes. Brush over cake.

GREEN TINTED COCONUT

1 tsp. milk or water	1⅓ cups flaked coconut
Few drops of green food coloring	

Place the milk or water in a bowl. Add the coloring and mix well. Add the coconut and toss it with a fork until the coconut is thoroughly tinted.

Makes enough to cover top and sides of a medium sized cake. (Before applying the coconut with the palm of your hand to the sides of cake, place a paper collar around the cake to catch loose coconut.)

HONEY NUT TOPPING (For Coffee Cake)

½ stick butter	4 Tbsp. honey
4 Tbsp. granulated sugar	½ cup chopped nuts
4 Tbsp. all-purpose flour	

Cream the butter with the sugar; mix well. Add in the flour and the honey and beat until mix is smooth. Stir in the nuts.

Spread on coffee cakes before baking.

LEMON MERINGUE TOPPING

⅓ cup granulated sugar	2 Tbsp. lemon juice
3 Tbsp. all-purpose flour	1 Tbsp. grated lemon rind
1 egg yolk	$\frac{1}{16}$ stick butter (1 tsp.)
⅛ tsp. salt	3 egg whites
½ cup water	1 Tbsp. granulated sugar

Blend the sugar and the flour. Add in the egg yolk, the salt, water, lemon juice, lemon rind, and the butter. Cook in a double boiler until the mixture is thick and creamy; stir constantly as it cooks. Remove the pan from the fire; beat the contents well and allow them to cool until they are lukewarm. Then spread this topping onto the baked cake.

Now make the meringue by beating the egg whites until they are stiff. Add in the 1 Tbsp. of sugar and beat again until the whites hold a peak. Put the meringue over the topping and brown it by placing the topped cake under the broiler for a few minutes. Serve the cake immediately.

STREUSEL TOPPING

¼ cup flour	4 tsp. cooking oil
½ cup granulated sugar	

Mix the flour and the sugar in a small bowl. Gradually add the cooking oil; toss to distribute well.

LEMON SAUCE

1 Tbsp. cornstarch	¾ cup water
¾ cup granulated sugar	⅛ stick butter
1 egg, separated	2 Tbsp. lemon juice
¼ tsp. salt	⅛ tsp. grated lemon rind

Mix the cornstarch, sugar, egg yolk, salt, and the water with a rotary beater. Place the mix in a double boiler and cook it for 5 minutes, stirring constantly. Remove the pan from the heat and add in the butter, the lemon juice, and the rind. Let the mixture cool.

Beat the egg white until it is frothy and fold it into the sauce.

LEMON RAISIN SAUCE

⅓ cup granulated sugar	½ cup raisins
1 Tbsp. cornstarch	1 tsp. lemon juice
¼ tsp. cinnamon	⅛ stick butter
1½ cups water	

In a saucepan blend the sugar, cornstarch and cinnamon. Add in the water and cook over medium heat, stirring constantly until the mixture comes to a boil. Add in the raisins and simmer 2 to 3 minutes. Remove the pan from the heat and add in the lemon juice and butter. Stir until the butter is dissolved, then let the sauce cool before serving it.

Common Causes and Remedies in Cake ∽ Baking Failures

COMMON CAUSES AND REMEDIES IN CAKE
BAKING FAILURES

LAYER CAKES, POUND CAKES, and so forth.

A) DEFECT: Cakes Sink in Center

CAUSE	REMEDY
1. Insufficient moisture.	1. Increase liquid to proper absorption.
2. Inferior shortening.	2. Use special hydrogenated shortening for best results.
3. Improper mixing.	3. Follow accurately the mixing speed and time specified in recipe being used.
4. Improper oven temperature.	4. For best results, use oven temperature of 350°—never over 375°.
5. Inferior flour.	5. Use only high quality cake flour for best results.
6. Under-baking.	6. Do not disturb cakes until batter has "set," or until baked in center.

B) DEFECT: Cakes Expand, Then Fall during Baking

1. Too much moisture.	1. Due to climatic conditions, flour will sometimes pick up moisture in storage, thus altering the moisture content of the formula. If batter is already mixed, add more flour.
2. Inferior flour.	2. Use high quality cake flour.
3. Poor emulsification.	3. Use special hydrogenated cake shortening, or half shortening and half butter.
4. Too much baking powder.	4. Reduce amount.
5. Over-creaming.	5. Reduce speed and creaming time of shortening.
6. Too low oven temperature.	6. Regulate oven temperature before placing cakes in oven.

C) DEFECT: Cakes Shrink or Pull from Sides of Pan

1. Too much liquid.	1. Balance formula. If batter is already mixed, add more flour.

CAUSE	REMEDY
2. Poor emulsification.	2. Check quality of shortening. Use high grade hydrogenated shortening or half shortening and half butter.
3. Wrong temperature of ingredients when mixed.	3. All ingredients, especially the eggs, liquid and shortening should be between 70 and 80° when mixed.
4. Unbalanced formula.	4. Check, measure and weigh all ingredients, as the case may be, carefully. Do not use guess work in this very important step.
5. Over-baking.	5. Bake only enough to set the cake.
6. Not enough batter in pans.	6. Increase amount of batter.
7. Oven too cold or too hot.	7. Regulate oven at 350° before placing cakes in it.
8. Improper cooling.	8. Remove cakes from pans as soon as possible and cool on special cake racks, free from drafts.
9. Inferior flour.	9. Use high grade cake flour.
10. Mix too plain and "bready."	10. Increase proportion of eggs, sugar and shortening.
11. Over-mixing.	11. Cut down speed and time of mixing.
12. Too much leavening.	12. Reduce baking powder.

D) DEFECT: Poor Volume

1. Oven too hot.	1. Regulate oven at 350° while mixture is being prepared.
2. Insufficient leavening.	2. Increase amount of leavening agent.
3. Excess leavening.	3. Cut down amount of leavening agent.
4. Under-mixing.	4. Use speed and full time given in the recipe especially in last stage.
5. Mix too plain and "bready."	5. Increase amount of eggs and shortening.
6. Weak or watery eggs.	6. Be sure eggs are fresh, if using shell eggs.
7. Improper measuring.	7. Check weights of ingredients carefully.

CAUSE	REMEDY
8. Poor emulsification.	8. Check shortening. Use only special hydrogenated shortening.
9. Excess moisture.	9. Reduce amount of liquid.
10. Not sufficient moisture.	10. Increase amount of liquid.
11. Improper mixing temperature.	11. Batter should be 70 to 80° and not over 80°.

E) DEFECT: Coarse Grain

CAUSE	REMEDY
1. Over-mixing.	1. Check formula and use correct mixing speed and time.
2. Cold oven.	2. Regulate oven at 350°.
3. Too much leavening.	3. Reduce amount of leavening agent, especially at high altitudes.
4. Unbalanced formula.	4. Measure and weigh all ingredients carefully.
5. Insufficient moisture.	5. Increase liquid.
6. Under-mixing.	6. Give correct speed and full mixing time.
7. Too much sugar.	7. Reduce amount.
8. Poor shortening.	8. Use special hydrogenated shortening.
9. Too high speed on mixer.	9. Use slower speeds in early stages.
10. Too much shortening or egg yolk.	10. Reduce amounts accordingly.
11. Wrong type of flour.	11. Use high grade cake flour.
12. Batter stands too long before baking.	12. Batter should be baked as soon after mixing as possible.

F) DEFECT: White Cakes Off-Color

CAUSE	REMEDY
1. Off-color shortening.	1. Use best quality shortening.
2. Poor flour.	2. Use high quality cake flour.
3. Poor baking powder.	3. Use best grade.
4. Poor egg whites.	4. Check for quality and freshness.
5. Wrong mixing temperature.	5. Best mixing temperature is between 70 and 80°.
6. Not enough acidity.	6. Add cream of tartar or phosphate.
7. Insufficient mixing.	7. Increase speed and mixing time.

G) DEFECT: White Cakes Bake Out Yellow

CAUSE	REMEDY
1. Too much soda.	1. Cut down on soda or use a little cream of tartar or phosphate.
2. Excess invert sugar.	2. Cut down on amount.
3. Poor shortening.	3. Use special hydrogenated shortening.
4. Poor egg whites.	4. Check for freshness.
5. Poor cake flour.	5. Use high grade cake flour.

H) DEFECT: Whole Egg Cakes Have Greenish Tint

1. Too much soda.	1. Reduce amount.
2. Frozen eggs too old.	2. Use fresh frozen eggs as soon as thawed.
3. Mixing temperature too low.	3. Use temperature between 70 and 80°.

I) DEFECT: Soggy Streaks in Cakes

1. Excess moisture.	1. Cut down on liquid.
2. Excess leavening.	2. Use less baking powder.
3. Excess acid in mixture.	3. Cut down on sour milk, phosphate, cream of tartar, and so forth.
4. Insufficient mixture of dry ingredients.	4. Sift together all dry ingredients one or more times.
5. Excessive top oven heat.	5. Bake in uniform oven.
6. Poor flour.	6. Use high grade cake flour.
7. Improper cooling.	7. Do not ice cakes until cooled.
8. Cakes knocked in oven.	8. Handle cakes carefully during baking, do not jar.
9. Under-baked.	9. Bake until cakes are well set.

J) DEFECT: Cakes Crack in Baking

1. Batter too stiff.	1. Add more liquid.
2. Over-mixing.	2. Cut mixing speed and time.
3. Oven too hot.	3. Lower heat and regulate to 350°.
4. Uneven oven heat.	4. Regulate oven to uniform heat before baking.
5. Excessive acid or soda.	5. Cut down on amount.
6. Mixture too poor and "bready."	6. Use more shortening and sugar.

K) DEFECT: Crust Too Thick

1. Too much sugar.	1. Reduce amount.
2. Oven too hot.	2. Reduce temperature.

CAUSE	REMEDY
3. Too long in oven.	3. Bake shorter time at higher temperature.
4. Weak flour.	4. Use best grade cake flour.

L) DEFECT: Crust Peels and Flakes Off

1. Too much steam in oven.	1. Open oven damper slightly.
2. Oven too cool.	2. Raise temperature accordingly and regulate.
3. Weak eggs.	3. Check for freshness and quality.
4. Weak flour.	4. Use best grade cake flour.
5. Poor formula.	5. Check for proper balance.

M) DEFECT: Cakes Peak Up in Center or on Side

1. Mixture too lean.	1. Add more shortening and sugar.
2. Not enough leavening.	2. Add more baking powder.
3. Insufficient moisture.	3. Add more liquid.
4. Over-mixing.	4. Cut mixing speed and time.
5. Flour too hard.	5. Use best cake flour.
6. Too much flour.	6. Add more liquid.
7. Oven too hot.	7. Reduce temperature accordingly.

N) DEFECT: Cakes Are Tough

1. Poor flour.	1. Use high grade cake flour.
2. Over-mixing.	2. Cut down on speed and mixing time.
3. Over-baking.	3. Cut baking time.
4. Mixture too plain and "bready."	4. Increase shortening and sugar.
5. Excess egg whites.	5. Cut down on amount accordingly.
6. Oven too cool.	6. Raise temperature accordingly.
7. Eggs not beaten enough.	7. Beat eggs to proper volume, especially in sponge cakes.
8. Insufficient richness.	8. Add more shortening and sugar.

O) DEFECT: Cakes Too Tender to Handle

1. Excess sugar.	1. Reduce amount accordingly.
2. Excess shortening.	2. Reduce amount accordingly.
3. Excess leavening.	3. Reduce amount accordingly.
4. Under-mixing.	4. Increase mixing time.
5. Over-mixing.	5. Cut speed and mixing time.
6. Poor flour.	6. Use good grade cake flour.
7. Not enough eggs.	7. Increase amount accordingly.

P) DEFECT: Cakes Dry Out Too Rapidly

CAUSE	REMEDY
1. Climatic conditions.	1. Use invert sugar.
2. Insufficient shortening.	2. Increase amount accordingly.
3. Insufficient sugar.	3. Increase amount accordingly.
4. Poor shortening.	4. Use hydrogenated cake shortening.
5. Too few eggs.	5. Increase amount accordingly.
6. Too much leavening.	6. Reduce amount accordingly.
7. Oven too cool.	7. Raise temperature accordingly.
8. Over-baked.	8. Bake only until cakes are set.
9. Insufficient moisture.	9. Increase amount of liquid or egg accordingly.

Q) DEFECT: Cakes Mold Quickly

1. Bad storage.	1. Store in dry, well ventilated room.
2. Contamination.	2. Check storage room for sources of contamination.
3. Improper cooling.	3. Do not pack or store until cool.

R) DEFECT: Uneven Texture

1. Poor shortening.	1. Use hydrogenated cake shortening.
2. Under-mixing.	2. Follow mixing instructions in formula.
3. Over-mixing.	3. Use low speed in first stages of mixing.
4. Too much liquid.	4. Reduce amount accordingly.
5. Insufficient sugar.	5. Increase amount accordingly.
6. Wrong oven conditions.	6. Check for temperature, drafts, and so forth.
7. Mixing speed too high.	7. Use low speeds.
8. Mixing temperature too warm or too cold.	8. Mix between 70 and 80°.

S) DEFECT: Dark Spots on Bottom of Cakes

1. Undissolved sugar.	1. Use fine granulated sugar.

ANGEL FOOD AND SUNSHINE CAKES

A) DEFECT: Cakes Shrink from Sides and Bottom of Pans

1. Oven too hot.	1. Regulate oven to temperature stated in recipe.

CAUSE	REMEDY
2. Air pockets between cakes and pans.	2. Gently knock pans to work mixture down before placing in oven.
3. Flour too hard.	3. Use best quality cake flour.
4. Grease in pans.	4. Wash in hot water and rinse in cool water just before using.

B) DEFECT: Spots and Thick Crust on Top of Cakes

1. Baked too long.	1. Bake until set only.
2. Poor flour.	2. Use high grade cake flour.
3. Undissolved sugar.	3. Use fine granulated sugar.
4. Temperature too slow.	4. Increase temperature.

C) DEFECT: Cakes Fall When In or Out of Oven

1. Oven too hot.	1. Reduce temperature accordingly.
2. Egg whites whipped too much.	2. Reduce whipping time. Do not whip whites dry.
3. Egg whites whipped at wrong temperature.	3. Whip at temperature between 70 and 80°.
4. Pans contain too much moisture.	4. Turn pans upside down and drain off excess water just before using.
5. Too much liquid.	5. Do not add water to mixture.
6. Improperly cooled.	6. Invert cakes in pans on rack to cool.

D) DEFECT: Cakes Stick In Pans and Cannot Be Removed

1. Pans too dry.	1. Rinse pans in cool water and drain just before filling with mixture.
2. Soiled pans.	2. Keep pans and other utensils thoroughly clean.

E) DEFECT: Dark Cakes

1. Poor acidity.	1. Use pure cream of tartar.
2. Old or weak eggs.	2. Check eggs for freshness and quality.
3. Soiled mixing utensils.	3. Utensils must be thoroughly clean and free from grease.
4. Unbleached flour.	4. Use best quality cake flour.

Important. Careless measuring usually means failure. Failure, in turn, means waste. Waste means loss of money, time, and energy, and—worst of all—discouragement.

Index

INDEX

BAKING
Basic tools, 7
Failures, causes and remedies, 181
General instructions, 14
High altitude, 16
How to test, 15
How to use this book, 3
Ingredients—
  baking powder, 6
  eggs, 5
  flavoring, 6
  flour, 4
  instructions, general, 14
  measurements and equivalents, 13
  measuring, 14
  milk, 5
  salt, 7
  shortening, 5
  sugar, 4
Terms, glossary of, 8
Time and temperature, 16
Tools, basic list, 7

CAKES (alphabetically by name)
Affluent Fruit, 64
Amber, 124
Angel Delight, 154
Apple Cider, 140
Apple Jam, 137
Apple Layer, 133
Apple Preserve, 116
Apple Raisin Coffee, 48
Apple Surprise, 118
Apple Treat, 78
Applesauce #1, 81
Applesauce #2, 28
Applesauce Cupcakes, 106
Apricot-Pineapple Cheese, 91
Banana Nut, 114
Banana Tea, 82
Basic Pound, 102
Biscuit Coffee, 156
Black Bear's, 139
Black Devil's, 28
Black Walnut, 130
Blackberry Jam, 128
Blueberry Coffee, 51
Bread Crumb, 88
Breakfast Crumb, 53
Bridal Shower, 128
Brunch, 52
Burnt Sugar Chiffon, 44
Buttermilk, 36
Buttermilk Cupcakes, 109

Campfire, 148
Carrot Eggless, 142
Cheesy Dutch Apple, 121
Cherry Angel Food, 46
Cherry Dream, 152
Cherry Upside Down, 77
Chiffon, 39
Child's Rainbow Birthday, 112
Chocolate Butter, 116
Chocolate Fudge, 23
Chocolate Loaf, 103
Chocolate Nougat, 126
Chocolate Refrigerator, 95
Chocolate Spice, 62
Chocolate Topside, 80
Chocolate Whipped Cream, 98
Chopped Apple, 140
Chopped Peanut, 136
Christmas Day, 90
Cinnamon Pineapple, 25
Cocoa Coconut, 35
Coconut Gold, 33
Coconut Jelly, 36
Coffee Angel, 42
Coffee Spice, 48
Colonial Fruit, 119
Coral Sanford's Company, 131
Cranberry Nut, 71
Cranberry Orange Cheese, 97
Crazy, 143
Creole Chiffon, 43
Crystal, 113
Danish White, 123
Dark Chocolate Angel Food, 41
Date, 70
Date Bar Fruit, 154
Date Crumb, 79
Delicious Fruit, 67
Delicious Honey, 24
Delight Oatmeal, 24
De Luxe Pound, 99
Dependable, 26
Double Butterscotch, 138
Dried Apricot, 30
Dutch Apple Bran, 79
Easy Apple Ginger, 155
Easy Cheese, 155
Easy-Does-It, 153
Easy Fruit, 70
Easy Method Angel Food, 41
Economy, 84
Eggless Chocolate, 87
Eggless, Milkless, Butterless, 88

191

CAKES (alphabetically by name)
(*Continued*)
Emma Stephenson's Fresh Coconut, 146
English Lemon Pound, 102
Ethel Brannon, The, 22
Famous Fruit, 68
Featherweight #1. 37
Featherweight #2, 39
Fig, 137
Fluffy Coffee, 50
Fresh Apple, 82
Frosted Mocha, 125
Fruit Salad, 81
Fudge Nut, 123
Ginger Crumb, 57
Gingerbread, 60
Golden Saffron Coffee Ring, 49
Graham Cracker, 35
Graham Flour Fruit, 69
Grandma's Molasses, 32
Grape Upside Down, 83
Green Apple, 143
Half-A-Pound, 104
Handy Andy, 74
Hilda Bracey's Pound, 101
Holiday, 120
Holiday Pound, 100
Honey Nut, 124
Hot Milk Sponge, 40
Hot Potato, 145
Icebox Ginger, 147
Iced Sour Cream Pound, 101
Irish Apple, 23
Jelly Roll, 27
Joanne Snider's Birthday, 113
Kansas Sunflower, 84
Large Birthday, 126
Lemon, 21
Lemon Gelatin, 150
Lemon Gingerbread, 151
Lemon Light Sponge #1, 44
Lemon Light Sponge #2, 45
Lemon Meringue, 27
Lemon Nut Coffee, 49
Lemon Pound, 153
Lemon Special, 152
Lemonade Cheese, 93
Low-Calorie Cupcakes, 107
Majestic, 131
Maple Snow, 125
Maple Upside Down, 76
Maraschino Cherry, 115
Marble, 101
Marmalade Refrigerator, 94

Maryland, 129
Midnight Mallow, 121
Milky Way, 142
Mince Meat Fruit, 66
Minted Chocolate, 21
Molasses Ginger, 58
Molasses Layer, 32
Molasses Pear, 55
Molasses Spice, 59
Mother Sanford's Special, 31
Mother-in-Law, 65
Mrs. Alice Peet's Eggless, 86
Mystery Fruit, 97
Nut Spice, 57
Nutty Apple, 29
Oatmeal Date Cupcakes, 107
Oldfashioned Lemon, 148
Orange, 76
Orange Raisin, 29
Orange Sponge, 38
Overnight, 145
Peanut Butter, 22
Pecan, 71
Pin Money, 86
Pineapple Delight, 95
Pineapple Whipped Cheese, 95
Pink Cupcakes, 109
Poppy Seed, 114
Potato Fudge, 134
Prune, 119
Prune and Apricot Upside Down, 73
Prune Coffee, 151
Pumpkin, 144
Quick, 34
Quick Cheese, 93
Quick Coffee, 54
Quick Orange, 80
Quick Orange Streusel, 50
Quickly Mixed Cupcakes, 106
Raised Coffee, 51
Raisin Coffee, 153
Raisin Nut, 56
Raisin Walnut Pound, 103
Raspberry Loaf, 89
Refrigerator Fruit, 92
Rhubarb Upside Down, 75
Ribbon Coffee, 53
Rich Soft Honey, 120
Rosy Applesauce, 149
Ruddy Devil's Food, 118
St. Nick's, 111
St. Patrick's Day, 112
Salad Dressing, 135
Salt Pork, 144
Scotch Oatmeal, 146
Silver White, 31

Silvery Moon, 117
Soft Gingerbread, 56
Sour Cream, 58
Sour Cream Chocolate, 104
Sour Cream Spice, 56
Spanish Layer, 117
Spiced Banana, 60
Spiced Coffee Layer, 33
Spiced Lemon Pound, 105
Spiced Prune, 62
Spicy Chiffon, 61
Spicy Cupcakes, 108
Spicy Pear, 59
Spud and Spice, 138
Strawberry Meringue, 115
Strawberry Pop, 136
Strawberry Ripple Coffee, 54
Strawberry Special, 155
Streusel Filled Coffee, 47
Sue Breeden's Chocolate, 127
Sugarless Angel, 43
Sugarless Orange, 85
Sunday Supper, 85
Sunshine Cupcakes, 110
Supreme Angel, 45
Surprise, 34
Sweet Buttermilk, 122
Sweet Potato, 141
Swiss Chocolate, 30
Sybil Hancock's Cocoanut, 78
Syrup Angel Food, 40
Texas Dark Fruit, 66
Three Egg Sponge, 42
Thrifty Pound, 100
Tomato Soup Spice, 135
Toothless Nell's, 134
Topsy Turvy, 74
Two Egg, 87
Unbaked Fruit, 92
Upside Down Ice Cream, 91
Vanilla Cupcakes, 108
Vanilla Marshmallow, 129
Vanilla Wafer, 130
Velvet Spice, 61
Velvety Icebox, 96
Vera Brannon's Orange Juice Date,
    141
Wacky, 147
Wedding, 127
White Butter, 25
White Fruit #1, 68
White Fruit #2, 69
Whole Wheat, 26
Yellow Angel Food, 38
Yellow Chiffon, 37

CAKES (by major ingredients and kind)
Angel Food
  Angel Delight, 154
  Cherry Angel Food, 46
  Coffee Angel Food, 42
  Dark Chocolate Angel Food, 41
  Easy Method Angel Food, 41
  Sugarless Angel, 43
  Supreme Angel, 45
  Syrup Angel Food, 40
  Yellow Angel Food, 38
Apple
  Apple Cider, 140
  Apple Jam, 137
  Apple Preserve, 116
  Apple Surprise, 118
  Apple Treat, 78
  Cheesy Dutch Apple, 121
  Chopped Apple, 140
  Dutch Apple Bran, 79
  Easy Apple Ginger, 155
  Fresh Apple, 82
  Green Apple, 143
  Nutty Apple, 29
Applesauce
  Apple Layer, 133
  Apple Raisin Coffee, 48
  Applesauce #1, 81
  Applesauce #2, 28
  Applesauce Cupcakes, 106
  Coral Sanford's Company, 131
  Irish Apple, 23
  Rosy Applesauce, 149
Brown Sugar
  Brunch, 52
  Carrot Eggless, 142
  Chocolate Topside, 80
  Chopped Apple, 140
  Cinnamon Pineapple, 25
  Date Crumb, 79
  Delight Oatmeal, 24
  Dutch Apple Bran, 79
  Easy Fruit, 70
  Economy, 84
  Eggless, Milkless, Butterless, 88
  Famous Fruit, 68
  Fruit Salad, 81
  Green Apple, 143
  Handy Andy, 74
  Holiday, 120
  Low-Calorie Cupcakes, 107
  Mother Sanford's Special, 31
  Peanut Butter, 22
  Prune and Apricot Upside Down, 73
  Prune Coffee, 151
  Pumpkin, 144

194   INDEX

CAKES (by major ingredients and kind)
                          (Continued)
    Ribbon Coffee, 53
    Scotch Oatmeal, 146
    Sour Cream Spice, 56
    Spicy Cupcakes, 108
    Spicy Pear, 59
    Sybil Hancock's Coconut, 78
    Topsy Turvy, 74
Buttermilk
    Applesauce Cupcakes, 106
    Blackberry Jam, 128
    Breakfast Crumb, 53
    Buttermilk, 36
    Buttermilk Cupcakes, 109
    Chocolate Loaf, 103
    Cocoa Coconut, 35
    Date Crumb, 79
    Dependable, 26
    Double Butterscotch, 138
    Emma Stephenson's Fresh Coconut,
                          146
    English Lemon Pound, 102
    Fresh Apple, 82
    Frosted Mocha, 125
    Gingerbread, 60
    Icebox Ginger, 147
    Joanne Snider's Birthday, 113
    Low-Calorie Cupcakes, 107
    Milky Way, 142
    Mother-in-Law, 65
    Mrs. Alice Peet's Eggless, 86
    Nut Spice, 57
    Orange, 76
    Orange Raisin, 29
    Pin Money, 86
    Raisin Walnut Pound, 103
    Rich Soft Honey, 120
    Ruddy Devil's, 118
    St. Nick's, 111
    Soft Gingerbread, 56
    Spiced Prune, 62
    Spud and Spice, 138
    Sweet Buttermilk, 128
    Texas Dark Fruit, 66
    Velvet Spice, 61
    Vera Brannon's Orange Juice Date,
                          141
Cheese
    Apricot-Pineapple Cheese, 91
    Cheesy Dutch Apple, 121
    Cinnamon Pineapple, 25
    Cranberry Orange Cheese, 97
    Easy Cheese, 155
    Lemonade Cheese, 93
    Pineapple Whipped Cheese, 95

    Quick Cheese, 93
    Raspberry Loaf, 89
Chiffon
    Burnt Sugar Chiffon, 44
    Chiffon, 39
    Creole Chiffon, 43
    Featherweight #1, 37
    Featherweight #2, 39
    Spicy Chiffon, 61
    Yellow Chiffon, 37
Chocolate
    Black Devil's, 28
    Chocolate Butter, 116
    Chocolate Fudge, 23
    Chocolate Loaf, 103
    Chocolate Nougat, 126
    Chocolate Refrigerator, 95
    Chocolate Spice, 62
    Chocolate Whipped Cream, 98
    Coffee Spice, 48
    Easy-Does-It, 153
    Eggless Chocolate, 87
    Fudge Nut, 123
    Hot Potato, 145
    Midnight Mallow, 121
    Minted Chocolate, 21
    Potato Fudge, 134
    Sour Cream Chocolate, 104
    Sue Breeden's Chocolate, 127
    Sunday Supper, 85
    Swiss Chocolate, 30
Cocoa
    Chocolate Topside, 80
    Cocoa Coconut, 35
    Crazy, 143
    Creole Chiffon, 43
    Dark Chocolate Angel Food, 41
    Dependable, 26
    Economy, 84
    Ethel Brannon, The, 22
    Frosted Mocha, 125
    Marble, 101
    Mrs. Alice Peet's Eggless, 86
    Ruddy Devil's, 118
    St. Nick's, 111
    Salad Dressing, 135
    Surprise, 34
    Wacky, 147
Coffee
    Apple Raisin Coffee, 48
    Biscuit Coffee, 156
    Blueberry Coffee, 51
    Breakfast Crumb, 53
    Brunch, 52
    Coffee Angel, 42
    Coffee Spice, 48

Fluffy Coffee, 50
Golden Saffron Coffee Ring, 49
Lemon Nut Coffee, 49
Prune Coffee, 151
Quick Coffee, 54
Quick Orange Streusel Coffee, 50
Raised Coffee, 51
Raisin Coffee, 153
Ribbon Coffee, 53
Strawberry Ripple Coffee, 54
Streusel Filled Coffee, 47
Cupcakes
Applesauce, 106
Buttermilk, 109
Low-Calorie, 107
Oatmeal Date, 107
Pink, 109
Quickly Mixed, 106
Spicy, 108
Sunshine, 110
Vanilla, 108
Eggless
Applesauce Cake #1, 81
Applesauce Cupcakes, 106
Apricot-Pineapple Cheese, 91
Biscuit Coffee, 156
Carrot Eggless, 142
Cherry Dream, 152
Chocolate Topside, 80
Chocolate Whipped Cream, 98
Chopped Apple, 140
Coral Sanford's Company, 131
Crazy, 143
Easy Apple Ginger, 155
Economy, 84
Eggless Chocolate, 87
Eggless, Milkless, Butterless, 88
Lemon Gingerbread, 151
Mrs. Alice Peet's Eggless, 86
Mystery Fruit, 97
Overnight, 145
Pineapple Whipped Cheese, 95
Quick Cheese, 93
Raspberry Loaf, 89
Refrigerator Fruit, 92
Salad Dressing, 135
Scotch Oatmeal, 146
Texas Dark Fruit, 66
Unbaked Fruit, 92
Upside Down Ice Cream, 91
Wacky Cake, 147
One Egg
Apple Raisin Coffee, 48
Apple Surprise, 118
Apple Treat, 78
Applesauce Cake #2, 28

Banana Tea, 82
Black Bear's, 139
Blueberry Coffee, 51
Breakfast Crumb, 53
Brunch, 52
Buttermilk Cupcakes, 109
Cheesy Dutch Apple, 121
Cherry Upside Down, 77
Cranberry Nut, 71
Date, 70
Delicious Honey, 24
Delight Oatmeal, 24
Dependable, 26
Dutch Apple Bran, 79
Easy Fruit, 70
Fruit Salad, 81
Ginger Crumb, 57
Holiday, 120
Mince Meat Fruit, 66
Molasses Ginger, 58
Molasses Layer, 32
Molasses Pear, 55
Oatmeal Date Cupcakes, 107
Orange Raisin, 29
Pin Money, 86
Prune and Apricot Upside Down, 73
Prune Coffee, 151
Quick Coffee, 54
Quick Orange Streusel, 50
Raised Coffee, 51
Raisin Coffee, 153
Ribbon Coffee, 53
Rich Soft Honey, 120
Rosy Applesauce, 149
Salt Pork, 144
Spicy Cupcakes, 108
Spicy Pear, 59
Strawberry Ripple Coffee, 54
Streusel Filled Coffee, 47
Sybil Hancock's Coconut, 78
Toothless Nell's, 134
Two Egg
Apple Jam, 137
Black Devil's, 28
Chocolate Fudge, 23
Chocolate Nougat, 126
Chopped Peanut, 136
Christmas Day, 90
Cinnamon Pineapple, 25
Cocoa Coconut, 35
Coconut Jelly, 36
Cranberry Orange Cheese, 97
Date Crumb, 79
Easy Cheese, 155
Easy-Does-It, 153
Fluffy Coffee, 50

CAKES (by major ingredients and kind)
(*Continued*)

Fresh Apple, 82
Frosted Mocha, 125
Fudge Nut, 123
Graham Flour Fruit, 69
Grandma's Molasses, 32
Grape Upside Down, 83
Green Apple, 143
Handy Andy, 74
Joanne Snider's Birthday, 113
Lemon Nut Coffee, 49
Lemonade Cheese, 93
Low-Calorie Cupcakes, 107
Maple Snow, 125
Marble, 101
Mother Sanford's Special, 31
Nutty Apple, 29
Orange, 76
Orange Sponge, 38
Peanut Butter, 22
Prune, 119
Pumpkin, 144
Quick, 34
Quick Orange, 80
Quickly Mixed Cupcakes, 106
Raisin Nut, 56
Rhubarb Upside Down, 75
Ruddy Devil's Food, 118
St. Nick's, 111
Soft Gingerbread, 56
Sour Cream, 58
Sour Cream Chocolate, 104
Spanish Layer, 117
Spiced Banana, 60
Spiced Coffee Layer, 33
Spiced Prune, 62
Sugarless Orange, 85
Sunday Supper, 85
Sweet Buttermilk, 122
Sweet Potato, 141
Swiss Chocolate, 30
Tomato Soup Spice, 135
Two Egg, 87
Vanilla Cupcakes, 108
Vanilla Wafer, 130
Velvety Icebox, 96
Whole Wheat, 26
Yellow Chiffon, 37
Three Egg
Apple Cider, 140
Apple Layer, 133
Apple Preserve, 116
Banana Nut, 114
Bread Crumb, 88
Chocolate Butter, 116
Date Bar Fruit, 154

Double Butterscotch, 138
Graham Cracker, 35
Honey Nut, 124
Jello Roll, 27
Maple Upside Down, 76
Marmalade Refrigerator, 94
Midnight Mallow, 121
Mother-in-Law, 65
Pecan, 71
Raisin Walnut Pound, 103
Sour Cream Spice, 56
Spud and Spice, 138
Strawberry Special, 155
Sue Breeden's Chocolate, 127
Surprise, 34
Three Egg Sponge, 42
Topsy Turvy, 74
Vanilla Marshmallow, 129
Velvet Spice, 61
Four Egg
Campfire, 148
Chocolate Loaf, 103
Chocolate Spice, 62
Colonial Fruit, 119
English Lemon Pound, 102
Famous Fruit, 68
Gingerbread, 60
Half-A-Pound, 104
Hot Milk Sponge, 40
Hot Potato, 145
Icebox Ginger, 147
Lemon, 21
Lemon Gelatin, 150
Lemon Pound, 153
Lemon Special, 152
Majestic, 131
Milky Way, 142
Molasses Spice, 59
Oldfashioned Lemon, 148
Pineapple Delight, 95
Potato Fudge, 134
Strawberry Meringue, 115
Thrifty Pound, 100
Vera Brannon's Orange Juice
Date, 141
Five Egg
Delicious Fruit, 67
Lemon Light Sponge #2, 45
White Fruit #1, 68
Yellow Angel Food, 38
Six Egg
Basic Pound, 102
Blackberry Jam, 128
Featherweight #1, 37
Golden Saffron Coffee Ring, 49
Iced Sour Cream Pound, 101
Lemon Light Sponge #1, 44

Spiced Lemon Pound, 105
Seven or More Eggs
Affluent Fruit, 64
Burnt Sugar Chiffon, 44
Chiffon, 39
Creole Chiffon, 43
De Luxe Pound, 99
Ethel Brannon, The, 22
Hilda Bracey's Pound, 101
Holiday Pound, 100
Spicy Chiffon, 61
Egg Whites
Angel Delight, 154
Black Walnut, 130
Bridal Shower, 128
Buttermilk, 36
Cherry Angel, 46
Child's Rainbow Birthday, 112
Chocolate Refrigerator, 95
Coffee Angel, 42
Crystal, 113
Danish White, 123
Dark Chocolate Angel, 41
Easy Method Angel, 41
Emma Stephenson's Fresh Coconut, 146
Featherweight Cake #1, 37
Featherweight Cake #2, 39
Fig, 137
Maraschino Cherry, 115
Maryland, 129
Pink Cupcakes, 109
Poppy Seed, 114
St. Patrick's Day, 112
Silver White, 31
Silvery Moon, 117
Strawberry Meringue, 115
Strawberry Pop, 136
Sugarless Angel, 43
Supreme Angel, 45
Syrup Angel Food, 40
Wedding, 127
White Butter, 25
White Fruit #2, 69
Egg Yolks
Amber, 124
Coconut Gold, 33
Dried Apricot, 30
Irish Apple, 23
Kansas Sunflower, 84
Large Birthday, 126
Lemon Meringue, 27
Minted Chocolate, 21
Nut Spice, 57
Sunshine Cupcakes, 110
Fruit
Affluent Fruit, 64

Colonial Fruit, 119
Cranberry Nut, 71
Date, 70
Date Bar Fruit, 154
Delicious Fruit, 67
Easy Fruit, 70
Famous Fruit, 68
Graham Flour Fruit, 69
Holiday, 120
Mince Meat Fruit, 66
Mother-in-Law, 65
Pecan, 71
Refrigerator Fruit, 92
Texas Dark Fruit, 66
Unbaked Fruit, 92
White Fruit #1, 68
White Fruit #2, 69
Gingerbread
Easy Apple Ginger, 155
Gingerbread, 60
Icebox Ginger, 147
Lemon Gingerbread, 151
Soft Gingerbread, 56
Graham Cracker
Apricot-Pineapple Cheese, 91
Cranberry Orange Cheese, 97
Graham Cracker, 35
Lemonade Cheese, 93
Pineapple Whipped Cheese, 95
Quick Cheese, 93
Refrigerator Fruit, 92
Unbaked Fruit, 92
Honey
Black Bear's, 139
Delicious Honey, 24
Honey Nut, 124
Rich Soft Honey, 120
Layer
Angel Delight, 154
Apple Cider, 140
Apple Jam, 137
Apple Layer, 133
Banana Nut, 114
Blackberry Jam, 128
Buttermilk, 36
Child's Rainbow Birthday, 112
Chocolate Butter, 116
Chocolate Fudge, 23
Chocolate Spice, 62
Chopped Peanut, 136
Cocoa Coconut, 35
Coconut Gold, 33
Coconut Jelly, 36
Colonial Fruit, 119
Crystal, 113
Danish White, 123
Double Butterscotch, 138

CAKES (by major ingredients and kind)
(*Continued*)
Easy-Does-It, 153
Eggless Chocolate, 87
Emma Stephenson's Fresh Coconut,
146
Featherweight #1, 37
Featherweight #2, 39
Fudge Nut, 123
Graham Cracker, 35
Kansas Sunflower, 84
Large Birthday, 126
Lemon, 21
Majestic, 131
Maple Snow, 125
Maraschino Cherry, 115
Maryland, 129
Midnight Mallow, 121
Molasses Ginger, 58
Molasses Layer, 32
Mother-in-Law, 65
Mrs. Alice Peet's Eggless, 86
Oldfashioned Lemon, 148
Orange Sponge, 38
Poppy Seed, 114
Prune, 119
Pumpkin, 144
Quick, 34
Raisin Nut, 56
St. Nick's, 111
Silver White, 31
Silvery Moon, 117
Spanish Layer, 117
Spiced Banana, 60
Spiced Coffee Layer, 33
Strawberry Meringue, 115
Strawberry Pop, 136
Sue Breeden's Chocolate, 127
Sugarless Orange, 85
Sweet Buttermilk, 122
Swiss Chocolate, 30
Two-Egg, 87
Vanilla Marshmallow, 129
Wedding, 127
White Butter, 25
Whole Wheat, 26
Yellow Chiffon, 37
Mixes, packaged
Angel Delight, 154
Biscuit Coffee, 156
Cherry Dream, 152
Chocolate Whipped Cream, 98
Date Bar Fruit, 154
Easy Apple Ginger, 155
Easy Cheese, 155
Easy-Does-It, 153
Lemon Gelatin, 150

Lemon Gingerbread, 151
Lemon Pound, 153
Lemon Special, 152
Mystery Fruit, 97
Prune Coffee, 151
Quick Cheese, 93
Raisin Coffee, 153
Strawberry Special, 155
Molasses
Black Bear's, 139
Black Devil's, 28
Date Bar Fruit, 154
Fig, 137
Ginger Crumb, 57
Gingerbread, 60
Graham Flour Fruit, 69
Grandma's Molasses, 32
Icebox Ginger, 147
Molasses Ginger, 58
Molasses Layer, 32
Molasses Pear, 55
Molasses Spice, 59
Mother Sanford's Special, 31
Nut Spice, 57
Raisin Nut, 56
Salt Pork, 144
Soft Gingerbread, 56
Texas Dark Fruit, 66
Toothless Nell's, 134
Pound
Basic Pound, 102
Chocolate Loaf, 103
De Luxe Pound, 99
English Lemon Pound, 102
Half-A-Pound, 104
Hilda Bracey's Pound, 101
Holiday Pound, 100
Iced Sour Cream Pound, 101
Marble, 101
Raisin Walnut Pound, 103
Sour Cream Chocolate, 104
Spiced Lemon Pound, 105
Thrifty Pound, 100
Practice cake, 17
Refrigerator
Apricot-Pineapple Cheese, 91
Chocolate Refrigerator, 95
Chocolate Whipped Cream, 98
Christmas Day, 90
Cranberry Orange Cheese, 97
Lemonade Cheese, 93
Marmalade Refrigerator, 94
Mystery Fruit, 97
Pineapple Delight, 95
Pineapple Whipped Cheese, 95
Quick Cheese, 93
Raspberry Loaf, 89

Refrigerator Fruit, 92
Unbaked Fruit, 92
Upside Down Ice Cream, 91
Velvety Icebox, 96
Sour Cream
  Apple Preserve, 116
  Iced Sour Cream Pound, 101
  Midnight Mallow, 121
  Raspberry Loaf, 89
  Sour Cream, 58
  Sour Cream Chocolate, 104
  Sour Cream Spice, 56
  Sybil Hancock's Coconut, 78
Spice and Spicy
  Affluent Fruit, 64
  Apple Preserve, 116
  Apple Raisin, 48
  Applesauce #2, 28
  Applesauce Cupcakes, 106
  Chocolate Spice, 62
  Coffee Spice, 48
  Colonial Fruit, 119
  Creole Chiffon, 43
  Delicious Fruit, 67
  Delight Oatmeal, 24
  Eggless, Milkless, Butterless, 88
  Famous Fruit, 68
  Ginger Crumb, 57
  Gingerbread, 60
  Graham Flour Fruit, 69
  Holiday, 120
  Hot Potato, 145
  Irish Apple, 23
  Low-Calorie Cupcakes, 107
  Molasses Ginger, 58
  Molasses Pear, 55
  Molasses Spice, 59
  Mother Sanford's Special, 31
  Mother-in-Law, 65
  Nut Spice, 57
  Nutty Apple, 29
  Overnight, 145
  Pecan, 71
  Potato Fudge, 134
  Prune, 119
  Pumpkin, 144
  Raisin Nut, 56
  Raisin Walnut Pound, 103
  Salt Pork, 144
  Soft Gingerbread, 56
  Sour Cream, 58
  Sour Cream Spice, 56
  Spanish Layer, 117
  Spiced Banana, 60
  Spiced Coffee Layer, 33
  Spiced Prune, 62
  Spicy Chiffon, 61

Spicy Cupcakes, 108
Spicy Pear, 59
Spud and Spice, 138
Surprise, 34
Sweet Potato, 141
Texas Dark Fruit, 66
Tomato Soup Spice, 135
Toothless Nell's, 134
Velvet Spice, 61
Sponge
  Hot Milk Sponge, 40
  Lemon Light Sponge #1, 44
  Lemon Light Sponge #2, 45
  Orange Sponge, 38
  Three Egg Sponge, 42
Syrup
  Chocolate Nougat, 126
  Refrigerator Fruit, 92
  Sugarless Orange, 85
  Syrup Angel Food, 40
  Two Egg, 87
Unusual
  Apple Cider, 140
  Biscuit Coffee, 156
  Black Bear's, 139
  Campfire, 148
  Carrot Eggless, 142
  Chopped Apple, 140
  Chopped Peanut, 136
  Crazy, 143
  Eggless, Milkless, Butterless, 88
  Emma Stephenson's Fresh Coconut,
                146
  Ethel Brannon, The, 22
  Grape Upside Down, 83
  Green Apple, 143
  Hot Potato, 145
  Mother Sanford's Special, 31
  Overnight, 145
  Peanut Butter, 22
  Potato Fudge, 134
  Pumpkin, 144
  Salad Dressing, 135
  Salt Pork, 144
  Scotch Oatmeal, 146
  Spud and Spice, 138
  Strawberry Pop, 136
  Sweet Potato, 141
  Tomato Soup Spice, 135
  Toothless Nell's, 134
  Wacky, 147
Upside Down
  Apple Treat, 78
  Applesauce #1, 81
  Banana Tea, 82
  Cherry Dream, 152
  Cherry Upside Down, 77

CAKES (by major ingredients and kind)
(Continued)
Chocolate Topside, 80
Date Crumb, 79
Dutch Apple Bran, 79
Easy Apple Ginger, 155
Fresh Apple, 82
Fruit Salad, 81
Grape Upside Down, 83
Handy Andy, 74
Lemon Gingerbread, 151
Maple Upside Down, 76
Prune and Apricot Upside Down, 73
Rhubarb Upside Down, 75
Sybil Hancock's Coconut, 78
Topsy Turvy, 74
Yeast
Brunch, 52
Fluffy Coffee, 50
Golden Saffron Coffee Ring, 49
Holiday, 120
Raised Coffee, 51

FILLINGS
Butterscotch, 158
Egg Yolk, 158
Lemon, 158
Lemon Custard, 159
Peanut Brittle, 159
Pineapple Egg Yolk, 159
Prune Nut, 160
Raisin, 160

FROSTINGS
Butter, 160
Candy Mountain, 160
Caramel, 161
Carrot, 161
Cocoa, 162
Coconut, 161
Coconut Pecan, 162
Cream Cheese, 162
Fudge, 163
Honey, 163
Hula, 163
Maple, 164
Mocha, 164
Nougat, 164
Nutmeat Coconut, 165
Orange, 165
Orange Coconut, 165
Orange Cream, 165
Ornamental, 166
Quick Caramel, 166
Sea Foam, 166

Snow White, 167
Strawberry, 167
Sugarless Orange, 168
Surprise, 168
Vanilla Marshmallow, 168

HOW TO FROST A CAKE, 157

ICINGS
Basic Boiled, 169
Broiled, 169
Brown Sugar #1, 169
Brown Sugar #2, 170
Burnt Sugar, 170
Buttermilk, 170
Chocolate, 171
Chocolate Butter, 171
Chocolate Chip Nut, 171
Cream Cheese, 172
Creamy Smooth, 172
Easy Jelly, 172
Egg Yolk, 172
Frozen Strawberry, 173
Honey Butter, 173
Lemon Cream Butter, 173
Maple, 173
One Minute Fudge, 174
Orange, 174
Peanut Butter, 174
Scotch Coffee, 174
Snow Peak, 175
Tutti Frutti, 175
Uncooked, 175
Yummy Pink, 175

**MEASUREMENTS AND EQUIVA-
LENTS,** 13

SAUCES
Lemon, 178
Lemon Raisin, 178

TESTING, methods for, 15

TIME AND TEMPERATURE CHART,
16
TOPPINGS
Almond Glaze, 176
Cinnamon Pineapple, 176
Crumb, 176
Glaze, 176
Green Tinted Coconut, 177
Honey Nut, 177
Lemon Meringue, 177
Streusel, 178

Lilith Rushing attended Oklahoma College for Women, Central State Teachers' College and Southwestern College in Oklahoma. She was class poet each year. For one year she taught school—girls' cooking classes and coaching girls' basketball. Later she began a business career during which she also wrote and sold many children's stories. For ten years she wrote two children's stories a month, called the Riverbottom Stories, for the *Farmer-Stockman* of Oklahoma City. She married a Kansan and has lived in Wichita for many years. Luther Rushing is his wife's best cake-taster. Mrs. Rushing maintains a lively interest in several local writers' groups of which she is a member.

Ruth Voss, the younger member of this sister team, also attended a teachers' college in Oklahoma, taught school for a year, then married and became a fulltime homemaker until her three children reached school age. Then she took a journalism course at Oklahoma University and embarked on a newspaper career. She was associate editor of the Thomas *Tribune,* Thomas, Okla., for two years, and news correspondent for the Kiowa *Star-Review,* Hobart, Okla., for ten years.

A widow, Mrs. Voss lives in semi-retirement with her bachelor son in Arkansas City, Kansas. She is also active in the local writers' groups.